Unfolded Tales

A. C. Hamilton. By Alec Ross. Courtesy of the Department of Public
Relations, Queen's University, Canada.

Unfolded Tales

Essays on Renaissance Romance

GEORGE M. LOGAN
and GORDON TESKEY

Editors

CORNELL UNIVERSITY PRESS

Ithaca and London

The contributors present this volume to
A. C. Hamilton, Cappon Professor
of English at Queen's University, Canada,
in recognition of his contribution
to English Renaissance studies.

Contents

Foreword

NORTHROP FRYE

This varied and fascinating collection of essays deals with aspects of one of the strangest success stories in English literature, the domination of the Elizabethan-Jacobean period by romance. This era had a strong sense of hierarchy in literary genres as elsewhere, and romance had, in theory, an inferior status. Romance stirred up sexual anxieties (see the quotation from Ascham in Carol Kaske's paper); it was constantly ridiculed for its extravagance, its neglect of the unities, the incredibility of its characters and their actions, its lack of attention to everything that critics of that time meant by "nature." Yet it is romance that takes over *The Faerie Queene*, the last period of Shakespeare, and the biggest work of Sidney. In Gordon Teskey's lively analogy, it is like the parasite of the medusa jellyfish that devours its host from the inside. Our own age is equally hierarchical, with certain "serious" genres studied in universities and others, mostly types of formulaic romance, consigned to the outer darkness of bedrooms, bus stations, and other places where fiction is actually read with some intensity. We may perhaps wonder if some of these subliterary conventions may not come in a distant future to show surprising powers of survival. One thinks of the remark of the garrulous drunk who tells the story of Nashe's *Unfortunate Traveler*: "*Architas* made a woodden Doue to flie; by which proportion I see no reason that the veryest blocke in the worlde shoulde dispayre of any thing."

The Elizabethan period and ours are not the only ones in which Hobgoblin has often snatched the garland from Apollo: in the "Romantic" period itself, and even more in the "pre-Romantic" age preceding it, romance formulas have outmaneuvered more highbrow preferences for what is called the "classical," the supposed opposite of romance in most ages. But in the period covered by this book there was an ambiguity in the conception of the "classical" itself. One of the most obvious and remarkable features of the period was its aspect as a "Renaissance," or re-creation of classicism, which gave it among other things an educational vision of great clarity and power, the vision for which the canon of classical writings provided the central content. By an educational vision I do not mean the forcible inserting of Latin paradigms into small boys, though there was a good deal of interest in that too: I mean the encyclopedic program of accomplishments set out in Castiglione's *Courtier*, in Elyot's *Governor*, and in courtesy books and miscellanies intended for the upper classes, such as Peacham's *Compleat Gentleman*.

The major classical models for this educational genre were the reconstituted society of Plato's *Republic*, the description of the magnanimous man (or however one translates it) in the *Nicomachean Ethics*, and the *Cyropaedia*, Xenophon's account of the life and education of Cyrus. These models reached sixteenth-century England in varied and often devious ways, but they are an informing presence in *The Faerie Queene* and, according to Fulke Greville, in Sidney's *Arcadia*. The fact that *The Faerie Queene* is among other things an educational treatise is emphasized in the "Letter to Raleigh." Even Shakespeare's most uninhibitedly romantic play *Cymbeline*, so prominently featured in this book, begins by praising Posthumus's achievements in the liberal arts, and can hardly find anything worse to say of the degenerate Cloten than that he cannot subtract two from twenty and get eighteen.

Education and romance seem very far apart in our minds today, because we think of education in a context of ideas, information, and the devoted efforts of a bureaucracy to prevent young people from getting it. The contemporaries of Spenser thought of it in a context of love, a word that had far less of the sentimental and rather embarrassing connotations that it has to us. The association of love and the arts had been inherited from the Middle Ages—one thinks of the famous opening stanza of Chaucer's *Parliament of Fowls*—and embellished with themes derived from the Italian Platonists. *The Faerie Queene* is really all about love, and three of its books, those devoted to Chastity, Friendship, and Courtesy, deal explicitly with recognized aspects of love. Britomart's chastity, in the completed poem, would have become the "married chastity" celebrated in Shakespeare's "Phoenix and the Turtle," as would also that of the invisible Faerie Queene herself. Love is also the climax of the courtier's education in Castiglione, and the interpenetration of love and learning in the literature of the time, from *Euphues* to *Love's Labor's Lost*, needs no further comment here. Even the so-called classics were read in a very romantic way: Virgil's *Aeneid*, for example, became essentially the love story of Dido. Before I read Patricia Parker's essay I had assumed that Shakespeare had no interest in the last six books of the *Aeneid*.

It takes a good deal of historical imagination to enter into this unity of learning and love: we tend to think of sexual and social relations, even relations within the individual psyche itself, as primarily adversarial, an antagonism that education normally intensifies instead of reconciling. Certainly Renaissance education was within a context of class and patriarchy, and knowing one's place in society was at the center of all other knowledge. But romance tries to give that knowledge a chivalric idealism that minimizes the arrogance that goes with class and sex distinctions. In a mistress's lament for her maid in Deloney's *Thomas of Reading* there is an exquisite blend of genuine personal feeling with class-inspired reflections about how hard it is to get good servants these days: "Farewell my sweet *Meg*, the best seruant that euer came in any mans house, many may I haue of thy name, but neuer any of thy nature, thy diligence is much, in thy hands I laid the whole gouernment of my house, and thereby eased my selfe of that care, which now will cumber me."

The concentrated training in words given by the trivium of grammar, rhetoric, and logic meant that Elizabethan education was verbal to a very intense degree. Perhaps the plethora of schools of critical theory today, most of which are at least referred to in the essays following, may be necessary to do justice to the intensity of the feeling for verbal texture in works of this period. Several aspects of it are featured here: multiple meanings of words (Judith Anderson), names (Alastair Fowler), recurring imagery (William Blissett), and complex patterns of verbal design like those of euphuism (the two essays on Greene). Spenser in particular was acknowledged to be a supreme master of rhetoric in his own day, but even what seem to be more casual writers demand very close attention to their texture, nor is all of it confined to English. To quote *The Unfortunate Traveler* again: "There was a Lord in the campe . . . sold syder and cheese by pint and by pound to all that came, (at the verie name of sider I can but sigh, there is so much of it in renish wine now a daies.) Well, *Tendit ad sydera virtus*, thers great vertue belongs (I can tel you) to a cup of sider."

Whatever the social or cultural conditions, friendship and courtesy will always be the essential social virtues in every age that they are in Spenser, and it is friendship and courtesy that have brought these essays together in honor of A. C. Hamilton. Whether explicitly referred to or not, his presence is everywhere throughout the book, which continually reflects the influence of his work on Sidney, on Shakespeare, on euphuism, and above all on Spenser, especially his monumental edition of *The Faerie Queene*. There could be no more impressive tribute to the fact that a first-rate scholar, simply by being what he is and by what he does, creates and fosters a community around him, a community not of discipleship but of a high morale sustained by the awareness that he is there.

Acknowledgments

The editors acknowledge the help given them by friends and colleagues, in particular D. O. Spettigue and Derek Crawley of the Department of English, Queen's University, who initiated the project; Kerry McSweeney of the Department of English, McGill University, and David Barnard of the Department of Computing and Information Science at Queen's for valuable advice; Andrew Currie (Queen's), John Ruffing (Cornell), and David Richardson (Cleveland State University) for technical assistance; Judith Bailey for copyediting; Elizabeth Teskey for help with proofs and index; Ann Stevens of the Queen's University Department of Public Relations for securing the photograph of A. C. Hamilton; and Karen Donnelly, who has been an invaluable friend to the project from its inception. We acknowledge with thanks the perspicacity of two anonymous readers for Cornell University Press and of Sylvia Söderlind (Queen's), who read a draft of one of the essays. We are grateful for the support of the Advisory Research Committee and the Office of Research Services of the Queen's University School of Graduate Studies and Research, Queen's University Computing and Communications Services, and the Cornell University Department of English. Our greatest thanks go to the authors.

George Logan, the senior editor, had the idea of creating a volume on Renaissance romance and was primarily responsible for corresponding with authors and editing copy. Gordon Teskey provided editorial assistance and discussed the project with Cornell University Press. The editors are pleased to be able to say that their collaboration on the volume was a very agreeable one.

G. M. L.
G. T.

Kingston and Ithaca

Abbreviations

CritQ	*Critical Quarterly*
ELR	*English Literary Renaissance*
HLB	*Harvard Library Bulletin*
JEGP	*Journal of English and Germanic Philology*
JWCI	*Journal of the Warburg and Courtauld Institutes*
MLN	*Modern Language Notes*
MLQ	*Modern Language Quarterly*
MP	*Modern Philology*
N&Q	*Notes and Queries*
PQ	*Philological Quarterly*
RenQ	*Renaissance Quarterly*
RES	*Review of English Studies*
SEL	*Studies in English Literature*
SP	*Studies in Philology*
TSLL	*Texas Studies in Language and Literature*
UTQ	*University of Toronto Quarterly*
Variorum	*The Works of Edmund Spenser: A Variorum Edition.* Ed. Edwin A. Greenlaw, C. G. Osgood, F. M. Padelford, et al. 11 vols. Baltimore: The Johns Hopkins Press, 1932–49.
YR	*Yale Review*

Unfolded Tales

Introduction

GORDON TESKEY

I

The essays in this book are concerned with some aspects of Renaissance romance as these appear in individual authors and works. This introduction, besides opening a small window into each of the essays, has the more general task of delineating the subject as a whole, which belongs to one of the most durable themes in the critical tradition: the relation of hierarchical exchange or, not infrequently, of symmetrical conflict between romantic and classical values. This theme is apparent in the title of the book, since the word *Renaissance* implies a rebirth of the classical ideals—wholeness, proportion, and clarity of form—to which everything we associate with *romance* is either opposed or indifferent. But when we examine this antagonism as it configures itself in the Renaissance, we find a symbiotic relation developing between episodic narratives of adventure and love and those kinds of literature—tragedy, comedy, and epic—which hold primary authority as the most select, or classic, forms of expression. What this relation is, and how some of its complexities are untangled in the following essays, we shall shortly consider. For the moment, however, a word must be said about the method implied in the title, if only to indicate that we are not here undertaking a survey of medieval and Hellenistic tales as told in the sixteenth and seventeenth centuries in England. Because the word *Re-*

I

naissance implies a historical perspective, the word *romance* a formal or generic one, a collection appearing under the two terms will be concerned in some measure with theoretical difficulties in coordinating the interests of both. Although the degree of concern on this point varies considerably in the essays that follow, the challenge of undertaking the sort of bifocal analysis implied in the title is a prominent theme. In this respect the volume contributes to a significant enterprise in Renaissance studies of the last two decades or so: that of treating literary history and critical theory as complementary modes of inquiry, illuminating at once the field under investigation and the instruments with which it is seen.[1]

There are two reasons for focusing on what Renaissance authors in particular did with romance, the first having to do with authority, the second with experiment. With regard to authority, we may remind ourselves first of the need for any serious investigation of romance to take into account its inferior literary status, romance being an expression, it is supposed, of the irregular impulses of the unlearned.[2] An author having classical principles will view the literature of romance either as a resource to be drawn on or as an example of bad taste to be shunned. In general, the first, or hierarchical, attitude is characteristic of the best classical works while the second, or adversarial attitude is evinced by arid neoclassicism. When Aulus Gellius describes an author as "classicus . . . scriptor, non proletarius," we note that the classical is defined not (to use a classic formulation) as in itself it really is but rather as what it is not: proletarian or popular.[3] A similar, Renaissance

1. For theoretically oriented discussions of Renaissance romance, based on the standard discussion in Northrop Frye's *Anatomy of Criticism: Four Essays* (Princeton: Princeton University Press, 1957), pp. 186–206, see James Nohrnberg, *The Analogy of "The Faerie Queene"* (Princeton: Princeton University Press, 1976), pp. 5–86 passim; Patricia A. Parker, *Inescapable Romance: Studies in the Poetics of a Mode* (Princeton: Princeton University Press, 1979), pp. 3–113; and Alastair Fowler, *Kinds of Literature: An Introduction to the Theory of Genres and Modes* (Cambridge, Mass.: Harvard University Press, 1982), pp. 251–52 et passim. See also Parker's entry on romance (with bibliography) in the forthcoming *Spenser Encyclopedia*, ed. A. C. Hamilton et al. (Toronto: University of Toronto Press). For remarks on the proximity of epic and romance in Renaissance authors and critical theorists, see Tomas Hägg, *The Novel in Antiquity* (Berkeley: University of California Press, 1983), pp. 1 and 197–201.

2. Northrop Frye, *The Secular Scripture: A Study of the Structure of Romance* (Cambridge, Mass.: Harvard University Press, 1976), p. 23.

3. Aulus Gellius, *Noctes atticae* XIX.viii.15.

statement of the classical ideal in terms of what it excludes may be found in Benedetto Varchi: "We shall term plebeian poets," he declares, "all those who without art and judgment . . . write only to delight the plebeians and to make the vulgar laugh."[4] Although Varchi is thinking of the deliberate buffoonery of Pulci's *Morgante* and not of Ariosto, whom he praises, his mood differs little from that of Thomas Nashe, who censures the authors of romances—"bable bookemungers" as he calls them—for desiring "to repaire the ruinous wals of *Venus* Court, to restore to the worlde that forgotten Legendary licence of lying, to imitate a fresh the fantasticall dreames of those exiled Abbie-lubbers, from whose idle pens proceeded those worne out impressions of the feyned no where acts, of Arthur of the rounde table, Arthur of litle Brittaine, sir Tristram, Hewon of Burdeaux, the Squire of low degree, the foure sons of Aymon, with infinite others."[5] Passages such as this, which are not uncommon in the Renaissance humanists, are very different in spirit from the generous opportunism of Sidney, who finds the basis of his classical values in the world of romance, just as he discerns the spirit of Pindar in an old man in the street singing of Percy and Douglas.

Sidney's attitude suggests that beneath the superficial antagonism between the classical and the romantic there is a more essential relation of mutual need: for as the classic work finds its imaginative ground in the world of romance, that world often achieves its fullest realization when presented in classical form, as in *The Tempest*. There are of course more than a few instances in Renaissance literature of classical values being affirmed in what would appear to be an antagonistic relation to the romantic, Trissino's *L'Italia liberata* and Jonson's *Sejanus* among them. But it is also a fact—a curious though undeniable one—that in this period more than in any other romantic and classical values not only engage in a fruitful relation with one another but are openly acknowledged to do so. Romance therefore enjoys an explicit authority—or, to speak more accurately, a prox-

4. Benedetto Varchi, *Della poetica* (1590), cited by Camillo Guerrieri Crocetti, in G. G. Cinzio, *Scritti critici*, Scrittori Italiani (Milan: Marzorati, 1973), p. 270 n. 9.

5. *The Works of Thomas Nashe*, ed. Ronald B. McKerrow, rev. ed. F. P. Wilson (Oxford: Basil Blackwell, 1958), I.11. The passage is cited and compared with Nashe's Preface to Robert Greene's *Menaphon* in G. R. Hibbard, *Thomas Nashe: A Critical Introduction* (Cambridge, Mass.: Harvard University Press, 1962), p. 15.

imity to authority—that it has yet to recover in subsequent literary history and that it had never acquired before. Nowhere is this more true than in England, where Sidney's *Arcadia* and Spenser's *Faerie Queene* were regarded as having attained to the dignity of epic. What one notices very soon while reading these works—and the history of criticism regarding them has never strayed far from this point—is the dynamism with which the forms of romance enter into relation with the classical principles informing the whole. This proximity in the Renaissance of romantic fancy to classical authority may explain why it would not have been thought odd to call Ariosto's web-work of tales a perfect, Aristotelian epic or to affirm that Spenser's heart "inharbours" Homer's soul.[6] In Renaissance works generally the imaginary antagonism between the classical and the romantic gives way to a relation in which the livelier patterns of romance energize the classical structures they support and inform.

Both *The Faerie Queene* and the *Arcadia* organize this hierarchical relation internally by treating the world of romance as the nursery of the heroic. Following the example of Tasso, Spenser proclaims in the first book of *The Faerie Queene* (and more tentatively in the "Letter to Raleigh") that his moralized romantic adventures are preparatory to a heroic struggle on the scale of an epic.[7] And Sidney, revising the *Old Arcadia* so that it would be, like the *Aethiopica* of Heliodorus, "an absolute heroicall Poeme," signals his intention of forming an epic by taking up the story in the midst of its action.[8] At the same time there is a sense in these authors, and in Renaissance epic poets generally, that

6. For Salviati's defense of Ariosto's poem as an Aristotelian epic, see Peter M. Brown, *Lionardo Salviati: A Critical Biography* (London: Oxford University Press, 1974), p. 180. For Spenser's heart and Homer's soul, see Charles Fitzgeffrey, *Sir Francis Drake* (1596), cited in *Spenser Allusions in the Sixteenth and Seventeenth Centuries. Part I: 1580–1625*, ed. William Wells, SP, 68 (1971), 48. For the classical unity achieved by romance, see G. G. Giraldi Cinzio, "Discorso intorno al comporre dei romanzi," *Scritti critici*, pp. 53 and 56.

7. *The Faerie Queene*, ed. A. C. Hamilton, Longman Annotated English Poets (London: Longman, 1977), I.xi.5–7. Cf. IV Proem 2.

8. *The Defence of Poesie*, in *The Prose Works of Sir Philip Sidney*, 4 vols., ed. Albert Feuillerat (1912; rpt. Cambridge: Cambridge University Press, 1962), III.10. See "The *New Arcadia*: 'an absolute heroical poem,'" in A. C. Hamilton, *Sir Philip Sidney: A Study of His Life and Works* (Cambridge: Cambridge University Press, 1977), pp. 123–74, esp. 125 and 201 n. 6. In "Structure and Rhetoric in Sidney's *Arcadia*," *Poetica*, 18 (1984), 68–81, rpt. in *Sir Philip Sidney: An Anthology of Modern Criticism*, ed. Dennis Kay (Oxford: Clarendon Press, 1987), pp. 245–64, John Carey notes that

because the heroic poem has its origin in the romance it is almost constantly in danger of an ethical and aesthetic relapse. This notion is common enough among the poets and the critical theorists.[9] And it generates in the Renaissance epic a thematic tension the imaginative center of which is brought into view, and unexpectedly resolved, in a work of a very different kind: Jonson's masque *Pleasure Reconciled to Virtue*.

The tension is more subtly captured, however, in an iconographical detail near the beginning of the *New Arcadia*. When the young prince Musidorus, having been shipwrecked, recovers his strength in the home of the Arcadian nobleman, Kalander, he visits a summerhouse in the garden, where he sees paintings of mythical subjects foreshadowing the passions that will emerge in the tale.[10] Just outside this house there

---

the *Arcadia*, in addition to being generally compared to the epics of Homer and Virgil, was cited by George Hakewill in his *Apology of the Power and Providence of God* as evidence of the greatness of the moderns as compared with the ancients (p. 245). See also Jon S. Lawry, *Sidney's Two Arcadias: Pattern and Meaning* (Ithaca: Cornell University Press, 1972), pp. 155, 173, 210; Mark Rose, *Heroic Love: Studies in Sidney and Spenser* (Cambridge, Mass.: Harvard University Press, 1968), p. 1. For an influential discussion of genre in the *Arcadia*, see Stephen J. Greenblatt, "Sidney's Arcadia and the Mixed Mode," *SP*, 70 (1973), 269–78, rpt. in *Essential Articles for the Study of Sir Philip Sidney*, ed. Arthur Kinney (Hamden, Conn.: Archon Books, 1986), pp. 347–56. J. C. Scaliger ranked Heliodorus's romance with Virgil's epic as a model of classical plot construction. For the importance of Heliodorus in relating romance to epic in Renaissance critical theory, see Merritt Y. Hughes, "Spenser's Debt to the Greek Romances," *MP*, 22 (1925), 75; C. S. Lewis, *English Literature in the Sixteenth Century Excluding Drama* (New York: Oxford University Press, 1954), p. 334; Alban K. Forcione, "Heliodorus and Literary Theory," *Cervantes, Aristotle, and the Persiles* (Princeton: Princeton University Press, 1970), pp. 49–87 (the fullest discussion); Gerald N. Sandy, *Heliodorus* (Boston: Twayne, 1982), pp. 97–106, which follows Forcione; and Henry C. Aiman, "Spenser's Debt to Heliodorus in *The Faerie Queene*," *Emporia State Research Studies*, 22 (1974), 5–6. One of the more telling instances of the desire to view Heliodorus's *Aethiopica* as an experiment in raising romance to the level of the epic is Abraham Fraunce's turning a portion of it into English hexameters, an effort ridiculed by Jonson in his conversations with Drummond. See Charles Whibley's introduction to *An Aethiopian History . . . Englished by Thomas Underdowne* (1587), Tudor Translations 5 (1895; rpt. New York: AMS Press, 1967), p. xxv.

9. Simone Fornari, "Apologia brieve sopra tutto l'*Orlando furioso*," *La spositione . . . sopra l'"Orlando furioso"* I (Florence, 1549), pp. 32–36. Torquato Tasso, "Allegoria del poema," *Gierusalemme liberata . . . con l'allegoria dello stesso autore*, ed. Febo Bona (Ferrara, 1581).

10. Maurice Evans, ed., *The Countess of Pembroke's Arcadia* (Harmondsworth: Penguin, 1977), p. 849 n. 1.

is another work of art that seems by its placement to condition the meaning of the pictures within: a fountain with a statue of Venus nursing a child. The child is not Cupid, as might be expected, but Aeneas, the quintessential hero of epic: "A naked *Venus* of white marble, wherein the graver had used such cunning, that the naturall blew veines of the marble were framed in fitte places, to set foorth the beautifull veines of her bodie. At her brest she had her babe *Aeneas*, who seemed (having begun to sucke) to leave that, to looke upon her fayre eyes, which smiled at the babes follie, meane while the breast running."[11]

The folly is that the child turns his gaze from Venus's breast to her eyes, which is not what a grown man would do. And it is the grown man, whose romantic involvement with Dido caused him to put off the task of founding an empire, that we think of when Sidney mentions Aeneas, recognizing the child as father to the man. We think of him because Aeneas's erotic temptation to delay his great task is the prototype of the experience of such Renaissance heroes as Tasso's Rinaldo who are similarly tempted. The hero of the romantic epic is never quite free of the goddess of love. And what is true of the hero is also true of the form, which by allowing itself to digress from the main action is in danger of falling back into its original and morally ambiguous state.

This danger is felt to be great, for the imaginative scope of romance is more ample than that of the epic and, like the naked Venus, a cause of more visible and immediate delight. And the "modern" epic poet, as Tasso remarked, cannot do without the narrative machinery of that delight: rapid variation of episodes and frequent supernatural marvels. The tendency to romance therefore establishes itself in every Renaissance epic, making it necessary, if the epic is to maintain its status, for the poet to subordinate that tendency to the larger, heroic concern. This subordination is accomplished by making the valor of the epic hero a kind of sublimated erotic desire, in keeping with the popular etymological connection between the words *eros* and *heros*: love, Spenser assures us, is the root of all honor and virtue.[12] Even as ro-

---

11. *Arcadia*, lib. I, chap. 3, pp. 17–18. The portrayal of Cupid as enamored of his mother appears in Renaissance art in Bronzino's *Allegory of Venus and Cupid* in the National Gallery in London.

12. *FQ* IV Proem 2. For *eros* and *heros*, see John Erskine Hankins, *Source and Meaning in Spenser's Allegory: A Study of "The Faerie Queene"* (Oxford: Clarendon

mance is subordinated, however, to the higher concerns of the epic, it provides an opportunity for the poet to modify and even to transform those concerns in the work as a whole. To summarize the point more abstractly, we may say that the Renaissance epic uses romance as a source of disorder, or potential for change, that is both necessary and dangerous to it.

The second reason for focusing on romance in the Renaissance follows in consequence of the first: having attained to a subordinate but not inconsiderable degree of authority in relation to tragedy, comedy, and epic, romance provides a kind of staging area where new ideas can be experimented with and introduced as innovations into the classical forms. When we think in these terms of the mechanical neoclassicism of those Tudor dramatists who follow Plautus and Seneca with all their might when not simply translating them—and even when we think of Marlowe and Kyd—we begin to see the importance of romance as an experimental medium for bringing Elizabethan drama to maturity. As is evident even in a neoclassical play like *The Comedy of Errors*, much of what makes Shakespeare different from his contemporaries is based in his reading of popular literature. Because romance provides Renaissance authors with an imaginative region where experiments can be allowed to take place, its relation to forms such as tragedy and epic is supplementary rather than adversarial or simply indifferent. Yet as a consequence of this unequal dialogue with higher forms, Renaissance romance borrows its episodes and motifs from medieval or Hellenistic sources rather than inventing its own. In proportion as it is innovative and experimental with respect to the alien forms in which it lives, it is conservative with respect to itself.

This proclivity in Renaissance romance to formal and stylistic experiment rather than to narrative invention is, in the broadest sense, the subject to which the essays in this collection address themselves.

Press, 1971), p. 47. To indicate that valor is sublimated desire, heroines in the Renaissance romance are given names like Philoclea and Gloriana. The most closely reasoned statement of the idea is in Tasso's prose allegory, where he first identifies the concupiscible and the irascible powers of the soul (demonstrated by Rinaldo's actions) as opponents of reason (represented by Goffredo). Tasso then argues that the conversion of the concupiscible into the irascible, followed by the obedience of the latter to reason, is necessary if reason is to have enough force to carry out its designs. Rinaldo is Goffredo's right arm.

We may define it more narrowly if we distinguish between naïve and sophisticated romance as extremes between which every romance situates itself by participating in some measure in both.[13] While *naïve romance* refers to a narrative basis in folk tales, sagas, and oral recitations of the exploits of heroes, *sophisticated romance* refers to the self-conscious literary structures that are sometimes raised on that foundation. These terms are not entirely satisfactory, because they imply value judgments not relevant here. Few romances could be more sophisticated as literary art than those of Chrétien de Troyes, which fall into the category of the naïve. And few works of literature worth reading at all are more simple-minded than Stephen Hawes's allegorical hybrids, which fall into the category of sophisticated romance. For our purposes, however, we may say that we have sophisticated romance when the author thinks of his medium as a distinct genre that can be brought into experimental relation with others.

This capacity for looking on the elements of romance with some detachment is necessary if it is to be put to work experimentally in the classical forms. For the values associated with the antique can only avoid arid reconstruction, as opposed to genuine rebirth, when those values are allied with others to which they appear, superficially, to be opposed. Consider, for instance, some examples of the revival of the classical genre of tragedy: *King Lear* and *Macbeth*, which have their narrative roots in the folktale; *Othello*, which is, like the mind of its hero, encircled by deserts where monstrosity and wonder abound; and *Antony and Cleopatra*, which derives much of its power not from Roman history but from our familiarity with similar temptresses and libidinous heroes in the world of romance. To a considerable degree it is the effect of romantic elements in these tragedies that distinguishes them from the more aridly classical *Gorboduc*. Only in some of Shakespeare's last works does it seem as if romance has liberated itself altogether from the strictures of classical form.

At this point it is necessary that the argument turn back on itself. I spoke of romance as standing in a hierarchically supplemental relation to the classical forms, which it nourishes, so to speak, from below, in

---

13. Frye's *The Secular Scripture*, p. 3, draws a distinction between naïve and sentimental romance from Schiller's essay "On Naïve and Sentimental Poetry."

the way that the *Oresteia* and the *Iliad* are nourished by a world of folktale and myth that they largely exclude. I then differentiated Renaissance romance by its closer proximity to the authority enjoyed by the classical forms and by the greater facility with which romantic elements, providing opportunities for experiments of a technical nature, make their way into those forms—or at least into works having an authority equal to what we call *classic*. The ambiguity of this last clause should alert the reader to a problem with the argument so far: when we speak of *The Faerie Queene* or of Shakespeare's late romances we are not speaking of classical works into which romantic elements have merely intruded themselves. We appear to be speaking instead of whole romances in which some classical elements have managed to survive by adapting themselves, like parasites, to the larger organism in which they are enclosed. In any canto of *The Faerie Queene* we will find classical formulas that while adapting themselves to the environment of chivalric romance can readily be traced to their origins in Virgil and Homer, where they exist as organic parts of the whole. But when these formulas are included in Spenser's poem it no longer seems as if certain elements of romance are nourishing the higher form of the epic: it seems as if the *disjecta membra* of the classical epic have managed to survive, as separate things, inside romance.

Now in trying to decide whether romance is being included in epic or epic in romance we encounter a problem larger than the one we have taken in hand. For genre theory has its basis in the categories of identity and difference and demands that the sameness of each thing, its *ethos*, remain true to itself, whatever complicated relations it enters into with others. And the relations into which romance and the various classical forms are brought in Renaissance literature are just the sorts of relations that undermine the categories on which genre theory relies, relations in which the host becomes the guest and the container becomes the contained. Since I have spoken, on the one hand, of the energies of romance nourishing the classical forms and, on the other hand, of little strips of the classic surviving like parasites in works of romance, it may now be useful to make more explicit the metaphor of feeding that has informed the discussion so far.

In his essay "The Medusa and the Snail," Lewis Thomas describes the symbiotic relation between a jellyfish, the medusa, and a common sea snail that in its mature state has a tiny, round, vestigial medusa attached to the skin near its mouth.[14] This vestigial jellyfish produces a full-sized offspring that will capture inside it a small snail of the same species as the large one on which its parent is anchored. Remaining undigested by the medusa, the engulfed snail will devour its host from within, growing larger as its host is correspondingly diminished in size. Finally, as the cycle is completed, the snail grows so large, and the jellyfish it devours so small, that its host is reduced to a tiny, round parasite clinging to the skin near its mouth.

The application of this cycle to the relation between the classical and the romantic is easily seen. We are used to thinking of *The Tempest*, for example, as a play in which Shakespeare imposes a rigorously classical form on the romantic experiments of *The Winter's Tale*. He does this by moving the tempest at the middle of the earlier play to the beginning of the later one and by having Prospero narrate to Miranda what had happened before the tempest occurred. But scrupulous order within a classical time scheme appears to be intrinsic to the action of the play, not imposed from without. It is Prospero who, like a classical author, governs the distribution of events in the play so that, like a wizard, he can capture the powers to be released when the previous age has completed its course in the stars. The classical perfection of *The Tempest* seems not to have been imposed from without on romantic materials but to have emerged from within to engulf them.

II

Having considered in general terms how romance provides Renaissance authors with an opportunity for technical innovation, we may turn now to the essays in this collection, which show how the opportunity is seized in particular cases. Beginning with the smallest structures of discourse, Judith H. Anderson and Alastair Fowler are concerned with Spenser's use of individual words to evoke two ideas of language that, by interfering with one another, give to the *The Faerie Queene* its rich and various surface. Anderson detects a persistent theme in the poem according to which certain words of power are

14. Lewis Thomas, *The Medusa and the Snail: More Notes of a Biology Watcher* (1974; rpt. New York: Viking, 1977), pp. 4–5.

drawn out of a *secretum* or "word-horde" and allowed to disseminate themselves in the open and mobile space of the story—just as the knights on their quests make their way outward from Faerie court. In Fowler's analysis of the Latin and Greek origins of Spenser's names, however, we can see how this idea of the poem's language would work at cross-purposes to the hieratic conception of language implied by these more difficult and (we are meant to suppose) more deeply significant words—words that exist on a level of meaning higher than that of the words used simply for advancing the narrative line. Taking these essays together, we notice that a lateral tendency of words away from a narrative center is interfered with by a tendency upward toward the universally inclusive Word, the one movement taking us away from Cleopolis, the other up to the "Sabaoths sight." It would seem that a familiar diegetical tension in *The Faerie Queene* is operating more subtly, and more pervasively, on the lexical plane.

Moving up to the next level of discourse—that of rhetorical tropes and syntactical patterns—we find a similar conflict evinced in Robert Heilman's essay on Greene and the history of euphuism. Euphuism is a hypertrophy of the most typically classical impulse of style: the balanced and harmonious arrangement of clauses. When John Lyly unclassically pursued this ideal in the extreme, he so thickened the texture of his medium that the story could advance only by forcing its way through the language. By the very extremity of this undertaking, Lyly exposed a tension in romantic fiction generally: the tension between narrative, which must push itself forward through time, and rhetoric, which tries to remove language from time altogether. While in Lyly's career rhetoric finally gains the upper hand, strangling any narrative interest, the opposite happens in Greene, leading to unexpected developments that are of larger importance, as Heilman shows, for the rise of the novel. An interesting twist is given to this line of reasoning by W. W. Barker, who argues that by recognizing and preserving this tension between rhetorical display and narrative drive, Greene forced himself to invent a more dramatic and naturalistic style—and to follow in his own career a course that would be followed on the larger stage of literary history.

At the next level of discourse we encounter lyrical effects imbedded in larger, narrative structures, as when a sonnet is jointly spoken by Romeo and Juliet when they first meet. The curious double perspective created by such moments is examined in A. Kent Hieatt's essay on the intrusion of lyric into romance in Shakespeare's last plays, particularly *Cymbeline*. Hieatt's argument is focused on a chain of images (originally forged in the sonnets) by which politics is associated with Roman themes, Roman themes with architectural ruins, ruins with a body contemplating its desolation by time, and that desolation as the overriding factor in the politics of love, where youth is reluctant to couch with age. The absurdity of the aging lover's predicament is captured in two statements taken from the same speech in *Cymbeline*: "The ruin speaks that sometime / It was a worthy building" and "nature doth abhor to make his bed / With the defunct."[15] Restored to their bizarre dramatic context—in which the speaker, Lucius, describes Imogen lying on the beheaded corpse of the wicked Queen's son, Cloten, whom Imogen has mistaken for her husband, Posthumus—the words say something quite different from what they seem, taken out of that context, to say about love. Hieatt is suggesting that as we strive, reading *Cymbeline*, to keep track of the story, we are touched, almost unawares, by the concerns of the sonnets. Cloten was a ridiculous wooer, now beaten and chopped.

Occupying the middle distance between language and style, on the one hand, and, on the other, inclusive genres, Carol Kaske focuses on Spenser's observation of another poet's experiment in combining allegory and romance. In the course of her analysis, Kaske is able not only to dispel a misconception as to which of Stephen Hawes's poems was most exploited by Spenser but to give us an example of how a major writer capitalizes on technical risks taken by others. This unclassical, experimental element in Spenser's writing, which Gabriel Harvey deplored, is examined by Donald Cheney in his essay on *The Shepheardes Calender*. Cheney demonstrates, among other things, that circular, calendrical patterns in that work anticipate the pattern of recurrence with difference, or "interlace," in Spenserian romance.

This concern with how Spenser conceived of his project is resumed in Thomas P. Roche, Jr.'s, striking discussion of one of the most venerable debates among Spenser scholars: the identity of Spenser's muse. Without entering into the particulars of that discussion, it may be noted that

---

15. *Cymbeline* IV.ii.354–58, ed. G. Blakemore Evans et al., *The Riverside Shakespeare* (Boston: Houghton Mifflin, 1974).

the very existence of uncertainty on this point is of interest because of the ambiguous position of Renaissance romance between history and epic, taking from the first the concern with orderly sequence in time (as in Spenser's line of Briton kings) and from the second the drive toward a culminating heroic battle between Christians and pagans. Is Spenser's muse therefore Calliope, singing of events preparatory to this great battle, or is she Clio, whose interests are sung whenever the dynastic theme comes to the fore? Even if it is possible to decide which muse governs Spenser's song, we will continue as we read to sense that there is a missing link in the chain of the muses between these lineal and oppositional modes, and that Hobgoblin wanders between them.

This proclivity of Renaissance romance to carry on a sustained negotiation of its identity, and to carry it on inside itself, is the most extreme manifestation of what I have called its experimental function with respect to the classical forms. For in its extreme stage the experiment becomes a conflict for the very identity of a literary kind, which struggles to digest an alien system that is struggling, in turn, to absorb and transfigure its host from within. A stage for this conflict is set in Patricia Parker's investigation of the Virgilian subtext of *Cymbeline* and of the play's notorious anachronisms, which are forced into view by the underlying struggle of generic codes. Serious anachronism is almost inconceivable in the world of naive romance, where the reader simply follows the story from one adventure to the next without any wider concern for its setting in time. But the *Aeneid* is an account of a past that has meaning only when juxtaposed, by deliberate anachronism, to later events in the history of Rome. In *Cymbeline* Jove describes the end of Posthumus's troubles as "the more delay'd, delighted . . . And happier much by his affliction made."[16] The difference of this statement from the famous one to which it alludes, Aeneas's "forsan et haec olim meminisse iuvabit" ("perhaps one day it will be a pleasure to remember even these sufferings")[17]—the one suggesting the necessity of delay in the economy of pleasure, the other the reality of suffering in the achievement of empire—marks the syncopation of genres in Shakespeare's play.

While the authors just mentioned are concerned with internal rela-

16. *Cymbeline* V.iv.102–08.
17. *Aeneid* I.203; cf. *Odyssey* XII.212.

tions between romance and the alien forms that it holds (or that hold it), Maureen Quilligan and Harry Berger, Jr., describe ideological patterns that become visible only when the formulas of romance are held at arm's length. Noting, for example, how Lady Mary Wroth, in her *Countess of Montgomerie's Urania*, reworks narrative codes that provide imaginary solutions to conflict between men and women, Quilligan shows how Wroth reverses the implications of such episodes of *The Faerie Queene* as Amoret's torture by Busirane. This reversal is not unlike feminist interpretations of Freud's effort, in Sarah Kofman's phrase, to "penetrate woman" with an alien discourse, as the Spenserian enchanter tries to do with his magical signs.[18] Berger is likewise concerned with the ideological implications of the discourse of romance, specifically with Spenser's difficulties in attempting a private reversal of the public, and hence given, codes of the genre. But in Berger's judgment Spenser not only recognizes the danger of trying to reverse the forces in a charged system but registers that awareness, and sets it apart, by allowing several discourses to strive for control in the poem.

In the final essay of this collection, William Blissett's "Caves, Labyrinths, and *The Faerie Queene*," we find that it is no longer possible to speak of romance in an experimental relation with other discourses or even, as in the last essays mentioned, in a critical relation with itself. We are brought instead into a wider area of concern to which the interests of this collection naturally tend. Blissett's title, with its judiciously indecisive conjunction, prompts us to ask whether romance is a verbal labyrinth or whether the labyrinth is merely a plan of the more complete form of life that we call, when we are thinking in literary terms, *romance*. Is the labyrinth, as it appears in Ariosto, for instance, contained by something larger, the cave of the romantic imagination? Or is the romantic imagination merely one cave hollowed out in the pathways of thought? The puzzle is captured, appropriately, in Blissett's description of Spenser's *Errour*, who is a cavelike gut entangled in the maze of her folds, which form a labyrinth inside a cave at the center of the labyrinth of the wandering wood.

We may conclude with this problem of identifying which is the

18. Sarah Kofman, *L'Enigme de la femme: La Femme dans les textes de Freud*, 2nd ed. (Paris: Galilée, 1983), p. 57.

container and which the contained. Each essay in this collection positions its subject inside something else: language and style *in* the romances of Greene, epic anachronicity and lyrical ruin *in Cymbeline*, imagination and ideology *in* Spenser and Wroth, discourse, *lexis*, and genre *in The Faerie Queene*. But while each of these things is said to be *in* a literary work, it is also supposed to belong to a much larger thing, Renaissance romance, which contains the containers. There is therefore a methodological uncertainty—that is, a legitimate and a necessary uncertainty—as to whether the subject of these essays is Renaissance romance and the literary works discussed merely the places in which it is seen, or whether the subject of each essay is a literary work examined in the light of something we may name, for convenience, Renaissance romance. It would appear that the first case applies only insofar as these essays belong to a book and the second insofar as each belongs to itself. But once this distinction is understood, and once we acknowledge that the two cases can never be made into one, we can dedicate these studies, both ways, to the same man.

1

"Myn auctour": Spenser's Enabling Fiction and Eumnestes' "immortall scrine"

JUDITH H. ANDERSON

Like Chaucer, Spenser often finds or pretends to find in earlier books the enabling source of his own poetry, and for this reason, among others, he describes Chaucer's writing as the wellhead of his own. Quite recently, Spenser's interpreters have sought the meaning of his deliberate reliance on a written tradition in pure textuality or in its effect on a community of readers.[1] While not rejecting their many valid perceptions, I would suggest that this reliance also be referred to the meaning Spenser gave it, particularly in *The Faerie Queene*. In Spenser's most massively allusive poem, the significance of earlier works is inseparable from the idea of antiquity, an idea in which these works are themselves implicated. "Whylome as antique stories tellen vs," Spenser wrote in imitation of the beginning of Chaucer's Knight's Tale—"Whylom, as olde stories tellen vs"—and thereby he specifically placed Chaucer's work in the tradition of antique writings, even as he recalled Chaucer's own placement of the Knight's Tale in such a tradition.[2]

1. See, for example, John Guillory, *Poetic Authority: Spenser, Milton, and Literary History* (New York: Columbia University Press, 1983), chaps. 2–3; and Maureen Quilligan's response to Guillory in *Milton's Spenser: The Politics of Reading* (Ithaca: Cornell University Press, 1983), pp. 157–71.

2. *FQ* VI.ii.32. Reference to Spenser's works is to the *Variorum*. Quotation of Chaucer's poetry is from *Works 1532, with Supplementary Material from the Editions of 1542, 1561, 1598, and 1602* (London: Scolar, 1969).

Antiquity, as Spenser develops this idea in *The Faerie Queene*, consists of plain truth and timeless admonitions; it is an idealized place of mythic patterns and an undefiled "well" of simple purity.[3] Antiquity resides in memorial scrolls and permanent records, and these participate in Clio's "volume of Eternitie," a volume that always surpasses yet ever illumines human memory (III.iii.4). For the Renaissance generally but more particularly for Spenser, the sense of a literary tradition and of the words and forms that constitute it is more idealistic and mysterious than in a modern poetics of loss and displacement. It is far more eclectic, including skepticism and doubt but also affirming wisdom, virtue, and truth. Often, as Spenser describes this tradition, it is recorded memory, tied intrinsically to the very idea of words, written records, and the mnemonic working of the human mind.

Predictably, many of the words Spenser uses to describe recorded memory are so revealing as to suggest his selecting them for the reminders—the associations or reminiscences—built into their history. Among these is the arresting word *scrine*, from Latin *scrinium*, which first appears in the Proem to Book I, where the poet asks his muse to "Lay forth out of" her "euerlasting scryne / The antique rolles" of Faerie Land.[4] Cooper's *Thesaurus*, or treasury, of the Roman language defines *scrinium* as "a coffer or other like place wherein jewels or secrete things are kept."[5] Stephanus's *Thesaurus linguae latinae* derives *scrinium* from *secernendum*, "setting apart, secreting, secluding," and defines it as a place in which precious things and mysteries (*secreta*) are preserved and protected (*servantur*).[6] Not surprisingly, in view of these definitions, the word *scrine* also carries the more specific meaning

3. See *FQ* II.vii.15, l. 7, IV.ii.32, l. 8. I have discussed Spenser's image of antiquity in greater detail in "The Antiquities of Fairyland and Ireland," *JEGP*, 86 (1987), 199–214.

4. Thomas H. Cain, *Praise in "The Faerie Queene"* (Lincoln: University of Nebraska Press, 1978), pp. 49–50, argues that *scrine* in Proem I transfers to Elizabeth I a phrase used in reference to papal authority, namely *in scrinio pectoris omnia*. While this dimension of meaning may well be present in Proem I, Cain seems to me to press its claims too far, treating them as primary and exclusive. Parodic reference to papal authority is already too narrow a meaning for *scrine* in Proem I and much too narrow for Spenser's second use of the word in II.ix.56, examined later in this essay.

5. Thomas Cooper, *Thesavrvs lingvae romanae & britannicae* (London, 1584). Cf. Thomas Thomas, *Dictionarivm lingvae latinae et anglicanae* (London, [1588?]).

6. Robertus Stephanus, *Thesavrvs lingvae latinae* (Basel, 1576–78).

"shrine" during the Middle Ages and the Renaissance.[7] Also in view of them, Spenser's description of the rolls that lie in his muse's "euerlasting scryne" as "hidden still"—that is, hidden always, secretly, silently, motionlessly—makes sense, but it is primarily in relation to the sacred meaning "shrine" that the word *everlasting* at this point does so. In the chamber of Eumnestes, or Good Memory, within the brain-turret of the House of Alma, the word *still* recurs in the phrase "recorded still" describing Eumnestes' operation and carries with it something of its mysterious force in the first Proem. In connection with Eumnestes' function, the word *scrine* likewise appears, characterized this time not as "euerlasting" but, with added point, as "immortall" (II.ix.56).

Both Cooper and Stephanus include among their illustrations of the meaning of *scrinium* Catullus's phrase "librariorum . . . scrinia"—the booksellers' containers of manuscripts or rolls.[8] Their illustration bears on the furnishing of Eumnestes' chamber, which is "all . . . hangd about with rolles, / And old records from auncient times deriu'd, / Some made in books, some in long parchment scrolles" (ix.57). The association of *scrinia*, or scrines, with books, records, and sacred relics goes deep into the past. Under the late Roman emperors, there were four types of public scrines for various kinds of historical records (*scrinia libellorum, memoriae, epistularum,* and *epistularum Graecarum*).[9] The scrines of monasteries or churches were the places, whether chests, cupboards, niches, or rooms, where the enabling instruments and authorizing documents that pertained to the rights of the institution were kept. In this context, the scrine is equivalent to the *secretum,* or "secret place," the treasury of the institution and, prior to the establishment of libraries, the depository for books.[10] Isidore of Seville, whose *Etymology* was a notable source for the Renaissance, describes scrines as containers in which books or treasures are protected—"ser-

---

7. *OED*, s.v. *scrine*; Du Cange, s.v. *scrinium.*

8. *Catullus,* ed. Elmer Truesdell Merrill (Cambridge, Mass.: Harvard University Press. 1893), XIV.17–18 and notes, p. 33: for my purpose the notes in this edition are most pertinent; for corroboration see *Catullus: A Commentary,* by C. J. Fordyce (Oxford: Clarendon Press, 1961), pp. 137–38 nn. 17–18.

9. Lewis & Short, s.v. *scrinium.*

10. Du Cange, s.v. *scrinium;* also Ronald E. Latham, *Revised Medieval Latin Word-List* (London: Oxford University Press, 1965). I am indebted on this point to Mary Carruthers, whose forthcoming work on memory in the Middle Ages has stimulated my own interest in the subject.

vantur libri vel thesauri"—and explains this to be the reason that those Romans who preserved the sacred books—"libros sacros"—were called *scriniarii*.[11]

From the ancient Roman past, through the Middle Ages, to the Tudor present, the fortunes of the word *scrine* suggest, in addition to its association with books and archives, equally persistent associations with memory or with things worth remembering—things worth keeping *in mind* and things of value: repeatedly and specifically *scrine* is associated with secrecy or seclusion (*secerno*, *secretum*), with a need to guard or preserve, and with the word and idea of a *thesaurus*, a treasure or a treasury of writing and, more fundamentally, of words. One moves easily, induced by the context of Spenser's usage, from these associations to Sidney's commonplace observation that, "memorie being the onely treasurer of knowled[g]e, those words . . . fittest for memory are likewise most conuenient for knowledge"; and then back in time to Plato's more mystically oriented idea that all knowledge is memorial, a kind of remembering, an idea reflected variously yet in turn by Aristotle, by the Neoplatonists, and by Saint Augustine.[12]

The word *scrine*, in itself and as Spenser employs it, also conveys the idea of communal or racial content—of resources that span generations.[13] Such resources may be accessible to individuals in time but

---

11. Du Cange, s.v. *scrinium*.

12. Sir Philip Sidney, *An Apology for Poetry*, in *Elizabethan Critical Essays*, ed. G. Gregory Smith (Oxford: Oxford University Press, 1904), I.182. Cf. Thomas Wilson, *Arte of Rhetorique*, ed. Thomas J. Derrick (1553; rpt. New York: Garland, 1982), p. 415: "The memorie [is] called the Threasure of the mynde." Francis MacDonald Cornford, *Plato's Theory of Knowledge* (1934; rpt. New York: Liberal Arts Press, 1957), pp. 2, 27–28; Étienne Gilson, *The Christian Philosophy of Saint Augustine*, trans. L. E. M. Lynch (1960; rpt. New York: Random House, 1967), pp. 71–76, 99–105. In *Aristotle on Memory* (Providence: Brown University Press, 1972), Richard Sorabji asks "why Aristotle should have devoted half his treatise" on memory to recollection or reminiscence (*anamnesis*) and then explains that "recollection played a major role in Plato's metaphysics and epistemology. And though Aristotle did not accept the metaphysics and epistemology, he did inherit [from Plato] the interest in recollection" (p. 35).

13. Harry Berger, Jr., *The Allegorical Temper: Vision and Reality in Book II of Spenser's "Faerie Queene"* (New Haven: Yale University Press, 1957), p. 79, makes a similar observation about the written documents in Eumnestes' chamber. Likewise, Michael Murrin, *The Veil of Allegory: Some Notes toward a Theory of Allegorical Rhetoric in the English Renaissance* (Chicago: University of Chicago Press, 1969), p. 82.

always exceed their direct and specific experience. Here, in connection with Spenser's two uses of *scrine*, one thinks of Bacon's traditional definition of history as both memory and experience and of Aristotle's and Aquinas's descriptions of experience itself as memory—as the fused product of many generations of memories of many things. When Aquinas considers the intellectual virtue of prudence, whose components the three sages of Alma's brain-turret represent, he follows Aristotle in explaining that *"intellectual virtue is engendered and fostered by experience and time"* and that "experience [itself] is the result of many memories." He concludes that "prudence requires the memory of many things," or, as he affirms elsewhere, "prudence requires experience which is made up *of many memories.*" Similarly, for Bacon's wise and prudent historian, whose knowledge belongs to the faculty of memory, "history and experience" are "the same thing." Heirs of such definitions, the sages of Alma's brain-turret represent imagination, rational judgment, and memory—the last in the figure of Eumnestes; they look in turn to the future, the present, and the historical past and together constitute Spenser's allegory of prudence.[14]

The content of Eumnestes' "immortall scrine" appears to be considerably purer than the books and scrolls, "all worme-eaten, and full of canker holes," that hang about his walls. These physically decrepit records are explicitly contrasted with the disembodied purity and seeming transcendence of the content of memory, which derives from

14. Francis Bacon, *Works*, ed. James Spedding, Robert Leslie Ellis, and Douglas Denon Heath, 15 vols. (Boston: Brown and Taggard [imprint varies; vols. 6–10: Taggard and Thompson], 1860–64), VI.182, VIII.408, 426, 433, II.187–88, 206, 214–15. Aristotle, *Works*, rev. Oxford trans., ed. Jonathan Barnes (Princeton: Princeton University Press, 1984): *Metaphysics* I.i.980b26–981a21, 981b30–982a2; *Nicomachean Ethics* II.i.1103a14–16; *Poetics* IX.1451b5–9. Saint Thomas Aquinas, *The "Summa Theologica,"* trans. Fathers of the English Dominican Province, 2nd rev. ed. (London: Burns Oates & Washbourne, 1929), X, II–II.47.16, 49.1; also *Summa Theologiae*, Blackfriars Edition (London: Eyre and Spottiswoode, 1974), XXXVI: "Sed ad generationem prudentiae necessarium est experimentum, quod fit ex multis memoriis, ut dicitur in princ. *Meta.*" (II–II.47.16); "Quid autem in pluribus sit verum oportet per experimentum considerare. Unde et Philosophus dicit quod *virtus intellectualis habet generationem et augmentum ex experimento et tempore.* Experimentum autem est ex pluribus memoriis, ut patet in I *Meta.*, unde consequens est quod ad prudentiam requiritur plurium memoriam habere" (II–II.49.1). On Spenser's allegory of prudence, see *Books I and II of "The Faerie Queene,"* ed. Robert Kellogg and Oliver Steele (New York: Odyssey, 1965), p. 343 n. 47.8–9, and the references in note 24 herein.

them. Well removed from physical worms, the content of Eumnestes' scrine belongs to a figure "of *infinite* remembrance," who

> things foregone through many ages held,
> Which he *recorded still*, as they did pas,
> Ne suffred them to perish through long eld,
> As all things else, the which this world doth weld,
> But laid them vp in his *immortall scrine*,
> Where they for euer *incorrupted* dweld. (II.ix.56; my emphases)

Like the content of any other shrine, including the body, the temple of the Holy Ghost, it is the content of Eumnestes' scrine—the "precious things and mysteries"—that is immortal, rather than the scrine itself, to which, in a way familiar to readers of *The Faerie Queene*, Spenser transfers the attribute of immortality. The immortal content of this scrine in which the past dwells uncorrupted is not far distant from the figurative use of *scrine* in Nicholas Udall's translation of Erasmus's *Apophthegmes*: "The mynde or solle of manne is couered, & . . . housed or hidden within the tabernacle or skryne of the bodye & dooeth in a mannes communicacion clerely appere and euidently shewe itself."[15]

Udall's translation would seem to apply to the House of Alma, to the chamber of Eumnestes, and to Eumnestes' scrine itself, with its transferred epithet "immortall": together, like so many Chinese boxes, these recesses are always receding, always hidden, but always there, always evident, always recorded—in words and (re-*cor*-dari) in the heart. As a gloss on Eumnestes' scrine, Udall's translation also returns us to Stephanus's derivation of *scrinium* from *secernendum*, "setting apart, secreting, secluding," which, along with "The antique rolles, which there [in the muse's scrine of Proem I] lye hidden still," suggests so hauntingly the Proem to Book VI:

> Such secret comfort, and such heauenly pleasures,
>   Ye sacred imps, that on *Parnasso* dwell,
> And there *the keeping* haue of *learnings threasures*,
>   Which doe all worldly riches farre excell,

---

15. (London, 1542), p. 145ᵛ. Cf. Wilson, p. 414: "The same is memorie to the mynde, that life is to the body."

> Into the mindes of mortall men doe *well*,
> And goodly fury into them *infuse*;
> Guyde ye my footing, and conduct me well
> In these strange waies, where neuer foote did vse,
> Ne none can find, but who was taught them by the Muse.

> Reuele to me the *sacred* noursery
> Of vertue, which with you doth there *remaine*,
> Where it in siluer bowre does *hidden* ly.
>
> (2–3; except *Parnasso*, my emphases)

Secrecy, seclusion, the preservation of learning's treasures, the welling or infusing of them into mortal minds, their sacred source at once immanent and hidden still—all again are present. Though all Spenser's muses are daughters of Dame Memory, his particular muse is most often Clio, History, which is memory itself, and the mnemonic resources this muse preeminently figures are finally the reason that "vertues seat is deepe within the mynd" (5). It is entirely appropriate that Spenser's mnemonic muse and Eumnestes should preside over the same scrine.[16]

The connections between Eumnestes' chamber and the Proem to Book VI lead, as do so often the traces or "tracts" of Spenser's "fine footing," to another, related passage in which the word *permanent* is a deliberately chosen paradigm of the provenance of recorded memory. This passage occurs at the outset of the Mutability Cantos and therefore affords some retrospect on Eumnestes' treasure. In it, Spenser

16. Whether the muse of *The Faerie Queene* is Clio or Calliope is a perennially vexed question: it is treated elsewhere in this volume by Thomas P. Roche, Jr. I suspect that Spenser saw his muses as he saw his Venuses, as so many expressions of a single power—related, continuous, and often blending—in the muses' case, the power of mnemonic song. When Spenser does not specifically name his muse, she is likely to be a composite figure, as in the first Proem and in the present quotation (VI Proem 2–3), where the "muse" is the focal referent for the power of the "sacred ymps, that on *Parnasso* dwell." In any case, the material I present in this essay argues strongly against the exclusion of Clio and her concerns from the figure he identifies as the "Muse," or inspiration, of his poem, "this famous antique history." It argues instead for the likelihood of her conflation at some crucial points with Calliope. A generally useful discussion of the muses is Wesley Trimpi's *Muses of One Mind: The Literary Analysis of Experience and Its Continuity* (Princeton: Princeton University Press, 1983), pp. i, xvii. Referring to Hesiod's *Theogony*, Trimpi observes that the poet's office embodies "the collective activities of the Muses," who themselves exist as "various aspects" of each other, "one implying all the others."

refers to the "antique race" and ancient lineage of Mutability and explains that he has "found it registred of old, / In *Faery* Land mongst records permanent" (vi.2). Like the word *scrine*, the phrase "records permanent" is arresting: a permanent record of change is puzzling on the face of it, albeit on reflection potentially ironic; the word *permanent* itself, moreover, has never appeared before this canto in connection with records or in the entire course of *The Faerie Queene* or, for that matter, with a single, relevant exception, in the rest of Spenser's poetry.

The word *permanent* occurs a total of four times in Spenser's poetry—twice more in later portions of the Mutability Cantos and once in *Amoretti* 79. These other occurrences accentuate the relation of the problematical phrase "records permanent" to Eumnestes' treasure and illuminate its importance. The two later uses of *permanent* in the Cantos come during the trial of Mutability's claims to sovereignty, and both emphasize the cosmic implications of this word. In the first of them, Mutability explicitly aligns permanence with an absence of movement—a stillness—which is only illusory, observing in her opening volley the ways in which "the Earth (great mother of vs all) . . . only seems vnmov'd and permanent" (vii.17). All that springs from the unstable Earth, Mutability maintains, necessarily changes restlessly; not only do the bodies of men "flit and fly: / But eeke their minds (which they immortall call) / Still change and vary thoughts, as new occasions fall" (19). The merely occasional nature of the mind's conceptions, of which its own immortality is clearly one, is the most disturbing extension of Mutability's argument, and it challenges directly the immortality of Eumnestes' treasure.

The final occurrence of *permanent* comes in the summation of Mutability's case: "Then since within this wide great *Vniuerse* / Nothing doth firme and permanent appeare," she concludes, "What then should let, but I aloft should reare / My Trophee, and from all, the triumph beare?" (vii.56). Again the implications of impermanence are comprehensive and total. Indeed, in the context of Mutability's seemingly overwhelming claims, the pun on the word *nothing*, which Shakespeare was to make so crucial in *King Lear*, momentarily threatens to assert itself: no *thing* is permanent, but nothingness is so.

In *Amoretti* 79, the word *permanent* belongs to a more positive context, yet one that similarly underlines its metaphysical charge. The sonnet links permanence to the characterization of "true beautie" as "free / from frayle corruption," like the "incorrupted," indwelling content of Eumnestes' "immortall scrine." Since *Amoretti* 79 immediately precedes the sonnet in which Spenser mentions having composed six books of *The Faerie Queene*, it is not wholly surprising that much of it should be relevant to my preceding discussion and especially to something permanent or immortal within the virtuous mind. "Men call you fayre, and you doe credit it," the poet begins the sonnet, but he soon observes how

> the trew fayre, that is the gentle wit,
>   and vertuous mind, is much more praysd of me.
> For all the rest, how euer fayre it be,
>   shall turne to nought and loose that glorious hew:
>   but onely that is permanent and free
>   from frayle corruption, that doth flesh ensew.
> That is true beautie: that doth argue you
>   to be diuine and borne of heauenly seed:
>   deriu'd from that fayre Spirit, from whom al true
>   and perfect beauty did at first proceed.
> He onely fayre, and what he fayre hath made,
>   all other fayre lyke flowres vntymely fade.

The concluding couplet is remarkably close to the end of Chaucer's *Troilus*, where the poet admonishes "yonge fresshe folkes" to look to God and think "al nys but a fayre / This worlde that passeth sone, as floures fayre," an ending which, as I have noted elsewhere, the penultimate stanza of the Mutability Cantos similarly recalls.[17]

The distinction throughout *Amoretti* 79 between "vertuous mind" and "glorious hew," permanence and corruption, spirit and flesh, resembles that between the content of Eumnestes' "immortall scrine" and his worm-eaten books; it also accentuates Spenser's care in referring Mutability's lineage to the "records permanent" *in* Faerie Land, rather than to those *of* Faerie Land. Only in Faerie are records permanent, and if we want to know where Faerie is, we need only remember the Proem to Book II, where we learn both that we can trace its whereabouts "By certaine signes here set in sundry place" and that "no

---

17. Judith H. Anderson, "'A Gentle Knight was pricking on the plaine': The Chaucerian Connection," *ELR*, 15 (1985), 173.

body"—that is, no one at all, none bodily, none in bodily form—"can know" where it is. Hardly by coincidence, we learn in this same Proem that *The Faerie Queene*, "this famous antique history," is the "matter of iust memory." Records are permanent only in Faerie Land, which is the only place Eumnestes' "immortall scrine" remains, resides, dwells uncorrupted, at once because the muse is the daughter of Memory and because she is also the daughter of Apollo—of poetic creativity—or elsewhere of Jupiter, of enabling power (III.iii.4, IV.xi.10). The content of memory is the source—the spring or well—but memory must be unfolded and fulfilled.

Like *scrine*, the word *permanent* comes to Spenser with a significant set of implications—a thesaurus of memories, reminiscences, associations. The etymological citations of a modern dictionary offer a shortcut to these and an introduction to the somewhat freer etymological associations familiar to the Renaissance from classical sources. *Permanent*, deriving from Latin *per*, "through," and *manere*, "to remain," is cognate to the word *manor*, or "desmesne, domain, area of dominium," which comes from Latin *manere* by way of Old French *manoir*, "to stay or dwell." The Indo-European base of *manere*, namely *men-*, is thought originally to have been identical with the Indo-European homonym *men-*, meaning "to think," which also underlies the word *mind*. The connection between *men-*, "to think," and *men-*, "to remain," is hypothesized to be the idea "stand in thought."[18]

While the finer points of Indo-European bases were hardly available to Spenser, such etymological speculations as those of the Roman Varro were, and they clearly fed the poet's own etymologically oriented and inventive imagination.[19] Like Spenser, Varro connects the ideas of remaining and thinking both with one another and with the idea of remembering or memory. He uses the Latin word *mens*, or "mind," to bridge them: thus, "*meminisse* 'to remember,' [derives] from *memoria* 'memory,' when there is again a motion toward that which *remansit* 'has remained' in the *mens* 'mind': and this may have been said from

18. *Webster's New World Dictionary*, s.v. *manor*; Lewis & Short, s.v. *maneo*.
19. See Ernest Weekley, "Our Early Etymologists," *Quarterly Review*, 257 (1931), 63–72; also A. C. Hamilton, "Our New Poet: Spenser's 'well of English undefyld,'" in *A Theatre for Spenserians*, ed. Judith M. Kennedy and James A. Reither (Toronto: University of Toronto Press, 1973), pp. 101–23; and K. K. Ruthven, "The Poet as Etymologist," *CritQ*, 11 (1969), 9–37.

manere 'to remain.'"[20] Developing further the association of *manere*, "remain," with *memoria*, "memory," Varro explains the expression *Mamurius Veturius* as an appellative signifying "memoriam veterem," what Chaucer might have translated as "a memory of olde times," and Spenser as "an antique image."[21]

The rest of Varro's etymologies in this section read like a gloss on Mutability, on Spenser's explicit recognition in the final Cantos that mutability and mortality are part of the abiding records in Faerie Land and of the undying content of human memory: "Et in Arcadia Ego," to quote the title of Panofsky's famous essay on the presence of transience and death in Arcady, the condition he defines as a "retrospective vision of an unsurpassable happiness, enjoyed in the past, unattainable ever after, yet enduringly alive in the memory," and elsewhere as "Sacrosancta Vetustas."[22] Varro's evolving derivations from *memoria*, "memory," also anticipate Spenser's recurrent interest in the idea that "moniments," or monuments, admonish, an idea relevant to Mutability and to the "records permanent" of her "antique race and linage ancient": from *memoria*, Varro explains, comes "*monere* 'to remind,' because he who *monet* 'reminds,' is just like a memory. So also the *monimenta* 'memorials' which are on tombs . . . *admonere* 'admonish' the passers-by that they themselves were mortal and that the readers are too. From this, . . . other things that are written and done to preserve their *memoria* 'memory' are called *monimenta* 'monuments.'" My point is not that mutability and mortality have never before been acknowledged as part of the content of memory in *The Faerie Queene*

---

20. Varro *De lingua latina*, trans. Roland G. Kent, 2 vols., Loeb (London: Heinemann, 1938), VI.49: "Meminisse a memoria cum [in] id quod remansit in mente rursus movetur; quae a manendo." Cf. Thomas, s.v. *maneo*: "To tarie, staie, stand still, remaine, continue, or persist . . . also to stick to, or to stick at: to remember, not to forget." Thomas has obviously been reading Varro, whether directly or through an intermediary.

21. Ibid.: "Itaque Salii quod cantant: 'Mamuri Veturi,' significant memoriam veterem." See Lewis & Short, s.v. *ancile* and *Mamurius Veturius*.

22. Erwin Panofsky, "*Et in Arcadia Ego*: On the Conception of Transience in Poussin and Wateau," in *Philosophy & History: Essays Presented to Ernst Cassirer*, ed. Raymond Klibansky and H. J. Paton (1936; rpt. New York: Harper & Row, 1963), pp. 223, 230, 232. Cf. *The Confessions of Saint Augustine*, trans. E. M. Blaiklock (New York: Thomas Nelson, 1983), p. 261 (X.21): "And since no one can say that they [sic] have not had the experience [of happiness], it is recognised because it is found in the memory."

but that they have not been the major focus of attention the way they are in Spenser's last Cantos. For example, both are present, though variously, in Eumnestes' registers, whether "*Briton moniments*" or "*Antiquitie* of *Faerie* lond," and in the admission in the Proem to Book II that "no *body* can know" Faerie's whereabouts, an admission that clearly refers to Faerie as more than simply a written record, the fragile document we hold in our hands or the poem whose location in our bookshelves we know.

Imprinted in the heart and embedded in the mind, enduring, memorial, admonitory, and written in the human past, "records permanent," and "mongst" them the memory of Mutability's origin, are the stuff that Spenser's Faerie romance is made on. The substitution of permanence for Eumnestes' "immortall scrine" may appear at first a real change and a retreat from intimations of visionary transcendence, but like everything else in the Mutability Cantos, it proves on closer inspection a sign of continuity. If a reminder of mortality is latent in the word *permanent*, one is similarly present not only in *immortal* but also in *scrine*, meaning "shrine," and specifically in the historical equation of *scrine* with a *feretrum*, or "bier," for the carriage or enclosure of *reliquae sacrae*, "sacred relics"—of what remains, *remanere*, and of what reminds, *rememorare*, *reminisci*.[23] If the claim to spiritual transcendence simultaneously present both in "scrine" and "immortall" is muted in "records permanent," it is, though still more deeply hidden, still there. It remains.

Like the resources of memory in Eumnestes' chamber, the House of Alma as a whole combines a number of philosophical traditions, which recent studies have gone far to identify.[24] These include both the Aristotelian and Platonic traditions and, where apt, in baptized form. As so often in the crucial centers, the houses or temples, of *The Faerie Queene*, to follow a single, competing doctrine would seem to have been, in Spenser's view, doctrinaire: to know rather than to recover and to renew truth. It would be to short-circuit the *process* of memory,

23. Du Cange, s.v. *scrinium*. Cf. Thomas, s.v. *recordor* and *permaneo*: "To abide till the end, or till all be done: to remaine still, to continue, to tarrie."
24. See, for example, Jerry Leath Mills, "Spenser, Lodowick Bryskett, and the Mortalist Controversy: *The Faerie Queene*, I.ix.22," *PQ*, 52 (1973), 173–86; Robert L. Reid, "Alma's Castle and the Symbolization of Reason in *The Faerie Queene*," *JEGP*, 80 (1981), 512–27.

to mummify its secrets and resources rather than to revive them in accessible forms.[25] As Alastair Fowler has argued, some form of Platonized or Neoplatonized reminiscence of truth of the sort present in Macrobius's *Commentary on the Dream of Scipio* was never far from Spenser's mind in Book II, and it would be difficult, in fact simply wrong, not to be reminded of this association by his mystically charged diction in Eumnestes' chamber and, more generally, in connection with that "sacred . . . noursling of Dame *Memorie*," his Muse (IV.xi.10).[26] But this reminiscence vanishes as quickly as the Graces on Mount Acidale when it is pressed and, even if not pressed, passes elusively within the subsequent movement, the *cursus*, of the poem itself into the de-mystified memory of an Aristotelian or more materialized system. And yet the inspiriting words recurrently attributed to memory *are* there still and still are "ment, / T'expresse the meaning of the inward mind" (VI.viii.26).

What is clear is that for Spenser the words and texts of recorded memory hold imprints of truth and sources of wisdom and that the "spirit" of these, infused into the poet, enables his Faerie vision (IV.ii.34). This is the reason he recalls so many overlapping yet various texts, so many "records permanent" of Mutability's true meaning in the final Cantos and, crucially among them, not just Chaucer's *Parlement* and *Troilus* but also his translation of Boethius, whose conspicuous references to a source or "well" Chaucer himself recalls near the end of the Knight's Tale. "And if," Chaucer's Boethius reads, the

25. Cf. Harry Berger, Jr., "Archaism, Immortality, and the Muse in Spenser's Poetry," YR, 58 (1969), 214–31: Berger's argument is more critical of primitivism in recorded or antique resources of memory than mine is; where he emphasizes a theory of evolution, I emphasize recovery and renewal. In "A Secret Discipline: *The Faerie Queene*, Book VI," Berger mentions *anamnesis* relevantly but is not concerned with its connection to sources, to texts, to recorded memory in *The Faerie Queene*; he locates reminiscence more exclusively in the self than Spenser appears to: *Form and Convention in the Poetry of Edmund Spenser*, ed. William Nelson (New York: Columbia University Press, 1961), p. 73. Cf. Murrin, pp. 90–97; also Gerald L. Bruns, *Inventions: Writing, Textuality, and Understanding in Literary History* (New Haven: Yale University Press, 1982), pp. 49–59. Bruns distinguishes between the imitation of a text and the "imitation of antique authority . . . that incarnates [and continues] rather than replicates," which he finds in a manuscript culture (p. 52, cf. p. 49).

26. Alastair Fowler, *Spenser and the Numbers of Time* (London: Routledge & Kegan Paul, 1964), pp. 99–100; Macrobius, *Commentary on the Dream of Scipio*, trans. William Harris Stahl (New York: Columbia University Press, 1952), pp. 133–37 (chap. XII). See also *FQ* VII.vii.2.

"kynge and lorde/ wele and begynnynge" did not govern and constrain all things, "they shulde departen from her wele/ that is to sayn from her begynnyng and . . . tournen in to nought" (fol. cclxiv^v). Alluding to this passage, the Knight's Tale aligns it more specifically with an acceptance of death:

> It helpeth not/ all gothe that ylke wey
> Than may ye se that al thyng mote dey
> What maketh this/ but Jupiter the kyng?
> That is prince/ and cause of all thyng
> Conuertyng all to his propre w[e]ll[27]
> From whiche it is deryued sothe to tell. (fol. xii^v)

Recalling the Boethian well of origin, Nature's judgment on Mutability's claims at the end of Spenser's seventh canto asserts that, though all things change,

> They are not changed from their first estate;
> But by their change their being doe dilate:
> And turning to themselues at length againe,
> Doe work their owne perfection so by fate. (VII.vii.58)

In Nature's answer, origin and destination, first cause and final effect, are one. The two stanzas of Canto viii, which follow closely on her answer and with which the poem ceases, poignantly express the poet's concern with personal mortality and with an ultimate destination. Their doing so suggests that in framing her answer not only the Boethian well but also Chaucer's adaptation of it in the Knight's Tale, which touches more directly on death, is present to the poet's mind and thus that the Chaucerian memory is infolded in the Boethian one.

Within Alma's brain-turret in Book II, Eumnestes seeks and reaches what has been lost or removed ("laid amis") and does so through the agency of a reminder or recollector, namely Anamnestes, the old man's young page (ix.58). Anamnestes' function corresponds to that which

---

27. In the Thynne family of editions of Chaucer's works, "well" here reads "wyll." Since "wyll" fails to rhyme with "tell," it is hardly conceivable that the correct reading "well" would not have occurred to the poet Spenser, especially if he recognized the source of the Knight's "well" in Chaucer's translation of Boethius, which is also to be found in the Thynne family of editions.

specific words and texts—like those of Chaucer—play for the Faerie poet, and to that which the Faerie poem, in turn, plays for us. Such words and texts are at once the "tract" and the way of tracing back as far as we are able, a process never finished, hence never perfected, until life itself is. Like memory as portrayed in Eumnestes' chamber and more generally like Alma herself, life, as used here, is at once collective and cumulative and individually and therefore partially realized. In this respect, it resembles experience, history, and time.

Spenser appears to have meant his avowed kinship with Chaucer, and especially with Chaucer's romances, as a paradigm of his relation to the recorded sources of memory. Because Chaucer's work, however profoundly human, is not memorably doctrinal or mystical, this paradigm is especially revealing. When Spenser begins his extension of Chaucer's Squire's Tale, he fuses the Knight's Tale with the Squire's and thus the father's with the son's. Together, these two romance tales become an image of the extension of experience through time, which is generically, although not uniquely, characteristic of romance. In this way Spenser affords us a paradigm of fusing parallel to that he claims between Chaucer's work and his own as-yet-unfinished extension of it. Notably, in characterizing his extension, he hopes not to complete the Squire's Tale (as is customarily assumed) but to follow the "footing" of Chaucer's "feete"—his "tracts" both spiritual and metrical—that he may "meete" the sooner with Chaucer's "meaning," something more deeply hidden toward which the tracks point (IV.ii.34). Pointing toward and participating in, rather than fully possessing or appropriating, are here the ideas that sustain and empower; in connection with them Spenser's particular engagement with Chaucer's *unfinished* romances—the Squire's Tale and the Tale of Sir Thopas—is remarkable. In the same passage in which Spenser describes the Squire's Tale as model and source, he characterizes Chaucer as the "well of English vndefyled" and speaks of the "infusion" of Chaucer's "spirit" into his own. He thus speaks of Chaucer much as he speaks in the sixth Proem of the muse's infusing and welling of "secret comfort, . . . heauenly pleasures," and the fruit of "learnings threasures . . . Into the mindes of mortall men," his own mind most specifically included.

At this point of my argument, it should almost have been predictable that the root word of *infuse* and of *fons/fontis*, "source or well," would prove to be the same, namely *fundere*, "to pour," a fact available to

Renaissance writers: "A *fons* 'spring' is that from which running water [*aqua viva*] *funditur* 'is poured.'"[28] Running water is moving, changing, hence living water, as Mutability would be among the first to remind us. One of the lessons Spenser learned from Chaucer, as he signals conspicuously in Arthur's dream of the Queene of Faerie, in the extension of the Squire's Tale, and in the half-jesting reference in the Mutability Cantos to Chaucer's own reference to *De planctu naturae*, is how to treat a source, be it Macrobius, Boethius, Alanus, Lollius, or Chaucer himself—that is, how to imbibe its spirit without being stagnated by its letter, how to use the resources of memory not as museum pieces, as mere authorities, but as the living voices of spirit.[29] Throughout *The Faerie Queene*, Spenser sought the traces of truth and the sources of inspiration not in an unmediated self but in the cumulative expression of the inward mind inscribed in the human past and present in human *records*, in human words and texts, from the beginning.

28. Varro, V.123: "Fons unde funditur . . . aqua viva"; cf. Isidori Hispalensis Episcopi, *Etymologiarvm sive originvm*, ed. W. M. Lindsay (Oxford: Clarendon Press, 1911), XIII.21.5; Thomas, s.v. *fons*: "A fountaine or water spring: a well: *per translationem*, the head, roote, principall cause, and beginning of a matter: also water."

29. I have discussed the Chaucerian source of Arthur's dream in Book I in "'A Gentle Knight was pricking,'" pp. 168–72.

2

Spenser's Names

ALASTAIR FOWLER

As gothicizing Elizabethan and great poet, Spenser occupied a uniquely strategic position between literary worlds. It would hardly be possible to recognize all his achievements in establishing features of English literature that later writers have come to take for granted. He not only wrote well but wrote first; so many aftercomers have modeled themselves on him, directly or indirectly, that one may say he invented much of poetic form as we know it. (He had predecessors, to be sure; but the changes in language and especially in versification that intervened between Chaucer and himself kept successors from looking back much before the sixteenth century.) This is strikingly true of names and naming. In his use of proper names, indeed, Spenser is in the strict sense more original than any subsequent poet. And it would be difficult to find comparable achievement in earlier romances, where names were cyclic rather than individual, presupposed rather than invented. Moreover, it was only in Spenser's time that the texture of English literature became close enough for allusion.

In his youthful work Spenser's naming already showed originality. The names of *The Shepheardes Calender*, for example, depart boldly from pastoral tradition in the direction of georgic or of early Tudor comedy. The eclogue speakers are not named after Theocritus's Daphnis and Corydon, or Virgil's Corydon and Lycidas, or Sannazaro's Lycidas and Mopsus, or Googe's Mopsus and Silvanus, but bear ordinary names like Piers and Cuddie (a familiar form of Cuthbert) and Diggon (a diminutive of Richard). The innovation was imitated by Spenser's "native" pastoral successors—especially Ambrose Philips, whose maladroit monikers offered targets for satire by Pope in *Guardian* No. 40 and by Gay in *The Shepherd's Week*. Gay pretends to praise Philips's Spenserian names as "right simple and meet for the Country"—ironically, since like Pope he was something of a generic purist, and disliked the free mixture of pastoral with georgic.[1] But the mixture established itself; so that Spenser's shepherd names no longer seem novel but natural and convincingly rustic.

So successful, indeed, is the name Colin Clout that it helps to set a tone of confident fictionality—"O *Colin, Colin*, the shepheards ioye"; "Poor *Colin Clout* (who knowes not *Colin Clout?*)."[2] Colin is Skelton's name for himself in an antiprelatic satire. But Spenser's reuse of it amounts to more than an allusion of the sort his "Piers" makes, in a more distanced way, to Langland's prophetic plowman. "Colin" does not merely nail political colors, still less provide a mere nom de guerre. Spenser makes it an archetypal poet's name—a name for the "new poet," just as Tityrus is his name for the *miglior fabbro* (of whom he discerns a new avatar), reassigning it from Virgil to Chaucer. The largeness of meaning was assisted by the fact that Colin was also Marot's name in "De Madame Loyse de Savoye." (No coincidence or fancied association, this, since Spenser arranged for "E. K." to point out the connection in his owlish way.)[3] The redoubled literariness is

1. John Gay, "Proeme," in *Poetical Works*, ed. Vinton E. Dearing and C. E. Beckwith, 2 vols. (Oxford: Clarendon Press, 1974), II.514, 522. John N. King suggests that Spenser's "Piers" alludes to Langland's, and his "Diggon Davy" to Churchyard's Davy Diker (another truth-teller): see "Spenser's *Shepheardes Calender* and Protestant Pastoral Satire," *Renaissance Genres*, ed. Barbara Kiefer Lewalski (Cambridge, Mass.: Harvard University Press, 1986), p. 383.

2. "August," l. 190; *The Faerie Queene* VI.x.16: imitating Ovid, *Fasti* II.83, as James Nohrnberg notes, *The Analogy of "The Faerie Queene"* (Princeton: Princeton University Press, 1976), p. 76. I am indebted to Nohrnberg for many suggestions incorporated in the present paper. Here and throughout, I cite Spenser from the *Variorum*.

3. "COLIN Cloute] is a name not greatly vsed, and yet haue I sene a Poesie of M. Skeltons vnder that title. But indeede the word Colin is Frenche, and vsed of the French Poete Marot (if he be worthy of the name of a Poete) in a certein Aeglogue. Vnder which name this Poete secretly shadoweth himself, as sometime did Virgil vnder the name of Tityrus, thinking it much fitter, then such Latine names, for the great vnlikelyhoode of the language" ("January," Glosse).

worth noticing: as we shall see, multiple aptness of this sort is a feature of Spenser's naming.

It would be pleasant to linger with Spenser's shepherds; canvassing perhaps the political allusions their incognitos disguise. But *The Faerie Queene* offers still greater onomastic interest. It is unusual among Renaissance and mannerist nondramatic works—only the *Orlando furioso* stands comparison—in that it mixes names of many different types. Matilda, George, Scudamour, Orimont, Numa, Burbon, Night, Perissa, Adonis, Celeno, Arthur, Tristram, Britomart, Florimell, Coridon, Cymothoe: ordinary Christian names and surnames, great historical names, allegorical and mythological names, names of legend and romance, Ariostan names, and names from classical poetry. In the very first canto the reader meets Gloriana, Errour, Morpheus, Hecate, and Archimago—a series that tells a story of its own. "Spenser varies his names from history, mythology, or romance, agreeable to his own scheme."[4] The redoubtable Upton recognized the characteristic well enough; although his bland explanation ("agreeable to his own scheme") dissatisfies as much as it intrigues.

The variety is generic. Renaissance theorists insisted on epic's encyclopedic inclusion of other genres; and of these the heterogeneous names are indicators. Thus, in varying mode and mood from canto to canto or book to book, Spenser depends a good deal on successive groupings of names—as with the pastoral concentration in Book VI or the astonishing mythological flood that is poured out in celebration of the spousals of Thames and Medway. But beyond such tonal variation one can sense in the names a drive toward creative realism. Spenser seems to pursue a cosmic image that will be comprehensive and diverse like the world itself.

The real world has a larger counterpart in Spenser's names than may at first appear. It is easy to say that some are obviously made up, others conceivably real. But if you are asked which names belong to which type—which are ordinary names and which allegorical—then difficulties arise. "Scudamour," at least, is beyond question; it must be allegorical ("the shield of love"), as the context confirms. Not at all: "Scudamoure" was a familiar surname in Spenser's time. And when Camden's *Remains* can cite as actual names Remedium amoris, Imago

4. Upton's note to I.ix.4.

saeculi, Free-gift, Reformation, Earth, Dust, Ashes, Delivery, More fruit, Tribulation, The Lord is near, More trial, Discipline, Joy again, From above, Acceptance, Thankful, Praise-God, and Live-well, why should not Spenser's Maleffort and Despetto have been credible? Orthography was still fluid enough for proper names to have uncertain variant forms, in which common nouns could often be found. Spenser took full advantage of this mutability—a licence Milton would still just be able to enjoy (as in his allusion to Fontarabbia, not quite Fuentarabbia).[5] Classical names, moreover, had become not uncommon: Spenser's first son was called Sylvanus; and the Brazen George at Cambridge was kept by one Troilus Atkinson. As for romance names, they were positively in vogue. Amyas (VI.viii.59) seems romantic now; but in Spenser's time it was also borne in everyday life, by Amyas Paulet among others. (The tendency had begun that would eventually bring things to the pass deplored by Isaac Disraeli: "The practice of romantic names among persons, even of the lowest orders of society, has become a very general evil").[6] Jonson's Puntarvolo courted his wife as Guinevere; and Drummond of Hawthornden hankered so keenly after a romance name that he made himself one by anagram; privately styling himself "Don Murmidumilla."

This possibility of overlap between quotidian life and the realm of romance is one that Spenser appears to have taken a special delight in. His names are so often diverse in their associations—far more often than Ariosto's or Tasso's, for example—that we can only conclude he sought the effect deliberately.

Most of Spenser's allegorical names use foreign-language components—Latin and Greek in the main, but also Italian, French, and Irish. In this, he might be regarded as reviving a medieval style of naming. Similar diversity of names, with much learned employment of Greek, is to be found in Platonic fiction such as Bernardus Silvestris's *Cosmographia* or Alanus de Insulis's *De planctu naturae*. But Spenser would also be aware of academic drama. And above all he must have been provoked by one of his most congenial sources—a great work, at

5. See Barbara Everett, "The End of the Big Names: Milton's Epic Catalogues," *English Renaissance Studies Presented to Dame Helen Gardner* (Oxford: Clarendon Press, 1980), pp. 260–61.

6. Isaac Disraeli, "Influence of a Name," *Curiosities of Literature* (rev. ed., London, 1881), II.71.

once powerful and currently fashionable—Francesco Colonna's *Hypnerotomachia polifili*, translated by R. Dallington as *The Strife of Love in a Dreame* (1592). This mysterious allegory makes elaborate play with names constructed from Greek elements, like Eleuterilida, Erototimoride, and Diapraxe. Spenser has many not dissimilar names, such as those of Perissa (Greek *perissos*), "who in excesse exceeded," and her sister Elissa (explained by Upton as "Elisse," an Italianization of *elleipsis*, "deficiency"). Here again, however, the rule of multiple aptness applies, since Elissa was also familiar from *Aeneid* IV as a name of unhappy Dido.

Some will say that in context the drift of "Elissa" is simple enough; and on one level this is true.[7] But other of Spenser's Greek names are more intricately derived. Few would now follow Pauline Parker and Arnold Williams in explaining "Calepine" simply as *kalos-epos* or Beautiful Speech: gone are the days when "epine" could be equated with "epos." Donald Cheney plausibly sees *kalos-pinē*, on the analogy of Ariosto's *Pinabello*, while John Erskine Hankins and James Nohrnberg prefer *khalepos*, "churlish" (improved by Cheney to *khalepainō*, "judge harshly"), and Berger finds the name of a standard Latin dictionary, Calepinus's. It seems to me likely that the main idea is *kalos-epinoeō*, "intend, contrive beautiful things." But Berger's and Cheney's suggestions cannot surely be excluded. They add complicating associations exactly in the style of nomination that characterizes *The Faerie Queene*. Similarly, "Calidore" points not only to *kallidōron* ("beauty-gift," "gift of grace") but also to *calidus* (Latin, "spirited") and perhaps to the innocent Calidorus in Plautus's *Pseudolus*.[8]

Spenser's learned names belong, as I have suggested, to the Platonic hermeneutic tradition descending from Bernardus Silvestris to Cristoforo Landino (in whose *Disputationes camaldulenses* (1489) such Greek names as Cymothoe, which also appears in *The Faerie Queene*, are interpreted etymologically).[9] But more immediately, the Spenserian

7. But what is Elissa deficiency of? See Alastair Fowler, *Spenser and the Numbers of Time* (London: Routledge & Kegan Paul, 1964), p. 112.

8. On "Calepine" see Nohrnberg, pp. xiii–xiv, 682–83; *Spenser Newsletter*, 8, no. 3 (1977), 50. For the Latin Calidores, I am indebted to Kenneth Borris, who draws my attention to Konrad Gesner's *Onomasticon proprium nominum*, appended to Ambrogio Calepino's *Dictionarium undecim linguarum* (Basel, 1590), where *Callidorus* is so etymologized.

9. See Paul Holberton, "Of Antique and Other Figures: Metaphor in Early Renaissance Art," *Word and Image*, 1 (1985), 53.

names also related to a contemporary vogue for the *figura etymologica*. The etymological conceit is everywhere in Spenser; although only explicit (as at *Prothalamion*, ll. 153–54) when too strained to stand on its own: "And endlesse happinesse of thine owne name / That promiseth the same" (Devereux, *devenir heureux*). Such wordplay belongs to a strand of lexical wit which runs throughout Spenser's work, and which is the subject of a brilliant article by Martha Craig.[10] She rightly connects it with Platonistic theories of appropriate naming, based ultimately (although perhaps mistakenly) on the *Cratylus*. Like most commentators on Spenser's names, she takes it for granted that they depend on the essentialist assumption that "every nomen conceals an omen." This view is encouraged by many phrases in *The Faerie Queene*—"his well deserued name"; "His name . . . did his nature right aread"; and the like. On the whole Spenser's names speak the natures of their bearers. But there are other instances where name and character are at odds: the Bower of Bliss is "of her fond fauorites so nam'd amis"; and Huddibras is "not so good of deedes, as great of name."[11] Or, a name may be irrelevant to its bearer's behavior. Or, it may contain several distinct meanings. In fact, there are so may different possibilities that nomination should be taken as an invitation to empirical investigation. With Spenser, omens are likely to be a good deal more numerous than nomens. There is no doubt that like most of his contemporaries he was to some degree an essentialist. But at the same time he shared Camden's skepticism about names, and his vision of apt language was not a simple one. Aptness was not automatic in a fallen world, where simple one-to-one equivalences of names and things might be out of the question.

Even seemingly obvious labels may turn out to be far from clearcut. For example "Braggadocchio" is usually and rightly taken to be English *brag*, *braggart*, *bragard*, or French *bragard*, with the Italian augmentative *-occio* or *-occhio*. But he is described as "auaunting in great brauery / As Peacocke" (II.iii.6), and *bravery* meant "finery" as well as "courage." In view of the prominence of wide slops as a commonly satirized feature of the Elizabethan swaggerer, it seems likely that

10. Martha Craig, "The Secret Wit of Spenser's Language," *Elizabethan Poetry: Modern Essays in Criticism*, ed. Paul J. Alpers (New York: Oxford University Press, 1967), pp. 447–72.

11. K. K. Ruthven, *The Conceit* (London: Methuen, 1969), p. 38. See *FQ* I.vi.20.4, I.viii.31, II.xii.69, II.ii.17.3.

Spenser also hints at *braga(s)* (Spanish and Italian: "breeches," "breeches leg"). And *bragado* (Spanish: "vicious") is also so close in form and apt in meaning as to be hard to exclude. The wit of such names lies in multiplicity of resonance; although the surface at best will seem simple and plausible. So "Trompart," as Nohrnberg observes (pp. 356n, 598), is not only "art of deception" (*tromper*) but also "art of the boastful tromp" or trumpet.

The devising of such names manifested a taste for a kind of verbal play that often found its outlet in the currently popular rebus. And indeed many rebuslike plays in *The Shepheardes Calender*—such as "Roffyn" for the Bishop of Rochester—lead one to expect similar disguised names in *The Faerie Queene*. Oddly, this putative strand of the poem has been largely neglected since the time of Greenlaw—with such honorable exceptions as A. C. Hamilton. Nevertheless, a few obvious instances, like Orimont (which surely refers to Ormond, recipient of a dedicatory sonnet), show that the strand exists. It would be interesting to trace it further—to know, for example, in view of the political and Irish dimensions of the Florimell-Marinell story,[12] whether "Dumarin," the name of Marinell's father, is an anagram of "Raimund" (Raymond le Gros, Raymond Fitzwilliam), the Norman conqueror of Ireland. But, although *The Faerie Queene* clearly contains historical allusions, Spenser does not encourage one to read it through the names as a roman à clef. He has another type of fiction in hand.

In naming, one might expect *The Faerie Queene* to be inferior to more novelistic works simply because it is allegorical and must therefore lack solidity of specification. Modern theorists regard allegorical names as the extreme of "essentialist nomination." Thus, a name like Occasion is supposed to contain the whole significance of the personage bearing it, so that subjective being is lost, and the character reduced to a mere *ficelle* of Guyon manipulated by the godlike author. The first appearance of a proper name ideally creates a "gap" or "semantic blank," which, as one reads on, is gradually filled or, as it were, implemented with the identity of the fictional character encountered. By contrast, allegorical names are mere labels (runs the argument), and have no such mysteriousness. An allegorical character cannot tran-

---

12. See, e.g., Isabel E. Rathborne, "The Political Allegory of the Florimell-Marinell Story," *ELH*, 12 (1945), 279–89.

scend the "labelling effect of the name by . . . being 'more' than the name's significance is allowed to encapsulate," since it has been exhaustively described already by its abstract label.[13] Although this doctrine is based on the weak presupposition that literary works are read only once, it may be true enough so far as single readings of naive allegories like Bunyan's go—although, even there, many of the personifications give occasion for realistic vignettes. But it by no means applies to the names of *The Faerie Queene*. For not even its most obviously allegorical labels can in the event be relied on to turn out obviously apt, let alone exhaustively descriptive. Perissa exhibits excess of something, but it is not immediately evident of what. Occasion is not occasion in the ordinary sense, but incorporates traits and attributes of previous abstractions like Penitenza and Incitement to Wrath, in ways that only become clear in the course of the narrative of Phedon and Pryene.[14] And there is nothing in Timias's name that befits his dishonor in IV.vii. Any Spenserian character is liable to disclose possibilities beyond its "label."

Or consider "Guyon." On first coming upon it in the proem ("this Faery knight / The good Sir *Guyon*"), or in the first Argument, or at II.i.19 ("Now by my head (said *Guyon*) much I muse"), an early reader may well have taken it for a romance name—perhaps thinking of Guy of Warwick, or Ogier's brother Guyon, or (as A. C. Hamilton notes) Guy of Burgundy, sometimes called Gyoun. Later, when Guyon's role as patron of temperance emerged, the reader might recall that Geon (Gaeon, Gyon) was the particular river of paradise associated by patristic authors with the cardinal virtue of temperance. Doubtless the name Guyon would then become partly a label. But the virtuous label was far from exhausting Guyon's characteristics—his lapses into intemperance, for example, and his nearly fatal disdainfulness in the House of Mammon. Later still, when Guyon's mission came to be understood as one of uniting the fountain of conscience in II.i with the fountain of will in the Bower of Bliss in II.xii, the reader might come to recognize that after all the river name amounted to more than a metonymic label of the virtue. Guyon was, in a sense, a river: a conduit

13. Thomas Docherty, *Reading (Absent) Character* (Oxford: Clarendon Press, 1983), pp. 50 and 47–50 passim.

14. See John Manning and Alastair Fowler, "The Iconography of Spenser's Occasion," *JWCI*, 39 (1976), 263–66.

of the fountain of temperance that mingled its cooling stream with the heating wine of excess and violence and concupiscence. Again, the wrestling prominent in Book II might recall a further interpretation of Geon, for example in Bersuire.[15] In some such surprising way, Spenser's personages have always the capacity to disclose new aspects of themselves. Appellative associations as complex as these are little different in principle from those of the novel—from the suggestions Ian Watt finds, for example, in the names Clarissa and Harlow.[16]

Many of Spenser's allegorical names form groups linked by formal similarities, like Pyrochles and Cymochles; Perissa and Elissa; Priamond, Diamond, and Triamond; Defetto, Decetto, and Despetto; Duessa, Fidessa, and Abessa. The bearers of such group names jointly constitute polarities, or triads, or variants of the same spiritual form. Indeed, in several cases they are specified to be brothers or sisters, which in allegorical genealogy signifies membership in the same category (just as the parent-child relationship means derivation or cause or subdivision). With all such personages, the group function is part of the content of the names. Only when the meaning of the group is understood, therefore, can the full aptness of such names be grasped. They are meant, admittedly, as helpful indicators; but if what lie at their hearts are mere labels, these labels can sometimes be mysteries not readily elucidated.

Typically elusive is the Sans foy–Sans loy–Sans joy group. The gothic suggestion of Saint Foy and Saint Loi (early noticed by Charles Fleming) will not satisfy for long. Clearly something schematic is also implied. But what scheme relates faith, law, and joy, or their absences? The genealogy of descent from Night and Aveugle (spiritual blindness) hardly takes us very far. A more useful hint comes in the signposting *propositio* allegory of II.ii, where Sans loy reappears with Huddibras as an opponent of Guyon's. It looks as if Sans loy, although he appears with his heathen brother in Book I, is to be a specific target of Book II.

---

15. See Nohrnberg, p. 304, where Gihon is related to the waters of Siloe at Jerusalem (Gihon in *Mandeville's Travels*); also Alastair Fowler, "The River Guyon," *MLN*, 75 (1960), 289–92, and "Emblems of Temperance in *The Faerie Queene*, Book II," in *Edmund Spenser: A Critical Anthology*, ed. Paul J. Alpers (Harmondsworth: Penguin, 1969), pp. 254–62.

16. See "The Naming of Characters in Defoe, Richardson and Fielding," *RES*, 25 (1949), 322–38.

If Guyon's purgative mission can be seen as directed against the moral disorder represented in epitome by the disorderly Sans loy—if, that is to say, the evil in Book II is Sans loy and Huddibras writ large—then the triadic scheme symbolized by the pagan brothers begins (but only begins) to take shape. We may be dealing, in fact, with the triad *illuminari-purgari-perfici*. This triadic scheme had wide distribution in the Middle Ages and the Renaissance, from Saint Bonaventura's *De triplici via* and other works in which he set out three aspects or stages of approach to God. Sans loy might be defeated by *purgari* in II, as Sans foy by *illuminari* in I. There is a glimpse in this of a possible structure. But it is not until we come to Book III with its various treatments of joylessness and joy (the House of Busirane, and the garden where Adonis "liueth in eternall blis, / Ioying his goddesse, and of her enioyd") that one can feel any stirring of confidence that Saint Bonaventura's scheme is alluded to. Only then does it become clear why the youngest heathen brother is named Sans joy, why his encounter with the Redcross Knight in I.v was inconclusive, and why the content of Sans joy called for treatment in a third book.

It is not, of course, Spenser's abstract "labels" that have most interest now but his other, less allegorical names. Yet this distinction proves to be one that Spenser seldom quite allows us to make. In his view, as in William Camden's, all names are originally and properly meaningful, although the corruption of language and of society may have concealed this fact. Even in his epic catalogues, he makes a program of etymologizing proper names. As Gordon Braden has shown, Spenser's river epithets in the spousals of Thames and Medway follow and improve on Mombritius's, revitalizing senses inherent in the names taken over from Hesiod.[17] Occasionally, I suspect, he will even find meaning in a name's sound or texture—as with "Maeander intricate" (IV.xi.21). Thomas Thomas (1587) defines *Maeander* as "a turning or winding: also in apparell wrought with the needle a winding in and out of the threds . . . or borders after the manner of a Labyrinth"; and Spenser's epithet weaves with the name a tricky, convoluted texture, repeating the /n dental r/ sequence almost exactly. The effect is to create a tortuously sinuate phrase and so to amplify the care in pronun-

17. Gordon Braden, "Riverrun: An Epic Catalogue in *The Faerie Queene*," *ELR*, 5 (1975), 25–48.

ciation forced in *Maeander* itself by hiatus. Throughout the catalogue, and indeed generally, Spenser makes names rise from meanings and give rise to others, in a continual metamorphic interchange between life and its abstractions.

Spenser's catalogue of rivers can be seen as almost pure poetry. It sets aside not only narrative but propositional communication. As James Nohrnberg puts it, "*thesis* yields back all its ground to *taxis*."[18] Spenser tells us that the names are listed "in order as they came," and he might have added that their existence is largely in the ordering. But the pleasures even of pure poetry are mutable, and the canto lists too many names for the modern taste. Not that this response is wholly irrelevant: critics have found in the passage a deliberate excess. Here one has to accommodate Spenser's desire to embrace factual information. For English poets were at last beginning to flex their georgic muscles, in belated emulation of Continental models. Even as the Second Part of *The Faerie Queene* appeared, Drayton may already have been planning his vast *Poly-Olbion* (1612; written ?1598–1612), with its minutely topographical river gazetteer.

Still, numerous though Spenser's names may be, they cannot make up anything like an exhaustive listing of rivers—even of English rivers. How, then, did he select the names he chose to include? The choices seem to be variously motivated—although always conscious, as his naming generally is. It might even be called self-conscious:

> But what doe I their names seeke to reherse,
>   Which all the world haue with their issue fild?
>   How can they all in this so narrow verse
>   Contayned be, and in small compasse hild? (IV.xi.17)

Confronted by the wide world, Spenser will include "only what needeth." One criterion is renown: some of the names are of "famous riuers" (Stanza 20)—not merely on the list of "endlesse memorie" but on the short list of fame. A second criterion is possession of natural resources, like the fish of the Darent (Stanza 29) and the adamant of the Avon (Stanza 31). The Dart is "nigh chockt with sands of tinny mines," (Stanza 31), while all "water . . . the . . . soile" (Stanza 30).

---

18. Nohrnberg, p. 683. Cf. Fowler, *Spenser and the Numbers of Time*, pp. 182–91, on the catalogue's elaborate numerological arrangement.

But a third criterion seems to have been lost sight of. Perhaps because we readily entertain the ancient idea of rivers as symbols of mutability—the aspect stressed by Braden—we find it difficult to grasp how much they also stood for permanence and order. We tend to forget that in Tudor times waterways were primary routes for travel and trade; so that to list rivers was to list lines (or, as we say, centers) of civilization.[19] River valleys were, in fact, the most settled parts of Britain. Of the rivers mentioned by Spenser, Thames, Medway, Lea, Humber, Ouse, Darent, Trent, Severn, and Yare were all used for communication in Tudor times, and doubtless many of the others were, too. It is the civilizing function of rivers that explains Spenser's mention of towns on their banks—and the especial prominence he gives to the academic towns, Oxford, Cambridge, and Stamford (Stanza 35). His catalogue, suitably for its position in Book IV, is a review of the national civilization that had developed historically out of alliance, accord, and peaceful communication. Even the sea gods included are "famous founders . . . Of puissant Nations" (Stanza 15).

Mythmaking or poeticizing is a part of civilizing. Hence the variety of river names, which Spenser "needeth" to illustrate the various sorts of poetic meaning. One is active mythmaking, as with "storming Humber"; another the use of existing myth or legend, as with "following Dee, which Britons long ygone / Did call diuine" (Stanza 39)—lore from Camden's *Britannia*. Yet another is historical association with "moniments of passed age" (Stanza 17). Or the poet can accept a suggestion in the name itself. So Ouze—

> whom men doe Isis rightly name;
> Full weake and crooked creature seemed shee,
> And almost blind through eld, that scarce her way could see (24)

—is made ancient beyond other English rivers through identification with the deity of an older civilization. (The connection fits in well with

19. See E. G. R. Taylor, *An Atlas of Tudor England and Wales* (Harmondsworth, Eng.: Penguin, 1951), p. 13: William Harrison mentions two thousand passenger boats on the Thames, besides "tide-boats, tilt-boats and barges for goods traffic. These were matched, though in less proportion, on the Severn, Trent, Yorkshire Ouse, and a score of lesser rivers." See further Taylor, "Lelands's England," in *An Historical Geography of England before A.D. 1800*, ed. H. C. Darby (Cambridge: Cambridge University Press, 1951), pp. 338–39, listing many rivers navigable in Tudor times.

other Egyptian mythological motifs in the spousals and elsewhere in the poem.) Mere topographical fact is enough to start the imagination working: Thame "seem'd to stoupe afore / With bowed backe" (Stanza 26) under the burden of Oxford, simply because of a bend in the river. The richly manifold intertexture of old associations and new senses makes for a very different style of catalogue from that favored by Milton. Although he is in many ways Spenser's successor as epic cataloguer, Milton prefers a more univocal style, assembling names that work all in the same way, to make the same moral or theological point.

Spenser's strange, half-mythological treatment of the river Isis serves as a reminder that he was the first English poet to make much poetic use of names—at least to create about them mood or atmosphere. There had been a few anticipations. Malory and others had used the great romance names effectively. And there was that remarkable passage in Chaucer's Prologue, listing the names of the Knight's battlefields—although they can hardly have been exactly atmospheric at a time when they had quite specific political connotations. Something very different, something new so far as English literature is concerned, began with certain of the names of *The Faerie Queene*. There, at last, the atmospheric potency of names was consciously dwelt on, and might even be explicitly invoked. Literature was acquiring new words of power. It formed them, ultimately, out of materials from romance and from religion; although the route by which the materials came was devious enough.

In the very first canto, the as yet unnamed hermit Archimago utters such words—words so terrible that they must not be read. (And yet the poem almost allows us to read them.) Archimago's aim is to raise spirits:

> Then choosing out few wordes most horrible,
>   (Let none them read) thereof did verses frame,
>   With which and other spelles like terrible,
>   He bad awake blacke *Plutoes* griesly Dame,
>   And cursed heauen, and spake reprochfull shame
>   Of highest God, the Lord of life and light;
>   A bold bad man, that dar'd to call by name
>   Great *Gorgon*, Prince of darknesse and dead night,
> At which *Cocytus* quakes, and *Styx* is put to flight. (I.i.37)

By writing the name Demogorgon (even if he perhaps avoided the *ipsissimum verbum* in the vocative case) Spenser himself framed verses of power and raised spirits that would not soon be laid. He here introduced into English (probably from Ariosto or Boccaccio or Hyginus) a name that was subsequently to resonate in Drayton and Milton and Shelley. I have called it a name; but in a way Spenser began with namelessness. For in Statius and Lucan, Demogorgon appeared only as a nameless deity, invoked to threaten the other eternal gods.[20] Scholiasts supplied the name itself, possibly through an act of creative misprision. (In some manuscripts of Plato's *Republic* the word *dēmiourgon* is written *dēmogorgon*.) And mythographers and lexicographers like Conrad de Mure (*Repertorium*, 1273) and Boccaccio and Conrad Celtis and Thomas Cooper in the process of time made him primeval father of the gods. They explained the name as *daimōngorgos* ("terrible daemon" or "terror to daemons") or *daimōn-geōrgos* ("god of the earth"). Gyraldi, who disapproved of the name as a mere textual corruption, was very much in a minority.

So far as English literature was concerned, however, Spenser had to start from scratch. It is instructive to see how he does it. At first he gives only a hint—a moiety of the name—in a sinister quiet line: "Great *Gorgon*, Prince of darknesse and dead night." This establishes the tone of gloom and the etymological sense "terrible"; and perhaps also borrows a suggestion of the terror of the other Gorgon. Spenser returns to Demogorgon next in Duessa's address to Night, where she alludes to a theogonic genealogy that overgoes even Boccaccio's. Boccaccio's mysterious Demogorgon is his first god and first cause. But Spenser pushes inquiry further back: Night is older than

> *Ioue*, whom thou at first didst breede,
> Or that great house of Gods caelestiall,

20. *Thebaid* IV.513–16; *Pharsalia* VI.742–49. Cf. Boiardo, *Orlando innamorato* II.13; Tasso, *Gerusalemme liberata* XII.10. See Raymond Klibansky, Erwin Panofsky, and Fritz Saxl, *Saturn and Melancholy* (London: Nelson, 1964), pp. 174n, 176; also Carlo Landi, *Demogorgone, con saggio di nuova edizione delle "Genealogie deorum gentilium" del Boccaccio e silloge dei frammenti di Teodonzio* (Palermo: R. Sandron, 1930); M. Castelain, "Demogorgon; ou le barbarisme déifié," *Association G. Budé Bulletin*, 36 (1932), 22–39; David Quint, "Epic Tradition and *Inferno IX*," *Dante Studies*, 93 (1975), 201–07.

Which wast begot in *Daemogorgons* hall,
And sawst the secrets of the world vnmade. (I.v.22)

As Hamilton notes, the spelling confirms part of Boccaccio's "god of earth" derivation; linking the name on the side of darkness with that of the Redcross Knight, Georgos, on the side of light. Later, Agape visits the Fates

Farre vnder ground from tract of liuing went,
Downe in the bottome of the deepe *Abysse*,
Where *Demogorgon* in dull darknesse pent,
Farre from the view of Gods and heauens blis,
The hideous *Chaos* keepes, their dreadfull dwelling is. (IV.ii.47)

This Demogorgon is a deep imagination indeed: a chthonic power possibly coeval with Night herself (if the syntax of I.v.22 makes him an alternative parent, with her, of Jove). And Spenser's Night is coeval with Herebus (II.iv.41), only a generation younger than Aeternitie. Nohrnberg (p. 739), following the mythographers, thinks we can identify Demogorgon as either Eternity or Chaos—as if he might go either way. However that may be, there is no doubt of the association with Chaos. Yet the ambiguity of Spenser's account (does Demogorgon, pent, keep Chaos, or keep Chaos pent, or does Chaos keep Demogorgon?) prevents us from sustaining any idol of Demogorgon, beyond a mystery of obscure power and limitation. And even these ideas are dim from interchange.

The unutterable name was subsequently much uttered. Perhaps in consequence it lost a little of its mystery. When Drayton took it up in *The Muses Elizium* (1630) he imagined only a susceptible earth god, whom a deity so junior as Apollo was able to disturb:

Great Demogorgon feeles thy might,
His Mynes about him heating:
Who through his bosome dart'st thy light,
Within the Center sweating. (IX.45–48)

Spenser had done better in keeping his deity less defined. Drayton's chthonic power is hardly indistinct enough for metaphysical capability. In the same way, Milton locates Demogorgon rather definitely, standing by the thrones of Chaos and Night: "by them stood . . . the dreaded name / Of Demogorgon" (*Paradise Lost* II.963–65). The mention is brief. All the same, it seems a lapse to make Demogorgon do anything so visual as *stand*.[21] Not until Shelley was the authentic mystery of Demogorgon reasserted. In *Prometheus Unbound*, the god is restored to a role of oracular and chaotic power. This power is based, however, on a significantly new etymology. Shelley's "Demogorgon" is indisputably to be derived from *dēmos*, "the people." Nevertheless, for the conception of formless power, for the language with which he adumbrates his new abstraction, and even, not impossibly, for the etymology itself, Shelley depends implicitly on Spenser.

But the point is not merely that Spenser's successors imitated or echoed his invention of names like Demogorgon. They owe him more than that. They owe to him nothing less than the entire idea that names in English could have atmospheric power. Before him, they were either absent altogether or introduced casually, without especial weight. Only with Spenser did they come to be used consciously for atmospheric effect.

Consciousness is particularly notable in Spenser's occasional avoidance or delay in naming. As many have noticed, he sometimes withholds names in the romance manner for long intervals, in a way that can make his story fairly difficult at times to follow. The Redcross Knight, indeed, receives his name only at I.x.61, although there have been earlier hints of it. And even then, Contemplation reveals "Saint George" as a future possibility, after canonization and writing up into legend—"thou Saint *George* shalt called bee." Yet "Georgos" (I.x.66), from *geōrgos*, husbandman (*gē*, "earth," *ergō*, "work"), has all along been the name conferred by his plowman foster father. It recalls the secret name of Christian individuation (Luke 10:20), enrolled "In heauenly Registers aboue the Sunne" (II.i.32). Yet individuation, it seems, is to be earned by humble georgic effort as much as appropriated by epic distinction. Apt naming may in some sense be essentialist. But there is a world of difference between names inherently apt, and

21. Nohrnberg defends Milton's passage, on the ground of the name's importance as the theogonic principle of pagan pantheons, Satan being on his way to a new avatar as a pagan god. See "On Literature and the Bible," *Centurion*, 2 (1976), 35–38.

those made so by adaptation. It is the difference between a mystique of order, and order achieved through change.

Demogorgon and Saint George are decisive instances of naming on a large scale. But Spenser also touches in delicate, fugitive effects that may easily go unnoticed. A virtuoso of names, he can evoke from them local atmospheres, shifts of tone, fine variations of mood. There is a subtle instance in the Book of Courtesy, where, as Berger and Nohrnberg have observed, several names have bookish connections. Calepine, as we saw, was the name of a common dictionary. And in the same way Aldus (Aladin) was a famous printer; Enius (Ennius) was the father of Latin poetry, just as Meliboe (Chaucer) was, of English; while Pastorella surely suggested the literary genre *pastourelle*. Such associations are not peculiar to this book—"Dony" at V.ii.3 (the name of Florimell's dwarf) would probably have suggested not only "gifts" but also Antonio Francesco Doni (1513–74), whose *Morall Philosophie* was translated by Thomas North (1570). But in the pastoral Book VI the literary names have an egregious effect, which cumulatively contributes to the civilized tone. Literature is a vital part of the cultured life there defended. And Spenser perhaps also senses that the names of books and authors carry associations of leisured security that may secretly amplify pastorality, even while they nominally break its rules.

Why have the beauties of Spenser's naming not been made more of? Probably in large part because of readers' uncertainty as to how much he can have meant in this direction. After all, he wrote without the support of any English tradition of allusion. With a later poet, such as Pope, uncertainties of this kind present less difficulty. We know reasonably well which authors Pope could allude to with any hope of uptake. But with Spenser these matters are pent in darkness. Is Matilde (VI.iv.29) named after Matilda, the foster mother in Tasso (*Gerusalemme liberata* I.59), or after Matelda in Dante (*Purgatorio* XXVIII–XXXIII), an image of the *vita activa*? Or both? The questions might be settled, but not very easily. Modern readers of *The Faerie Queene* have no comfortably secure knowledge how many associations they are likely to be expected to pursue. Through establishing allusive poetry in English, Spenser incurred a certain penalty, imposed on his poem in the shape of an occasional arduousness of difficulty.

3

Greene's Euphuism and
Some Congeneric Styles

ROBERT B. HEILMAN

I

Robert Greene's *Card of Fancy* (1584) provides excellent prime materials for an inspection of euphuism and hence of some later developments of euphuistic style.[1] There are two reasons for its especial utility. The first is that Greene's work, as a romance, permits us to see the impact of a given style upon a given type of fictional material; thus we have a good perspective for glancing at several later novels that have a partly comparable duality. The second reason for the usefulness of *The Card of Fancy* is Greene's indefatigable application, in almost every sentence, of the various procedures that we know as euphuism. He provides copious data for the description of what we might call fundamentalist euphuism, from which we can then see an evolution to a more centrist practice of the style. And it is of course relevant that A. C. Hamilton has recently published some observations on the modal and stylistic traits of *The Card of Fancy*.[2]

---

1. For a concise account of the sources, relationships, spread, and duration of euphuism and of studies of these matters, see the article "Euphuism" in James E. Ruoff, *Crowell's Handbook of Elizabethan and Stuart Literature* (New York: Crowell, 1975), p. 140.

2. A. C. Hamilton, "Elizabethan Prose Fiction and Some Trends in Recent Criticism," *RenQ*, 37 (1984), 21–33.

The character of this fiction as a "romance"[3] is apparent enough to eliminate the need for full-scale demonstration. English readers, of course, would feel the romance of the exotic: the action begins in Metelyne (Mytilene), continues in Barutta (Beirut), and has its main body in Alexandria. There is the old identity problem: Gwydonius succeeds as courtier and lover at Alexandria, where it is not known that his father is the hostile duke of Metelyne. There is a love triangle at Alexandria: Valericus becomes vindictively jealous when Castania, the duke's daughter, prefers Gwydonius to him. Then war breaks out between the dukes of Metelyne and Alexandria, and their sons and daughters suffer the conflict between love and political loyalty. But all problems are solved happily in the end: the two dukedoms are united in peace through the marriage of Gwydonius and Castania. We need no further evidence of the generic status of Greene's work.

As for Greene's euphuism, the first task is to describe it fully, both its central schemata and all the variations of these. We should have more than an impressionistic sense of it and hence a better base for observing the modifications in the works of certain epigones. Since a record of stylistic practices is extensive, I shall restrict discussion to dictional and syntactic matters, which are the main survivors in later uses of the euphuistic manner.[4]

Once the style has been analyzed, I can proceed to two other topics—the relation of euphuism to romance, and the relation of original euphuism to later stylistic developments. Euphuism and romance: the singular marriage of an old generic type and a young stylistic mode. What we find, I think, is this: the overall management of the romantic plot is influenced by the euphuism that Greene relentlessly practices; the structuring of the narrative units shows the impact of euphuistic procedures that had, as it were, taken possession of the author's mind, whether or not he was wholly conscious of this. In brief, certain syntactic principles, and their tonal impact, helped determine the general narrative configuration.

Euphuism and later styles: this coordination may seem a bit odd. Since sixteenth-century euphuism carried "everything to excess" (as

3. Hamilton offers an urbane description of the genre, ibid., pp. 27–28.
4. I shall omit the "unnatural natural history," the classical references and quotations, the proverbs, and the echoes of fable and myth that appeared in sixteenth-century euphuism.

Hamilton says of *The Card of Fancy*), it may well seem incapable of survival. Yet we can argue that it did not die by the time of *Love's Labor's Lost*. For under the blazing features and the ornamental devices that make us speak of "excess" there is a much simpler essence: a persistent quest for order that would continue, or recur, in comparable ways. To anticipate briefly my later argument: the quest appears, in less spectacular form, in various manifestations of neoclassical style, which are most visible in Samuel Johnson's prose. The Johnsonian style had many practitioners in the eighteenth century; then it influenced Scott and, even less probably, Charlotte Brontë. In both of these writers, too, there is much of the Latinate diction that appeared in the original euphuists and, most famously of course, in Johnson; it is picked up by later autodidacts such as Hardy, and hits bottom in the modern style we call "bureaucratese." Since the elements common to these various styles appeared first in euphuism, it seems permissible to use the original term for them.

II

The main constituents of Greene's euphuism are alliteration, parallelism, balanced elements, and antithesis. He uses alliteration in virtually every sentence, and with all possible variations. There are pairs of connotatively related nouns (counsel/comfort, pleasure/profit, ruth/ruin, wealth/weal), adjectives (sad/sorrowful, cruel/coy), adverbs (charily/chastely), and combinations of several parts of speech (flattering mates/fawning merchants) (173).[5] Since alliteration and meaning do not coincide as often as the euphuist might wish, such pairs are used again and again. Still more frequent, however, are the pairs of words with contrasted or opposing meanings: treasure/trash, vice/virtue, nature/nurture, woe/weal, bale/bliss, sweet/sour, cherish/chastise, loathe/like. The opposed elements may be phrases: "young years,"/"hoary hairs" (168) and "merry devices"/"mournful dumps" (209), pairs that illustrate two alliterative patterns often used by Greene: *aabb* and *abab*. Such combinations are almost uncountably

5. All page references are to the 1587 text reprinted in *Shorter Novels: Elizabethan and Jacobean*, Everyman's Library No. 824 (London: Dent; New York: Dutton, 1929). I give no page references for phrases often repeated. Since the spellings in the text are inconsistent, I regularize by modernizing.

frequent. Perhaps less frequent, but still persistent, are triads: "favored and fostered up by fortune" (165) and "inflamed with friendly affection" (177), in the second of which Greene uses a frequent device, alliteration both by vowels and by internal consonants.[6] Greene sometimes uses a pair, or even sets of pairs, to follow up a triad: "her beauty bred his bane, her looks, his loss, her sight, his sorrow, her exquisite perfection his extreme passions" (178), where the overall pattern is *bbb, ll, ss, epep*. Now and then he manages a foursome: "doleful days in dumps and dolors" (166) or a quartet of phrases: "more care than commodity, more pain than profit, more cost than comfort, more grief than good" (179). He often goes into combinations, such as a triad plus a pair, or a pair plus a triad. Here is a foursome plus a pair: "salve thy sores with sweet syrups, not with cutting corrasives" (217). Of course he can pile up still larger numbers of phrases and even clauses, too space-consuming to record here. The best case of multiplicity that I have noted has some twenty adjectives, distributed through five consecutive sentences, preceded by *so* (166).

In the struggle to combine alliteration and meaning in every sentence, Greene may fall back on phonetic echoes without orthographic identity ("cease from thy suit" [190]), or the converse, the orthographic without the phonetic ("woe and wretchedness" [256]). In relating more than two words, he regularly uses certain patterns, such as the *abab* type already mentioned ("smelled the fetch, and smiled at the folly" [199]). But he always strives for what variety the system permits. Occasionally with a foursome he uses a chiasmic form, *abba*: "hearty love, with loathing hate" (216), which, to a reader well-nigh overcome by routine alliteration, seems a shade less mechanical, as does an occasional interwoven effect: "his merciless cruelty in correcting his faults, and his moodless rigor in rebuking his folly" (230), in which the alliterative pattern is *abbc, addc*. Greene may struggle against the obvious by avoiding close contiguity of key phrases, as in "the su*gar*ed *p*oison of your divine beauty, as through the extremity of *p*inching *gr*ief" (218), with separation, chiasmus, and use of an internal sound (*gar*) in the alliterating group. In "sleepeth without repentance" (200) both key

6. The dominance of *f* in these quotations calls to mind the thematic word *fancy*, whose structural role I had planned to discuss but had to omit for lack of space. Commenting on the role of *fancy*, Hamilton remarks that the work "builds increasingly to an elaborate rhetorical fugue in F." He adds that the "elaborate hunting of the letter . . . is designed to reveal states of intense conflicting passion" (p. 27).

sounds are internal. "Privy friend . . . open foe" (216) uses a familiar *abab* pattern but varies it in two ways: in the *pfpf* series, all the consonants are labials, illustrating the alliteration by consonantal class that Greene uses occasionally; and in the closing pair there is the assonance that often appears (cf. "lawless liberty"/"slavish captivity" [194]). Occasionally a repeated metaphor may substitute for a repeated sound but be combined with a repeated sound: "so *snared* with thy *beauty*, and so *entangled* in the *trap* of thy *bounty*" (227). There is a fairly regular use of rhyme: "not imbrued with vice, but endued with virtue" (205) and "rid us from blame, and reward him with shame" (247). Both examples combine rhyme and alliteration, as does one sentence that I rearrange typographically to emphasize its devices:

> What desire, what lust,
> what hope, what trust,
> what care,
> what despair,
> what fear, what fury? (207)

Still another connective is the pun. Castania writes Valericus that "thy doggish letters favor of *Diogenes* doctrine, for in truth thou art such a cynical kind of dunce" (192). Greene's "doggish"/"cynical" is not an accident.

Let us look, finally, at euphuistic management of longer units—clauses and sentences. I shall present most of these in typographic arrangements that will make overall design unmistakable. Here is a triad of verb phrases which, containing a clause and three alliterated words each, achieve a more elaborate effect than we have so far seen:

> Shall I grudge when the gods are agreed,
>   or defer it, when the destinies drive it:
>   or frown at it, sith fortune frames it? (223)

A quartet of parallel predications containing if-clauses and conclusions produces a more clipped and perhaps more sophisticated effect through the omission of verbs. The passage is about love, which

> if it be lawless, it is lewd:
> if without limits, lascivious:
> if contained within no bounds, beastly:
> if observed with no order, odious. (202)

Another series of four parallel if-clauses is managed differently: the first three (all parts of a quite long sentence) contain respectively 13, 16, and 15 words, and then the fourth, which replaces the *if* with inversion, is as follows: "be she virtuous, be she chaste, be she courteous, be she constant, be she rich, be she renowned, be she honest, be she honorable" (179), the eight brief elements giving a touch of speed in a leisurely sentence that then goes on for another 140 words, with various euphuistic schemes throughout. Finally, a group of four verbal phrases, while using repetition, also aspires to some differentiation:

> for an inch of joy, to reap an ell of annoy,
> for a moment of mirth, a month of misery:
> for a dram of pleasure, a whole pound of pain,
> and by procuring mine own delight,
>   to purchase my father's death and destruction. (237)

In the four statements of indulgence-cum-nemesis, Greene uses four different metaphors—linear measurement, temporal measurement, weight measurement, and purchasing; the fourth is longer than the others; and the first uses both vocalic alliteration and rhyme.

To conclude this sampling of sentence patterns, I will quote two passages with slightly longer units: these should give some feeling of more massive euphuized effects and more complex applications of the system. The first is this:

> how pinching a pain is it to be perplexed with diverse passions,
> what a noisome care it is to be cumbered with sundry cogitations,
> what a   woe it is to hang between desire and despair,
> what a   hell it is to hover between fear and hope. (254)

The almost identical arrangement of words in the four predications is modified by the omission of adjectives in the third and fourth units, and this is compensated for by the use of two objects in the closing prepositional phrases; "perplexed" and "cumbered," parallel passives, are parallel in meaning, as are "diverse" and "sundry" and of course the alliterated "hang" and "hover"; "cumbered" and "sundry" are assonant, and there is some interweaving in the alliteration. My final example is briefer, and it leads in a somewhat different direction:

Did my Father promote thee to this thou art, from the state of a beggar,
   and
wilt thou now presume   to be my better? (213)

Here the antithetical clauses are so different in length as hardly to seem balanced at all, the two pairs of alliterated words (unusually few) are far enough apart to suggest a delicate accent rather than a pressing insistence, and the assonance of *beggar* and *better*, in a context only mildly euphuized, might elude the ear.

So much for the basics of Greene's euphuism, and for the considerable spread of devices by which he seeks to vary and multiply the patterns of alliteration and repeated, balanced, or opposed syntactic elements. Within the school of euphuistic stylists there must have been strong competition in devising variations and refinements of the standard procedures and, among the consumers, a vast admiration for agility in modification and innovation. It is well to see how much invention could be practiced, and how much apparent novelty encompassed, within an essentially closed style. On the other hand, of course, the presence of variables within a system that would seem to exclude them cannot much modify our sense of a monotony that closes off the almost infinite varieties of prose rhythm to which writers of succeeding centuries have accustomed us. Whatever euphuists and their cousins marinists, gongorists, and *les précieuses* might have intended, or even in some cases accomplished, by way of countering a lack of structure, a bumbling inelegance they perceived in general prose practice, their prescriptions for reform—applied with a rigorous mechanical invariability that seemed compulsory—led to a fairly rapid exhaustion of the possibilities.

III

These truisms are useful mainly as a way into another issue—the relationship of style to narrative design in *The Card of Fancy*. In brief, the habit of mind which appears in euphuistic style appears also in the structure of relationships and events. In verbal and syntactical patterns, whether the semantic direction is toward repetition, elaboration, and reinforcement or toward contrast and opposition, the essential quality evident through many variations is symmetry. Symmetry also appears in the main plot lines. There are two rival rulers, the dukes of Metelyne and of Alexandria. Each has a son and a daughter. The children of Clerophontes of Metelyne are Leucippa and Gwydonius; the children of Orlanio of Alexandria are Castania and Thersandro. In the families there is just one asymmetry, which we can see is analogous to a break in an alliterative pattern: three of the children are conspicuously virtuous, whereas Gwydonius is initially a ne'er-do-well and has to reform, as he does in Barutta and Alexandria. Indeed, his sharp turnaround from the disobedient, dissolute, and rowdy son of the ruling duke to knightly lover, man of principle, and military and political hero has a euphuistic character: it is the narrative form of the syntactic antithesis (which also appears in the total contrast between all-bad Gwydonius and his all-virtuous sister Leucippa). Gwydonius falls in love with Castania, and Thersandro with Leucippa. Each brother has a rival lover. But after many vicissitudes, including a large war between Clerophontes and Orlanio, the Montague-Capulet situation comes to a happy ending in two brother-to-enemy's-sister marriages that unite two dukedoms. Symmetry leads to total unity.

But this euphuistic conception of situation and development is perhaps less striking than the local means by which the plot is advanced. Here, I think, we not only see a parallel between sentence management and plot management but can reasonably assume an impact of stylistic habit upon narrative method. The euphuistic manner—alliteration, series, balance, opposition—is obviously not the natural style of spontaneous, undisciplined, or explosive feeling, for it is planned, controlled, regularized, formalized. It is the method of the disciplined speaker, who is not driven toward incoherence by the pressure of thoughts and emotions but is always aware of the stylistic medium. It is the rhetoric of conscious address, not of strong and unruly expression; of public rather than private life. It is planned and calculated rather than free-swinging and unpredictable. It suggests less the domestic scene than the public platform, less the private room than the stage.[7] A few stage directions punctuate the dialogue. But the dialogue is euphu-

7. Hamilton argues that "the highly rhetorical speeches that replace narrative and become the soul of the work, an end in themselves without further meaning or purpose," were effective in their day (p. 28).

istic; it has little of informal briskness, snap, and free-wheeling give and take. Greene's people speak as at a lectern, like debaters with set speeches; brevity, overall or in the parts, is rarely a goal. Their speeches somewhat remind us of the *tirades* in French classical drama and English heroic drama, but there is little or no infusion of the stichomythy that gives variety, for instance, in Racine. Greene's dialogue is usually an exchange of monologues, an antithesis of paragraphs rather than of short, sharp statements. Euphuistic style determines these ordered exchanges, and they provide plenty of opportunity and space for the exercise of that style. Letters do too, and hence parts of *The Card of Fancy* anticipate the epistolary novel that would become a vogue a century and a half later.

We can detect the impact of the euphuistic consciousness in Greene's distribution of space, which can best be represented in number of lines occupied by this or that narrative element (in the text I am using, there are forty-three lines to the printed page). Greene's opening narrative, describing Clerophontes, duke of Metelyne, his beautiful and virtuous daughter Leucippa, and his handsome reprobate son Gwydonius, occupies sixty-two lines of text. Then Greene shifts to Clerophontes' reflections on his son's misbehavior, and this section goes on for fifty-five lines. The passage is in effect an internal monologue, a form which Greene uses again and again. But while the modern internal monologue proceeds by associative connections that ignore or deny rational order, Clerophontes' internal monologue is euphuistic, that is, a highly organized product of a mind making points as it goes. His longest sentence occupies seventeen lines, his shortest four. To show the euphuistic composition of the words supposed to denote inner turmoil, we may diagram his longest sentence as follows:

Now (quoth he) I prove by experience,
the saying of *Sophocles* to be true,
that the man which hath many children shall never live without some mirth,
                              nor die without some sorrow:
for if they be virtuous, he shall have cause whereof to rejoice,
     if   vicious,   wherefore to be sad,
which saying I try performed in myself,
          for as I have one child   which delights me with her virtue,
          so   I have another   that despites me with his vanity,
          as the one by duty   brings my joy,

so the other by disobedience breeds me annoy:
yea, as the one is a comfort to my mind,
  so the other is a fretting corrasive to my heart:
  for what grief is there more griping,
    what pain more pinching,
    what cross more cumbersome,
    what plague more pernicious,
yea, what trouble can torment me worse,
    than to see my son,
      mine heir,
  the inheritor of my Dukedom,
which should be the pillar of my parentage,
    to consume his time in roisting and riot,
        in spending and spoiling,
        in swearing and swashing, and
        in following willfully the fury
          of his own frantic
            fancy. (166–67)

This is a characteristic Greene sentence. It suggests declamation rather than a spontaneous surfacing of painful emotions; the rhetoric of inner disturbance is, to say the least, different from Hamlet's. However, the point is not to disparage the method but to see how it determines the nature of both internal and external monologue. Brevity, disordered syntax, and the rat-a-tat of normal dramatic dialogue were not compatible with the stylistic preconceptions of the euphuist.

Clerophontes' internal monologue is followed by seventeen lines of authorial narrative about the duke's verbal attack on his son. Gwydonius replies in a hostile monologue of twenty-four lines divided into only three sentences (168)—the first spoken lines in the tale. He'll go abroad, he says. Greene uses ten lines to report that this idea pleases Clerophontes and then turns the lectern over to Clerophontes for a massive pre-Polonius Polonial address to his son—actually 108 lines or over two pages (169–71). The remaining space in the first section is allotted as follows: action (Gwydonius travels to Barutta, continues his dissolute ways, and is jailed), thirty-five lines; Gwydonius's internal monologue (self-blame and resolve to reform), fifty lines; action (he travels to Alexandria), eighteen lines (171–74). Greene has now devoted 142 lines to authorial narrative, and 237 lines to four massive monologues—the form of "action" toward which the euphuistic manner regularly drives him.

Greene describes the ducal household in Alexandria, which balances that in Metelyne, rather quickly (174–78). In one respect he proceeds antithetically: in Metelyne the central situation involved father and son, whereas now it is father and daughter. Duke Orlanio employs Melytta as "companion and counsellor" to his fourteen-year-old daughter Castania, enabling Greene to balance, against Clerophontes' Polonial advice to his departing son, Orlanio's instructions to Melytta—a fifty-five-line monologue followed by her twenty-two-line speech of acceptance (175–77). Gwydonius shows up with an assumed but noble identity, makes a twenty-line speech of application for a job, and is promptly appointed companion to Duke Orlanio's son Thersandro (177–78). In this short second "chapter" Greene has so much external action going on that he has to devote seventy-eight lines to it, with only a few more—ninety-two—to the set speeches. Hence these occupy only 54 percent of the text, as against 62 percent in the opening section.

Then Greene is relieved, one imagines, to put situation building behind him and shift to a central theme much more amenable to euphuistic expression—love affairs, which occupy fifty-two of his total of ninety-six pages and loom large in a final thirty pages in which war and politics are nominally the central issues. In a love story, little connective tissue is required, and people can talk or write at length in euphuistic manifestos. Greene provides two suitors for Castania—Valericus, who fails (fifteen pages), and Gwydonius, who succeeds (thirty-seven pages). The Valericus-Castania affair goes on for 598 lines, the author assigning only 122, or about 20 percent, to connective tissue, and 476, or roughly 80 percent, to the characters—the highest proportion yet for euphuistic discourse. In Greene's handling of Valericus's failure to win from Castania anything more than a temporary jesting interest in the game, three matters are interesting. One is the apparent apportioning of lines according to intensity of feeling: Valericus has 266 lines of internal and external monologue (in five passages), and Castania has only 39 lines (in one passage). The second is that Greene hits upon letters as excellent carriers of euphuistic formalism: Valericus writes two (sixty lines), and Castania a balancing two (forty lines). Third, at one point Greene even makes an approach to "normal" dialogue. Valericus, Castania, Melytta (and the author) split up a seventy-nine-line exchange as follows: C, 13; author, 6; V, 17; M, 10; V, 11; C, 7; V, 3; C, 2; V, 3; M, 7. Only three speeches, however, approach brevity, and these are less heavily euphuized. True euphuism led to length.

In the thirty-seven pages required for Gwydonius and Castania to arrive at a mutual acknowledgment of love, the author's connective tissue occupies 251 lines, Gwydonius's monologues, internal and external, 352 lines, Castania's 301, and Valericus's 51 (his anger against them). For these figures the overall percentages are: third-person narrative, 26 percent; characters' speeches, 74 percent. These figures change somewhat when we take into account Greene's introduction of some variations analogous to those he employed in the earlier Valericus-Castania section. Again there is an exchange of letters, two by each lover: Gwydonius, eighty-nine lines, Castania, ninety-one lines, with forty-one descriptive lines by the narrator. Whereas in the Valericus-Castania story there was one approach to dialogue with shorter speeches, in the Gwydonius-Castania story there are three such shifts. In the most complex of these there are four speakers—the two lovers, Castania's brother Thersandro, and her tutor Melytta. The subject is love, and the discussion starts off a little like a Castiglione round table, with four initial papers on a program as it were: Thersandro, eight lines; Gwydonius, twenty-one; Melytta, forty-eight; and Castania, forty-one. But then it gets a little looser, more informal, almost enough to suggest dialogue in a Restoration comedy; the numbers of lines in the series of speeches are 9–6–22–7–2–10–3–4–5–4–5–7–6, and the narrator stays out of it entirely. In a second alteration, though less marked than the first, Castania and Melytta have an exchange in which the parts somewhat reduce the usual euphuistic amplitude: M, 31; C, 15; M, 13; C, 16, and M, 8, with the narrator having only 5. In the third such exchange the speeches are cut down a shade more: Castania, 29; Gwydonius, 7; C, 5; G, 5; C, 4.

But though one should notice this occasional thinning down of speeches, they are all essentially in the euphuistic mode, so that they can be included in the overall account of the distribution of space. From beginning to end the Gwydonius-Castania story includes 295 lines of narrative, and 1,225 lines of dialogue composed mostly of monologue, 19 and 81 percent; the latter percentage is the highest of all the five sections.

In the final thirty pages, where a war and two three-cornered love affairs are brought to a happy ending, there is so much going on that Greene is driven to a more extensive use of third-person narrative—46 percent of the space, leaving a relatively low 54 percent for mono-logues.[8] Thus the total spatial design of the book can be seen in the accompanying table.[9]

Narrative material	Pages	Third-person narrative	Monologues
Metelyne and Barutta:			
Gwydonius leaves both	9	38%	62%
Alexandria: Gwydonius arrives	5	46%	54%
Valericus-Castania affair	15	20%	80%
Gwydonius-Castania affair	37	19%	81%
War, love, honor, peace	30	46%	54%

Greene unmistakably prefers the one-on-one situation, which is most conducive to long speeches and internal monologues and hence to the highly euphuistic prose style of which he makes less use in the passages of connective tissue.

IV

Despite the larger presence of authorial narrative, the long final section still has what we might call a euphuistic rhythm. The principle of antithesis controls the actual patterns. The dominant element is the war between Clerophontes and Orlanio. Within this central opposi-tion, other opposing elements are carefully balanced. Clerophontes' son Gwydonius loves Orlanio's daughter Castania, and she him. Or-lanio's son Thersandro loves Clerophontes' daughter Leucippa, and

8. Approaching the end, Greene tended to hurry things, as if he were getting weary of the double labors with style and plot. Indeed, a twelve-line paragraph at the end covers so much ground that one could read it as a consciously jesting dismissal of the project. A critic who wanted to pursue this argument could call attention to the generic terms that Greene uses: "this tragical comedy" (211), when Gwydonius is concerned about the apparent illness of Castania; "this tragedy" (246), when Orlanio has Castania and Melytta jailed because Castania loves Gwydonius, the son of a political enemy; and finally "this strange tragedy" (260), of a final solution happy for everybody. He may, of course, be using *tragedy* as a loose synonym for *drama*.

9. The table concludes my use of statistics, which I know are tedious, but which have seemed the only way to present, in relatively brief compass, the distribution of space as a significant reflector of the influence exerted by the euphuistic habit of mind.

she him. Thus all four lovers have similar divided feelings. Valericus wants to break up the Gwydonius-Castania affair; for balance, Greene dredges up at the last moment, as if he had just remembered his narrative design and cared more about it than about any probability at all, a Lucianus to whom Clerophontes wants to marry Leucippa. Topping off this system of balanced antitheses is a duel between Clerophontes and his son Gwydonius, a complement to the early quarrel that inaugurated the situation now being resolved. Gwydonius is disguised, so that we have the Sohrab-and-Rustum situation,[10] but with a difference: the son nominally wins the duel, not hurting his father but displaying an apologetic and magnanimous style that permits the resolution of all antithetical elements into an embracing harmony.

A modern reference book lists *The Card of Fancy* among Greene's "romances of pure adventure and entertainment."[11] This description ignores the vast euphuism in the tale and its impact on the tone and hence on the generic character of the book. Granted, the exotic scene, love affairs, war, the love-and-honor motif, and the happy ending are the traditional stuff of romance. But the severe discipline of euphuistic style and organization changes the romantic cast. Exotic scenes lose their distance and become almost domestic classrooms. When adventure is patterned, it becomes illustrative rather than unpredictable; it obeys design rather than gives the illusion of spontaneity. If romance connotes escape from the patterns of ordinary life, euphuism imposes rigorous patterns that assert an inescapable modeling of life. This does not mean that the presentation of human nature is always coerced by artifice. Some motives are plausible enough: the jealousy of Valericus and, in Castania, a certain gamesomeness and a certain unsureness about Gwydonius's devotion that faintly anticipate the style of Congreve's Millamant. Still, hanging over everything is a predetermined orderedness that inhibits the sense of freedom requisite for romantic tone.

Compare *The Tempest*, in which the mingling of love and politics and the ultimate resolution of the conflicts between the two and within each are not unlike Greene's basic plot. But there is only one love

10. One wonders whether this is the earliest English appearance of a motif that dates from Firdausi, c. 950–1020. For the spread of the motif from the Renaissance on, see my book *The Iceman, the Arsonist, and the Troubled Agent* (Seattle: University of Washington Press, 1973), pp. 346–47 n. 25.

11. *Crowell's Handbook of Elizabethan and Stuart Literature*, p. 177.

affair, and hence an absence of imposed parallelism. More important, Shakespeare creates a sense of a gradual evolution, both emotional and moral, toward a workable solution—a free will of the plot, as it were, against a predestination executed by the ever-present hand of Greene. It would be frivolous, no doubt, to propose that blank verse is a less tyrannical mode than the quasi poetry of euphuism, but the metaphor does have some suggestive value.

If romance embodies a dash toward the wonderful and the libertine, euphuism goes along to insist on the inevitable presence of likenesses, relationships, parallels, repetitions, and contrasts that constrain free-floating adventure, novelty, strangeness, and the attractions of disorder. It would be too radical to assert that euphuism turns romance into something else. It is better to reintroduce the shaggy beast that has slouched through much modern criticism, namely, tension, and to say that in euphuistic romance there is always a pulling-apart between opposing ways of managing narrative art, a struggle for different modes of response in the reader (a struggle not present, for instance, in such a combination of euphuism and didacticism as we find in Lyly's *Euphues*). Furthermore, this tension exists not only between a narrative mode and a stylistic vogue but also between larger forces—the romantic and classical impulses that emerge from human nature into cultural manifestations. Though such categories have inspired some revisionist paradoxes, we can use them for their convenience and beg the question of their metaphysical status. Romanticism is so large a subject that here we need do no more than note its inclusion of the world of romances, which Greene somewhat modified. We can go a little further with classical style, or what is better called neoclassical style, for euphuism, as I noted at the very beginning, is the matrix of one distinct neoclassical style and of related stylistic methods traceable in subsequent writing. The practices of later centuries evidence the residual force of the basic euphuistic idea, which appears in a specialized and exaggerated form in the sixteenth-century vogue. The idea embodies the neoclassical aspiration to rational ordering and control.

V

"Specialization and exaggeration": these words immediately suggest what we usually call decadence, the phase of a style that occurs when, as a result of overfamiliarity and hence weakening impact, the consumers require, and the producers supply, ever stronger and more bizarre versions of the stimuli characteristic of the mode. In euphuism we then have a remarkable historical anomaly in that decadence, or at least what looks very much like it, precedes what we might call "normal" practice. If we move ahead almost two centuries to Samuel Johnson's didactic romance *Rasselas* (1759), we find a euphuism that is, as it were, purged of all the tyrannical thoroughness of Elizabethan euphuism. Johnson omits virtually all the learning, literal or fantastic, that decorates Greene's fiction, all the spectacular comparisons, the citations of myth and fable, the exclamations and the rhetorical questions so visible in Greene. What he retains is something of the conceptual euphuism and a considerable amount of the stylistic euphuism that we have described.

By "conceptual euphuism" I mean, of course, the overall patterning of the narrative materials. Johnson's central design is antithetical: the opposition between the more or less ideal but restricted life of the "happy valley" in Abyssinia, and the more mixed, complex life of different individuals in the outside world, that is, Egypt. Rasselas, his tutor Imlac, and his sister Nekayah escape from their safe haven and explore Egypt (of which they see a great deal more than Greene's characters see of Alexandria). The antithetical principle largely governs the narrative pattern: the explorers meet different types and strata of people, believe them to possess and exemplify a "happy" life, and then on closer inspection find that these prospective models also suffer from the dissatisfactions, worries, and troubles natural to humanity generally. Or they contrast different modes of life, such as marriage and celibacy, secular and monastic living; Johnson writes balanced paragraphs of opposing views. Things are not balanced up as neatly as they are in Greene, however; there are intelligent free-wheeling discussions that can end indecisively; and indeed at the end the explorers retain different views of a desirable mode of life even when, rather mechanically, they opt for a return to native Abyssinia. There is enough play of thought and feeling to vary considerably the antithetical sense of things that determines the narrative design.

In style Johnson is remarkably euphuistic—a fact that will be more or less striking in accordance with a reader's expectations or prior reading. If one comes to him from such Augustans as Addison and Steele and Swift, Johnson seems overabundantly euphuistic; if one comes to him from Greene, Johnson seems relatively easy flowing. That is to say that a freedom from dominating euphuistic habits marks enough of his sentences to give an overall sense of a much less constrained rhythm than one finds in Greene. But still the euphuistic tendency is always there; one can find few paragraphs without balance, parallelism, or antithesis. The frequency of Johnson's euphuistic sentence designs can be inferred from the fact that all my illustrations are from the first few pages of the novel and that I am being highly selective in quoting from these pages.

Johnson often comes up with a rather short antithetical sentence such as is fairly rare in Greene: "His wish still continued, but his hope grew less" (617).[12] He frequently uses a more extensive balance to govern part of a sentence: "to forget those lectures which pleased only while they were new, and to become new again must be forgotten" (612). There Johnson uses a chiasmus of meaning (forget-new-new-forgotten) which he relies on more frequently than Greene does. Here is a somewhat more complex example: "He that can swim needs not despair to fly: to swim is to fly in a grosser fluid, and to fly is to swim in a subtler" (618). Johnson often writes a series of three parallel elements, for instance, "to make seclusion pleasant, to fill up the vacancies of attention, and lessen the tediousness of time" (608). Such parallels may prevail in more extended predications—"he neglected their officiousness, / repulsed their invitations, / and spent day after day on the banks of rivulets sheltered with trees, where he sometimes listened to the birds in the branches, / sometimes observed the fish playing in the stream, / and anon cast his eyes upon the pastures and mountains" (610)—where the extra long third element in the first triad of verb phrases creates some variation in the overall pattern of successive triads.

Finally, alliteration. There is some of it in the passages just quoted, but it is incidental rather than enveloping, as it is in Greene. On the other hand, it is a regular tool of Johnson's; he uses it more frequently—no page is without it—than later writers would, though less than pure euphuists did. It appears pretty frequently in phrases and clauses: "the *i*gnorance of *i*nfancy, or *i*mbecility of *age*" (615), "neither

12. References are to the text in Samuel Johnson, *"Rasselas," Poems, and Selected Prose*, ed. Bertrand H. Bronson (New York: Holt, Rinehart and Winston, 1952).

labor to be endured nor danger to be dreaded" (613; note also the run of medial and final rs); "no power of perception which is not glutted with its proper pleasure" (611). It may add emphasis to a balanced sentence: "They wandered in gardens of fragrance, and slept in the fortresses of security" (610). Since Johnson manages a moderate infusion of short, neat sentences, as several of the preceding quotations show, his euphuistic effects are much less massive and relentless than those of Greene. But he is capable of longer and more highly organized sentences that combine clear structural patterns with alliteration. Here is one of these, typographically arranged to emphasize the internal relationships:

> On one part were flocks and herds feeding in the pastures,
> on another all the beasts of chase frisking in the lawns;
> the sprightly kid was bounding on the rocks,
> the subtle monkey frolicking in the trees, and
> the solemn elephant reposing in the shade. (608)

And of course beasts, bounding, frolicking, and reposing are held together by dominant labials, three of them initial; three of them are participles; and the three animal names—kid, monkey, elephant—are arranged according to increasing number of syllables. Finally, here is a whole paragraph made up of one euphuistic sentence:

> His chief amusement was to picture to himself that world which he had
> never seen;
>> to place himself in various conditions;
>> to be entangled in imaginary difficulties, and
>> to be engaged   in wild adventures:
> but his benevolence always terminated his projects in
>> the relief of distress,
>> the detection of fraud,
>> the defeat of oppression, and
>> the diffusion of happiness. (614)

Still, the balances emphasized by alliteration are rather less monumental than those which Greene constructed on nearly every page.

The eighteenth-century revival, with modifications, of a style highly fashionable for a decade or two in the sixteenth century argues for a certain enduring utility and even attractiveness in the central devices of that style. One might argue (1) that it is a linguistic way of representing a perceived or sensed reality in the objective world, or (2) that it is a gratifying way of ordering phenomena whose objective nature is not known, or (3) that it is a natural emanation of the structure of the mind as it comes into contact with an objective world. But while I acknowledge these epistemological problems, I will not pursue them, for my interest is simply in the durability of a mode which, in its first historical manifestations, came to seem fantastically improbable. It is important to see how it sobers up in "classicism," shedding a singular initial excess, a merciless hyperbole, an all but loony paradise of dainty devices of ordering and ornamental intent, but retaining its essential modi operandi and thus expressing the "aspirations towards symmetry, decorum, rationality" that Frank Warnke includes in a more extensive definition of classicism.[13]

VI

Johnson's classicism or neoclassicism of prose style had somewhat of a run in Frances Burney and Maria Edgeworth, though with some thinning out of the dominant equationism and oppositionism. These continued to undergo further purification, or perhaps we should say subordination to other syntactic practices. Not that they should or could disappear entirely but that they began to be reserved for special functions rather than freely indulged on every page. Here are a number of sentences from the last page of the fourth chapter of *Pride and Prejudice*. Austen is characterizing two men who later would marry two of the Bennet sisters (the sentence numbers are of course my additions):

> [1] Bingley was endeared to Darcy by the easiness, openness, ductility of his temper, though no disposition could offer a greater contrast to his own and though with his own he never appeared dissatisfied. [2] On the strength of Darcy's regard Bingley had the firmest reliance, and of his judgment the highest opinion. . . . [3] Bingley was by no means deficient, but Darcy was clever. [4] He was at the same time haughty, reserved, and fastidious, and his manners, though well bred, were not inviting. . . .
> [5] Bingley was sure of being liked wherever he appeared, Darcy was

13. Frank Warnke, "Metaphysical Poetry and the European Context," in *Metaphysical Poetry*, Stratford-upon-Avon Studies, 11 (New York: St. Martin's Press, 1970), p. 274.

continually giving offence. . . . [6] Darcy, on the contrary, had seen a collection of people [the Bennets and friends] in whom there was little beauty and no fashion, for none of whom he had felt the smallest interest and from none received either attention or pleasure.[14]

In characterizing Darcy and Bingley entirely by contrast, Austen chooses not to do separate vignettes of a paragraph each but to portray them simultaneously, with alternating specifications. Hence it seems natural for her to rely on syntactic devices that we have seen in both Greene and Johnson. These are, in the sentences as numbered: (1) a main clause, with a three-word series, opposed by two parallel *though*-clauses, and with the only traces of alliteration, and these hardly detectable, in the whole paragraph; (2) two balanced pairs of interlocking prepositional phrases, an initial group balanced against a final group; (3) antithetical clauses; (4) symmetrical clauses, one with a series, the other with an antithesis; (5) antithetical clauses; (6) three parallel subordinate clauses.

Though my series of compact annotations may suggest a euphuistic density of devices, no reader is likely to feel that the passage suffers from oppressive formalism. It is not heavily Latinate, and the devices seem to serve the meaning rather than the author's determination to achieve a certain ring. The relative lightness of the passage would be even more marked if I had included several sentences that have no euphuistic devices at all. Further, this passage does not seem the product of a compulsive pattern: Austen writes pages and even chapters in which there is no euphuism or only a light touch of it. In her hands the classical or euphuistic manner is purged of excess and hence reserved largely for local functions to which it is especially adapted.

VII

If in Austen the style was cut back to what, in contemporary argot, we might call minimalist status, one might predict its ultimate disappearance, especially in such a time as our own, when logicalist perception, if we may so call it, is not a widespread gift among fictionists. A

14. I quote from *Pride and Prejudice*, ed. Robert Daniel (New York: Rinehart, 1949).

history from then to now would be an interesting one. My own guess is that it would not be, indeed could not be, a history of a declining and finally lost form, detectable only in fossil state. But what one would certainly not expect would be a new development away from the bare-bones Austen condition, a restoration of full-fleshed euphuism resembling the earlier grandiose manifestations. Yet oddly enough such a recovery of an earlier rich panoply of stylistic accoutrements does occur at least once, and, still more surprisingly, in a romantic writer in whom it would a priori seem wholly improbable—Charlotte Brontë. Her *Villette* has a rather remarkable infusion of euphuistic practices. Brontë's style is so varied and innovative—it even contains elements of what we can only call the surrealistic—that we can easily lose sight of her resemblances to Austen and even Johnson.[15] Balanced structure, series, antitheses are everywhere; a few examples hardly begin to suggest the pervasiveness of these stylistic alignments in her text. Of students, "the stirring of worthy emulation, or the quickening of honest shame" (chap. 9, p. 73) of Mme Beck, "watching and spying everywhere, peering through every keyhole, listening behind every door (chap. 8, p. 63).[16] "The school gossiped, the kitchen whispered, the town caught the rumor, parents wrote letters" (chap. 11, p. 87), where the series registers a comic sense not always present in euphuistic writers. She can serialize antithetic pairs: "Her service was my duty—her pain, my suffering—her relief, my hope—her anger, my punishment— her regard, my reward" (chap. 4, p. 30). A man looked "high but not arrogant, manly but not overbearing" (chap. 7, p. 53). Brontë's alliterative groups are so constant, surprisingly so in a nineteenth-century text, that it has been a bit of a problem to find, for my initial illustrations, passages without evident alliteration. Brontë's pairs don't become all-service clichés, as many of Greene's do, but they are well-nigh

15. A full description of the unusual stylistic varieties appears in my "Tulip-Hood, Streaks, and Other Strange Bedfellows: Style in *Villette*," *Studies in the Novel*, 14 (1982), 223–47. In that more complete account of Brontë's euphuism than is possible here, I describe her use of other relevant devices—rhetorical questions, exclamatory statements, apostrophes, classical and mythological allusions, habitual inversions, and borrowings from the later neoclassical versions of the style, such as abstract terms, personification by capitalization, Latinate vocabulary, etc.

16. References are to *Villette*, Everyman's Library, No. 351 (1909; rpt. London: Dent; New York: Dutton, 1949). I supply chapter numbers for the convenience of anyone who may be using another edition.

as frequent: "prodigal and profligate," "flaw or falsity," "drooping draperies." There are frequent threesomes, such as "pain, privation, penury," "wind was wailing at the windows," "his supple symmetry, his smile frequent," with a chiasmus of parts of speech.[17] Alliteration, direct or overlapping, may emphasize an antithesis: "lapsing from the *p*assionate *p*ain of *c*hange to the *p*alsy of *c*ustom" (chap. 21, p. 215); and, of a dressmaker who could "*u*nite the *u*tterly *u*npretending with the *p*erfectly becoming" (chap. 33, p. 344), the connection between the parts further marked by the two combinations of an adverb and a gerund. Brontë can manage a sort of wit in a predication that is both more alliterative and more Latinate than Austen would use, as when she describes the progress of lovers: "out of association grows adhesion, and out of adhesion amalgamation" (chap. 25, p. 263), with an added effect through the echo of -*ation* between the beginning and the end of the passage. Brontë writes that Mme Beck preferred "such associates as must culti*vate* and ele*vate*, rather than those which might *d*eterior*ate* and *d*epress" (chap. 26, p. 266), in which there are two internal *v*s, two initial *d*s, and three words ending in -*ate*. She not only uses assonance but does not hesitate at rhyme, even a dactylic one: "He watched tearlessly ordeals that he exacted should be passed through fearlessly" (chap. 30, p. 319).

On the other hand, she can be relatively subtle in the use of such devices. Take, for instance, the phrase "—too terribly glorious, the spectacle of clouds, split and pierced by white and blinding bolts" (chap. 12, p. 96), where there is a sensory concreteness absent from the work of her predecessors, where the two participles and the following pair of adjectives do not seem like a mechanical arrangement, and where the alliterations might well escape our eyes entirely. One has almost to make an effort to detect the related *sp*, *spl*, and *p*, and the *bl* and *b-l* in the last two words. What happens, I suggest, is that these specific sound echoes are subordinated to an overall flowing, almost rhythmical effect traceable to sounds that we hardly notice: the presence in all the major words but *white* of liquid consonants—the internal *r*s in three words and, in seven words, various combinations with *l* (in order, *bl*, *gl*, *cl*, *cl*, *spl*, *bl*, and *b-l*).

17. The quoted passages are located, in order, as follows: chap. 14, p. 112; chap. 35, p. 365; chap. 3, p. 23; chap. 21, p. 207; chap. 4, p. 31; chap. 2, p. 11.

What that series of words communicates is less a logical ordering of experience than the emotional impact of experience. And this is where we see Brontë parting company with our other employers of euphuism, however much they have in common technically. Brontë can use all the devices we have sketched for ends that would hardly seem to be congruent with such means. Here is how she describes a riding accident that results in a man's death: "I saw the horse; I heard it stamp—I saw at least a mass; I heard a clamor" (chap. 4, p. 33). The symmetry is exceptional. We could hardly find four predications more squared up than these. They constitute almost a mathematical formula: three of the four clauses made up of exactly four words, "I saw" used twice, "I heard" used twice, and, rather less apparent, a tie through assonance more subtle than many of her phonetic echoes, the short-a sound in three major words. But one would never mistake it for a logical triumph over disaster; it may try to control the response, but it registers the almost hysterical feeling of the observer and survivor. Again, the well-worn series of parallel adjectives, arranged 3–3–2–2–1, in the following description of Mme Beck, may seem like no more than a wholly dispassionate, almost scientific roll call of personal qualities: "Wise, firm, faithless; secret, crafty, passionless; watchful and inscrutable; acute and insensate—withal perfectly decorous—what more could be desired?" (chap. 8, p. 64). Each segment of this superb characterization applies the principle that governs the first: though the series implies sameness of direction in all of its constituents, the closing adjective takes off on its own, antithetically. But then we see that the apparent contradiction is absorbed into the overall identity: in this case being "faithless" is indissolubly tied to being "wise" and "firm." The parallelism voices a great shock, the shock of the conception and, behind that and more telling still, the observer's pained recognition of the nature of the world she inhabits.

An antithetical statement may turn on a metaphor that can only be a carrier of strong feeling. Paul Emanuel unsparingly characterizes the narrator, Lucy Snowe, as one who "would snatch at a draught of sweet poison, and spurn wholesome bitters with disgust" (chap. 21, p. 210). Again the antithesis (with an alliterative effect subdued, as it were, by the intensity of the metaphor) less "controls" experience by identifying its contradictions than it underscores the perversity of a troubled nature. Finally, when Lucy is encouraged to "cultivate happiness," she picks up the metaphor and uses it to hit back with intense feeling. Happiness, she asserts with passion, "is not a potato, to be planted in mould and tilled with manure" but "a glory shining far down upon us out of Heaven . . . a divine dew which the soul . . . feels dropping upon it from the amaranth bloom and golden fruitage of Paradise" (chap. 22, p. 227). The antithesis is there, but without the compactness that can make it seem like a gadget; the alliterative patterns abut on open spaces that soften their usual self-assertiveness; and the concrete words that work out the metaphor are a hedge against the logical abstractness inhering in repeated patterns. The passage registers not rational control but the force of emotion.

In sum, Brontë has done a remarkable thing: while she uses various euphuistic methods in traditional ways—for order and ornament, epigram and wit—she also adapts them to wholly different ends, that is, to the powerful expression of the contradictions and pressures of the world and of the psyche. With her, verbal and syntactic repetitions and oppositions, while they may simply be conveniences in descriptive and analytical tasks, take on a new life as means of emphasizing and driving home the stresses of emotional life or its conflict with efforts at rational ordering. Thus a series can be less an elucidating catalogue than a succession of blows from disturbing passions within or drastic pressures from without; and an antithetical structure less an attractively neat presentation of felt or perceived oppositions and contrasts than a registering of deep contradictions in conduct, personality, and encircling humanity.

Whether or not she knew Elizabethan euphuists, Brontë revived or perhaps reinvented some central elements of their style and used them, if not with the mad indefatigability of the original users, still with a regularity and fullness that probably surpassed Johnson's and vastly surpassed Austen's. In Johnson the style was consistent with the attitude he wished to instill, the rational control of longings and illusions; and in Austen with an instinctive clearheadedness and good sense in observing an imperfect world. What Greene and Brontë shared was the combination of an apparently rationalistic style with a romantic substance. But the combinations differed because the romantic substance differed. Greene's romance derived from a traditional conception of a world of mainly outer action in which the participants had standard roles and only minimal subjective reality on their way to success or failure; they are subordinate to a hyper-euphuistic style in which relentless formalism competes against the romantic spirit of love, adventure, conflict, the exotic, and so on. On the other hand, Brontë's romantic substance is the passion of the individual soul, more or less "privileged," as we say nowadays, in its conflicts with a larger world that often seemed indifferent, difficult, or downright hostile. And she has so managed her version of an old style—ordinarily used for and, as it seems, inherently committed to a logical, rational mediation of reality—as to make it an unexpected but nonetheless impressive vehicle of the disturbances and tensions in the personality and in the life that impinges on the personality.

It is a nice rounding out of this story, which is a fragment of a quite incomplete history.

4

Rhetorical Romance: The "Frivolous Toyes" of Robert Greene

W. W. BARKER

I

Among the scores of literary characters created by Robert Greene during his short career none is so interesting to us as the one he presents in his last books—himself. This "Robert Greene" is a wastrel who has left his wife and now lives in sin. He has been overcome by a profound feeling of self-disgust and is appalled by what he has written—the "frivolous toyes" and "follies" of romance. He publicly renounces these earlier works and begs his readers to learn from his example as a sinner who now repents. Greene's self-abasement is almost embarrassing to the reader; what turns embarrassment into poignancy is the death of the author, who is reported, in one of his own books, to have been cut down in this moment of self-realization and repentance.

Readers have long recognized that the "Robert Greene" of the late works is a direct descendant of the prodigals in earlier tales by Greene. The drama of Greene's repentance may seem more real because of the circumstances of his death, yet the character is not far removed from Pharicles, Gwydonius, Arbasto, Philippo, Francesco, and other prodigals in his various romances. What I am concerned to show, however, is that the figure of "Robert Greene" is the developed form of a narrative voice as much as it is the refinement of the author's own character of the prodigal. "Greene" is not just a character in his last works, he is also the teller of his life's tale, and the affecting quality of his story derives as much from the way it is presented as from its apparent facts.

The late Greene is a distracted narrator; his stories begin to fly apart, ending in random collections of episodes or poems or documentary exhibits (letters, testaments, and so on). Yet despite the piecemeal presentation and the apparent lack of integration—especially when compared to the formal dialectic of the early romances—our sense of character is heightened. The voice becomes stronger, more immediate, more dramatic, more novelistic.

The transformation of Greene's narrative style may be described, in the terms of the Russian critic M. M. Bakhtin, as a movement from a monologic discourse in the early works (constrained as they are by the formal requirements of a humanist rhetoric) to increasingly varied and interruptive forms of dialogism—a movement toward parody (including self-parody) and a general carnivalization of language. In his essay "Epic and Novel," Bakhtin says about the "novelization" of genres that "they become more free and flexible, their language renews itself by incorporating extraliterary heteroglossia and the 'novelistic' layers of literary language, they become dialogized, permeated with laughter, irony, humor, elements of self-parody and finally—this is the most important thing—the novel inserts into these other genres an indeterminacy, a certain semantic openendedness, a living contact with the unfinished, still-evolving contemporary reality."[1] Although Bakhtin is describing a vast historical shift, I argue that the same kind of change also takes place in the prose fiction of Robert Greene.

To trace this shift in the narrative style, I consider four works—*Carde of Fancie*, *Menaphon*, *Never Too Late* (with its second part *Francescos Fortunes*), and *Groats-worth of Witte*. I show how narrative formulas in both plot and style interact, how a transformation in rhetoric is accompanied by transformations in characterization, how certain elements of the narrative are retained during this shift from romance to putative autobiography.

II

Carde of Fancie is the second of ten extended narratives and eight story cycles that have come to be known as Greene's romances. To his

1. M. M. Bakhtin, *The Dialogic Imagination: Four Essays*, trans. Caryl Emerson and Michael Holquist (Austin: University of Texas Press, 1981), p. 7.

contemporaries, familiar with the chivalric romance of Malory or *Amadis de Gaule*, these were, however, romances with a difference.[2] "No great adventures, but . . . many passions full of repentant sorrowes" (VIII.118), they are primarily love stories written specifically for "gentleman readers."[3] They have a close relationship to Greek romance,[4] the *erōtika pathēmata*, or tales of suffering in love, by Achilles Tatius, Heliodorus, and others, but are modified in the style of Lyly's *Euphues* by a strikingly academic preoccupation with debate, language display, and the proving of moral positions. Indeed, it is the style that is the first and most difficult barrier for the modern reader. We shall, however, begin with the form, or formula, of the plot.

Carde of Fancie is typical of Greene's patterned fiction. His principal romance subject is love—whether sought, refused, envied, discovered, enjoyed, or endured. His stories are structured around variations of a pattern in which there are a limited number of actors: one or more Elders, the Young Gentleman, the Young Lady, the Gentleman's

2. Roger Ascham, in his *Scholemaster*, attacks the work of Malory: "What toyes, that dayly readyng of such a booke [as *Morte Arthure*], may worke in the will of a yong jentleman, or a yong mayde, that liveth welthelie and idlelie, wise men can judge, and honest men do pitie" (*English Works*, ed. William Aldis Wright [Cambridge: Cambridge University Press, 1904], p. 231). This is the standard view, although there were attempts to recuperate chivalric romance as a noble form. Sidney, for instance: "Truly, I have known men, that even with reading *Amadis de Gaule* (which God knoweth wanteth much of a perfect poesy) have found their hearts moved to the exercise of courtesy, liberality, and especially courage" (*An Apology for Poetry*, ed. Geoffrey Shepherd [London: T. Nelson, 1965], p. 114). Ironically Greene would agree with Ascham's condemnation: part of the pleasure of the love romance may be that it is forbidden or at least not beneficial to the reader and is, despite the moral message, always a "frivolous toy." On the long-standing suspicion of romance by modern critics and on the need for fresh reading of the texts, see two essays by A. C. Hamilton: "Elizabethan Romance: The Example of Prose Fiction," *ELH*, 49 (1982), 287–99, and "Elizabethan Prose Fiction and Some Trends in Recent Criticism," *RenQ*, 37 (1984), 21–33.

3. All parenthetical references are to Robert Greene, *The Life and Complete Works*, ed. Rev. Alexander B. Grosart, 15 vols. (Privately printed, 1881–86). Quotations have been lightly regularized (i/j and u/v modernized and contractions expanded). The passages from *Groats-worth of Witte* have been adjusted according to the edition of 1592 (Grosart follows 1596). For a most useful survey of the texts, see A. F. Allison, *Robert Greene, 1558–1592: A Bibliographical Catalogue of the Early Editions in English (to 1640)* (Folkestone: Dawson, 1975).

4. The relationship is explored in Samuel Lee Wolff, *The Greek Romances in Elizabethan Prose Fiction* (New York: Columbia University Press, 1912); and Arthur F. Kinney, *Humanist Poetics: Thought, Rhetoric, and Fiction in Sixteenth-Century England* (Amherst: University of Massachusetts Press, 1986).

Friend, and the Lady's Friend. There is also a Rival; sometimes the Lady's or Gentleman's Friend or Elder is replaced by or becomes this Rival. The narrative is a working out of their relationships (like those chemical interactions in Goethe's *Elective Affinities*). In *Carde of Fancie* we find two Elders, the Young Gentleman, the Lady, the Friend, the Rival; the story is sealed up when the intergenerational and intersexual conflicts are brought into parallel and jointly resolved. As in other romances by Greene, the double seal becomes one: through marriage a lover also becomes part of the partner's family. The formula has a recognizable relation to the complications and resolutions in Greek New Comedy and the plays of Terence and Plautus.

The story begins as a typical tale of the prodigal. Gwydonius leaves the city of Metelyne after hearing lengthy advice from his father, Duke Clerophontes, who despite his fatherly advice is glad to see this wastrel go. He travels to Barutta, where (disguised) he recklessly overspends, is thrown into jail, and is later released, somewhat wiser. According to the prodigal son story (Luke 15:11–32, retold at length in *Greenes Mourning Garment*), Gwydonius should now be sufficiently chastened to head home, but in Greene's narratives the son returns with a wife. Gwydonius now travels to Alexandria, to the court of Orlanio, where (now in a second disguise) he becomes companion to Orlanio's son Thersandro. Orlanio also has a daughter, Castania, who is being pursued by Valericus, a courtier; the narrative dwells on his unsought and improper advances, preparing us for the parallel but much more correct suit by Gwydonius, whom Castania at first coyly refuses, then accepts. In Greene, the complication between the lovers is often followed by an external complication, usually caused by parental rivalry or interference. Orlanio renders annual tribute to Clerophontes, but this year he refuses to pay. Clerophontes threatens war, and Thersandro is sent as ambassador to the court at Metylene to settle the dispute. No sooner does the young man arrive than he falls in love with Gwydonius's sister Lewcippa (the good child, who stayed at home). Clerophontes is enraged; Thersandro is sent home; both sides prepare for war. For Gwydonius, this conflict between his father and future father-in-law is difficult, especially now that he has been made Orlanio's chief lieutenant in the field. He laments to himself his frightful position, but is overheard (in a remarkable violation of the soliloquizer's right of privacy) by the old rival Valericus, who reports

Gwydonius's real identity to Orlanio. Gwydonius is taken prisoner (for the second time) as a spy, but is released by Thersandro, who begs him to say a good word on his behalf to Lewcippa. The crisis is now at its height: the fathers are at war; Thersandro and Lewcippa are apart; Gwydonius, separated from his beloved Castania, is in hiding, unable to act. The battle is to be resolved in a contest between champions; Clerophontes appoints himself for his side, but no champion is found for Orlanio until Gwydonius, at his own offer and Castania's prompting and in a third disguise, comes forward. Father and son battle it out and the son wins; when Gwydonius reveals himself, Clerophontes is delighted to rediscover his long-lost son. In a swift and typically chiastic ending, the brother Gwydonius and the sister Lewcippa marry the sister Castania and the brother Thersandro. The only loose end in the story is the fate of Valericus (who according to the pattern in Greene's other romances should either be publicly shamed or cheerfully forgiven and married off).

The pattern found in *Carde of Fancie* is played with in other narratives. *Mamillia*, Greene's first work, shows it established tentatively: the Gentleman Pharicles loves the Lady Mamillia, then improperly loves her cousin (and Friend/Rival) Publia; his inconstancy is discovered and he leaves Padua, disguised as a palmer; in Sicily he falls under the spell of the courtesan Clarynda; he is accused of being a spy; only the sudden appearance of the faithful Mamillia saves him from execution. The story is ended by the marriage of Pharicles and Mamillia; Publia enters a convent. There are Elders in the story—Gonzago, father of Mamillia; Gostino, father of Publia; the old men of Sicily who imprison Pharicles—but the fathers are removed from the narrative complication by death, not reconciliation. The pattern is also found in later works. In *Ciceronis Amor*, for instance, Flavia (the Lady's Friend) loves Lentulus (the Rival who becomes a Friend) who loves Terentia (the Lady) who loves Cicero (the Gentleman). The narrative problem is resolved with the unions of Cicero to Terentia and Lentulus to Flavia, though these pairings are briefly impeded by Fabius (a second Rival in love with Terentia, who is content in the end to marry Cornelia, second Friend of the Lady). In *Arbasto*, both Ladies die, the Friend proves to be a Rival, and the Gentleman loses his kingdom and becomes a priest (not so much reconciled with an Elder as becoming one himself). Such structural variations are played with throughout the longer fictional works of Greene and often enough in the story cycles as well.

Within the combinatory mathematics of Greene's plots there is, however, a quality of danger that always threatens to disrupt the movement toward a formulaic conclusion. Principally this danger is the threat from and to love. In *Carde of Fancie* love is found between parent and child and between man and woman and can be either disruptive or reparative. Love is a risky business until the very end. The story begins with the failed love of father and son, and continues with the unconsummated love of Gwydonius (who, according to the rules of the narrative, must remain in disguise until Castania loves him) and the reluctance of Castania (she cannot initially trust Gwydonius because he is a man, and hence given to the same kind of deceitful jealousies as the Rival Valericus). In its initial stages, love is always disruptive; it is a crime, an intrusion, it engenders guilt and excessive emotion, it is a threat to reason, it must be concealed—all the anxieties traditional in love narrative. Yet the lovers' story is not finished until love culminates in the marriage union in which the mutual possession of the lovers is made fully public and all the disguises and hesitations are dropped. It seems as if the young man can only be reconciled with the father when he is ready to become a father himself, a father now married to a mother (the missing mother is a problem for the children in Greene's romances). Marriage, one must also note, is not just a solution for the characters; in Greene's earliest narratives it is also the final solution to the "crime" or "folly" of romance, for marriage is the final punctus to the complications of the romance narrative.

The general patterns of love in Greene's romances are recognizable to us (especially since they are also to some extent imbedded in present-day mass-produced romances), but the rhetoric perpetrated and suffered by the characters is not. We wonder, for instance, what Greene's readers relished in Clerophontes' lengthy advice to his son, Castania's elaborate refusal of Gwydonius, Gwydonius's moments of self-doubt. Yet these set speeches, not smaller narrative episodes or subplots or even characteristic actions or descriptions of places or emotions, provide the basic dilation of the narrative. Direct discourse, which takes up well over two-thirds of *Carde of Fancie*, consists almost entirely of monologues in a surprisingly limited number of forms. There are speeches of advice, meditations in solitude, speeches of supplication in which a character asks for a boon (usually love), or speeches in which a character rejects a supplication or a proposed course of action. There are also letters, which are similar in form and which demand of their fictional readers the same counterresponse as direct discourse. These letters and speeches operate from a single rhetorical principle; of the three classical types—forensic, epideictic, and deliberative—they are almost all deliberative, arguing for or against a position or a suggested action. As Thomas Wilson says in his *Arte of Rhetorique*, deliberation is used to "perswade, or disswade, entreate, or rebuke, exhorte, or dehorte, commende, or comforte."[5]

When, for instance, Thersandro, ambassador from his father to the court of Clerophontes, declares his love to Lewcippa, he presents a formal and elaborate suit for her favor. This speech argues that unreasoning creatures have foresight whereas human beings have reason but lack foresight; the speaker is a man, and therefore not prescient of the transformative effects of love; he should therefore be forgiven, his "heavinesse" eased, by Lewcippa. This speech, planned and delivered as a unit, must be quoted in full.

> Madame (quoth hee) if any creature hath just occasion to accuse either nature or the gods of injustice, man onelie hath the greatest cause to make this complaint: for there is none either so deprived of reason, so devoide of sence, which by some naturall instinct doth not skilfully presage of perills before they come, & warily prevent ere they be past.
>
> The Goates of *Lybia*, know certainlie when the Canicular daies beeginne, wherein commonlye they fall blinde, and therefore by eating the hearbe *Polopodium*, they providentlie prevent their disease. When the Lion leaveth his Lawnes, and raungeth in forraine Deserts, hee alwaies foresheweth a drought. When the Fish called *Uranascapos* sinketh downe to the bottom of the Sea, hee beewrayeth great tempestes to bee imminent. But man is so farre from this secret foresight, that not onely he cannot devine of these ensuing daungers, but rather wilfully or willing: pusheth himselfe into most manifest perills, which Madame, I speake, as feeling my selfe distressed with this want. For if I had bene indued with this sacred prescience, perfectly to presage of ensuing perills,

5. Thomas Wilson, *Arte of Rhetorique*, ed. Thomas J. Derrick (New York: Garland, 1982), p. 76. As Derrick points out, Wilson follows Aristotle's *Rhetoric* (I.iii.3) and the *Ad Herennium* (III.ii.2) but modifies these sources by reference to Erasmus's *De conscribendis epistolis*. The deliberative letter, analyzed so intensively by Erasmus, is an essential part of the euphuistic style, especially in Greene's writing.

I had not bene crossed with such cares as I am like to incurre, nor hadde cause to repent this my present arivall. But sith lacke of such skill hath procured my losse, and that when the hurt is hadde it is too late to take heede, though revealing of my mishappe cannot heale my miserie, nor repeating of my paines redresse my sorrow: yet, I meane to participate my passions to your good grace, that though you cannot or will not mittigate my maladie, yet you may pittie my estate, which will somewhat ease my heavinesse.

I came to your Fathers Court, Madame, a free man of *Alexandria*, and am like to retourne a captive of *Metelyne*: I arived devoide of care, and like to departe, drenched with calamitie: I landed free from affection, but feare to passe hence fraught with fancie: my charge was onely to *parle* of peace, but my chaunce is to discourse of passions. Yea, your beautie hath so fettered my freedome, and so snared my heart in the linkes of your love, that it shall never bee raced out by anie sinister meanes of Fortune, although I see it is almost impossible to obtaine it.

For I doubt our parents are lyke to proclaime themselves professed foes, and the urgent necessitie of my affaires, forceth mee to depart so speedelie, as want of time will not suffice to make tryall of my love, whereby I might claime a sufficient guerdon for my good wil: yet howsoever the matter shall happe, whether my hope be voide, or my happe be vaine, I meane madame to remaine yours for ever. (IV.142–44)

Although Thersandro's speech seems to be a simple declaration, there is a strongly implied action required of the listener Lewcippa, that she supply him with the "sufficient guerdon" of her favor. The argument proceeds in stages: the first proposition is stated in the opening paragraph: the support of this argument is given in the beginning of the second paragraph by *testimonia* (the natural similitudes); the redirection of the argument to Thersandro's own problem then follows; the third paragraph gives a closer interpretation of his position (he is imprisoned and therefore himself incapable of restraining his love); the fourth paragraph returns to the necessary circumstances surrounding his request. His deliberative argument is skillful, because he is able to make concessions, because he is attentive to his audience, and because he does not ask for much more than his audience is initially willing to give. He may be besotted by Lewcippa, but he shows that he is a worthy lover because his rhetorical control remains intact; he does not ask for too much and thereby shows that he is worthy to receive all. As Castania had been earlier with Gwydonius, however, Lewcippa is wary, unwilling to appear "light of love" (145), and so immediately puts him off in a speech of almost equal length. Thersandro is unwilling to accept her decision, her "verdite" (146; in deliberation, audience and judge are in a sense conflated)[6] and counterresponds, to which she again speaks, begging him to "rest uppon this point, that I wil alwaies like thee as a friend, though not love thee as my phere" (148). Characters always speak in *Carde of Fancie* toward a particular end; the speech is, in accordance with the rules of rhetoric, direct and focused. The debate begun in the speeches, moreover, is always resolved by narrative action. Thersandro sues for love; his suit is expressed not in his bodily perfection, his family, his reported nobility (although these are always indirectly present) but in his words; it is from his language and through hers that Lewcippa is able to respond to him. Thersandro's suit is, however, not resolved by words; in *Carde of Fancie* speech expresses desire, but narrative action fulfills desire. So Thersandro and Lewcippa are united only after actions outside of their control have taken place: namely, the battle of Gwydonius with his father and their reunion in parental and filial forgiveness and love.

The deliberative function of the discourse is also found when characters speak to themselves. They think aloud in direct discourse, but they always deliver formal addresses in which speaker and audience are the same—a curious violation of classical rhetoric in which the speaker and audience are always quite separate, the former attempting to please, teach, or move the latter. Thus the lengthy first sentence of the speech made by Gwydonius to himself after he has been imprisoned in Barutta:

> Alasse (quoth hee) now have I bought that by haplesse experience, which if I had beene wise, I might have got by happie counsaile: Nowe am I taught that with paine and perill, which if selfe-love had not besotted my senses, I might have learned with profite and pleasure, that in the fayrest Sandes is most ficklenesse, out of the bravest Blossome moste commonlie springeth the worste Fruite, that the finest flower seldome hath the best smell, that the moste glistering Stone hath often-times the least vertue, and that in the greatest shewe of good will, lyes ofte times the smallest effect of friendshippe, in most flatterie, least fayth, in the

6. Forensic speech is central to the arguments in Louise Labé's *Debate between Follie and Love*, translated by Greene and regularly appended to editions of *Carde of Fancie*. Although very different, these works in their contrasting rhetorical methods may profitably be read against each other.

fayrest face, the falsest heart, in the smoothest Tale the smallest Truth, and the sweetest gloses most sower ingratitude: Yea, I see nowe (quoth hee) that in truth lies treason, that faire wordes make fooles faine, and that the state of these fained friendes are lyke to the Mariegolde, which as long as the Sunne shineth openeth her leaves, but with the least Clowde, beginneth to close, lyke the Violettes in *America*, which in Summer yeelde an odoriferous smell, and in Winter a most pestilent savour: so these Parasites in prosperitie professe most, but in adversitie performe least: when Fortune favoureth, they laughe, when shee frowneth they lowre: at everie full Sea, they flourish, but at every dead Neape, they fade: Like to the fish *Palerna*, which beeing perfectlie white in the Calme, yet turneth passing blacke at everie storme: to the trees in the desarts of *Affrica*, that flourish but while the South winde bloweth, or to the *Celedonie* stone, which retaineth his vertue no longer than it is rubbed with golde. (IV.25–26)

Gwydonius's speech to himself might be compared to that made by his father to him only a moment before, in the way one ostensibly wiser character addresses one less wise. Yet here Gwydonius is speaking only to himself, a wise Gwydonius addressing a weak Gwydonius. The convention of such a bifurcated personality strikes us as odd: how can one person be two? Yet for the purposes of the deliberative discourse this doubling is absolutely necessary: the argument requires a convincing speaker and a receptive audience. Gwydonius is using himself as the example of failure to teach himself to be better; now the adviser is the "father" as well as the reformed son; the audience is the unreformed son who seeks to become the father. The dialectical bifurcation is apparent in the language, not just in the repetition of isocolon and alliteration, but in the parallel structure of the imagery: the friends appear true but are false, "the Mariegold" is open but closed, "the fish *Palerna*" is white but black, and so Gwydonius is foolish (as the son who ignores the father) but wise (as the son who repeats the words of his father). The speech resolves itself in the same way the entire narrative does—"after miserie alwaies insueth most happie felicitie." The character has convinced himself. It comes as no surprise that having caused his own reform, he should immediately be released from prison, the narrative action responds to the needs of the rhetorical debate.

In a valuable brief discussion of *Carde of Fancie*, Walter Davis comments on the dialectical form of the narrative (Gwydonius's first two disguises are resolved in his third), but does not comment on the way the language of the speeches parallels the movement of the narrative. He claims that the work celebrates "the power of experience."[7] I am arguing for a different emphasis. Although experience resolves the dialectical conflicts, these conflicts are often generated within speech. *Carde of Fancie* can be seen as the celebration of language, specifically the language of deliberation, as it is worked out in the lives and actions of the characters. This language in its highly formal structures moves always toward completion or closure; the speeches and debates request action and the action moves to resolve these closely worked rhetorical moments. Characters move and act according to dialectical relationships with themselves or others.

III

Any argument about the development of Greene's style must concern itself with one of his best-known works, *Menaphon*, published five years after *Carde of Fancie*. A different kind of work, *Menaphon* is much closer in setting and theme to the Greek pastoral romance. Modern readers, charmed by the Arcadian landscape, the disguises, the variations in plot, the reversals, often claim that this is Greene's masterpiece.[8] They are also attracted by the style—above all by the poems sprinkled throughout the narrative—and in this they agree with the work's earliest commentator, Thomas Nashe, who praised its verbal "attire" as "not so statelie, yet comelie," an example of "that *temperatum dicendi genus*, which *Tullie* in his *Orator* tearmeth true eloquence" (VI.11). If the style is not full-blown euphuism but of a middle range, we might expect a different kind of narrative. And indeed, the work is no longer structured around bifurcations in characterization or by strictly dialectical confrontations between characters. Now a greater variety of voices and styles is accompanied by a greater complexity in characterization and narrative form.

Menaphon unfolds the familiar themes of familial and sexual love, and the problem of their reconciliation, within a political framework. In this work, however, the two kinds of love become confused in incest.

7. Walter R. Davis, *Idea and Act in Elizabethan Fiction* (Princeton: Princeton University Press, 1969), pp. 141–43.
8. E.g., Davis, p. 171.

Despite the innocence of the Arcadian world and the final harmless resolution of the narrative, the reader cannot forget that for a while the main character Sephestia/Samela has been wooed by Pleusidippus her impulsive son and Democles her tyrannical father. The danger the characters are exposed to in the last third of the narrative gives *Menaphon* its edge. That the near violation of Sephestia has been due but to a comic problem of identity does not blunt the sharpness of the tale.

The entire action of the romance is the working out of an answer to a riddle posed by an oracle. The characters go through their actions unaware that they are merely providing this answer, which comes in an unveiling of identities by an unnamed old woman who suddenly appears at the very end. The riddle is a series of dialectical impossibilities (*adynata*) in the millennial mode of the Virgilian fourth eclogue, in which opposing forces or attributes are to be resolved in a happy future time: "When Lambes have Lions for their surest guide, / And Planets rest upon th'*Arcadian* hills" (VI.34). The union or reunion of the characters at the end is the narrative response to this oracle. Between the poles of riddle and response, the story is unexpectedly complex.

After Democles decides he can do nothing to solve this oracular riddle, the narrative shifts to the seashore of Arcadia. Menaphon the shepherd sees an old man (Lamedon), a young woman (Sephestia), and an infant boy (Pleusidippus) come ashore after a shipwreck. Menaphon falls in love with Sephestia, who has now assumed the name Samela, but despite his care to establish her and the small family in the shepherd community of Arcadia, she holds him off. Melicertus, actually the gentleman Maximius disguised as a shepherd, hears of Samela, and finds her as beautiful as his lost wife Sephestia, and she is quite taken with him, seeing that he seems so much like her lost husband. For the reader the remarkable inability of husband and wife to recognize one another might seem to be a profound difficulty in the narrative, but it becomes clear that this story is not so much about being able to see as about being able to name someone properly. Other characters have the same problem. When Pleusidippus returns to Arcadia as a young man (after having been as a boy stolen by pirates and carried off to Thessaly) and falls in love with Samela, and Democles, Sephestia's father, comes in disguise to Arcadia to woo this famous shepherdess, neither knows the real name of his beloved. The last third of the story is the working out of the competing claims of Melicertus/Maximius,

Pleusidippus, and Democles for Sephestia/Samela. Only the old proph-
etess at the end can name people as they really are and so allow the
final pairing of the characters (Maximius with Sephestia; Pleusidippus
with Olympia, the Thessalian princess; Menaphon with Pesana, the
shepherdess). Democles is forgiven and abdicates his throne for
Pleusidippus. And, "lest there should be left any thing unperfect in this
pastoral accident" (VI.145–46), Doron and Carmela are married too.

Greene's principal romance story (the Gentleman, the Rival, the
Lady, the Elder) has been retained and exuberantly varied in *Menaphon*. The work seems to us more confident, more playful, and more
artful than the early works. Yet characters still please, instruct, and
move one another through the power of speech. In addition to the
deliberative addresses that are central to Greene's earlier romances, we
now find a new form of verbal contest—the conversation—and, in the
poems, a greater variety of rhetorical display. Lamedon's "perswasive
argument" (VI.47) after the shipwreck is in the older style, with its
dialectical oppositions: "*Sephestia*, thou seest no Phisick prevailes
against the gaze of the *Basilisckes*, no charme against the sting of the
Tarantula, no prevention to divert the decree of the Fates, nor no
meanes to recall backe the balefull hurt of Fortune: Incurable sores are
without *Avicens* Aphorismes, and therefore no salve for them but patience" (VI.45). Yet this kind of discourse is quickly dropped in the
story. Speech is increasingly a series of elaborate contests, often framed
as debates or suits—Menaphon to Samela, Melicertus to Samela,
Pleusidippus to Olympia, Pleusidippus and Democles to Sephestia. At
the same time, the characters have become subtler stylists: their speech
is more conversational, less like a series of formal exercises.

This new conversational style is nowhere so clear as in the debate
during the shepherd's celebrations in Arcadia, when Melicer-
tus/Maximius, ostensibly "to set time free from tediousnesse" (VI.74)
but really to see whether Samela/Sephestia is "as wise as beautifull"
(73), proposes an apparently innocent *quaestio*: "Then gentle shep-
heardesse tell me, if you should be transformed through the anger of
the Gods, into some shape; what creature would you reason to be in
forme?" (74). Samela immediately grasps Melicertus's gambit—"pithie
questions are mindes whetstones, and by discoursing in jest, manie
doubts are deciphered in earnest"—acknowledging that even her most
offhand comments will be used to judge her. Her choice is to be a

sheep, a suitable jest for Arcadia; she argues that a sheep lives comfortably (good water, clear air, and so on, and "thoughts at ease") and, when pressed, adds that a sheep in Arcadia is in the constant presence of beauty—"would not a sheepe so long fed with beautie, die for love?" (76). In her argument, based on physical pleasure but delivered allusively and ironically, she declares herself ("in earnest") to be an intellectual sensualist and ready for Melicertus's advances. The characters judge each other by their eloquence. Yet they must guard against stylistic excess, for at their next meeting, soon after, Samela finds Melicertus "superfine," perhaps speaking with "an inkhorne desire to be eloquent," whereas he thinks she has "learnd with *Lucilla* in *Athens* to anatomize wit, and speake none but *Similes*" (82). It is a bit like Juliet's rejoinder to Romeo: "You kiss by th'book." This contest, it must be noted, is not just between the two characters—in the *quaestio* other characters playfully interrupt. The exchange is no longer academic; it has more of the *sprezzatura* of Castiglione. Of course it is still performance, but the place of the performance has shifted from the hall or the classroom to the sitting room, the garden, or the dinner table.

The use of verse in *Menaphon* is another departure from Greene's earlier practice. It is sometimes used in competition—as when Melicertus and Menaphon compete for the honor of saving Samela—but more often it serves to express the feeling conveyed in earlier works by the solitary meditation. Characters may be divided (many of them are of course in disguise), but they rarely express the anxiety of this division. Menaphon, for instance, does not deliberate with himself when he lies in bed; instead he sings about the "sweete griefe" he feels and never tries to convince himself to do a thing about it. The riddle, the eclogues, the various roundelays, the fable, the "jigge," Melicertus's "Description of his Mistresse" and his madrigal, the narrator's "Sonetto"—all these greatly enhance the expressiveness of the work through a variety of styles. Even the comic love dialogue between Doron and Carmela ("Thy breath is like the steeme of apple pies" [VI.138]) further extends the range of the work; we get another way of speaking, even if it is a topsy-turvy version of the courtly language of the narrator and his characters. This carnivalization of the language serves to ground the narrative in the way that the distorted rhetoric of certain Shakespearean characters parodies the higher rhetoric of their social superiors. In this clownish parody there is a hint of a social order emerging, of "higher" and "lower" estates in the representation of styles. In Greene's late works this parody will be much more broadly expanded in the enclosed language, private morality, and curiously refined attitudes of the criminal world.

Menaphon shows an opening up of language, a greater variety of styles. Although the narrative is no more complicated than the story of *Carde of Fancie*, the work seems more complex, more resonant, because of this variety of styles. Yet *Menaphon*—with all its hints of tyranny and incest—is still like the early works in the way the narrative is so firmly concluded in the comic resolution provided by the marriages. In later works the styles become even more mixed, the endings less certain.

IV

Never Too Late and its second part *Francescos Fortunes* both appeared a year after *Menaphon*. In the two works, which are usually discussed under the single title *Never Too Late*, Greene leaves Arcadian romance and returns to the prodigal narrative. Yet there are slippages in both the formal structure of the narrative and in the confidence of the moral expressed. Although the prodigal is reclaimed, the resolution of the narrative is far from neat. By setting the long story of Francesco's infidelity within the frame of the Palmer's narrative of unfulfilled love and setting it against the comic tale of Mirimida's rejection of marriage, the whole work seems to deny the possibility of love, at least within the final completion of marriage. The two earlier stories, *Carde of Fancie* and *Menaphon*, both worked toward a satisfying closure. *Never Too Late* rejects this closure within both the plot and the language of its narrative. It is a step toward a more open and dialogical style.

The work begins with a frame story, set in Bergamo, in which a pilgrim (in Greene usually a former reprobate or a rejected lover) tells a story about Francesco, an Englishman living in the days of Palmerin. Francesco loves Isabel, but her father Fregoso is absolutely opposed to the match. When the couple elopes, the father has them thrown into prison. The two behave in an exemplary way and are released by the authorities. They move to a cottage, Francesco teaches school, they have a baby, and five years later Fregoso forgives them. At this point, or even sooner, the story should end, given the logic of Greene's earlier prodigal narratives. Yet this is just the beginning of the real tale, one of obsessive marital infidelity. Francesco goes to Troynovant on business, falls for the courtesan Infida, and for the rest of the first part of *Never Too Late* seesaws back and forth between his passion for Infida and his intense guilt for having abandoned Isabel. The second part, though called *Francescos Fortunes*, is actually about what happens to Isabel, as we shift from the prodigal narrative to another favorite story in Greene, a version of Susanna and the Elders (Daniel 13 in the Apocrypha; retold at length in *Myrrour of Modestie*).[9] The solitary Isabel is approached by Bernardo, but she rebuffs him in several lengthy speeches. He accuses her of adultery and she is sent to prison; she is placed on trial before the city and is about to be condemned when the young witness suborned by Bernardo confesses his perjury. Isabel is freed; Francesco returns, repents, and is forgiven. The reconciliation, however, seems incomplete in comparison with those of Greene's earlier stories. There is no marriage to seal up the prodigal's reform—the marriage has long since taken place and has only provided opportunities for sin and guilt. Moreover, there can be no reconciliation with the Elders, for Francesco, a father, is virtually an Elder himself.

The notion of the marriage union as an inadequate solution to conflict is also played with in the second narrative in *Francescos Fortunes*, a comic tale told to Francesco and Isabel by the Host of the Inn. In this story, Mirimida rejects her three suitors, the ugly clown Mullidor, the handsome shepherd Eurymachus, and the dashing gentleman Radagon. This rejection is an unlikely fantasy within a male-dominated context—what woman would or could reject all her suitors? Yet for the purposes of the overall narrative, what is being rejected is not the suitors but marriage in general. Immediately following this story, we shift to the surrounding frame of Francesco and Isabel, and from

---

9. Greene was a relentless borrower—from his own work as well as that of others. One example may serve. When Isabel rejects Bernardo, she says: "But alas, it is unfit for the young Fawn to lead the old buck: for a blind man to be guide to him that hath his sight: and as unmeete for a simple woman to instruct a Bourgomaister and Elder of the Citty" (VIII.152–53). She echoes the words of Susanna in *Myrrour of Modestie*: "But alas it is unfite for the yoong fawne to leade the old bucke, for a blind man to be a guid to him which hath his sight, nor meete for a seelie simple woman to instruct the Elders and Judges of the people" (III.23).

there to the outer frame of the Palmer, who speaks to his (apparently happily) married host and his wife. Why, asks his host, is the Palmer traveling to Venice? To examine the vanities of "Loves Paradise" (Venus's Venice). The Palmer is a disappointed lover; apparently by examining how love works, by telling his tales, he tries to come to terms with its mysteries. He expresses his wandering in a zodiacal poem about the movement from sin to repentance to wisdom. The poem is called a "circle," but the Palmer leaves before his own narrative circle is completed: the narrator promises that "what there he did, or howe hee lived, when I am advertised (good Gentlemen) I will send you tidings" (VIII.229). By comparison with *Menaphon*, this work has a most "*un*perfect" ending.

Although the internal story of Francesco and Isabel still relies on the deliberative mode of suit and countersuit, the language of *Never Too Late* is remarkably varied. There are sonnets, odes, roundelays, songs, canzones, letters, public addresses, private meditations, even a list of "precepts" drawn up by the reformed Francesco. There is the high style of Francesco's extravagant suit to Infida and of his moments of anxiety; there is the middle style of the Palmer (who serves as a narrator for most of the work); and there is the comic low speech of Mullidor ("You *Mirimida* are the Eaw [ewe] that hath so caught *Mullidor* captive" [VIII.192]). The movement from one story frame to another is facilitated by the various styles.

One example will serve to show Greene's increasing mastery of characterization through language. Francesco is in the midst of his affair with Infida. Isabel, back in Caerbranck, has been told of his philandering; although she publicly discounts it as a "frivolous tale," she knows that it may be the truth. Yet in the letter she writes to him, she does not try to argue that he should mend his ways (as a character in one of Greene's earlier, more euphuistic works might have). Instead, "like a good wife" (as the Palmer says), she displays her own sincerity and patience and directs her *suasio* against his feelings of guilt:

> Isabel to Francesco *health*.
> If *Penelope* longde for her *Ulysses*, thinke *Isabel* wisheth for her *Francesco*, as loyall to thee as she was constant to the wily *Greeke*, and no lesse desirous to see thee in *Caerbranck*, than she to enjoy his presence in *Ithaca*, watering my cheekes with as manie teares, as she her face

with plaints, yet my *Francesco*, hoping I have no such cause as she to increase her cares: for I have such resolution in thy constancie, that no *Circes* with all her inchantments, no *Calipso* with all her sorceries, no *Syren* with all their melodies could pervert thee from thinking on thine *Isabel*: I know *Francesco* so deeply hath the faithful promise and loyall vowes made and interchanged betweene us taken place in thy thoughtes, that no time how long soever, no distance of place howsoever different, may alter that impression. But why doo I inferre this needlesse insinuation to him, that no vanitie can alienate from vertue: let me *Francesco* perswade thee with other circumstances. First my Sweete, thinke how thine *Isabel* lies alone, measuring the time with sighes, and thine absence with passions; counting the day dismall, and the night full of sorrowes; being everie way discontent, because shee is not content with her *Francesco*. The onely comfort that I have in thine absence is thy child, who lies on his mothers knee, and smiles as wantonly as his father when he was a wooer. But when the boy sayes: Mam, where is my dad, when will hee come home? Then the calmes of my content turneth to a present storme of piercing sorrowe, that I am forced sometime to say: Unkinde *Francesco*, that forgets his *Isabell*. I hope *Francesco* it is thine affaires, not my faults that procureth this long delay. For if I knewe my follies did any way offend thee, to rest thus long absent, I woulde punish my selfe both with outward and inward penaunce. But howsoever, I pray for thy health, and thy speedie returne, and so *Francesco* farewell.

> *Thine more than her owne*
> *Isabel.*   (VIII.97–99)

She argues from *his* fidelity: no matter how he may wander, he will, like Ulysses, return to his Penelope. Then she argues from her loneliness, from their son's. And she concludes with the possibility of her own guilt. The image is of an ideal woman (from the perspective of the gentlemen readers, of course), who is long-suffering, guilty, restrained, and reasonably quiet. She is certainly not angry. The style is relatively restrained—no elaborate reaching for comparisons, no elaborate counterpoint. There are certainly parallel constructions ("it is thine affaires, not my faultes"), but not extended strings of them. Instead of formulaic repetition, there is an opposite effect in the use of dramatic reversal and shift in style. Thus the remarkable dramatic touch in the boy's question: "Mam, where is my dad, when will hee come home?" (the son now reprimanding the prodigal father). The whole speech is in marked contrast to Francesco's nervous meditation, which begins:

Nowe *Francesco piscator ictus sapit,* experience is a true mistresse, but shee maketh her Schollers treade upon Thornes: hast thou not leaped into the ditch, which thou hast long foreseene, and bought that with repentance which thou hast so greedily desired to reape. Oh now thou seest the difference betweene love and lust: the one ful of contented pleasure, the other of pleasing miseries: thy thoughts were feathered with fancie, and whether did they flie so farre that they freeed themselves, and thou rest consumed? Oh *Francesco,* what are women? (VIII.106–07)

Here the balance and the heavy alliteration serve to emphasize mental division. The language of the speech recalls the excesses of euphuism, now an indication not of wisdom but of insincerity.

With the variation in voices, characterization becomes more complex in the narrative. The story becomes increasingly layered, although these layers are held together by strong thematic parallels. Yet the two parts of *Never Too Late* form an interesting experiment in style and in the increasing fragmentation of the prodigal narrative. The tale, despite its comic pretensions, has a worrying darkness to it that sets it apart from the earlier stories. Principally this darkness comes from the lack of clear resolution at the end. The story trails off into incompletion; we have no guarantees that Francesco will not start misbehaving all over again.

V

Greene's critics usually read the works separately—the romances, crime pamphlets, autobiographical confessions, and plays are rarely discussed together. Yet there are many close connections among them, in narrative structure and in the language of characterization. In the very late works (when we call them this, we must remember that Greene died when he was just thirty-four) there is still the fascination with the arts of language, a kind of latent academicism in the form of display. Still, as I have shown in tracing Greene's path from *Carde of Fancie* through *Menaphon* to *Never Too Late,* this formality gradually diminishes. Language becomes more heterogeneous as more and different voices begin to speak in internally characteristic styles. It is tempting to call this mixed style more "dramatic," and indeed it may reflect

Greene's work for the stage. The dramatic quality is found to a marked degree in the extraordinary last work *Groats-worth of Witte*.[10]

This surprising narrative begins in familiar territory. Old Gorinius (the Elder) has decided to divide his property. To Lucanio, the elder son, he gives his estate; to Roberto, the younger, he gives a groat, the worthless coin he started with, so that this scholarly wastrel might have a "groatsworth of wit." Gorinius dies, and Roberto decides to entrap Lucanio (now his Rival), deprive him of his fortune, and turn him into another prodigal. To this end, he introduces his brother to the prostitute Lamilia, but she decides to keep the prey for herself. Roberto goes off penniless but soon finds work writing for a company of players. Over the next two years, Lamilia bleeds Lucanio dry; he leaves her, and becomes a panderer. By contrast, Roberto finds success to be his undoing: he drinks too much, gambles, and in the end is unable to pay his bills. All he has left is the groat. He begins a speech typical of Greene's prisoners. At this moment, quite unexpectedly, the narrative breaks off in a sudden unmasking, much like the revelation of true identity in earlier romances: "Heere (Gentlemen) breake I off *Robertos* speech; whose life in most parts agreeing with mine, found one selfe punishments as I haue doone. Heereafter suppose me the saide *Roberto*, and I will goe on with that hee promised: *Greene* will send you now

---

10. Some of the piquancy of *Groats-worth of Witte* stems from the mysterious circumstances of its publication—circumstances disputed by Greene's contemporaries. Henry Chettle, the editor of the posthumous publication, claims in his *Kind-Harts Dreame* of 1592 that "it was all *Greenes*, not mine nor Maister *Nashes* as some unjustly have affirmed" (ed. G. B. Harrison [London: John Lane, the Bodley Head, 1923], pp. 6–7). The debate over the authorship is presented by Chauncey Elwood Sanders, who rejects Greene's authorship, in "Robert Greene and his 'Editors,'" *PMLA*, 48 (1933), 392–417; and by Harold Jenkins, who accepts it, in "On the Authenticity of Greene's *Groatsworth of Wit* and *The Repentance of Robert Greene*," *RES*, 11 (1935), 28–41. Two more recent studies reject Greene's authorship: Warren B. Austin, *A Computer-Aided Technique for Stylistic Discrimination: The Authorship of Greene's "Groats-worth of Wit"* (Washington, D.C., 1969 [H.E.W. Project 7-G-036]), and Norbert Bolz, *Eine statistische computerunterstützte Echtheitsprüfung von "The Repentance of Robert Greene": Ein methodischer und systematischer Ansatz* (Frankfurt am Main: Peter Lang, 1978). What may be more important than the authorship is how Greene is perceived from this work. The circumstances of the publication of *Groats-worth of Witte* will never be known to us. The main point is that a created image serves the needs of contemporary readers; the dying and repentant Greene is extremely satisfying to those prepared for such a scene by certain moments within his fictional romances.

his groats-worth of wit, that neuer shewed a mites-worth in his life: &
though no man now be by, to doo mee good: yet ere I die, I will by my
repentaunce indevour to doo all men good" (XII.137).

From here on the narrative, if it may be called that, disintegrates far
more radically than any earlier work. First, there is a poem in which
Greene presents himself as an utter failure who was deceived by the
"alluring toyes" of this world, who abused the "bountie" of his "gifts,"
who "loosely spent" his time, and who is now "undone." Now in
prose, he rejects all he has written: these "vaine fantasies" and "follies"
are, in an interesting twist to the struggle between father and son in this
story and elsewhere in Greene, "so many parricides." Greene is both a
father of folly and a foolish son—a double bind this prodigal must
somehow work through. He lists ten rules for behavior, learned too
late but set down for the edification of his gentlemen readers. He
addresses his friends, his fellow playwrights, in a letter (it is here, in
perhaps the most quoted passage in all of Greene, that he warns them
of that "upstart Crow" Shakespeare). A fable of the ant and the
grasshopper in verse and prose is followed by the concluding document, "a letter written to his wife, found with this booke after his
death." In this he portrays himself as a failed husband and, even more
important, a failed father. His son is "yet Greene, and may grow
straight, if he be carefully tended: otherwise apt enough (I feare me) to
follow his fathers folly" (XII.149).

Much has been written about the theme of the prodigal in Elizabethan drama and fiction.[11] Greene's fiction is often treated as if it
were entirely encompassed by this theme, even though, as I hope I have
shown, the theme of the prodigal son in Greene must be seen within a
larger thematic structure of the love relationship as it is worked out in
the personal, familial, and even political spheres. A story like *Carde of
Fancie* is clearly structured around the prodigal theme, although
Gwydonius's prodigality is quite restrained. *Menaphon* does not fit
quite so neatly into the theme, because the real problem of the story is
not so much a prodigal son (though Pleusidippus is one briefly) but a
prodigal and incestuous father who must be forgiven by his daughter.

---

11. The most thorough and suggestive treatment is Richard Helgerson, *The Elizabethan Prodigals* (Berkeley and Los Angeles: University of California Press, 1976);
chap. 5 is on Greene.

Yet not just these two but all the stories tell of the failure of love by individuals who must recognize their failure and learn to repent. Greene, who styled himself "Loves Philosopher" (IX.122), is obsessed with the breakdown of love and other social relations and with their restitution. The history of the prodigal is merely the most recognizable and most easily namable story that he tells about love.

In *Groats-worth of Witte* we do have the story of the prodigal, however seriously incomplete. In other stories the pattern usually runs: advice from father; advice rejected; departure from home; a short period of pleasure, usually associated with the love of a woman and friends; destitution, sometimes brought on by the dishonesty of the woman or a friend; imprisonment; a realization of the crimes; release from prison; a period of restitution and good behavior; union with a good woman; acceptance by father (often after a direct conflict with him); marriage. As I have noted, this pattern does not jibe very closely with the parable in Luke, but this is the story in Greene. The prodigal is not just a wastrel, he is a social reprobate, and what brings him back into society is marriage. Of course, *Groats-worth of Witte* leaves both Roberto, the first prodigal, and Lucanio, the second, in the abyss that separates the incomplete family at the beginning and the promised completion of the family at the end. What is especially striking is that they are left there permanently. But even more surprising, and frightening, the narrator/author has left himself there too. Unlike the earlier works, this one has no happy ending.

The possibility of an open-ended prodigal story had already, as we have seen, been presented in *Never Too Late*. There are strong connections between Francesco and the two Robertos in *Groats-worth*. They drink, they gamble, they consort with prostitutes, they dissemble, they write plays, they desert their wives and children. They are or behave like criminals, they are social outcasts. Moreover, they feel extraordinary guilt for what they have done, and they wish to repent. The difference is that in *Never Too Late* it is never too late, whereas for the Robert Greene in *Groats-worth* it *is* too late. The reconciliation is never effected. He is left permanently in the "prison" stage of the prodigal narrative, aware of his crimes, suffering a punishment imposed by himself as well as his society, but with no hope of release, no chance for the joy of the marriage that will end his story happily.

The language that expresses this lost state is very different from the bifurcated dialectic of the early stories. All the documents at the end of *Groats-worth* show that the narrative moves away from resolution into chaos and dissolution. The fable of the ant and the grasshopper is one example of this entropy. The story begins as a prose fable, slips into quatrains, and then after a prose break becomes sixaines, then turns into alternating quatrains and sixaines for the grasshopper's epitaph and the warning to "Greene springing youth." The narrator/author concludes not with a formal elaboration and application of the moral but with a simple statement: "Now faint of my last infirmitie, beseeching them that shal burie my bodie, to publish this last farewell, written with my wretched hand. *Felicem fuisse infaustum.*" The modesty of the style, rarely apparent in the copious rhetorical flow of an earlier Greene, suggests his exhaustion, dramatized in the broken form of the fable and in the brief conclusion.

In Greene's last works (we should here include his *Repentance*), a new kind of character and style emerge. The early euphuistic narratives present characters built around oppositions with others and within themselves. The later works are increasingly made up of smaller units of narrative mixed in with bits and pieces of poems, lists, speeches, reports, and the rhetoric relies less and less on dialectical opposition. The inner vicissitudes of character seem less programmatic, more varied. And in the course of these changes the narrator becomes increasingly central to his tale, until in *Groats-worth*, character, narrator, and author collapse into a single subject. This subject is presented through a montage of scraps that seem on first glance to be anything but unified. Yet the character is more tightly, more dramatically presented than any other in Greene's writing. The drama comes from the rhetorical disintegration that happens even as one reads. The self-consciousness of the narrator, drawing attention to his own publicity-seeking and blatant use of the press to present his life, further heightens the immediacy. Friends are exhorted to behave, to help in publication, to defend the author. And the story merges into the moment of publication. There is all the excitement (a regrettably unpleasant excitement—and therefore perhaps more morbidly engaging) of the confession of the condemned man speaking from the gallows—virtually the same kind of story Greene had already written in *Blacke Bookes Messenger*, in the autobiography of Ned Browne. Greene's willingness to be so public in his confession is remarkably shameless. Yet isn't that what his earlier characters have done? Through the display of language they act out moments of anxiety, moral indecision, and desire. Greene, like many of his contemporaries (sonneteers, preachers, and so on), relished this transformation into a character.[12] And despite all the moral posturing, which of course only serves to intensify the reader's sense of guilt (for enjoying the death and for not following the advice), Greene's death may have served less as instruction than as a last-ditch effort to provide a remarkable entertainment. Even his death becomes a "frivolous toy." Its unseriousness is devastating.

Oddly enough, death did not and cannot end the story of Robert Greene, certainly not the way marriage ends the story in the conventional prodigal narratives. The story of the prodigal Greene becomes expanded in subsequent posthumous narratives.[13] *Greenes Newes Both from Heaven and Hell* is an anonymous pamphlet of 1593 that places the author outside of both heaven (he has sinned too much) and hell (he has told the truth about sinners and prostitutes, and Satan has therefore denied him hell). He comes back to earth to dictate a story to John Dickenson in *Greene in Conceit. New Raised from his Grave to Write the Tragique Historie of Faire Valeria of London* (1598), and his ghost pursues unpunished thieves in S. R.'s *Greenes Ghost Haunting Conie-Catchers* (1602). Hardly was Greene dead than Gabriel Harvey revived him by an intemperate attack, a response to Greene's vilification of the Harvey brothers in *Quip for an Upstart Courtier*. (The debate between Harvey and Nashe grew out of this attack.) Greene's most lasting literary character was himself: the condemned man, the criminal who has special insight into criminal language and behavior, the sinner and reprobate who is the scourge of sinners and reprobates, the permanent outsider, the ironist, the master of arts and master stylist who prides himself on being able to outwrite his enemies. Similar characters speak in the Martin Marprelate tracts, Nashe's pamphlets, and the satires of the late 1590s and can still be heard in the beginning of the next decade in the self-recriminations of that prodigal son, would-be playwright, university man, and scourger of sinners, Hamlet.

12. See Stephen Greenblatt, *Renaissance Self-fashioning: From More to Shakespeare* (Chicago: University of Chicago Press, 1980).

13. René Pruvost, *Robert Greene et ses romans (1558–1592): Contributions à l'histoire de la Renaissance en Angleterre* (Paris: Société d'Edition "Les Belles Lettres," 1938), pp. 41–43.

5

Cymbeline and the Intrusion of Lyric into Romance Narrative: *Sonnets,* "A Lover's Complaint," Spenser's *Ruins of Rome*

A. KENT HIEATT

When Shakespeare used *choir* figuratively for the last time we know of, in *Cymbeline* III.iii.43,[1] he had not used any noun or verb form of it or *quire* in his plays and narrative poems for twelve years, since *quiring* in *Merchant of Venice* V.1.62, the choir of birds at *2 Henry VI* I.iii.89, and occurrences in *Venus and Adonis* and *Midsummer Night's Dream*. His using it in *Cymbeline* triggered an association with Sonnet 73, or more likely the association triggered the word, in the following way in contiguous speeches (my emphases):

> *Arviragus.* . . . Our cage
> We make a *choir*, as doth the prison'd *bird*,
> And *sing* our bondage freely. (42–44)

My obligation to my associates Charles W. Hieatt and Anne Lake Prescott for their help continues in this case as in all others connected with the larger Spenser-Shakespeare project in which we are engaged. I wish to thank particularly Thomas G. Bishop and Eric A. Nicholson, my assistants in 1985–1986, during my visiting fellowship at Yale, for their help with this article. Their knowledge, intelligence, resourcefulness, and integrity conduced to bring more to light and avoid more errors than I could have done by myself in four times the time.

1. It occurs twice nonfiguratively, meaning the location and the singers in Westminster Abbey, in *Henry VIII*. Here and below I depend on Marvin Spevack, *The Harvard Concordance to Shakespeare* (Cambridge, Mass.: Harvard University Press, 1973) (with occasional use of his longer edition) and *The Riverside Shakespeare*, ed. G. Blakemore Evans et al. (Boston: Houghton Mifflin, 1974).

98

> *Belarius.* . . . Then was I as a tree
> Whose *boughs* did bend with fruit; but in one night,
> A storm or robbery (call it what you will)
> *Shook* down my mellow hangings, nay, my *leaves*,
> And left me *bare* to weather. (60–64)

The first quatrain of Sonnet 73:

> That time of year thou mayst in me behold
> When yellow *leaves*, or none, or few, do hang
> Upon those *boughs* which *shake* against the cold,
> *Bare* ruin'd *choirs*, where late the sweet *birds* sang.

Aside from the twelve-year hiatus in the use of *choir*, there is the much longer hiatus between the idea of a choir of birds in *Cymbeline* and the same idea in 2 *Henry VI*. And it is not only the words and the two figures of a bird-choir and a weather-beaten tree losing its leaves that are similar in the two passages. The "I" who speaks here—the "I" of the Young Friend sonnets as a whole—stands in a loving and quasi-tutelary relationship to someone younger of higher social standing, and Belarius stands in the same relationship (as defined here) to Guiderius and Arviragus, princes of the blood although they do not know it.

I argue in this essay that Shakespeare was intensely concerned with his nondramatic poetry (sonnets and the affectively lyrical complaint in this case) when he wrote *Cymbeline*—very likely as much as at any time since *Venus and Adonis* (1593), *Lucrece* (1594), and the drafting of many of his sonnets (now usually supposed to have begun in the early 1590s). There is a strong verbal relation between parts of *Cymbeline* and "A Lover's Complaint," the final item in the first edition of *Sonnets*. I argue as well that Spenser's *Ruins of Rome*, which has been shown to play so large a part in the embodiments of time's rule and defeat in *Sonnets* and *Lucrece* and in the bitterly emphasized need for English unity in the history plays,[2] returned to Shakespeare's imagination in the composition of this Roman and British romance. Of all his romances, this lyrically affective, experimental one probably gives the best chance of testing precisely the now popular notion[3]—one of the

2. A. Kent Hieatt, "The Genesis of Shakespeare's *Sonnets*: Spenser's *Ruines of Rome: by Bellay*," *PMLA*, 98 (1983), 800–14.

3. Widespread, but perhaps best defended by Patricia Parker. It is a constant premise in her *Inescapable Romance* (Princeton: Princeton University Press, 1979), passim, but see especially pp. 4, 172, 233.

most powerful modern extensions of genre criticism—that lyrical affect and romance narrative stand close together.

Cymbeline is usually thought to have been written in 1609–1610, and *Sonnets*, ending with "Complaint," was first published in 1609. Katherine Duncan-Jones has recently demonstrated the hollowness of all the usual reasons for regarding *Sonnets'* publication as unauthorized.[4] It is next to inconceivable that Thorpe, its publisher, would have pirated the edition at this stage of his career. On the known evidence, as Duncan-Jones shows (and others have long thought), the arrangement of the contents is likely to be Shakespeare's own and follows contemporary precedents. Perhaps Shakespeare established a general order for his sonnets much earlier, when he had completed drafts of the majority of them (by 1599 at the latest, on the most authoritative verbal evidence, but see below). Around 1600, as others and I have already tried to show,[5] he was almost surely trying to round out the collection with "Complaint" (often supposed not to be by him). Whatever inhibited him from publication at that point, it seems clear that he was busy in the period just before the 1609 publication with the completion of "Complaint" in the form we now have. That he busied himself then as well with the ordering and final form of his sonnets seems to me more than a live possibility. The reminiscence of Sonnet 73 in *Cymbeline*, which is the verbally densest, most extensive reminiscence of one of his sonnets in all the works, is certainly not conclusive, but it points in this direction.[6]

The studies of Kenneth Muir, MacD. P. Jackson, and particularly

---

4. Katherine Duncan-Jones, "Was the 1609 *Shake-Speares Sonnets* Really Unauthorized?" *RES*, 34 (1983), 151–71.

5. A. K. Hieatt, T. G. Bishop, E. A. Nicholson, "Shakespeare's Rare Words: 'Lover's Complaint,' *Cymbeline*, and *Sonnets*," *N&Q*, n.s. 34 (1987), 219–24. The article builds on Eliot Slater's work.

6. Since initial formulation of this article in 1985, my associates and I have examined this matter further and expect to publish our results shortly. On the basis of what seems impregnable verbal evidence we are able to show that in the period roughly after 1600 Shakespeare heavily revised and/or added to some sections of those sonnets (1–126) in which all references to the young beloved appear. We are as yet unable to say how much of this composition fell in the period of *Cymbeline* itself but continue to be impressed by the "anecdotal" evidence relating to the first quatrain of no. 73. An additional point (which as teachers many of us have previously been at pains to combat) is that no. 73 is autobiographically much closer to the seventeenth-century Shakespeare than to the sixteenth-century one.

Eliot Slater impose the very strong likelihood that "Complaint" (at the end of a group of sonnets, like the complaints in Samuel Daniel's *Delia* and Thomas Lodge's *Phillis*) is Shakespeare's.[7] Further, Slater's demonstration that Shakespeare worked on the poem in the time of *All's Well* and finished it as we have it in the time of *Cymbeline* is almost impossible to resist once it is understood. Many stylistic arguments (others' and my own) for Shakespeare's authorship do not need to be gone into here. The most important point for our present purposes is Slater's demonstration that "Complaint" is closely allied to *Cymbeline*. It is the close verbal connection of the complaint with this play and those around the time of *All's Well*, so disproportionate to the connection with plays of the rest of Shakespeare's career, that constitutes Slater's most important, although not his only, proof of Shakespeare's authorship. The reasons that his study has not received due attention are probably that it is extraordinarily compressed and rhetorically resistant and that it does no more than summarize the statistical evidence that is indispensable for comprehension of his claims.[8]

Slater's most important argument is easy to summarize once it is grasped. Envision a class of the words most rarely used by Shakespeare in his plays, comprising every word that is used in no more than five plays. Establish which words of this class are used in "Complaint" (and in Shakespeare's other poems, which Slater also studies). Of these rare words isolated in "Complaint," determine the number in each of the plays where they occur. Considering how rarely these words are used,

7. See Kenneth Muir, "'A Lover's Complaint': A Reconsideration," in his *Shakespeare the Professional and Related Studies* (London: Heinemann, 1973); MacD. P. Jackson, *Shakespeare's "A Lover's Complaint": Its Date and Authenticity*, University of Auckland Bulletin 72, English Series 13 (1965); and Eliot Slater, "Shakespeare: Word Links between Poems and Plays," *N&Q*, 220 (1975), 157–63. In his recent New Penguin edition, *"The Sonnets" and "A Lover's Complaint"* (Harmondsworth, Eng.: Penguin, 1986), John Kerrigan agrees with this conclusion, on very similar grounds.

8. Slater (now deceased) did not list the hundreds of words with which he was dealing. He simply gave totals. In this he followed the habit of Alfred Hart (see note 11), who with the help of Schmidt's *Shakespeare Lexicon* manually assembled all the words in Shakespeare's vocabulary, discriminated by individual works and other criteria, and then published his results in reputable journals. Slater was a highly distinguished psychiatrist and writer of psychiatric texts—a C.B.E.—in the Institute of Psychiatry of the University of London, with a secondary interest in Shakespeare. He describes Bartlett's *Concordance* as his only source.

any play in which the number of them shared with "Complaint" is very far above average is likely to have a significant relationship to it.

Slater's "rare word" technique is in fact a variation of that used by Gregor Sarrazin, later the editor of the third edition of Schmidt's *Shakespeare Lexicon*, in a two-part article in the 1890s.[9] Having isolated the words used by Shakespeare no more than two or three times, Sarrazin showed that in nearly all the forty-one Shakespearean works he studied the greatest number of such words were shared with works believed on other grounds to be chronologically near it. When the forty-one works are ranged in the traditional sequence of four periods, with totals of shared words in each work being given in separate columns for each of the four periods, his evidence—a kind of lexical bludgeon—constitutes one of the few successful nineteenth-century efforts to convert aspects of textual study to a science.[10] If Shakespeare had not been verbally so acquisitive from year to year throughout his working life,[11] Sarrazin's evidence would not have shown statistically appreciable variations. It does show them in the Shakespearean case, and his success goes far to validate Slater's method.

Sarrazin's evidence concerning "Complaint" is, as far as it goes, consistent with Slater's, but, working with a much larger class of rare words (in addition to the work under study, occurrences in five plays instead of two or three occurrences in the works), Slater was able to perceive relationships with this fairly short work that escaped Sarrazin. On Slater's evidence, the association of *Cymbeline* with "Complaint" is 232 percent of normal expectation (thirteen words [but see below], instead of the five or six that one would expect on average)—the highest association with a play not only for "Complaint" but for any of

9. Gregor Sarrazin, "Wortechos bei Shakespeare," *Shakespeare-Jahrbuch*, 33 (1897), 121–65, 34 (1898), 119–69. As far as I know, Slater was unaware of this article.

10. His evidence enabled him (II.168) to decide correctly that *Troilus* was not, as often supposed in the 1890s, a late play but belonged in the third period. His data, like Slater's, suggest that the majority of work in *Sonnets* belongs in the first period, but, as he points out (II.169), this evidence is not conclusive, since the smaller totals of agreeing words for the other three periods might bespeak further composition in the case of a work traditionally supposed to have been composed over a long period. Spot checks indicate that his error rate in manipulating material from the *Shakespeare Lexicon*, his only source, was 10–15 percent, insignificant in this context.

11. Alfred Hart, "Vocabularies of Shakespeare's Plays," *RES*, 19 (1943), 128–40; "The Growth of Shakespeare's Vocabulary," *RES*, 19 (1943), 242–54.

Shakespeare's nondramatic works, entailing far less than a .05 probability of being random. On the same basis Slater shows that *Hamlet*, *Troilus*, and particularly *All's Well* (all around 1600) also have strong verbal associations with "Complaint."[12] He concludes that "Complaint" was drafted about 1600–1603 and then deeply recast around 1609.

Such statistical arguments are hard to come to terms with, but the relation between *Cymbeline* and "Complaint" shows up very convincingly when the rarest words shared by them are *identified*, as they have been in a recent article,[13] where further details are available. The contexts of these fifteen shared words (not thirteen, Slater's figure) suggest that Shakespeare was working on *Cymbeline* and "Complaint" at nearly the same time and that they affected each other. In most cases the contextual relationship of pairs of rare words used in these two works is much closer than with any occurrences of these words in any other works. Three of the words (*commix, outwardly,* and *slackly,*) are used only in *Cymbeline* and "Complaint." Six of the remaining words (*gyve, physic, spungy, rudeness, usury,* and *pervert*) are used in one or another of the cited three plays around 1600, in accord with the premise that Shakespeare was first formulating "Complaint" then; perhaps some of them recur in *Cymbeline* because Shakespeare was reminded of them while recasting "Complaint" around the time of the play's composition.

Three of the cited fifteen occur in one brief scene (II.ii) in *Cymbeline*, within twenty-eight lines, starting with line 8, where, just before falling asleep, Imogen prays for protection from the night's "tempters." As the term is used in "Complaint," it suits Jachimo even better than it does the angellike, fiendish seducer operating on defenseless women in

12. Slater extends his statistical analysis by five gradations of frequency, arriving finally at all words (not simply rare ones) which "Complaint" shares with the rest of the canon. Here again, *Cymbeline*'s association with "Complaint" is the closest of any play (169 percent of normal expectation—107 words instead of an expectable 63), although the association of the other three plays with it is slightly less impressive (greatest for *All's Well*, at 160 percent).

13. See notes 5 and 8. Our "Shakespeare's Rare Words" describes the method of arriving at the words. The fifteen are: *amplify, aptness, blazon* (vb.), *commix, feat* (adj.), *gyve* (noun), *outwardly, pervert* (vb.), *physic* (vb.), *ruby* (noun), *rudeness, slackly, spungy, tempter, usury*. Their locations in the works are readily available in Spevack's *Concordance*.

"Complaint": "th' unexperient gave the tempter place, / Which like a cherubin above them hover'd" (318–19). Narratively, it is Jachimo who, a moment after, hovers over the sleeping Imogen; the hoverings of the seducer in "Complaint" are not part of the story. The other two shared rare words in this scene in *Cymbeline*—the noun *ruby* and the adverb *outwardly*—show similar symptoms of overlaps at the workshop stage, but comparison with their counterparts needs to be postponed for a moment, so as to consider the additional point that these counterpart words form part of another brief passage, this time one in "Complaint." At line 17 of the scene in *Cymbeline*, Jachimo, having emerged from his chest, compares Imogen's lips to "rubies" (very rarely used as a noun by Shakespeare). Jachimo reflects in lines 35–37 that the bracelet he has just taken from her wrist "will witness *outwardly*, / As strongly as the conscience does within, / To th' madding of her lord." It is tempting to suppose that Shakespeare worked on this scene around the same time as "Complaint," particularly because, in the latter, *rubies* and *outwardly* (which is unique in Shakespeare to this play and this poem) reemerge in the single stanza beginning the passage in which the seducer is presenting his exhibits of spurned loves as a tribute to the present object of his lust. In the 329 lines of "Complaint," no fewer than six of the fifteen specified words of "Complaint" are restricted to lines 197–259, in the nine stanzas of this self-contained passage. It seems likely, therefore, that most of this passage belongs to the time of *Cymbeline*. The first stanza (197–203) contains *rubies* and *outwardly*, closer together than in the scene in *Cymbeline*:

> Look here what tributes wounded fancies sent me,
> Of pallid pearls and *rubies* red as blood
> Figuring that they their passions likewise lent me
> Of grief and blushes, aptly understood
> In bloodless white and the encrimson'd mood,
> Effects of terror and dear modesty,
> Encamp'd in hearts but fighting *outwardly*.

The rubies here become a metaphor, as in the play, for a color in a woman's face. It is possible to see, as well, an accommodation of the slightly off-key *terror* and *modesty* (why terror and modesty, when grief and sexual desire are the prime meanings in context?) in a recall of the situation in II.ii: the breathless spectacle of a chaste woman, unconscious and helpless, in physical contact (the removal of the bracelet) with a villain who has tried to seduce her and has just expressed sharp physical appetite. *Outwardly* applies here to the outer evidence, the complexion and consequently the metaphoric aspect of the jewels that the seducer's victims have given to witness their inner passion. *Outwardly* in *Cymbeline* applies to another adornment, the bracelet Jachimo has just stolen. It will be an outward token to spur the inner madness he will implant in Posthumus: "this will witness outwardly, / As strongly as the conscience doth within, / To th' madding of her lord" (35–37). In both cases, an aspiring seducer and a desired woman are two sides of a triangle, which is completed in one case by spurned women and in the other by a husband. In both cases an outward adornment is a token of a frantic inner state.

The self-contained passage of "Complaint" (197–259) also contains a third, fourth, fifth, and sixth word of the fifteen rare words which make the poem's relation with *Cymbeline* so singular. The third of these six is *amplify* (209). In *Cymbeline* the vicious queen, receiving new supplies, claims (I.v.15–18) to be amplifying her judgment in the art of poisoning; in "Complaint" the unchaste women practicing their arts on their seducer are said to have amplified their gifts of jewels with what amounts to a new art: "deep-brain'd sonnets that did amplify / Each stone's dear nature, worth, and quality." *Blazon,* the fourth of the six, follows in the "Complaint" passage at 217. It is the art of sonnets by which their creators effortfully blazon their gifts of jewels here: "each several stone, / With wit well blazon'd, smil'd or made some moan." On the other hand, it is an opposite principle that is automatically self-blazoned in creating Guiderius and Arviragus in *Cymbeline*: "Thou divine Nature, thou thyself thou blazon'st / In these two princely boys!" (IV.ii.170–71). The fifth of the six words in the "Complaint" passage, *gyve* (242), correlates more exactly with its counterpart in the play. The early history of one of the seducer's conquests in "Complaint" is that she had happily entered a nunnery, preferring "eternal love" to what previous suitors had offered. What seemed to others penitent incarceration was for her a joy; she was "Playing patient sports in unconstrained gyves." At *Cymbeline* V.iv.13–15, Posthumus, held prisoner by the British, mirrors her feelings: "Must I repent, / I cannot do it better than in gyves, / Desir'd more than constrain'd." The sixth word, *physic* (259), verbalizes the encouragement of love, as by a medical compound. The seducer puts together the offering of all his other loves "As compound love to physic your cold breast." Imogen on Posthumus's sorrow at absence from her: "let that grieve him: / Some griefs are med'cinable, that is one of them, / For it doth physic love" (*Cymbeline* III.ii.32–34).

Of the remaining eleven rare words shared by *Cymbeline* and "Complaint," *tempter* has already been mentioned. The others are studied elsewhere.[14] *Feat* (adj.), *rudeness, usury,* and *pervert* show no special association. *Aptness* relates in both play and poem to shifts of amorous technique according to need. (The queen advising Cloten how to win Imogen: "Frame yourself / To orderly solicits, and be friended / With aptness of the season; make denials / Increase your services" [II.iii. 46–49]. The seducer in "Complaint" makes use "Of burning blushes, or of weeping water, / Or sounding paleness; and he takes and leaves, / In either's aptness as it best deceives" [304–06].) *Commix* (unique to the two works) appears in similar contexts. Two faculties of the female speaker are yoked but opposed at "Complaint" 28: "The mind and sight distractedly commix'd"; in the play the smiling and sighing of the disguised Imogen are yoked but opposed in the commixing of the sigh with the wind:

> Nobly he yokes
> A smiling with a sigh, as if the sigh
> Was that it was for not being such a smile;
> The smile mocking the sigh, that it would fly
> From so divine a temple to commix
> With winds that sailors rail at. (IV.ii.51–56)

Spungy carries a certain connotation of deceitfulness (*Cymbeline* IV.ii.348–49; "Complaint" 326). *Slackly* (unique to the two works) covers the degree of abrogation of a safeguarded status quo (the children of Cymbeline stolen away by Guiderius were "slackly guarded" [I.i.64]; some of the female's hair in "Complaint" "in her threaden fillet still did bide, / And true to bondage would not break from thence / Though slackly braided in loose negligence" [33–35]).

There are naturally many other close verbal fits between *Cymbeline* and "Complaint." These fifteen are no more than an earnest of many

14. Hieatt, Bishop, Nicholson, "Shakespeare's Rare Words."

other shared words (ninety-four according to Slater) of less rarity in the canon. If Slater's initial restriction to words used in five plays is only slightly relaxed, many other relations spring into view. For instance, three significantly rare words in *Cymbeline* I.i—*feated, slackly, swathing*—are found in similar form in corresponding contexts among five such words in the first eight stanzas of "Complaint": *commix, enswath'd, feat, slackly, usury*.[15] Enough has been said, however, to show how heavily the verbal textures of passages in the two works are implicated in each other, across the generic boundary between a romance and a lyrical complaint which has no more story line—is no more a narrative—than Shakespeare's sonnets.

Shakespeare's putative approval of the publication of *Sonnets* 1609 and his having busied himself with completing what we have of its final item at that time can, then, licitly form part of a larger argument concerning the lyric aspect of the verbal substance of *Cymbeline* itself. It may be that the plague years 1608–1609, during which the theaters were closed (see Duncan-Jones), were for Shakespeare something of a replay of the same circumstances in 1592–1593, during which he may have had more time for poetry (cf. publication of *Venus* in 1593 and *Lucrece* in 1594, and the authoritative opinion that he was also working on his sonnets in those years).[16] What the role of the sonnets themselves may have been in the gestation of *Cymbeline* is a question for future treatment.

Beyond largely verbal problems, however, there is one way in which the participation of concepts first formulated in a lyrical way can be teased out in *Cymbeline*. The large part Spenser's *Ruins of Rome* played in the inspiration of *Sonnets* and *Lucrece* and its smaller but significant part in the histories seem to have their counterparts in recently gathered evidence from the end of Shakespeare's career. A major surprise in accumulating initially verbal information about this sequence and Shakespeare's work has been that the overlap of vocabulary between the two falls off very markedly in Shakespeare's middle period—even in his Roman plays and particularly *Julius Caesar*, where an influence might be expected—but increases in the romances. It is

15. I am indebted to Eric Nicholson for this point.

16. To these circumstances Duncan-Jones adds in her cited article that Shakespeare's enforced inactivity in the later plague years may have led to a need for money, which the sale of a manuscript of *Sonnets* would help to satisfy.

often generally remarked that in his latest plays Shakespeare seems to return to some early preoccupations, but in the case of verbal and conceptual echoes of this early sonnet translation by Spenser something much more specific seems to have happened in *Cymbeline*, the only romance combining British interests (resembling those of the early histories) and Roman ones.

Eagle and its inflected and hyphenated forms belong to an interesting class of words of which the pattern of frequency in Shakespeare's career is hourglass shaped, although not drastically broken like the pattern of *choir*: the sixteen works through *Romeo* (1589–1595/6, but arbitrarily including *Sonnets*, which has no eagles), show seventeen occurrences; the ensuing twenty works through *Coriolanus* (1595/6–1607/8), only ten occurrences; the seven works from *Timon* through *Two Noble Kinsmen* (1607/8–1613), thirteen occurrences.[17]

If, however, one omits *Cymbeline*, the frequency on the more accurate basis of line counts is only insignificantly higher in the last period than in the middle one, because *Cymbeline* is Shakespeare's play of the eagles: nine out of all forty occurrences. It contains more eagles than any other Shakespearean work, even if one discounts those eagles that are centrally thematic to it in delivering the goods of romance. These two thematic ones are, first, the expressively auspicious (feather-preening and bill-"cloying") eagle that, in Posthumus's enacted dream in the next-to-last scene, flies Jove down from and back up to the heavens (perhaps the upper stage) so that the god can promise the family of Posthumus Leonatus final union with Imogen; and, second, the eagle which the Romans' soothsayer has seen in a vision bestowed by the gods. This second eagle, a both Roman and Jovial one flying from South to West and disappearing into the sunbeams, initially leads the soothsayer into the mistaken prophecy of a Roman victory (IV.ii.350–52) but in the last scene allows a recovery of vatic credit when (as "Philarmonus" now) he perceives that disappearance into sunbeams means final harmony between Augustus and the English sun, Cymbeline. Philarmonus interprets as well in this last scene the missive that Jove, just before his eagle flies off with him in the next-to-last scene, had left behind for Posthumus: not only was Imogen to be restored to Posthumus but her two brothers, long ago carried off by Belarius,

17. Trusting Riverside's chronological table and Spevack's *Concordance*.

would be restored to Cymbeline, and Britain would flourish in peace and plenty.

The personal and national harmonious reconciliations that are the final aims of the play and of its last scene yoke these two flying, visionary eagles in a structural pattern. They are actors in the symbolic embodiments of the two sides of the play. Posthumus's eagle of Jove carries a god imperiously but justly concerned to impose beneficent reconciliations; the seer's Roman eagle (also of Jove) enacts a political reconciliation. The literature on the play, however, suggests no source for these eagles, and classical and Renaissance treatments seem to offer no parallels.[18] One of Spenser's sonnets, however—*Ruins of Rome* 17—fuses Jove's eagle and a Roman one in a similar visionary, political milieu. Shakespeare's seer says "I saw Jove's bird, the Roman eagle, wing'd / From the spungy south to this part of the west, / There vanish'd in the sunbeams." Spenser, like Shakespeare, capitalizes on

18. The association of the eagle with Jove and with Rome and its legions was naturally well known, but the fairly extensive classical references to *auspicium* by means of eagles ignore the position of the sun and suggest only that a preliminary sighting southward is unfavorable (contrary to the seer's conclusion). Cicero's *De divinatione* produces *auspicia* by eagles, but nothing more relevant here than, quoting Ennius, a bird appearing on the left at sunrise (XLVIII, Romulus and Remus). No significance for the present case arises in the sections devoted specifically to auspices (XXXIII-XXXIX). G. P. Valeriano Bolzani, *Hieroglyphica* XIX (p. 188 in the Garland 1976 reprint of Lyon 1602), commends eagles and their indication of success in war (going back to Jove's struggle with the giants, before which an eagle flew toward him, presaging victory; see Cartari, "De Jove," following Anacreon) and recounts numerous stories of their predictive behavior, but nothing at all like Shakespeare's. He claims Aristotle's authority in associating men with either the raven or the eagle according to the shapes of their noses, and associates eagles with monarchs. Many emblems show, or concern, an eagle flying toward the sun or in some other relation to it, but the significance is always moral, and very distant from what Shakespeare points to. See *Emblemata: Handbuch zur Sinnbildkunst des XVI und XVII Jahrhunderts*, ed. Arthur Henkel and Albrecht Schöne (Stuttgart: J. B. Metzler, 1967), columns 775–78, and for other eagles, 757–59. Closest to Shakespeare is the aged eagle who combines flying to the sun to singe his feathers and bathing in water so as to regenerate himself (cols. 776–77. In the second reference the sun is Christ. The tradition goes back to the *Physiologus*). See also Jupiter mounted on an eagle (col. 1726), as in *Cymbeline*, but with an entirely different significance. Also, in connection with the possible associations of the raven in *Cymbeline*, baring its eye to the dawn in the play, see cols. 881–82 (below, the raven as rumormonger, spying on two naked lovers [cf. the Manciple's Tale and the raven as a bad reporter for Noah, Gen. 8.7]; above, as procrastinator croaking "cras" as he watches the sun rise). I have consulted many encyclopedic treatises without finding more than this.

the Roman habit of priestly auspices, and his sonnet contains "Jove's
. . . bird," "Romane eagle," the influence of the sun upon a flying
eagle, the relation between the Roman Empire and a northern opponent, and other features and words found in *Cymbeline*'s two eagle
visions; but it is tragic rather than reconciliatory and tragicomic:

> So long as *Ioues* great Bird did make his flight,
> Bearing the fire with which heauen doth vs fray,
> Heauen had not feare of that presumptuous might,
> With which the Giaunts did the Gods assay.
> But all so soone, as scortching Sunne had brent
> His wings, which wont the earth to ouerspredd,
> The earth out of her massie wombe forth sent
> That antique horror, which made heauen adredd.
> Then was the Germane Rauen in disguise
> That Romane Eagle seene to cleaue asunder,
> And towards heauen freshly to arise
> Out of these mountaines, now consum'd to pouder.
> In which the foule that serues to beare the lightning,
> Is now no more seen flying, nor alighting.

I must return here for a moment to the connection I have recently
described between *Ruins of Rome* and Shakespeare's *Sonnets, Lucrece,*
and early history plays. It is not only that the physical ruin of Rome
and its poetic survival find their echoes in the two poetic works; the
equally important theme in *Ruins of Rome* of the self-destruction of
Rome and its empire through the internal strife of its sons plays a less
important but striking part (much more so than I have indicated in my
former article) in Shakespeare's thinking in his histories, with the
proviso that England finally avoids the fate that *Ruins of Rome* must
assign to Rome.

It is often noted that Milford-Haven (completely absent from Shakespeare's sources) is a place where almost everyone wants to go in
Cymbeline (Posthumus, Imogen, Cloten, Lucius, and other Romans; it
is named four times), and that its importance here relates the play to
Shakespeare's other great English reconciliatory gesture: the arrival of
Richmond at Milford-Haven so that he could end Richard III's rule,
marry into the opposing family, end the Wars of the Roses, and institute Tudor unity. Perhaps just as the early Shakespeare imagines
England as winning through there to the reconciliation that Rome

could never find for her civil wars in *Ruins of Rome,* so Rome attains, at the other end of the hourglass, an external pacification that *Ruins of Rome* never envisioned. But here the path of the heroic is clearly rejected, is reduced in fact to the level of Cloten and his mother, as it never was so clearly in, for instance, the scruples of Hamlet, the satire of *Troilus,* and the complexities of *Antony.* As a way to a worthy solution the heroic will appear in no more of Shakespeare's work. Perhaps *Ruins of Rome* had nothing to contribute to the specifically Roman plays of the middle period, because its paradigm did not work there: the only resort the ethical, in the case of Brutus, and the personal, in the case of Antony, can seek in the face of the coming, not particularly heroic, but efficient empire is suicide.[19] This has nothing to do with *Ruins of Rome.*

On all the assumptions sketched so far (experiences like those of the earlier plague years, some enforced inactivity, concern with his most important nondramatic poetry, possible need for money, rumination on his only play combining Roman and British themes), it is plausible to think that Shakespeare would have returned to his earlier concern with *Ruins of Rome*: not simply to the theme in *Sonnets*—physical ruination in time but spiritual survival—but also to the analogy in the histories between Roman and English destiny, paradoxically qualified by a happy outcome for the English in contrast to the pathetic downfall through strife which is described in *Ruins of Rome.* A similar analogical paradox in the case of *Cymbeline* is interpretively attractive: in place of the destructive gigantism of Rome's enemies in *Ruins of Rome,* Shakespeare gives us in the people of Thames's banks an imagined perpetuation of a Roman idea of universalism and order, but through honorable give-and-take in accord with his growing disenchantment with heroic measures.

Nothing is more obvious now to the student of Shakespeare's imagery than that families of consonant lyric images march through each play on paths that are not always in consonance with the narrative. The five references to the two thematic eagles I have mentioned do not

19. Cf. G. K. Hunter, "A Roman Thought," in *An English Miscellany Presented to W. S. Mackie,* ed. Brian S. Lee (Cape Town: Oxford University Press, 1977), pp. 93–117. See also, on *Cymbeline,* Robert S. Miola, *Shakespeare's Rome* (Cambridge: Cambridge Unversity Press, 1983), pp. 206–35. I cannot follow him and G. Wilson Knight in their picture of the play as a glorification of British values against Roman ones.

exhaust the eagle census in *Cymbeline*. Augustus is naturally a princely eagle. Posthumus is an eagle[20] (versus Cloten as puttock). Having attacked like eagles, the Romans flee like chickens. Additional birds make *Cymbeline* Shakespeare's probably most avian play: beyond eagle, puttock, and chicken lie crow, raven, wren, robin, jay, phoenix, the lark at heaven's gate, and sets of unspecified birds. It is tempting to suppose that the raven of Jachimo's appeal as he climbs back into his casket is a reminiscence of the raven adversary to the eagle of *Ruins of Rome* 17: "Swift, swift, you dragons of the night, that dawning / May bare [Folio: "beare"] the raven's eye!" (II.ii.48–49). Furness considered that Jachimo was identifying himself with the raven, and Nosworthy accepted this view.[21]

Birds are much invoked by Belarius in III.iii—the same scene in which the reminiscence of Sonnet 73 occurs—in a pastoral lesson to Guiderius and Arviragus. Having romped up a hill, he tells them, they will see him below as no more than a crow in significance, because mere appearances are like class: it is opportunistically attained place that "lessens and sets off" those who have not attained it from those who have; often to our comfort we find "the sharded beetle in a safer hold / Than is the full-wing'd eagle." In this pastoral period, Belarius lives with his young companions in a cave. He will be reconciled with Cymbeline and rejoin the eagles, but at this point his pastoralism is as aggressive in its condemnation of the court as Meliboe's is in *Faerie Queene* VI. Belarius takes satisfaction in the low-roofed humility and the secure rock-substance of his dwelling, which teaches rightly to adore the heavens. The pastoralism of the scene is full of transparent references, not only to court generically but to courtly dangers in the thematic world of the play, as for instance one prominent motif—"We will fear no poison, which attends in place of greater state" (77–78)— even though, as in *As You Like It*, a pastoral-courtly somersault is being executed here, like Meliboe's assurance of the safety of his lowly state shortly before he is slain by robbers. The potion from Cym-

20. As others have noted, his ability to stare into the sun like an eagle is indicated at I.iv.12 and at III.iv.94. Imogen applies the verb "tirest" to him, as though he were a ravenously feeding eagle.

21. *Cymbeline*, ed. J. M. Nosworthy (Arden Edition) (London: Methuen, 1969), p. lxxiii. The tradition usually referred to here, however, is that the raven roosts so as to face the sun at dawn.

beline's queen, which is thought by her to be a poison but is not, will be consumed in this cave by Imogen, who thinks it is a restorative, which it is not.

One of the most pregnant metaphors suggesting the court, however, is Belarius's mobilization of the Renaissance significance of giants as chthonic, violent, rebellious, tyrannical forces, by nature destructive of divine order. It is Shakespeare's most striking use of this sense of *giant* since the giant-systems in the imagery of the other end of the hourglass, the earlier histories,[22] which also seem to me to have much contact with similar giant images in *Ruins of Rome* (one of them, "antique horror" in *Ruins of Rome* 17, above). In praising his low-ceilinged rocky structure and its lowly gate, which teach a right respect for heaven, Belarius says at 4–7:

> The gates of monarchs
> Are arch'd so high that giants may jet through
> And keep their impious turbands on without
> Good morrow to the sun.

(Compare, incidentally, "this vaulted arch," near Jachimo, to which he calls Imogen's attention in Cymbeline's palace at I.vi.32, and the sun, which is Cymbeline and toward which the eagle flies.) In the imaginative world of the play, the giantlike forces of disorder in *Cymbeline* are, at the personal level, Jachimo and his deep-laid malice but more pointedly, at the political level, those forces of brutal disorder Cloten ("that irregulous devil") and his mother-queen, who second their personal antipathies and liking for poison, violence, malice, or rape with their obstreperous advocacy of making Britain a "world to itself" by throwing off the Roman connection and tribute (III.i and V.v.462–63).

Such extensive national, biblical, and classical traditions as those of giants in the Renaissance cannot be completely localized. The Saracen

---

22. In the earlier histories are "Giant world enrag'd" (*John* V.ii.57); "put the world's whole strength / Into one giant arm, it shall not force / This lineal honor from me" (2 *Henry IV* IV.v.44–46, relating to *John*'s "Come the three corners of the world in arms, / And we shall shock them" [V.vii.116–17]; this in turn relates to *Ruins of Rome* 21: "Sustein'd the shocke of common enmitie . . . all the world in armes against her bent"); "to whip this dwarfish war, this pigmy arms" (*John* V.ii.135), etc. The only uses of *giant* and its other forms in this sense in the time intervening between the earlier histories and *Cymbeline* are *Measure* II.ii.107–09 and *Hamlet* IV.v.121–22.

touch of turbans came of course from elsewhere;[23] and it would be wrong to neglect A. E. Thiselton's suggestion that a sermon by Henry Smith[24] comes close to several items in Belarius's speech. There are nevertheless reasons for thinking of *Ruins of Rome* here.

The appearances of giants in *Ruins of Rome* are colored by a phenomenon common to all good sonnet sequences. These exploit a productive ambiguity in the slippage of meaning which a sequence permits: sonnets are separate entities, more so than narrative stanzas are, but their ordering in a sequence holds the option of continuity open. (In this they are distantly like the speeches in a Shakespearean play.) Du Bellay exploits this feature more than is usual in *Antiquitez* (which Spenser translated as *Ruins of Rome*) and in *Songe*, which ends Du Bellay's sequence, because in writing visionary, or Orphic, poems he finds the riddling, puzzling aspect of prophecy useful, as Petrarch had done before him. So, consequently, does *Ruins of Rome* exploit this feature. In *Ruins of Rome* 4, Jove fears that the growth of Rome may bring about another uprising of the old giants. In 11, Mars, ashamed that his offspring—Roman mortal puissance and pride in hardihood— seemed to exceed heaven's power, cooled the Roman heat and blew new ardor into the cold Gothic north, to the effect that, first, that northern nation, the "earths new Giant brood," beat down Rome's walls into the earth, their mother, and, second, that no one, even Jove the sire of Mars, should boast of the Roman Empire. In 12, just as the giants (the children of the earth) rebelled against the gods, piling hills on hills to reach the sky, and were quelled with Jove's thunderbolts, so Rome, lifting her front on hills against the heaven, has been conquered, and the gods no longer fear. In the already quoted 17, uniquely, Jove's bird and the Roman eagle are one, and as long as it flew, carrying the lightning with which heaven instills fear into us and shading the earth from scorching heat, heaven had no fear that the former, ardently unruly violence of the giants (now not Romans but northern barbarians) would again threaten them. But that eagle, once scorched by the sun and (in *Ruins of Rome* only) cloven by the German raven in the

---

23. E.g., *Faerie Queene* VI.vii.41, 43.

24. Alfred Edward Thiselton, *Some Textual Notes on "The Tragedie of Cymbeline"* (London: R. Folkard, 1902), p. 28. Noted by Nosworthy without particulars. Henry Smith's sermon *A Disswasion from Pride* is in *The Sermons of Master H. Smith gathered into one volume. T. Orwin f. T. Man* 1592 (STC No. 22718), sig. E.e.7–sig. G.g.2.

disguise of the Roman, Jovial bird,[25] no longer protects and controls us: fiery violence is let loose on the world. In 18, the imperial eagle is again, in passing, opposed by heaven. The giants are not mentioned, and with *Antiquitez/Ruins of Rome* 17 and 18 the theme of the giants ends with the last reverberation concerning the eagle, which has played a role in only these two sonnets.

At least at one point in Shakespeare's plays something indubitably from Du Bellay via Spenser is joined with giants of Du Bellay's kind. In the series leading from one item in *John*, "world in arms," "self," and "shock," which is surely in a strong relation to *Ruins of Rome* (see note 22), the item in a corresponding context when Hal first puts on the crown at *2 Henry IV* IV.v.44–46 ("Put the world's whole strength / Into one giant arm, it shall not force / This lineal honor from me") anglicizes, and seems to fuse, the Roman hardihood of *Ruins of Rome* 21 and Roman resistance to inimical giant forces at other places (e.g., 17) in the sequence. The thematic relation between the eagles in *Ruins of Rome* 17 and in *Cymbeline* is likely, therefore, to be seconded by such a relation between the rebellious northern giants referred to in number 17 and elsewhere in this sequence (and, of course more distantly, between the ravens of this sonnet 17 and *Cymbeline*).

Certain other parallels are of interest. My attention was first drawn to the soothsayer's description of his vision to the Roman general Lucius in IV.ii.346–52 because this description is immediately followed by two images that are also reminiscent of *Ruins of Rome*. Lucius, seeing the beheaded body of the queen's son, Cloten, says:

> Soft ho, what trunk is here?
> Without his top? The ruin speaks that sometime
> It was a worthy building. (353–55)

The notion of a tree that has been harmed belongs to a family of images in *Cymbeline*: Cymbeline himself is a cedar from which two branches, his sons, have been lopped and to which they are finally restored (in the

---

25. The German raven, which in Du Bellay's version simply replaces the eagle, points in one sense to northern barbarian incursions, but what Du Bellay probably had most in mind was the Holy Roman Empire, enemy of France, which was so ineffectual a replacement for Roman power and justice. See Joachim Du Bellay, *Les Regrets et autres oeuvres poëtiques*, ed. J. Jolliffe and M. A. Screech (Geneva: Droz, 1966), p. 290 n. 10. Shakespeare is unlikely, perhaps, to have attended to this refinement of meaning.

soothsayer's last-scene interpretation).[26] The matter of the reminiscence of Sonnet 73 and its bare tree in Arviragus's and Belarius's speeches has already been noted. It is in the case of the passage in *Sonnets* 73 that I formerly tried to make a connection to *Ruins of Rome* 28, concerned with the bare, aged oak that is a symbol of present Rome. It now seems to me that participation rather than derivation is the better term for this relationship: it would be hard to find a more frequent verbal and visual figure in the Renaissance than the tree.[27] But if *Ruins of Rome*'s participation is right in this earlier case, it holds as surely for the tree image Belarius applies to himself, and the participation stretches out, if more remotely, to the tree images concerning Cloten and Cymbeline.

The matter of Cloten's appearing to Lucius as a ruin that sometime was a worthy building is a little clearer. Shakespeare's three validated uses of the verb *ruinate* belong to *Sonnets* 10 ("seeking that beauteous roof to ruinate"), *Lucrece* 944 ("To ruinate proud buildings with thy hours"), and *3 Henry VI*, V.i.83–84 ("I will not ruinate my father's house / Who gave his blood to lime the stones together"). The concern with ruined buildings, as so frequently in *Ruins of Rome*, and the use of Spenser's *ruinate* (*Ruins of Rome* 7, concerning Rome's ruins, monuments, arches, spires: "though your frames do for a time make warre / Gainst time, yet time in time shall ruinate / Your workes and names, and your last reliques marre"), seem to associate these early images surely with Spenser's sequence. Once that association is made, however, it is difficult not to see *Ruins of Rome* somewhere behind many of Shakespeare's other evocations of ruined buildings,[28] as in the case of Cloten (whose body, once it is headless, is worthy enough to be mistaken for Posthumus).

Cymbeline's reconciliation of the English and the Romans is Shakespeare's strangest. Earlier his quieters of strife had been victory, marriage, or death. This time such ambiguities as the decision of *Troilus*'s

26. The relation of these features to the dying speech of Warwick in *3 Henry VI* V.ii.11–15 has been pointed out by Wilson Knight. It is further evidence of the connection of *Cymbeline* with Shakespeare's early English histories.

27. Cf. Orgoglio's fall as both tree and ruin, *FQ* I.viii.22–23.

28. E.g., *2 Henry IV* I.iii.50–62, *Troilus* IV.v.219–24, *Coriolanus* III.i.204–06, *Pericles* II.iv.37.

Trojan council and the attack of Fortinbras on the Poles when honor's at the stake are explicitly rejected (as they are implicitly criticized, no doubt, in their plays). Instead the laws of nations are affirmed and a nationally humbling engagement is kept, but at the honorable juncture of national victory. (The reconciling marriage and Posthumus's forgiveness towards Jachimo belong to a different order of business.) "The world unto ourselves" of Cloten is rejected; in its place is an affirmation of the Roman idea and pax; and an empire stretched to its limits by the Balkan revolts of Dacia and Pannonia can maintain its integrity. Whatever the agreements here with James I's foreign policy, or the allusions via Milford-Haven to the coming of the Tudors, this idea of the significance of the imperium is very much like that of *Ruins of Rome* (e.g., *Ruins of Rome* 8, but also a general thesis), except in one sense: if, uniquely among the crowd of far-flung but unsuccessfully mutinous subjects in *Ruins of Rome* 31, the "bolde people by the *Thamis* brincks" ("*Thames* inhabitants of noble fame" in 22) had not been made to act magnanimously in *Cymbeline*, the otherwise invincible empire would have been in trouble. One wonders what Augustus could have done if the victory won by Posthumus, an old man, and two boys had entailed the loss of Lucius and all his legions: the emperor was already scraping the bottom of the barrel (more so than after the almost contemporary historical defeat of Varus and his eagled legions). The preeminent honor of England among nations is maintained both martially and pacifically, at the moderate cost to Cymbeline's exchequer of three thousand pounds per annum.[29]

Cymbeline reinforces our sense of the proximity of the affects of lyric to the affective, unrealistic romance patterns of figured calamities surmounted by transfigured fulfillment, but does it in a way that is often less generic than it is specific to individual lyrics. Yet against its lyrical affectiveness stands a contrary tendency. One of the reasons that this play is not so entirely a romance as are *Winter's Tale* and *Tempest* is that it is "historical." The two political entities—Britain and Empire— are parts of a developing world important to Shakespeare, Spenser,

---

29. Without further specification a contemporary listener would, it seems to me, have supplied pounds sterling here (cf. Shakespeare's usual meaning for *pounds*, in such a context), although Nosworthy claims that 3,000 lbs. avoirdupois of gold or silver is meant. Under *OED sovereign* A.4.a, a historical quotation of 1726–31 entails that 3,000 pounds of gold would have been worth about 108,000 pounds sterling in 1599.

and us in a way that brings romance into a more daring relation, apparently, with actuality than the other Shakespearean romances show. The rapprochements between Sicilia and Bohemia in *Winter's Tale* and between Milan and Naples in *Tempest* are efficiently romantic in being aspects of individuals' fortune in winning through to happiness and marriage, but there is a grave, annalistic purity in *Cymbeline*'s ranging of the marriage, the reunion of father and sons, and the attainment of harmony between Empire and Britain as separate, if parallel, effects. It now seems likely that the degree of historical specificity in *Cymbeline*, like that in the early histories, related in Shakespeare's mind to a sonnet sequence in which Spenser, led by Du Bellay, had demonstrated that history and politics can be made lyrical.

6

How Spenser Really Used Stephen Hawes in the Legend of Holiness

CAROL V. KASKE

I

In two influential educational treatises, Roger Ascham castigates chivalric romances, particularly those of Malory. In *The Schoolmaster* (1570), he says:

> In our forefathers' time, when papistry, as a standing pool, covered and overflowed all England, few books were read in our tongue, saving certain books of chivalry, as they said for pastime and pleasure; which, as some say, were made in monasteries by idle monks or wanton canons. As one for example *Morte Arthur*; the whole pleasure of which book standeth in two special points, in open manslaughter and bold bawdry. In which book those be counted the noblest knights that do kill most men without any quarrel, and commit foulest adulteries by subtlest shifts; as Sir Launcelot, with the wife of King Arthur his master.... This is good stuff for wise men to laugh at, or honest men to take pleasure at; yet I know when God's Bible was banished the court and *Morte Arthur* received into the prince's chamber. What toys the daily reading of such a book may work in the will of a young gentleman, or a young maid, that liveth wealthily and idly, wise men can judge and honest men do pity.

I wish to thank Geraldine Heng and Karen Cherewatuk, students in my Spenser seminar at Cornell University, for valuable suggestions. Mary Ann Radzinowicz and Deborah MacInnes of Cornell University and Anne Lake Prescott of Barnard College criticized earlier drafts of the essay.

And yet ten *Morte Arthurs* do not the tenth part so much harm as one of these books made in Italy and translated in England.[1]

Disregarding these moral strictures, Spenser chose romance of one variety or another as the generic common denominator of his major literary effort *The Faerie Queene*; and in Book I, as everyone knows, he even attempted to use romance to deal with biblical themes and characters. As he made this seemingly frivolous generic choice, with the Lodge-Gosson controversy (1579) still ringing in his ears, Spenser must have been haunted by criticisms of romance like Ascham's. I propose that in the Legend of Holiness Spenser revised romance to take account of Ascham's criticisms. Indeed, the biblicism of this book seems to reflect Ascham's contrast of romance with the Bible as ideal reading matter.

That Spenser was impressed by objections of the kind Ascham raises is most clearly apparent in the figure of the hermit Contemplation. In the Proem to Book I, Spenser forthrightly announces, "Fierce warres and faithfull loues shall moralize my song."[2] Yet Contemplation—whose views have considerable normative force—asserts that "bloud

---

1. Roger Ascham, *The Schoolmaster*, ed. Lawrence V. Ryan (Ithaca: Cornell University Press, 1967), Book I, ad fin., pp. 68–69. For the original spelling and marginal notes, see William A. Wright, ed., *English Works* (Cambridge: Cambridge University Press, 1904), pp. 230–31. See also Ascham's Preface to *Toxophilus, the School of Shooting* (1545), ad init., ed. George R. Potter, *Elizabethan Verse and Prose (Nondramatic)* (New York: H. Holt, 1928), p. 285 (for original spelling, see Wright, pp. xiv–xv): "English writers by diversity of time have taken divers matters in hand. In our father's time nothing was read but books of feigned chivalry, wherein a man by reading should be led to none other end but only to manslaughter and bawdry. If any man suppose they were good enough to pass the time withal, he is deceived," and so on to the same effect. In similar vein, Spenser's editor E. K. in his gloss on "Ladyes of the Lake" in "April" enters on an irrelevant tirade against "fine fablers and lowd lyers such as were the authors of King Arthure the great and such like, who tell many an unlawfull leasing of the Ladyes of the Lake, that is, the Nymphes." There were of course political motives for the revival of romance, such as, in the Netherlands, to help throw off the Spanish yoke, a motive which would have done much to allay Ascham's doubts about adequate motivation for bloodshed. See Gordon Kipling, *The Triumph of Honour: Burgundian Origins of the Elizabethan Renaissance* (The Hague: Leiden University Press, 1977), pp. 160–64; and Frances Yates's fundamental study, "Elizabethan Chivalry: The Romance of the Accession Day Tilts," *JWCI*, 20 (1957), 4–25, reprinted with slight revisions in *Astraea: The Imperial Theme in the Sixteenth Century* (London: Routledge & Kegan Paul, 1975), pp. 88–111.

2. Throughout, I quote Spenser from the *Variorum*.

can nought but sin and wars but sorrowes yield" (I.x.60); in heaven, "battailes none are to be fought"; and "as for loose loues, [they] are vaine, and vanish into nought" (62)—presumably because in heaven, as Christ says, there is not even "marriage nor giving in marriage" (Matt. 22:30).[3]

Elsewhere in the poem, Spenser sometimes defies Ascham, as in the Proem to Book IV, where he boldly defends a serious and high-minded love interest against "Stoicke censours." At other times he simply complies with Ascham, purging his entire romance of certain things Ascham found objectionable. While his heroes still "kill without any quarrel," thus preserving the open manslaughter, Spenser purges his romance of any hint of adultery between characters for whom we have sympathy; he not only omits Guinevere and her adulterous lover Lancelot, which greatly reduces the bold bawdry, but replaces Guinevere with Gloriana. Such bawdry as he retains involves characters for whom we have little sympathy.

This essay will explore one of the ways in which Spenser compromised with Ascham in Book I: by crossing the medieval romance with a genre distinct in itself in the Middle Ages though almost extinct today, the moral and philosophical allegory. *The Faerie Queene* has never been aligned with its romance and allegorical sources in the light of our new appreciation of the hybrid genre and of the more adversarial kinds of imitation; nor has Book I been properly isolated from the others in considerations of its genre.[4] These projects lead to a new assessment of

3. In another essay I have assessed the effect of having a normative character condemn most of the concerns of the poem he appears in. See "Spenser's Pluralistic Universe," in *Contemporary Thought on Edmund Spenser*, ed. Richard Frushell and Bernard Vondersmith (Carbondale: Southern Illinois University Press, 1975), pp. 122–23. Rosemond Tuve denies that Ascham's criticism of romance had any effect on Spenser and that Spenser's elimination of Lancelot and Guinevere from his romance was motivated by moral scruples such as Ascham's about their adultery. See *Allegorical Imagery: Some Mediaeval Books and Their Posterity* (Princeton: Princeton University Press, 1966), pp. 340 n. 3, 341 n. 4, and 346.

4. A. C. Hamilton observes that "Spenser's possible relation to the Arthurian traditions and medieval romance, particularly Malory, has not been seriously investigated except by Tuve." See General Introduction, *The Faerie Queene* (London: Longman, 1977), p. 6. He ignores—perhaps because of its brevity—Kathleen Williams, "Romance Tradition in *The Faerie Queene*," *Research Studies* (Washington State University, Pullman), 32 (1964), 147–60. Studies of generic hybridization are exemplified by the chapters "Transformations of Genre" and "Generic Modulation" in Alastair Fowler's

recognized sources, one which foregrounds a hitherto unappreciated subtext—*The Example of Vertue* by the pre-Reformation Tudor poet, Stephen Hawes. I propose that in the Legend of Holiness Spenser exploitatively imitated the second half of this work in his genre and purpose, in some themes, characters, and episodes, and in the whole outline of the quest, while silently transforming and excelling it in style and technique.

Unlike Ariosto's influence, which Spenser acknowledges by clear imitation in the proposition (I Proem 1.9), Hawes's influence is never acknowledged. I cannot claim Spenser was rewriting Hawes conspicuously, as he did Ariosto. Yet a genetic study such as this can contribute to the understanding of meaning insofar as the author's adaptations of these raw materials provide clues to his emphasis— clues that are especially helpful in a genre like romance, whose individual exemplars are, as A. C. Hamilton has recently remarked, so much alike.[5] Such a study can also highlight the distinctive aesthetic qualities of the author.

As Alastair Fowler says, *The Faerie Queene* is to a rare degree a hybrid of romance and allegory. In most works of literature, he explains, allegory is not a genre but a mode or structural principle that simply modulates a genre, as it does the romance-epic genre of Tasso's *Gerusalemme liberata*. In *The Faerie Queene*, allegory is more definitive than this and "may be thought prominent and pervasive enough to constitute a hybrid." Fowler does not consider Hawes, but some have challenged for him the distinction of creating this hybrid. In the mind of C. S. Lewis, allegory makes Spenser the heir of Hawes: "In order to fulfil the demand that the poet should be a moral teacher he decided that he would follow Hawes as well as the Italians. His poem was to be a romance of chivalry, but it was also to have a secondary meaning

---

Kinds of Literature: An Introduction to the Theory of Genres and Modes (Cambridge, Mass.: Harvard University Press, 1982). Barbara Lewalski traces Milton's practice of a genre that is mixed in the sense not only of hybridization but of alternation—one genre set within another—in *"Paradise Lost" and the Rhetoric of Literary Forms* (Princeton: Princeton University Press, 1985), pp. 5, 23, et passim. Studies of adversarial imitation are exemplified by Harold Bloom, *The Anxiety of Influence* (Oxford: Oxford University Press, 1973), and its multitudinous and rebellious progeny.

5. A. C. Hamilton, "Elizabethan Prose Fiction and Some Trends in Recent Criticism," *RenQ*, 37 (1980), 21–33. My defense of source criticism is indebted to Professor Alice Colby-Hall, Cornell University.

throughout."[6] While these generalizations may not apply to some books of *The Faerie Queene*, they apply fairly well to the Legend of Holiness. But they fail to specify which book of *The Faerie Queene* they refer to, and Lewis focused on the wrong poem of Hawes. Once the right poem of Hawes is aligned with the right book of *The Faerie Queene*, we shall find that Hawes even predominates and that he showed Spenser how to bring the Italians into accord with the moral and religious norm invoked by Ascham. Patrick Cullen gives the best summary to date—because of its emphasis on the *Example* and on Book I—of Spenser's indebtedness to Hawes: "If we were to combine the *Example of Virtue*'s triumph over the infernal triad through a true love with the *Pastime of Pleasure*'s succumbing to the infernal triad through a false love, we would be very close to the general outline of Book I of *The Faerie Queene*."[7] Yet even his fundamental study, close to the mark as it is, overstates and misplaces the influence of the *Passetyme* and thereby underestimates that of the *Example*. While both romances admittedly adumbrate Spenser's genre, I propose that the *Example* alone contributed anything distinctive to Redcross's part of the legend.

II

Romance and allegory took several steps toward each other in the Middle Ages, but it was not until the sixteenth century that they fused. The difference that for centuries appeared irreconcilable was the central and at least potentially positive place which romance accords to sexual love. Prudentius couched his *Psychomachia*, a pure allegory about the personified Seven Deadly Sins, in terms of warfare—plot material characteristic of epic and contributory to romance (a genre as yet unborn in the West); and works of verbal and visual art imitated

6. Fowler, *Kinds*, p. 192; C. S. Lewis, *Studies in Medieval and Renaissance Literature*, ed. Walter Hooper (Cambridge: Cambridge University Press, 1966), p. 131; see also *The Allegory of Love* (Oxford: Oxford University Press, 1936), p. 310. Helen Hennessy concludes her article "The Uniting of Romance and Allegory in *La Queste del Saint Graal*" with some interesting remarks on *Faerie Queene* I in particular as a marriage of romance and allegory (*Boston University Studies in English*, 4 [1960], 199–200).

7. Patrick Cullen, *The Infernal Triad* (Princeton: Princeton University Press, 1974), p. 13.

Prudentius's fusion. In the thirteenth century, the erotic side of romance (which chiefly distinguishes it from epic) was made the subject,
not the vehicle, of an allegory in the *Roman de la Rose*, with again
some imagery of warfare. In the same century, romance had been
discordantly yoked with its Christian counterpart, the saint's legend,
and even with passages from the Bible, by the Cistercians and their
imitators in the Grail romances. Their hermits and other *raisonneurs*
cast aspersions on the principal goals of romance heroes, winning a
lady and achieving martial exploits, thus anticipating Ascham and the
hermit Contemplation.[8] Any major hero except Galahad can sin and
make mistakes as does Redcross. Isolated passages—first in the *Queste
del Saint Graal* in the Arthurian Prose Cycle and then in Malory's
Sankgreal—even allegorize the Seven Deadly Sins as is done in pure
allegories and in *Faerie Queene* I.v.[9] Here was a type of romance which
would have measured up to Ascham's standard of seriousness. But
these pre-Spenserian romances, like Tasso's romance-epic, are not allegorical enough to hybridize the genre. They are not even true romances, as Tasso's is, only romances manqué, because the element of
"faithfull loues" is absent or summarily condemned. According to
these works, knights ought ideally to vow perpetual virginity, and they
should under no circumstances follow their usual practice of taking
their ladies with them on their quest. The only women of a virtue

8. When I refer to the Grail romances, I mean Chrétien's unfinished *Perceval*, the
Queste del Saint Graal in the Arthurian Prose Cycle, and Malory's Books 13–17.
Nancy Freeman-Regalado points out in particular that in them, "knights . . . worry
about bloodshed." See "*La Chevalerie Celestiel*," in Kevin Brownlee and Marina Scor-
dilis Brownlee, eds., *Romance: Generic Transformations from Chrétien de Troyes to
Cervantes* (Hanover, N.H.: University Press of New England, 1985), pp. 95–96. In the
introduction to her translation of the *Quest*, Pauline Matarasso goes even further: "All
the accepted values are inverted. The *Quest* sets out to reveal the inadequacies and the
dangers of the courtly ideal." See *The Quest of the Holy Grail* (Harmondsworth, Eng.:
Penguin, 1969), Introduction, p. 15. Furthermore, in *The Redemption of Chivalry*
(Geneva: Droz, 1979), Matarasso argues that the *Quest* carries a sort of allegory—a
biblical typological level—throughout. In an as yet unpublished study, "Transformations of Romance in the Legend of Holiness," I make similar claims for parts of *Faerie
Queene* Book I.
9. Seven knightly antagonists are allegorized as the Seven Deadly Sins, their castle
full of captive maidens as the souls in hell, and Galahad their deliverer as Christ
harrowing hell in Malory, *Works*, Book XIII, ed. Eugène Vinaver (Oxford: Clarendon
Press, 1967), II.892, ll. 2–6 and 9–10, and in *The Quest*, trans. Matarasso, chap. 4, p.
79.

worth remarking upon who are encountered on the Grail-quest are Perceval's sister and his aunt.

Not only high seriousness but allegory prevailed over romance in 1483 in *Le Chevalier délibéré* by Olivier de La Marche, the Burgundian court poet who also played a role in the court of Edward IV of England. In 1569, La Marche's work was translated into English (with adaptations to his own creed and country) by Stephen Batman or Bateman as *The Travayled Pylgrime*. Many editions were printed by Spenser's time, including three—a French edition, a Spanish edition which Bateman used, and Bateman's English version—which were enhanced by attractive woodcuts.[10] Then *Le Chevalier délibéré* was imitated on the Continent by the Carmelite Jean Cartigny in *Le Voyage du chevalier errant* (Antwerp, 1572), which was in turn translated into English by William Goodyear in 1581 as *The Wandering Knight*.[11] Throughout these four related and most serious works, romance is pervasively diluted with allegory to about the same thinness as in the House of Holiness (*FQ* I.x). These works anticipate Spenser's allegorization of the armor of a romance hero according to the armor of a Christian in Ephesians 6. So familiar was this strategy that Goodyear-Cartigny's very errant knight wears armor that parodies it—a Buckler of Shamelessness, for example, instead of the Shield of Faith. Indeed, the message of these works is sometimes sermoned at large by the authorial persona to the reader, not couched in narrative at all; Goodyear-Cartigny quotes the Lord's Prayer and the Ten Commandments *en bloc*. Bateman-La Marche's authorial sermons are shorter and more closely related to the story. In Spenser's more organic fusion of

10. La Marche's first edition was in French, 1486, published either at Gouda or at Antwerp. I cite from Stephen Bateman's translation, *The Travayled Pylgrime* (London, 1569), STC No. 1585. I owe most of my knowledge of La Marche to Anne Lake Prescott, both to her essay "Spenser's Chivalric Restoration," *SP*, forthcoming, and to our exchanges of ideas. For a bibliography of *Le Chevalier délibéré*, see Gordon Kipling, *The Triumph*, p. 154 n. 11. Kipling claims that other allegorical romances were composed in Burgundy, but he cites only the imitation of La Marche by Cartigny (1572); staged allegorical tournaments, which cannot be classed as romances; Deguileville's *Pèlerinage*, which I call a romance manqué because it lacks a love interest; and courtesy books, chivalric manuals, and books of advice to princes (see pp. 19, 22, 154). See also Kathryn Koller, "*The Travayled Pylgrime* by Stephen Batman and Book Two of *The Faerie Queene*," *MLQ*, 3 (1942), 535–41.

11. I cite from William Goodyear's translation of Cartigny, *The Wandering Knight*, ed. Dorothy Atkinson Evans (Seattle: University of Washington Press, 1951).

romance with allegory, the brief and rare moral addresses of the author to the reader are usually relegated to a special place—the stanza introducing a canto.

As Anne Lake Prescott has pointed out, *The Travayled Pylgrime* evinces some situational and narrative similarities to the Legend of Holiness. The Pilgrim strays into the minor error of rather enjoying a visit to a Castle of This World or Palace of Disordered Livers, which is decorated with gold and inhabited, as in Spenser, by lustful, ambitious worldlings. (A similar castle appears also in Goodyear-Cartigny, and the hero participates in the sins of the inhabitants [I.7–13 ad init.].) Without actually participating, the Pilgrim departs on the advice of his companions Memory and Reason, thus prefiguring Redcross's departure on the advice of the Dwarf, who is sometimes interpreted as Reason. (There is no comparable adviser in Goodyear-Cartigny.) Like Redcross, though with less cause, he subsequently feels guilty before God, repents, and is restored. As Prescott concedes, the last part of the romance—the struggle with Age, Dolor, Debilitie, and Death—seems to have contributed nothing to Spenser. Indeed, Age is central to the entire poem in a way quite alien to the Legend of Holiness. Less romantic still, the Goodyear-Cartigny romance contains no combat, only a quest. All four works are innocent of any love interest and hence qualify only as romances manqué. Although Spenser borrowed some motifs from this group of related works, they are piecemeal rather than pervasive sources, and they constitute only rudimentary generic precedents.

While he must have admired the pervasiveness of their allegory, Spenser evidently disliked the summary way in which the allegorical would-be romances purged all sexual emotion. Part of his delight in allegory sprang from the fact that *eros* could be made to symbolize *agape*. One way of doing this is to make the beloved symbolic. Within the romance genre, his heroine Una represents a combination of the romance damsel in distress (to be won in marriage by fulfilling a quest) with the romance damsel as guide—Lunette in Chrétien's *Yvain*, Lynette and the Damsel Maldisaunt in Malory. So much might account for her role in the plot, but the imagery tells us that she symbolizes something transcendent. While not unknown in other genres, a symbolic beloved had recently been introduced into romance, as we shall see, in Hawes's *Example of Vertue*.

A few critics have recognized that at times Una symbolizes among other things the biblical Sapience.[12] Sapience appears chiefly in the deuterocanonical books of the Bible, books still familiar in Spenser's time but little read today, especially by Protestants and Jews, who designate them as "Apocrypha."[13] Sapience is extolled by name in Spenser's "Hymne of Heavenly Beauty," occupying more than twice as many lines as God himself (God, 134–82; Sapience, 183–287). The biblical Sapience provided the model for several magisterial person-ifications in a number of medieval allegorical works: Sapientia in Au-gustine's *Soliloquies*, Philosophy in Boethius's *Consolation*, Sapientia in Prudentius's *Psychomachia*, Sapienza in Dante's *Convivio*, Beatrice in his *Commedia* (who has occasionally been associated with Una),[14] and Sapience in the late medieval *Court of Sapience*, which served as a model for both the poems by Hawes which Lewis and others relate to *The Faerie Queene*. Unlike the typical romance heroine, a Sapience figure quests for the man she has in charge; he need not quest for her. The biblical Sapience and Una compete for dominance and sometimes for sexual status with a bad female: just as Una competes with Duessa for Redcross, so Sapience (Prov. 7–9), like the wife (Prov. 5), competes with the strange woman (Prov. 4–6) for the attentions of Everyman. The principal guide in *The Example of Vertue* is named Sapience; while her relationship to the hero is not sexual, she too follows him around and warns him against a bad female. As William Murison says, "the prominent part assigned to Wisdom and Discretion" (her sister and deputy) manifests "the influence of the wisdom-literature of the Old Testament and the Apocrypha."[15] Una as allegorical female tour

---

12. F. M. Padelford says accurately, if somewhat confusedly, that Una is sometimes "more social" than is Sapience "for purposes of romance," but that finally she "reveals herself to [Redcross] in her eternal aspect" (*Variorum* I.434). In *The Structure of Allegory in "The Faerie Queene"* (Oxford: Oxford University Press, 1961), A. C. Hamilton identifies Una with Wisdom both because she reenacts Ecclus. 4:17–19 (p. 35) and because she uses proverbs (p. 87). See also his edition of *The Faerie Queene*, at I.i.13.4. James Nohrnberg identifies Una with Wisdom because she reenacts Ecclus. 21.22–23: *The Analogy of "The Faerie Queene"* (Princeton: Princeton University Press, 1976), pp. 142–43, 221.

13. For evidence of their liturgical prominence, see Article VI of the Thirty-Nine Articles, and Carol Kaske, "Bible," in *Spenser Encyclopedia*, ed. A. C. Hamilton et al. (Toronto: University of Toronto Press, forthcoming).

14. See, e.g., Hamilton, *Structure of Allegory*, pp. 30–43, passim.

15. William Murison, "Stephen Hawes," *The Cambridge History of English Litera-ture*, ed. A. W. Ward and A. R. Waller (Cambridge: Cambridge University Press, 1907–27), II.223–38.

guide and Sapience figure within a romance plays the same role as Hawes's magisterial personification Sapience and hence derives most immediately from her. We shall see that Una as allegorical beloved derives from Hawes's heroine Clennes.

III

As several perceptive literary historians have pointed out, Stephen Hawes was the first original English poet to effect a genuine fusion of allegory and romance,[16] thus challenging and contributing to the generic uniqueness of the Legend of Holiness. Hawes wrote *The Example of Vertue* in 1503/4 and published it in 1509/10; his *Passetyme of Pleasure* appeared soon after, in 1510. Thus, it is possible that he knew La Marche, but not the other allegorical would-be romances or Ascham. Incidentally, Hawes's works likewise contained custom-made woodcuts, which added to the vividness of the text, though the workmanship was poor.

The pervasive but unacknowledged generic model of *Faerie Queene* Book I is *The Example of Vertue*. Granted, the first and overtly didactic part of the *Example*—the debate of Sapience with Fortune, Hardiness, and Nature—seems to have contributed nothing to the Legend of Holiness beyond the characterization of Sapience (chap. v), which Spenser admittedly could have found in the other Sapience figures

16. C. S. Lewis says, "The combination of allegory on a large scale and chivalrous romance which Hawes wants to revive, could not be revived because it had not existed. There had been some approach to it in Deguileville: but Hawes carries it much further, and we shall not find the thing in perfection till we reach *The Faerie Queene*" (*Allegory*, p. 279); "in order to fulfil the demand that the poet should be a moral teacher he decided that he would follow Hawes as well as the Italians. His poem was to be a romance of chivalry, but it was also to have a secondary meaning throughout" (*Studies*, p. 131). Cullen, because of his loose definition of romance as including pilgrimage allegories, credits Deguileville with the invention of "allegorical romance" (p. 5), but he also stresses the generic innovativeness of Hawes (pp. 5–67, passim, esp. pp. 7–13). See also John N. King, "Allegorical Pattern in Stephen Hawes's *The Pastime of Pleasure*," *Studies in the Literary Imagination*, 11 (1978), 57, 59; A. S. G. Edwards, *Stephen Hawes* (Boston: Twayne, 1983), esp. p. 94. I have used *The Works of Hawes*, ed. Frank J. Spang (Delmar, N.Y.: Scholars' Facsimiles & Reprints, 1975); like the original, it contains neither line nor stanza numbers, only chapter and signature numbers. For the *Example*, I have also used *Minor Poems*, ed. Florence W. Gluck and Alice B. Morgan, EETS OS 271 (Oxford: Oxford University Press, 1974), and for the *Passetyme*, *The Pastime of Pleasure*, ed. William E. Mead, EETS OS 173 (London: H. Milford, Oxford University Press, 1928).

mentioned above. This first section (along with the poet's conventional concluding pleas for tolerance of his faults, the favor of his ruler, and the salvation of his soul) is also the only part of the work that resembles a free-standing sermon.

I begin with a synopsis by a disinterested interpreter of the *Example*, A. S. G. Edwards: "It makes a more compressed attempt [than does the *Passetyme*] to focus centrally on the problems of man's spiritual health and well-being, eschewing the . . . digressions" (p. 60); and the latter half of the poem . . . crams five distinct episodes into barely a thousand lines: the encounter with temptations, the meeting with the King of Love, the fight with the dragon, the marriage, and the final vision of Heaven and Hell. . . . The briefly described battle with the three-headed dragon is wholly Christian in the orientation of its allegory" (p. 67).

All five episodes are paralleled in *Faerie Queene* I. In each work, a sovereign sets as a condition of winning the hand of his daughter in marriage the conquest of a dragon—in the *Example*:

> As to scomfyte the dragon with heedes thre
> That is a serpent of grete subtylte
> Which well betokeneth as we do fynde
> The world the flesshe and the deuyll. (chap. 11, sig. ee viii)

In *The Faerie Queene*, the dragon likewise betokens the devil (Argument to I.xi). Spenser's dragon was "bred in the loathly lakes of Tartary" (vii.44). Hawes's dragon "lay in a marys in a grete lake / Whiche was moche stynkynge foule and blake" (sig. ee viii) and Tartarus or hell is the dragon's home, as Hawes tells us later (sig. ff ii^v). In contrast, in the other allegorical would-be romances (and indeed for the most part in medieval romance at large), none of the antagonists are animals, let alone dragons.[17] Spenser split two of the episodes: he parceled out Hawes's king into two sovereigns—the Faerie Queene, who gave Red-

---

17. Similar dragon fights of some importance do occur in a few other pure romances before Spenser, but without the hybridization of allegory, and each lacks some essential feature: the popular Saint George legend, a Christian romance cited by Spenser, does not reward the dragon slayer with the princess's hand in marriage; conversely, the romances that do give a princess in marriage to the dragon slayer—*Sir Bevis of Hampton* and *Guy of Warwick*—while ending on a religious note, are not pervasively religious like the Legend of Holiness. See *The Romance of Sir Beues of Hamtoun*, ed. Eugen Kölbing, Part I, EETS ES 46 (1885), and Part II, EETS ES 48 (1886); *The Romance of Guy of Warwick*, ed. Julius Zupitza, Part I, EETS ES 42 (1883), and Part II, EETS ES 49 (1887).

cross the quest (I.vii.46–47; "Letter to Raleigh"), and Una's father the king of Eden, who, according to a hitherto unmentioned proclamation, rewards Redcross with his daughter's hand in marriage (I.xii.19–20)—and he parceled out Hawes's final episode, the vision of heaven and hell, giving the vision of hell to the villain (I.v) and making the vision of heaven a prelude to the dragon fight (I.x), so that it might serve as additional inspiration to the hero. The vision of heaven cannot come at the very end as it does in Hawes's poem (and in Goodyear-Cartigny's *Wandering Knight*), because within the time covered by *The Faerie Queene* Spenser's hero does not die or even retire permanently from his martial career as do the others.

And there are further correspondences. Hawes's hero is initially said to be naive and is tempted, although unlike Redcross he does not fall.[18] Like Redcross, Hawes's hero improves, winning in the process a new and more honorific name. Sapience promises him victory through the virtues his arms symbolize—

This is the armure for the soule
That in his epystole wrote saynt Poule
Good hope thy legge harneys shall be
The habergyn of ryghtwysnes gyrde with chastyte (chap. 11, sig. ee viii^v)

—and so on through the armor of God listed in Ephesians 6.11–17, just as Spenser allegorizes the armor Una presents to Redcross in the "Letter to Raleigh."[19] As Cullen notes (pp. 8–9), Hawes, like Spenser, confronts the hero with two bad women, one offering him her body, the other holding a cup and ensconced in a castle—figures that would have been easily recombinable into the literal and moral levels of Duessa and Lucifera.[20]

---

18. The romance precedents for Redcross's fall are found in the Grail romances—in the erring knights Lancelot, Bors, and Perceval—and in Goodyear-Cartigny, the only allegorical would-be romance in which the hero falls into a sin of a gravity comparable to that of Redcross. Aside from this similarity of plot and the many biblical references that inevitably accompany sermons such as those in Goodyear-Cartigny, the analogies Evans draws to the Legend of Holiness are not very close (Introduction, *Wandering Knight*, pp. xliii-xlvii).

19. Armor explicitly identified as that in Ephesians occurs also in *Passetyme*, chap. 23, sig. l v-v^v.

20. Furthermore, in the *Example*, the hero's intended sends him into battle with a speech—"O vertuous knyght you for me have dured / In grete wo and payne"—

The secondary guide of Redcross (Una's Dwarf) and of Hawes's hero (Sapience's sister Discretion) resemble each other in their respective actions and divisions of labor with their superiors. Discretion helps Hawes's hero resist the lady with a castle who carries a cup of gold and offers him worldly advancement, just as the Dwarf, appealing to practical reason, admonishes Redcross to leave Lucifera's castle. Critics have not seen this parallel, perhaps because of the different sexes of the secondary guides. Since Discretion is almost a double of her sister Sapience, some of her other actions, such as the condemnation of the lustful woman, are simply transferred to Una. Before Hawes's hero meets the bad women, there is a purely verbal resemblance to Spenser's title, the undeveloped remark that on a green beside a river "there daunst also the fayre [fayrye] quene" (chap. 9, sig. ee ii^v).

Hawes's damsel Clennes resembles Una in being at the same time a literal woman, loving and lovable on the literal level, yet something more, bringing as her dowry the right to heaven. Redcross's fiancée acquires overtones of the New Jerusalem, "the bride, the Lamb's wife" (Rev. 19:7–9, 21:2, 9–11), thus becoming a fit mate for someone who in the preceding canto symbolized Christ; Hawes's bride Clennes symbolizes that purity of heart and body which will merit the Beatific Vision (Matt. 7:8).[21] The symbolism of each heroine here becomes eschatological, thus contributing to the eschatological overtones of her betrothal or wedding.

Another way to rehabilitate sexual love is to make the *eros* itself a symbol or a synecdoche of something higher. This consideration recalls the striking thematic resemblance that C. S. Lewis noted between the *Example* and another of Spenser's poems: "the sort of unification or ambiguity" between *eros* and *agape* "on which Spenser's sixty-eighth sonnet is based" (*Allegory*, p. 286). The wedding in the *Example* resembles Redcross's betrothal in ways beyond the conventional: each

---

anticipatory of Una's speech at a similar point: "Deare knight . . . / That all these sorrowes suffer for my sake" (*Example*, chap. 11, sig. ff i; *FQ* I.xi.1.7–9). At one point the dragon catches Hawes's hero in his claws as in *Faerie Queene* I.xi.18–19. One of the hero's early trials is a "mase," glossed as "the besynes of worldely fastion" (i.e., "fashion"; see Gluck and Morgan's note, chap. 9, 1206–11), suggesting, as Cullen points out (pp. 8–9), the Wandering Wood. A door to an allegorical castle is opened by its "warde" Humility (*Example*, chap. 3, sig. aa viii; cf. *FQ* I.x.5).

21. For the early history of the concept "Clenes," after which the heroine is named, see Michael Twomey, "The Anatomy of Sin: Violations of *Kynde* and *Trawpe* in 'Cleanness,'" (Ph.D. diss., Cornell University, 1979), pp. 1–21.

has both erotic appeal and eschatological symbolism—in Hawes, angels and long-dead saints and doctors of the church officiate. Both poets make their respective ceremonies into mystical experiences for the lover. But Spenser overgoes his predecessor in subtlety. Whereas Hawes chiefly expresses the unification or ambiguity through the lady's father, the King of Love, who has the attributes of Cupid and acts and is addressed like God the Father, Spenser does not strain to equate God with Cupid but simply fuses the divine and human songs and leaves larger unities to the reader's imagination:

> one sung a song of loue and iollity.

> During the which there was an heauenly noise
> Heard sound through all the Pallace pleasantly,
> Like as it had bene many an Angels voice,
> Singing before th'eternall maiesty,
> In their trinall triplicities on hye;
> Yet wist no creature, whence that heauenly sweet
> Proceeded, yet eachone felt secretly
> Himselfe thereby reft of his sences meet,
> And rauished with rare impression in his sprite. (I.xii.38–39)

Besides Revelation 19:6–7, inspiration for this passage came from Hawes's wedding music, with its fusion of heavenly and earthly joy:

> And aungels came downe from heven hye
> As saynt Mychell with gabryell and the gerachye
> To helpe saynt peter the masse to synge
> The organs went and the bellys dyd rynge
> My penne for feblenes may not now wryte
> Nor my tonge for domnes may not expresse
> Nor my mynde for neglygence may not endyte
> Of the aungelycall Ioye and swete gladnesse
> That I sawe there without heuynesse.[22]

Hawes also anticipated Spenser's Christian-humanist fusion of heavenly and earthly love in setting the initial courtship in Clennes's garden of innocent "recreacyon." The garden serves not only as a literal moral

---

22. Chap. 13, sig. gg iv[v]. The concrete details, though not in this case their symbolism, may also have contributed to the wedding music in the "Epithalamion."

example but as an anagogical foretaste of her promised inheritance, heaven, which is also described as a garden (chap. 12, sig. gg ii) and to which the couple go at the end of the poem (chap. 12). "Loue is the lesson which the Lord vs taught."

It may be helpful to fictionalize the order of composition to express the relation of various borrowings. Eclectic though he is, Spenser seems to have used the *Example*'s plot as the principal framework for Redcross's plot. He fleshed this out from widely scattered sources, including the Grail-quest romances, Goodyear-Cartigny's *Wandering Knight*, Bateman-La Marche's *Travayled Pylgrime,* the Book of Revelation, and, in spots, the Italian romance-epic.

IV

Even those critics who have pursued in detail the importance of Hawes for Spenser have made too much of the *Passetyme*. Lewis said it was "the English poem which probably influenced him most" (*Studies,* pp. 130–31). Perhaps misled by this remark, Cullen blames its heroine La Belle Pucell for such evil as the hero falls into, and makes her the prototype of Spenser's false love Duessa.[23] But there is nothing false about La Belle Pucell, nor is she the motive or occasion for the decision the hero finally regrets. She is if anything the opponent of the infernal triad; her limitation is that she is merely a damsel, a temporal good. It was not anything in the *Passetyme*, but the outright seductress in the *Example*, along with the biblical Whore of Babylon of course, who served as model for Spenser's false love. To be sure, the love of Grand Amour for La Belle Pucell in the *Passetyme* reads like a preliminary sketch of Arthur's love for the Faerie Queene, associated as it is with fame and proving one's worthiness to wed a woman of higher rank, and limited as it is to this world. But many parts of the *Passetyme*, such as the long Godfrey Gobelive episode, were unused by Spenser,

---

23. Cullen, pp. 9–13; cf. King, pp. 57–64, passim. Close as he is to the mark on the influence of Hawes and of the *Example* in particular, Cullen seems to me to exaggerate when he says the infernal triad and the pilgrimage are dominant motifs in the Legend of Holiness. King, on the other hand, by not specifying that La Belle Pucell actually anticipates Duessa but simply identifying her with earthly joy and pleasure, escapes my criticism; he simply asserts in general terms the influence of these episodes of the *Passetyme* on *The Faerie Queene.*

whereas in the romantic last thousand lines of the *Example*, only the crossing of the sword-bridge does not find its way into *Faerie Queene* Book I in some form. It is therefore appropriate to rephrase Cullen's statement (quoted at the outset) as follows: if we were to combine Hawes's two romances—the *Example* focused on salvation and the *Passetyme* focused (until the very end) on temporal success in love and honor—we would be very close to the general outlines of Redcross's story in Book I and of Arthur's story both in the poem as we have it and in its projected though unachieved end.

Aside from our difference as to which poem is more important for Spenser, Lewis, King, Cullen, and I stand united against those who deny or minimize the influence of Hawes on him—chiefly Tuve, the editors of Hawes, and the general editor of the first volume of the *Variorum*, whom I take to be Padelford.[24] The current focus on hybrid genres and on unities more artificial than organic highlights the generic innovation of Hawes. In Spenser's creative process, Hawes acted as go-between (with a little help from the Grail romances and Olivier de La Marche and his translators and imitators) by crossing romance, especially its female character types, with corresponding elements in the medieval allegorical poem. In the past, Spenser's indebtedness to the *Example* has been concealed by two different assumptions about intertextuality, the one too atomistic, the other too holistic. Those who think in terms of isolated topoi and motifs see the similarities but, like the *Variorum* editor, are persuaded by the commonness of the individual motifs to find them unremarkable: "The list of resemblances is certainly impressive when regarded in its entirety, but when examined item by item it is found to contain only the commonplaces of the romances, of the homilies, of the morality poems and plays, and allegorical paintings and tapestries." For example, "the armour of the Christian as described by St. Paul is constantly referred to in homilies and ecclesiastical writings." Naturally; but what other *romancier* besides Hawes and Spenser portrays an allegorical female guide giving such armor to the hero before he fights a dragon in order to win a

---

24. *Variorum* I.418. For Tuve see below. Of the editors of Hawes, Mead's doubts regarding Spenser's debt to the *Passetyme* are expressed on pp. cxi-cxii; Gluck and Morgan's regarding the *Example*, on p. xlvii. See also Kipling, *Triumph*, p. 155.

princess? Indebtedness can be established even though the material consists of commonplaces when a constellation of them recurs, as here, and in similar order.

The second kind of dismissal comes from those who view the source as a cause of the work, somehow determining the author's greatness. They say correctly with Tuve that *"The Faerie Queene . . .* resembles Hawes so little in all that makes us enjoy reading" but falsely continue that "all the parallels in the studies have been unable to tie the two men together in an important way" and conclude that Spenser "is no more likely than we to have read the poor and neglected the good" (p. 371 and n. 24). A recent and interesting failure may inspire a poet, unlike a common reader, to improve upon it. Next to doing something unattempted yet in prose or rhyme, perhaps it is most satisfying to do something that has been attempted and done badly, even if the source was so bad as to be not worth acknowledging. This is a kind of imitation that G. W. Pigman—refining Thomas Greene's second kind, "eclectic" or "exploitative"—calls "dissimulative" and "transformative" imitation; and he acknowledges that establishing it requires a genetic study such as this one.[25] The Saint George story to which Spenser alludes had been rendered "ridiculous" both by popularization in the crude art of village churches and, as William Nelson says, in the "accretions of impossible adventure and the buffoonery of village St. George plays."[26] Indeed the romance genre as a whole, though gloriously reborn in Italy as the romance-epic, had never, with a few notable exceptions, attained much literary distinction in England. *The Shepheardes Calender* contains in its title, emblems, and calendrical structure a more overt and clearly transformative imitation of the almost subliterary form the farmer's almanac (*The Calendar of Shepherds* and its French predecessors), a form appealing to a taste much

---

25. G. W. Pigman III, "Versions of Imitation in the Renaissance," *RenQ*, 33 (1980), 1–32, esp. 3–11, 26 and n. 36, and 32; Thomas Greene, *A Light in Troy: Imitation and Discovery in Renaissance Poetry* (New Haven: Yale University Press, 1982), pp. 39–40.

26. William Nelson, *The Poetry of Edmund Spenser* (New York: Columbia University Press, 1960), p. 150. This represents a class-conscious view of something C. S. Lewis celebrated, Spenser's use of popular material (*Allegory*, pp. 310–12). A few readers defend Hawes for being at least experimental: Alistair Fox has recently praised Hawes for putting romance conventions to a new use in another work. See "Stephen Hawes and the Political Allegory of *The Comfort of Lovers*," *ELR*, 17 (1987), 3–21.

lower than that which could stomach Hawes.[27] Spenser seems from these examples to have enjoyed improving upon vulgar and even crude models: so why not upon Hawes? The denials that Hawes influenced Spenser often seem to spring from fear that if Spenser borrowed from an inept poet he too must be judged inept; but the current recognition of the active and even adversarial nature of imitation allows us to acknowledge at last his imitation in Book I of Hawes's *Example of Vertue.*

27. The *Calender*'s imitation of *The Calendar of Shepherds*, mentioned by E. K., has been acknowledged by critics at least as early as J. J. Jusserand (*Variorum* VII.581; see also Courthope, 582, and Greenlaw, 594). For an important recent treatment, see Ruth Samson Luborsky, "The Allusive Presentation of *The Shepheardes Calender*," *Spenser Studies*, 1 (1980), esp. 30, 43 and n. 36, 54–57. See also, in the same volume, Bruce R. Smith, "On Reading *The Shepheardes Calender*," esp. pp. 71–73 and n. 3, 82–85.

7

The Circular Argument of
The Shepheardes Calender

DONALD CHENEY

Spenser's determination, in *The Shepheardes Calender*, to acknowledge and assimilate the fullest possible range of literary predecessors, as well as some predecessors that might be called sub- or extraliterary, produced a work that frustrates attempts at systematic analysis. Since his allusions are to texts that are themselves highly allusive or ambiguous, the meanings generated multiply too rapidly for a reader to accommodate them. A reading of the poem is an experience of flickering glimpses of rustic calendar and classic eclogue-book, goat-talk and sheep-talk, or what E. K. distinguishes as the "three formes or ranckes" of plaintive, moral, and recreative song.[1] We see here something like the "interlace" found in romance narrative: alternating motifs call attention to each other and to the variations of detail or context in which they recur. This multifariousness can be delightful in itself; for the anonymous "Immeritô" it is a necessary strategy as well. Spenser's presentation of himself as England's new poet gains authority in proportion as he can stake out a domain of national dimensions and show that in all respects he is heir to a literary tradition that has been recast in a distinctively British form and made to survive because of his mastery of it.

At the same time, and by the same logic, he must do more than point

---

1. Throughout, I quote Spenser from the *Variorum.*

to these various regions of language and gesture: he must provide a structure that contains or comprehends them. In an essay that has influenced a generation of Spenser studies, A. C. Hamilton described one such structure as the linear "argument" of generic progression, classically associated with Virgil, whereby the neophyte poet proves himself in pastoral before proceeding through georgic to the full maturity and responsibility of an epic undertaking.[2] By this argument, at the end of the *Calender* the young poet has exhausted the possibilities of the pastoral genre and "died" to it, as Colin Clout claims to do, leaving its world and concerns behind him; we are not surprised, therefore, when *The Faerie Queene* opens with a translation of Virgil's own announcement of his transition from pastoral to epic. In the present essay, I want to supplement Hamilton's thesis, and suggest that we should not be surprised, either, to find Spenser's poetry returning to Colin Clout and even to that cycle of the months which both evinces Mutabilitie's claims and finally denies them. In merging the tradition of classic pastoral with that of the calendar or almanac (as embodied by such different works as Ovid's *Fasti* and the popular *Kalender and Compost of Shepherdes*), Spenser enclosed his linear argument within a circular framework that implied renewal and return. The one argument points toward epic and the celebration of historical fulfillment; the other implies the recurrences of romance. I think that careful attention to the intertextual patterns of Spenser's allusions will reveal that the importance of the calendar to his shepherds is even greater and more pervasive than we have thought.[3] Spenser invokes tragic figures—Hip-

2. A. C. Hamilton, "The Argument of Spenser's *Shepheardes Calender*," *ELH*, 23 (1956), 171–82. This sequence from pastoral through georgic to epic was known as the *rota Vergilii*, in reference to the display as segments of a circle or wheel of the various social ranks, trees, locales, etc., associated with each genre. See Ernst Robert Curtius, *European Literature and the Latin Middle Ages*, trans. Willard R. Trask (New York: Pantheon, 1953; first pub. 1948), p. 232. I know of no suggestion of cyclical return in this term as it was traditionally conceived or employed.

3. Mary Parmenter, "Spenser's 'Twelue Aeglogues Proportionable to the Twelue Monethes,'" *ELH*, 3 (1936), 190–217, demonstrated that contemporary debate over calendar reform gave a topical urgency to Spenser's choice of a calendrical format. Gregory XIII had proposed in 1577 (and would enact in 1582) a revision of the Julian calendar that was broadly opposed by English Protestants as a symbol of Roman hegemony. The uncertain state of contemporary chronography, and the conflicting interests at stake, are reflected by E. K.'s discussion of whether the year should begin in January; by the poet's concluding uncertainty whether he has "marked well the starres reuolution"; and (perhaps) by the fact that the volume appeared with the imprint of the controversial Hugh Singleton, publisher of John Stubbs's *Discoverie of a Gaping Gulf*.

polytus, Adonis, Dido—only to deny them their tragic valence: although his calendar ends in wintry December, a counterplot opposes Colin Clout's pessimistic view of the year as mirror of his life, and reminds us that spring is not far behind.

Iniusta Nouerca

In an apparently simple instance of Spenser's quoting of pastoral *topoi*, Willye urges Thomalin to describe his encounter with Cupid, promising to watch the other's sheep in the meantime:

> Thomalin, haue no care for thy,
> My selfe will haue a double eye,
>   Ylike to my flocke and thine:
> For als at home I haue a syre,
> A stepdame eke as whott as fyre,
>   That dewly adayes counts mine. ("March" 37–42)

E. K. notes that the last lines imitate Virgil's third eclogue, where Menalcas is about to engage in an amoebaean singing match (like that which Willye undertakes in the other eclogue where he appears, "August"): "est mihi namque domi pater, est iniusta nouerca, / bisque die numerant ambo pecus, alter et haedos" (33–34: "for at home I have a father, and a cruel stepmother, and twice a day both of them count the sheep, and the latter counts the goats as well").

There is nothing unusual here about the offer to watch while the other sings; this is a fixture of pastoral, and in fact the same Menalcas makes such an offer (promising that Tityrus will do the watching) in Virgil's fifth eclogue, when he urges Mopsus to sing his lament for Daphnis: "incipe; pascentis seruabit Tityrus haedos" (12). But in the lines from the third eclogue Menalcas is explaining why he cannot put up any of his flock as a prize; his problems at home have nothing to do with his willingness or ability to watch two flocks at once. Willye, if not Spenser, seems to have confused two different kinds of "double eye" in this borrowing of pastoral gesture.

Perhaps this misappropriation of *topoi* is part of the eclogue's comedy, an instance of "comic cross-purposes" in a dialogue between shepherds who are too young to know love and too rustic to speak well about it.[4] But there is a further transformation of Virgil in the reference to a stepdame "whott as fyre." Menalcas' stepmother is merely *iniusta* ("Epitheton generale nouercarum," observes Statius: the term characterizes the *genus* of stepmothers), a detail expressive of the threat to property rights that hangs over Virgilian pastoral;[5] Willye's carries a sexual threat, as befits the subject of this eclogue. In fact, the non sequitur of line 42, together with the ambiguity of reference in "mine," may suggest that what she is daily evaluating may be young Willye's fire, not his flock.

Willye's stepmother may be more important to the poem than those critics have recognized who complain about the eclogue's abrupt and anticlimactic ending. The bulk of "March" is devoted to Thomalin's story of attacking Cupid and of being wounded by his arrow in return: "And now it ranckleth more and more, / And inwardly it festreth sore, / Ne wote I, how to cease it." In the anacreontic tradition, this is Cupid's normal way of taking revenge. Willye, however, has had no direct experience of Cupid and knows him only "by a token," from his father's story of having once caught him in a fowling net "(Whereof he wilbe wroken)." Here, the form of that revenge is left unspecified; and Willye abruptly notes that night is falling and "Yts time to hast vs homeward." Yet it seems clear that Spenser meant to balance the two boys' stories (as the woodcut emphasizes),[6] and the poem becomes more shapely if the stepmother is recognized as the prospective agent of Cupid's revenge. The young Thomalin (like Colin) is punished by being denied the object of his desire; the older man, by being granted it, in the form of a passionate young wife. As Willye nonchalantly hastens homeward, we may sense that the pattern of paired revenges is about to be completed, willy-nilly.

4. Patrick Cullen, *Spenser, Marvell, and Renaissance Pastoral* (Cambridge, Mass.: Harvard University Press, 1970), pp. 100–05.

5. For a discussion of the ominous overtones of this eclogue, see Michael C. J. Putnam, *Virgil's Pastoral Art* (Princeton: Princeton University Press, 1970), pp. 121–35. Virgil is imitating Theocritus VIII.15–16 but changes the stern father and mother to a father and stepmother. Virgil's concern for the loss of his country property is a traditional reason for his writing the *Eclogues*. Robert Coleman, in his edition of the poem (Cambridge: Cambridge University Press, 1977), notes that the conventional *saeua nouerca* appears also in *Georgics* II.128, there, with a hint of murderous intent.

6. Ruth Samson Luborsky, "The Allusive Presentation of *The Shepheardes Calender*," *Spenser Studies*, 1 (1980), 29–67, argues for the specificity with which the woodcuts are adapted to the details of Spenser's poem.

In tracing that pattern, and seeing its place in the *Calender* as a whole, we might look more closely at Spenser's ingenious juxtaposition here of lines spoken by the same Virgilian character in different eclogues. Both passages share a common reference to young goats (*haedos*). Is it pertinent that E. K. has earlier suggested that eclogues (anthologized "selections"—and Spenser's more than live up to that traditional etymology in their intense eclecticism) are really aeg-logues, talk of goats and/or goatherds? An association of goats with sexuality may have pointed Spenser toward this "whott" stepmother, whom he places in a March eclogue celebrating the world's awakening from its wintry sleep (under the sign of the Ram, like the opening of *The Canterbury Tales*). Further, the rather odd choice of "dewly" in line 42 may constitute a pun on Virgil's *bisque die*, twice daily: she dually counts the flock, and considers them her due. If she "will lye" with Willye, that too is both due and dual.

Such puns (and there are surely many readers who will refuse to make or let themselves hear them) seem discordant and indecorous, a willful violation of the tone of Virgilian pastoral. It is comparable to Ezra Pound's rendering of Pindar's "tina theon, tin' hērōa, tina d'andra keladēsomen" as "What god, man, or hero / Shall I place a tin wreath upon."[7] In 1579 Spenser's assignation of classical motifs to an English context must have risked seeming as radical and quirky as Pound's claim to defend and illustrate an American vernacular. Here, though, the *translatio studii* involves character, setting, and language at once. Willye is recognizably English in the no-nonsense terms with which he enunciates classical topics. His name may "translate" that of Hippolytus, since will or sexual desire is an unreined steed; but although there is a passionate stepmother in both their households, Willye's story promises to be a comic deflation or denial of tragedy. Spenser's Willye and Shakespeare's Bottom are both participants in festive comedy; their unflappable acceptance of whatever befalls them implies that a reliable English yeoman can take anything in his stride, be it Phaedra or fairy queen. We may remember, too, that Spenser's Hippolytus is not merely a tragic victim but also (by way of Virgil, *Aeneid* VII.761–82, or Ovid, *Metamorphoses* XV.531–46) the "twice-born" Virbius restored to life by Aesculapius.[8]

7. *Olympian II*, l. 2; *Hugh Selwyn Mauberley*, pt. 3.
8. Spenser develops the story of Hippolytus in *FQ* I.v.36–39. It is striking that *A*

Willye's other appearance in *The Shepherdes Calender* is in keeping with this characterization, and it illustrates the play of rustic and courtly perspectives that is typical of the poem. In "August," he and Perigot engage in an amoebaean song celebrating the vision of a "bonilasse" who has wounded the shepherd's heart:

> *Per.* I saw the bouncing Bellibone,
> *Wil.*   hey ho Bonibell (61–62)

In "Aprill," Colin had said of Eliza that "*Pan* may be proud, that euer he begot / such a Bellibone" (91–92). There, the French *belle et bonne* was Englished fairly straightforwardly: Colin sees and praises a maiden who is beautiful and good.[9] So do the rustics; but they complete the process of translation by unfolding the phrase and displaying the earthy English physicality that the French phrase had idealized: the bouncing belly-bone, the bony belle. Their lusty and optimistic song stands in contrast to the despairing (and dreary) sestina of Colin's that Cuddie recites by way of response, in the second half of "August."

The pastoral laments of the more courtly shepherds, Cuddie and Colin, dominate the second half of the *Calender*. In "October" Cuddie "complayneth of the comtempte of Poetrie," and in "November" and "December" Colin first commemorates Dido's death and then anticipates his own. Though these laments may be appropriate to the declining phase of the year's cycle, they tend to be willfully pessimistic in their view of human possibilities for survival. This is especially true of Colin's sestina, which Cuddie describes as a "doolefull verse / Of Rosalend" although it makes no mention of Rosalind or of any other source of the generalized woe that overwhelms the singer. As a sestina,

---

Midsummer Night's Dream, Shakespeare's most overtly Spenserian work, is framed by the wedding of Theseus and Hippolyta and ends with the blessing of the marriage bed that will produce Hippolytus; that its comic treatment of Pyramus and Thisbe burlesques the tragic themes of *Romeo and Juliet*; that the play's action is explicitly—and confusedly—contained within the completion of a lunar month. These elements may give some evidence of how a sensitive contemporary read Spenser.

9. E. K. notes that Colin's "Bellibone" is "homely spoken" and prefers such synonyms as Bonibell or Bonilasse; it remains for Perigot to animate the Bellibone and make its homeliness fully apparent.

it is irregular in repeating its end words in the same order throughout, with the last end word of one stanza simply becoming the first of the next. The effect is to heighten a sense of bathetic monotony, of "rehearsing" woes and imposing personal grief on an otherwise happy landscape. It is an extreme instance of the tendency of the sestina form to beat, as Empson put it, "with a wailing and immovable monotony, for ever upon the same doors in vain."[10]

The *Calender*'s reiterated expressions of frustration and stasis doubtless glance at the limitations imposed by Elizabeth on her courtiers;[11] the *otium* of the pastoral world is comparable to that of the leisure class, and Rosalind's intransigency looks forward to the "imperious feare" that Spenser will increasingly urge his queen to banish, "That she may hearke to loue, and read this lesson often" (*FQ* IV Proem 5). Presiding over both worlds are imperious virgins associated—justly or not—with a generalized blockage of sexual expression. But the placement of the courtly laments in a calendrical framework, juxtaposed with the songs of humbler, more frankly "goatish" figures, suggests that the blockage can be removed or circumvented with the passage of time. Colin sings of a "Bellibone" begotten by Pan and borne by Syrinx: she is the fictive Eliza created by poetry at least as much as she is the unapproachable Elizabeth. The bouncing Bellibone seen and celebrated by Perigot and Willye is closer to that "poore handmayd" of the Faerie Queene whom Colin will later celebrate in

---

10. The sestina, especially in its English career, seems well suited to the expression of erotic obsession. William Empson—*Seven Types of Ambiguity*, rev. ed. ([New York]: New Directions, 1947)—is describing Sidney's double sestina, where the shepherds Strephon and Klaius alternate stanzas, competing in their zeal (comparable to Colin's here) to turn the landscape into an image of their own desolation. Strephon opens with an appeal to "Yee gote-heard Gods"—another instance where a sexually charged pastoral is identified with goatherds rather than shepherds. The extreme instance (and surely designed to overgo Sidney) is Barnabe Barnes's triple sestina (*Parthenophil and Parthenophe*, sestine 5), in which the frustrated lover calls on "threefould *Hecate*" and the vengeful furies, by whose means he forcefully brings his reluctant beloved to his bed, carried on the back of a goat. Though he borrows the theme of enchantment from Theocritus's second idyll and Virgil's eighth eclogue, Barnes presses on where earlier poets stopped: Parthenophil possesses the weeping Parthenophe, and parthenophilia ends with the loss of virginity.

11. See Louis Adrian Montrose, "'The perfecte paterne of a Poete': The Poetics of Courtship in *The Shepheardes Calender*," *TSLL*, 21 (1979), 34–67.

Book VI, the Elizabeth whom Spenser will later marry. Even in 1579, one Bellibone suggests another.[12]

Alter Adonis

Spenser's choice of names for his pastoral figures demonstrates some of the taste for riddling and multiple etymologies that we find in those of *The Faerie Queene* as well. Although the recovery of these etymologies is necessarily speculative, there is no doubt that such playful speculation was popular at the time, as may be seen in the etymologies and anagrams developed (in Latin and other languages) in the genre of the onomastic *allusio* by such continental figures as Du Bellay and Charles Utenhove. The latter's collection of *allusiones*, the *Xenia* (Basel, 1568), contains one that he had presented to Queen Elizabeth, playing on the Hebrew etymology of her name and identifying her as a protectress of religious exiles: evidence, if any were needed, that *nomina* could produce *omina* to fit specific needs or desires.[13]

One characteristic of the names by which the anonymous poet characterizes himself in the *Calender* is a potential for multiple and even contradictory implications—as is perhaps to be expected of a poet at the threshold of his career, eager to leave his options open. Thus he may call himself, most directly, "Immeritô" in the primary sense (taking the word as an Italian adjective or substantive) of one who has not yet won or earned a name for himself. Alternatively, if the word is taken as Latin, its meaning is shaded toward a context of unfair or undeserved treatment; Thomas Cooper's *Thesaurus* (1569) cites examples from Plautus where the word appears in this form both as ablative noun and as adverb, defined as "with out cause or deseruyng." Both meanings seem applicable to the name as it appears at the end of the

---

12. I have discussed the later development of such parallelisms in "Spenser's Fortieth Birthday and Related Fictions," *Spenser Studies*, 4 (1983), 3–31.

13. See J. A. van Dorsten, *The Radical Arts: First Decade of an Elizabethan Renaissance* (Leiden: Leiden University Press; London: Oxford University Press, 1970), chap. 2. In the same work (pp. 42–45), van Dorsten describes a 1565 medal by Steven van Herwyck which shows Elizabeth as signifying anagrammatically (in Greek) "divine fountain of the realm"; the existence of a similar anagram for Leicester suggests a Franco-Flemish interest in their marriage and provides a further link between such ingenious onomastics and the circle with which the young Spenser identified himself.

epigraph "To his booke"; its accent may perhaps suggest a Latin form.[14]

In choosing the name of Colin Clout for his pastoral persona, Spenser seems to be following a program hinted at by E. K.: it is "a name not greatly vsed, and yet haue I sene a Poesie of M. Skeltons vnder that title. But indeede the word Colin is Frenche, and vsed of the French Poet Marot (if he be worthy of the name of a Poete) in a certain Aeglogue. Vnder which name this Poete secretly shadoweth himself, as sometime did Virgil vnder the name of Tityrus, thinking it much fitter, then such Latine names, for the great vnlikelyhoode of the language" (*Minor Poems, Variorum* I.17–18). The borrowing of sixteenth-century names rather than classical ones is a gesture by which the "new Poete" asserts his modernity (and, in so doing, distances himself from his great predecessor Chaucer, whom he honors under the very name of Tityrus). His choice of a name that is used by an English poet as well as a French one further signals the mingling of Continental and native strains in the *Calender*. That the French poet in question should be Clément Marot is not surprising, in that Spenser imitates two of Marot's poems in his final two eclogues: the elegy to Louise de Savoye, the queen mother, in "November," and the *Eglogue au Roy* in "December." Clearly, despite E. K.'s disparaging remarks, Marot was an important near-contemporary model for Spenser; recent studies have argued that his Virgilian imitations, royal patronage, and Lutheran associations would have made him an attractive example of what the new English poet was hoping to become.[15]

14. The distinction between these two shades of meaning is blurred; and a comparable blurring may be found in the motto that follows the Envoy, "Merce non mercede." Judith M. Kennedy, "The Final Emblem of *The Shepheardes Calender*," *Spenser Studies*, 1 (1980), 95–106, offers a possible interpretation. I think that Spenser may wish to keep the distinction between *merx* and *merces* vague, since he hopes to be "graced" with both glory and patronage. A similar vagueness is found in the last line of the Envoy: "The better please, the worse despise, I aske nomore." However this is parsed, the meaning seems to include a mutual scorn from and toward the "worse" that constitutes a kind of moral victory over the forces of envy. Spenser is imitating the conclusion of the *Thebaid*, where Statius looks forward to the "meriti . . . honores" that will come with time, after the clouds of envy have passed. Until then, the poet will be "Immeritô."

15. See Luborsky (1980), pp. 56–57, and Annabel Patterson, "Re-opening the Green Cabinet: Clément Marot and Edmund Spenser," *ELR*, 16 (1986), 44–70. Patterson may overstate the importance of Marot's Lutheran leanings (equivocal as they were) to his English reputation: Anne Lake Prescott, in *French Poets and the English Renais-*

The *Calender* concludes, then, with a pair of highly wrought songs that constitutes the new poet's claim for a rank comparable to Marot's. "December," addressed to "soueraigne *Pan* thou God of shepheardes all" (in Marot, explicitly identified with the monarch), urges: "Hearken awhile from thy greene cabinet, / The rurall song of carefull Colinet." That someone was listening to this plea for laureate status is suggested by a curious detail: in the third through fifth quartos of the *Calender*, of 1586, 1591, and 1597, "rurall song" (Marot's "chant rural") is replaced by "laurell song." Henry J. Todd (1801) saw this as evidence of Spenser's laureate status by that time; and in 1586, too, William Webbe writes that Spenser "may well were the Garlande."[16]

Skelton's aptness as a model for Spenser's pastoral self-figuring, alongside Marot, would seem to be based on similar criteria. Churchyard had remarked on Marot's comparable royal patronage in an introductory poem to Skelton's works (1568);[17] Skelton's came from Henry VIII, who was to be figured as "Pan" in the *Calender*. His ecclesiastical satires, directed against Wolsey, would appear to Elizabethans to contain (as Milton said of Spenser's in reference to his own era) "some presage of these reforming times." Less directly, then—since Spenser's Colin Clout is not identified with the *Calender*'s "moral" eclogues—an allusion to Skelton could serve as a cautious pledge by the new poet and prospective laureate to serve his queen in a distinctively English and Protestant vernacular.

---

sance (New Haven: Yale University Press, 1978), pp. 1–36, surveys the confusing evidence of references to him during the Elizabethan period, and suggests that he may have been seen as comparable to Skelton, a lively and rather disreputable precursor of vernacular Protestant poetry. In France, Marot and his detractors punned variously on his name's association with Virgil ("Maro"), clownishness (*marotte*, a fool's bauble), and mischief (*maraud*, vagabond or marauder); in England, the additional sense of "marrow" or pith could seem apt as well. I am grateful to Professor Prescott for a copy of her unpublished essay "Musical Strains: Marot's Double Role as Psalmist and Courtier."

16. *Minor Poems, Variorum* I.419; *Spenser Allusions in the Sixteenth and Seventeenth Centuries. Part I: 1580–1625*, ed. William Wells, *SP*, 68 (1971), 8. Marot's speaker, Robin, appears as Robinet in this line; since "robinet" also means "faucet," there is a curious foreshadowing here of the famous Spenserian signature, the song tuned to the water's fall. Whether or not the change to "laurell" was accidental, it could not have been better placed.

17. Churchyard's poem is discussed in relation to Skelton and Spenser by Prescott (1978), p. 18, and Luborsky (1980), p. 56.

A mingling of Continental sophistication and English downrightness is seen not only in the pairing of Marot and Skelton, but in the two names of Colin Clout, the one French and the other Anglo-Saxon. A clout is a clod of earth; "Colin" comes from Latin *colonus* (French *colon*), a countryman or farmer, one who cultivates (Latin *colo*) the earth.[18] Though the name may suggest no more than a rustic lout well suited to the undemanding work of a shepherd, it also carries a hint of the georgic, especially perhaps in its religious aspects. We may recall Chaucer's pairing of his Parson with the Plowman his brother, or Spenser's pairing of Chaucer (Tityrus) with Langland's Piers ("the Pilgrim that the Ploughman playde a whyle") in the Envoy.[19] Perhaps Spenser's own Piers can be seen as something of an alter ego to Colin, embodying the Skeltonic aspects of the name.

By Spenser's time, the expanding forces of empire had located the lands to be cultivated or colonized beyond the boundaries of England itself; and the southern shepherd's boy was to spend most of the rest of his life in Ireland. When Colin Clout "comes home again" it is no longer clear whether home is the court in England or the pastoral society in Ireland that hears his tale. Although his career in Ireland may not have been what Spenser had in mind when he presented himself in the *Calender*, it is what someone named Colin might have expected. Comparable trials await George, the Redcross Knight, before he too can return home and become "Saint *George* of mery England" (*FQ* I.x.61).

Beyond figuring those forces in the *Calender* that E. K. would associate with the "moral" rank of eclogues, Skelton may have given Spenser a precedent for the larger structure of his poem; for there is one point in Skelton's works where his laureate ambitions are expressed in terms that are explicitly pertinent to Spenser's calendrical context and to the themes of return and rebirth that I would attribute to it. This point is

---

18. A separate *colon*, derived from Greek *kōluō* "to cut off," carries the sense of a rhetorical period and thence a mark of punctuation. Evidence of one such reading of Colin's name appears in Thomas Blenerhasset's *Reuelation of the True Minerva* (1582), where a shepherd complains: "Poore *Colon* I, and careful *Comma* shee / My weded wife, once happie, nowe forlorne . . ." (sig. B1ʳ).

19. Though I think it clear that Spenser is referring to Langland in this passage, the theory that he may have in mind the pseudo-Chaucerian *Plowman's Tale* does not seriously affect my argument.

seen in a pair of woodblocks that appear on the recto and verso of the title page to the 1523 *Garland of Laurel*. The recto (Figure 1) shows an elderly man seated at his desk; figures approach him from behind at the left. Since Skelton was approximately sixty-three years old at the time of publication, the picture can be taken as a plausible illustration of the scene of laureation that his poem describes. It is possible that the block was carved specifically for this work, since I have found no source for it elsewhere; but in any case it resembles other humanist portraits (such as the portrait of Petrarch in the Sala dei Giganti at Padua) in its essential elements: desk, elevated bookstand, window with a view, ecclesiastic garb, pointing finger.

On the verso, by contrast, appears a portrait of a young man clutching a flower in one hand and a leafy branch in the other (Figure 2). Above it appears the title *Skelton Poeta*, and beneath it four lines of Latin:

> Eterno mansura die dum sidera fulgent
> Equora dumque tument hec laurea nostra virebit.
> Hinc nostrum celebre et nomen referetur ad astra
> Undique Skeltonis memorabitur alter adonis

(While the stars last and shine with eternal daylight, and while the seas continue to swell, this laurel of ours shall be green. Hence our glorious name will be borne to the stars and everywhere Skelton will be remembered as another Adonis.)

This figure of Skelton-the-poet as an Adonis is copied from a block that appears in the French *Compost et Kalendrier des bergeres* (Paris: Guy Marchant, 1499; Figure 3), where the young man is a personification of April, and his attributes of flower and branch represent the seasonal rebirth of bloom and leaf; the inscription adds that the month is "le plus joly" because God suffered and was reborn then.[20] By identifying the figure as Adonis, Skelton introduces a contrast in the at-

20. A set of blocks for the twelve months appears in editions at Paris of 1493 and 1499, and at Troyes of 1529 and 1541, according to A. H. Diplock (*The Kalender of Shepherds: being devices for the twelve months* [London: Sidgwick & Jackson, 1908]). I have seen only the editions of 1499 and 1529, both at the British Library. So far as I know, no English edition of the *Kalender and Compost* has any but the January block; this is confirmed by Luborsky, "The Illustrations to *The Shepheardes Calender*," *Spenser Studies*, 2 (1981), 47–48 n. 24.

FIGURE 1. John Skelton, *Garland of Laurel*, 1523, title page (recto). By permission of the British Library.

FIGURE 2. John Skelton, *Garland of Laurel*, 1523, title page (verso). By permission of the British Library.

Auril

Auril suis ou quel de verdure   Je suis auril le plus iolp
Bois et buissons sont couuerture   De tous en honneur et vaillance
Et la terre pareillement   Car en mon temps fut confranchi
A pres ie veulz soudainnement   Le monde du fer dune lance
Que mes tresors leur soient couuers   Par sa saincte digne souffrance
Et tout soient de mes fleurs couuers   De dieu qui se monde crea
Mon temps si est doulx et begnin   On en doit auoir souuenance
Mais q la ceue gist le venin   Car en mon temps resuscita

FIGURE 3. *Compost et Kalendrier des bergeres*, Paris: Guy Marchant, 1499; sig. C1ᵛ. By permission of the British Library.

tributes where originally there was identity. The branch is the laurel
that will remain ever green, while the flower is the short-lived symbol
of Adonis's early death. The same contrast is made by the two illustrations: Skelton the frail human grows old and dies, albeit (a very important proviso for this particular individual, as his poems make clear)
heavy with honors, but the poet's name and works will remain eternally youthful. Nelson compares the imagery here with the figure of
another "green" persona of Skelton, Parrot, who is based on Boccaccio's Psyttacus, a son of Deucalion granted transformation into an
eternally green shape.[21] Spenser's Colin Clout, who "dies" prematurely
in "December," may be derived in part, then, from a similar understanding of *Skelton Poeta* as another Adonis.

Anna Perenna

Adonis has a place as well at the beginning of the tradition of pastoral
elegy; so the generic background of the "November" eclogue recapitu-
lates and extends the associations just discussed. Bion's lament for
Adonis establishes the main elements in the subgenre; and when
Moschus in turn laments the death of Bion on his precursor's model,
the reflexive nature of the elegy has been firmly established: a clear line
extends from these two poems to "Lycidas," in which Milton similarly
broods over the failure of poetry to triumph over death. Yet the poems
end on a hint of something more positive. Bion concludes with the
statement that Venus's lament for her lover is an annual occurrence, so
the death is contained within the seasonal celebration of the vegetative
cycle. Moschus similarly ends with the statement that Bion is held by
Kore, Persephone; but he adds that she has been known to be moved
by song, when she gave up Eurydice to Orpheus; it is the poetry of
lesser and later mortals that lacks efficacy. In his lament for Daphnis in
the fifth eclogue, Virgil introduces an element of enigmatic and apparently discontinuous reference that will also be seen in Spenser. This
Daphnis has little explicit connection with the minor mythological
figure who bears his name in earlier poems. As master shepherd, associated in name with the laurel, Daphne, he may suggest the pastoral

21. William Nelson, *John Skelton, Laureate* (New York: Columbia University Press,
1939), p. 193n.

poet's dream of glory; as bringer of civilization and Bacchic dance, he is a culture hero like Hercules or Bacchus; his deification is felt to allude to that recently bestowed on Julius Caesar. Like Virgil, Spenser seems to be aiming for an unresolved and suggestive blend of contemporary and generic allusions.

In "November," Colin laments the recent death of "Dido." The song itself is explicitly patterned on Marot's pastoral elegy "vpon the death of Loys the frenche Queene," as E. K. puts it—Louise de Savoie, mother of his royal patron François Ier. E. K. makes much of the mystery of Dido's identity: she is "some mayden of greate bloud. . . . The personage is secrete, and to me altogether vnknowne, albe of him selfe I often required the same." Again, in a gloss to the identification of Dido as "the great shepehearde his daughter sheene," E. K. insists that the shepherd "is some man of high degree, and not as some vainely suppose God Pan. The person both of the shepehearde and of Dido is vnknowen and closely buried in the Authors conceipt. But out of doubt I am, that it is not Rosalind, as some imagin: for he speaketh soone after of her also" (*Minor Poems, Variorum* I.104, 110). After so much protesting, it is no surprise that readers have recalled that Virgil's Dido is also named Elissa, and that the Elisa of "April" is the daughter of "*Pan* the shepheards God" whom E. K. has explicitly identified as "her highnesse Father, late of worthy memorye K. Henry the eyght." Or that the most satisfactory interpretation to date should see her as a combination of Elisa and Rosalind, her death and joyous transfer to the Christian "*Elisian* fieldes so free" a revision both of Virgil and of the pastoral project of the earlier eclogues, "of both pagan imperial epic and Anglican dynastic eclogue."[22] Without disputing the general validity of this judgment, as regards the linear argument of the poem, I would suggest that more can be recovered of the implications of this Elizabethan Dido for the *Calender*, and for its calendrical theme.

We may begin by observing that Virgil's treatment of Dido was startlingly and controversially revisionist. He took the story of an exemplary Dido who killed herself out of loyalty to her dead husband Sychaeus, refusing to remarry, and made her the victim of a destructive love for Aeneas. As a type of the later African queen, Cleopatra, whose defeat was a necessary prelude to the emergent hegemony of Augustan

22. Montrose, p. 51.

Rome, this "traduced" Dido was doubly a victim of bad faith, on the part of the Roman poet as well as of his Trojan hero. Perhaps some of the mysterious power of our last view of her, in the *lugentes campi* on Aeneas's route to the underworld in Book VI, derives from the fact that even though Virgil is through with her, he has not been able to deliver her to the Elysian fields; she has been reunited with Sychaeus and has nothing to say to the stammering Aeneas, but she is still in the shadows.[23] Spenser may have known the glosses of Servius on IV.682 and V.4, in which he reports that Varro claimed that it was not Dido but her sister Anna who was seduced by Aeneas and killed herself. And he would certainly have known Petrarch's *Triumph of Chastity*, in which the chaste Dido is honored and Virgil's version of her story rejected.

Since Elizabethan Britons traced their ancestry from a Brutus who was a descendant of Aeneas, it is easy to see that Dido could figure as a richly contradictory icon of Elizabeth. As a queen who does not let her passions stand in the way of duty to country, as an immensely effective virago (*dux femina facti*), she can be at once an Aeneas to Virgil's Dido and an embodiment of the "true" Dido who had been defamed by Roman propaganda. One example of such a presentation of her is seen in the "Sieve" portrait of Elizabeth in Siena.[24] There, Elizabeth is por-

23. The edition of *Aeneid* VI by Robert G. Austin (Oxford: Clarendon Press, 1977) discusses the scene (ll. 450–76) in detail. The vacuity of Aeneas's defensive comment to Dido here—"inuitus, regina, tuo de litore cessi" (l. 460: "against my will, O queen, did I leave your shores")—is underscored by its echo of Catullus LXVI.39, where the lost lock of Berenice's hair addresses its former mistress: "inuita, o regina, tuo de uertice cessi," "against my will, O queen, did I leave your head." Jacques Perret, "Les Compagnes de Didon aux enfers (*Aen.* 6.445–449)," *Revue des Etudes Latines*, 62 (1964), 247–61, suggests that the description here, immediately before Dido, of Caeneus, whom mythographers had described as a woman changed into a man (cf. Ovid, *Metamorphoses* XII.459–535), and whom Virgil places in the *lugentes campi* restored to her former sex, implies a similar restoration of Dido, who no longer needs to be a virago. Barbara J. Bono, in *Literary Transvaluation: From Vergilian Epic to Shakespearean Tragicomedy* (Berkeley and Los Angeles: University of California Press, 1984), has provided a valuable treatment of the Renaissance Dido.

24. The portrait is described by Roy C. Strong, *Portraits of Queen Elizabeth I* (Oxford: Clarendon Press, 1963), and more fully in his *Gloriana: The Portraits of Queen Elizabeth I* (London: Thames and Hudson, 1987), pp. 94–108. A review of the latter book by Malcolm Rogers, *TLS*, August 14, 1987, p. 867, accepts Strong's attribution of the Siena portrait to Cornelius Ketel but challenges his late dating and proposes that it be assigned to around 1578, when Ketel is recorded as having painted the queen. Strong interprets the queen as representing an Aeneas here; Stephen Orgel, who discusses the painting in "Shakespeare and the Cannibals," in *Cannibals, Witches, and*

trayed holding a sieve, figuring the Roman vestal virgin, Tuccia, who, like the virtuous Dido, appears in the *Triumph of Chastity* (I.148–51). Behind her is a column with scenes of Dido and Aeneas; at its base, the crown of the Holy Roman emperors, which seems here for the first time to have been used (with Charles V's impresa of the pillars of Hercules and the motto *Plus Ultra*) to figure Elizabethan ambitions to extend empire to the New World. A figure in the background has been identified as Sir Christopher Hatton, a favorite of Elizabeth who had been knighted in December 1577 and made vice-chamberlain of the royal household in 1578. Not surprisingly, Hatton was an opponent of the French marriage and a supporter of the voyages; he was associated with the Henry Bynneman who printed Van der Noodt's *Theatre* in 1569 and the two Harvey-Spenser *Letters* volumes of 1580 and who describes himself as "servaunt" to Hatton on a 1578 title page.

Whether or not the Siena portrait is a "source" for Spenser's allusion to Dido in "November," it does illustrate a problematic use of Dido that seems very similar to what E. K. is apparently encouraging. Furthermore, this problematic looks forward to contrasts of being and seeming that are more usually associated with *The Faerie Queene*; the two Didos, or the one Dido properly "read," can be seen in the pairing of Una (embodying the "semper eadem" of Elizabeth's motto) with her Romish counterpart, Duessa. And the dividing of Elizabeth into such complementary pairs as Gloriana and Britomart reflects a sense that the queen contains both Didos in important ways, as passionate woman and royal virago. Some of what is implied here is not likely to be welcome to Elizabeth, and the identity of Dido in "November" is rightly described as "closely buried" and veiled. Spenser's way, here and in his later works, is to aim for a multiplicity of references by which no single one need be definitely affirmed. For instance, the reference to the grief of "Lobbin" (lines 167–69), whom E. K. identifies here as "a shepherd, which seemeth to haue bene the louer and deere frende of Dido," momentarily gives the song a very specific and dangerous thrust: if Lobbin is Leicester, he may be taken as grieving at the loss of Elizabeth's favor after the discovery of his marriage to Lettice Knollys;

Divorce, ed. Marjorie Garber (Baltimore: The Johns Hopkins University Press, 1987), pp. 40–66, identifies her as the non-Virgilian Dido. The portrait is reproduced by Strong and Orgel; since its details are difficult to show clearly it is not included here.

he is then being offered the prospect of being able to worship his beloved queen in a more platonic fashion, presumably, but the offer is really to the queen to let herself be so worshiped, while walking the Elisian fields of her virginal status.[25] But the moment that suggests this application quickly passes, and the elegy as a whole will scarcely support such an interpretation.

Beyond the major riddle of Dido's identity, "November" contains two notorious cruces or "errors"; and since they appear in symmetrical positions in the thirteen quatrains of the eclogue's opening section,[26] they seem to ask to be taken together. In the fourth quatrain, Colin observes that

> Phoebus weary of his yerely taske,
> Ystabled hath his steedes in lowly laye,
> And taken vp his ynne in Fishes haske.

E. K. duly notes in his gloss that "the sonne, reigneth that is, in the signe Pisces all Nouember." Yet it takes very little knowledge of the calendar to be aware that Pisces is the sign associated with February, or more precisely with the latter part of February and the earlier part of March; the sun does not reign in any sign all of any month, although Spenser's Calender diverges from the tradition (as typically seen in Figure 3) by associating each month with a single sign. And in fact the illustrations to "February" and "November" show Pisces and Sagittarius respectively as their signs. At the same time, the tenth quatrain— the fourth from the end of the introduction—has Thenot observing that Dido is "dead alas and drent," a victim of drowning rather than of the fires of passion and her own funeral pyre. In fact, there is nothing in "November" beyond the name of Dido (and the presumed pun on Elissa in the Elisian fields) to confirm our assumption that this is either Virgil's Dido or the chaste "widow Dido" of the alternate tradition.

The Pisces reference has proved the more troubling of the two (since drent might be forced into a transferred sense of "forgotten" or "re-

---

25. Charles E. Mounts, "Spenser and the Countess of Leicester," ELH, 19 (1952), 191–202, suggests that the reference to "Lettice" in "March" 20 is a tactless allusion to the Leicester disgrace.

26. Marianne Brown, "Spenserian Technique: The Shepheardes Calender," REAL: The Yearbook of Research in English and American Literature, 2 (1984), 90.

pressed," or perhaps taken as a misprint for *brent*). Critics have suggested that the eclogue was originally designed for February and
moved at the last moment, although that would explain neither E.
K.'s explicit association of Pisces with November nor Colin's remark in the
same quatrain that Phoebus was "weary of his yerely taske"— unless
we also posit that this would have been a February eclogue in a
Calender that started the year with March. More promising is the
recent observation that a *Calender* that begins in January as Spenser's
does (and that chooses the end-of-month sign for each month) acquires
a symmetrical structure that is based on the night and day houses of
each planet: January and December are the night and day houses,
respectively, of Saturn; February and November, of Jupiter.[27] Although this theory does not make sense of the claim that the sun is in
Pisces in November, it does link the two signs of Pisces and Sagittarius
and perhaps suggests that a royal figure analogous to Jupiter inhabits
them.

It happens that the association of Pisces with the threat of drowning
recalls a specific historical moment earlier in the sixteenth century,
when the prospect of an extraordinary conjunction of the planets in
February of 1524, when the sun was in Pisces, led to extended debate
during the preceding years as to what cataclysm, if any, might result.[28]
Astrologers debated the predictive force of conjunctions as opposed to
horoscopes; at the same time, the prospect of a major prediction that
might not be fulfilled gave hope to those skeptics who would deny any
validity to astrology. Evidence of wickedness at home or abroad
seemed reason enough to predict divine punishment, with the planets
merely gathering to witness it. Specifically, the peasants' revolts and
the spread of Lutheranism were associated with the ominous prospect.
The genre of the Practica, or annual prediction, which accompanied

27. Norman Farmer, Jr., "Spenser's Homage to Ronsard: Cosmic Design in *The
Shepheardes Calender*," *Studi di Letteratura Francese*, 12 (1986), 249–63.
28. The debate is summarized by Lynn Thorndike, *A History of Magic and Experimental Science* (New York: Columbia University Press, 1941), V.178–83. For more
recent studies, see Delio Cantimori, *Umanesimo e religione nel Rinascimento* (Turin: G.
Einaudi, 1975), pp. 164–74; Carlo Ginzburg, *Il nicodemismo. Simulazione e dis-
simulazione religiosa nell'Europa del '500* (Turin: G. Einaudi, 1970), chap. 2; and the
numerous books edited by Paola Zambelli, especially *'Astrologi halucinati': Stars and
the End of the World in Luther's Time* (Berlin: De Gruyter, 1986).

popular almanacs, flourished in this climate of anticipation. Leonhard
Reynmann's (Nürnberg, 1523) is typical, albeit with a title page that
illustrates the prominence of Pisces more eloquently than others (Figure 4). A giant fish dominates the sky; inside of it are a dead body and
the planets. From it issues a torrent which engulfs a village below. On
the left, Saturn (the god of country folk) leads a peasant uprising, with
a fife and drum corps and comet above. On the right, emperor, pope,
and prelates look on in impotent dismay. The traditional association of
sibylline prophecy with the promise of Virgil's fourth eclogue—"Iam
redit et virgo, redeunt saturnia regna"—takes on a violent, revolution-
ary aspect with this prediction of Saturn's return.

If Spenser's invention of a drowned "Dido" associated riddlingly
with Pisces does glance at the predictions for 1524, it does so from the
comfortable perspective of a half century later. The world did not come
to an end, though floods were reported in German territory and
Lutheranism continued to spread; Luther himself published a sermon
attacking the idolatry of astrologers and specifically these false predictions of a second flood.[29] In Spenser's England, now, there is a virgin
on the throne, replacing Catholic figures of Mary there and in the
churches; so it might be said that the Dido of "November" is a beneficent complement to the darker figures of the past. But there is one final
date in Pisces, and another calendrical text, that should be taken into
consideration when discussing the watery death and transformation
that appear at the climax of Spenser's calendar.

If Virgil's *Eclogues* are the classic model for later eclogue books,
Ovid's *Fasti* must be expected to serve that role for calendars or almanacs. And for a Spenser who was compiling his calendar at a time when
the Julian calendar was notoriously out of joint and a Gregorian one
was proposing to supplant it—so that Protestants were forced to a
choice between Roman and Romish authorities—one date from the
Roman calendar must have had particular interest, as marking the
death of the man who gave the current calendar its name. Ovid's entry
for the Ides of March (*Fasti* III.523–710) mentions Caesar's death only
incidentally in its final lines; it consists chiefly of a description of the
origins of the feast of Anna Perenna which takes place on that day.

---

29. Martin Luther, *Ain Sermon von der Beschneydung am newen Jaretag. Item ain
gaystliche Auslegung der Zaichen in Son, Mon, unnd Gestirn* (Augsburg, 1524).

FIGURE 4. Leonhard Reynmann, *Practica vber die grossen vnd manigfeltigen Coniunction der Planeten . . .*, 1523. By permission of the British Library.

Anna is of course a female personification of the returning year (*annus*); she is celebrated with much drinking and loss of virginity (Martial refers to her grove as delighting in virgin blood, IV.lxiv.16). Ovid identifies her with Dido's sister, inventing the story that she stayed for three years in Carthage before being banished by Iarbas, Dido's rebuffed suitor, who had taken over the city on her death; then she spent two years on Malta before its ruler in turn banished her out of fear of Pygmalion, her murderous brother; finally, after failing to land in southern Italy, she was swept to Laurentium outside Rome. There she is welcomed by an Aeneas who is still guilty at having betrayed her sister. His welcome awakens the jealousy of Lavinia, and the ghost of Dido warns her in a dream to flee; she is embraced by the river Numicius and becomes a water nymph: "Amne perenne latens Anna Perenna vocor" ("Hiding in an endless river, I am called Anna Perenna").[30]

Ovid concludes by mentioning the death of Caesar on this feast day, noting laconically that Caesar's killers have met bad ends at the hands of Augustus. Virgil's *Aeneid*, with its implicit comparison of Dido and Cleopatra, is the canonical statement of the glories and costs of the *pax Augusta*. In bringing Anna from Carthage to Rome, Ovid locates a feminine figure of seasonal Roman rebirth at the precise point where Virgil's story had left off and marginalized the passion of his African queen; Dido's ardor (the transgressive "veteris vestigia flammae" that Virgil had detected in that model of marital loyalty) is answered by the watery transformation of her sister. This act of recuperation (reminiscent perhaps of the *translatio studii* of the Arethusa myth, or the transformation of Furies into Athenian Eumenides) is advanced tentatively—Ovid reports that others identify Anna Perenna with the moon, or Themis, or Isis—but its effect is to assert a benevolent female presence at the center of Augustan Rome, one that both challenges and blesses the male establishment.

The mystification of Spenser's treatment of Dido in "November" seems to point toward a comparably rich and paradoxical celebration of renewal; for the elegy ends by emphasizing Dido's translation to

30. *Fasti* III.654. See also *Metamorphoses* XIV.596–608, where Venus brings the dying Aeneas to Numicius, who washes away "whatever in Aeneas had been mortal" prior to the hero's deification. Ovid is speaking in both passages of the first Roman settlement near Ostia.

enduring joys. Although this apotheosis may be taken as anticipatory of the heavenly joy that Elizabeth herself will know eventually, it seems to fit as well the situation of noble women who are already dead. That Marot's elegy was directed to the *mother* of his royal patron might lead us to suspect that Spenser had in mind Anne Boleyn, the Syrinx to Henry's Pan in "April"; Ovid's pairing of Dido with an Anna would underscore such an allusion. At the same time, the association of Marot's Queen Louise with the poet's prosecution for Lutheranism might point toward royal and Catholic "sisters" of Elizabeth, Mary Tudor or Mary Stuart; Ovid's pairing of Dido with a sister encourages these associations. Finally, earlier moments of historic crisis associated with Pisces (February 1524, the Ides of March in 44 B.C.) serve both to assert the seriousness of the issues confronting Elizabeth in 1579 and to place them in a context of repetition and renewal. Whether the "herse" that Colin rehearses is light or heavy depends on whether we take the poem as a calendar for one year or for every year. Spenser lets us have it either way.

8

Spenser's Muse

THOMAS P. ROCHE, JR.

"For people who like that kind of thing, that is the kind of thing they like."

Zuleika Dobson

The occasion of the present volume seems the proper time to reconsider a once burning question of Spenserian scholarship: who is the muse of *The Faerie Queene*? The question is still smoldering, and we seem not to have profited from that early battle now embalmed as Appendix IX in the first volume of the Spenser *Variorum*. Apparently not until 1930, when F. M. Padelford published "The Muse of the *Faerie Queene*," did any reader give the problem much thought. Padelford claimed that editors, from Upton on, assumed that Clio was the muse of the poem, and he was out to challenge such complacency by proposing Calliope for the position. Less than two years after the publication of Padelford's piece, Josephine Waters Bennett issued a defense of Clio's claim which would have taught Mutabilitie much about the ways of argumentation. The court of appeals in this case was the editors of the Spenser *Variorum*, headed by Padelford, who reprinted his entire article in Appendix IX, had his friend and coeditor Charles Grosvenor Osgood write a one-page summary of Bennett's article, and appended a one-page rebuttal by the editor himself: "and them destroied quite; Yet not so quite," for in that same year of 1932 Henry Gibbons Lotspeich, Osgood's student, following in the tradition of his mentor's *Classical Mythology of John Milton's English Poems* (1900), published his *Classical Mythology in the Poetry of Edmund Spenser*, in which he came out strongly in favor of Clio. Repercussions are not recorded, particularly in Appendix IX. Except for D. T. Starnes's support for Calliope in 1942, supplemented in his collaboration with E. W. Talbert in 1955, the problem has not again been broached in print except as addenda to one side or the other of the basic argument or in the footnotes to modern annotated editions, with the Cliophilists represented by Bayley, Maclean, and Hamilton and the Calliopeans represented by Kellogg and Steele, and Roche.[1]

It must be admitted at the outset that the Cliophilists outnumber the Calliopeans, but for that very reason the case for Calliope must be presented anew, if only to challenge the attractive, even sensible, hypothesis in favor of Clio. Stated most simply, the Cliophilist argument runs that since Clio's name is derived from the Greek word for fame (*kleos*), and since she bestows glory on those heroes who seek it, Clio is the obvious muse for a poem about Gloriana and a hero Arthur, who is searching for her. The only difficulty with this hypothesis is that it runs counter to the entire history of the muses and their interventions in epic poetry.

Although my primary purpose in this essay is to correct the vagaries of Spenser's critics, ancient and modern, I would also like to suggest why such vagaries occur so often in Spenserian scholarship. No other major poet has been so patronized as Spenser: we expect him to be wrong, to forget the name, or not to finish the story, and therefore his muse allows us our muddled readings because of the inaccurate ques-

---

1. F. M. Padelford, "The Muse of the *Faerie Queene*," *SP*, 27 (1930), 111–24; Josephine Waters Bennett, "Spenser's Muse," *JEGP*, 31 (1932), 202–19; *Variorum*, I.506–16; Henry Gibbons Lotspeich, *Classical Mythology in the Poetry of Edmund Spenser* (Princeton: Princeton University Press, 1932), pp. 83–85; D. T. Starnes, "Spenser and the Muses," *University of Texas Studies in English*, 22 (1942), 31–58. Starnes's findings have been elaborated in his collaboration with E. W. Talbert, *Classical Myth and Legend in Renaissance Dictionaries* (Chapel Hill: University of North Carolina Press, 1955), pp. 96–102; E. R. Gregory, "More about Spenser and the *De musarum inventis*," *American Notes & Queries*, 14 (1976), 67–71, and "Spenser's Muse and the Dumaeus *Virgil*," *Spenser Newsletter*, 5 (1974), 10–11; P. C. Bayley, ed. *The Faerie Queene, Book 1* (Oxford: Oxford University Press, 1966; Hugh Maclean, ed., *Edmund Spenser's Poetry*, Norton Critical Edition (New York: W. W. Norton, 1968); A. C. Hamilton, ed. *The Faerie Queene* (London: Longman, 1977); Robert Kellogg and Oliver Steele, eds. *Books I and II of "The Faerie Queene," the Mutability Cantos and Selections from the Minor Poetry* (New York: Odyssey Press, 1965). See also Thomas H. Cain, *Praise in "The Faerie Queene"* (Lincoln: University of Nebraska Press, 1978), pp. 44–47, which argues for the conclusion I reach in this essay.

tions we address to his poem. Finding him out in one of his presumed nods urges us as Spenserians to justify his "error," rarely to ask why he should be doing it his way. That Spenser should have a muse does not move us to ask why, since we all know that every epic poet has one or more of them, but this shows us much closer to Byron's breezy disclaimer of the epic tradition in "Hail, Muse, etcetera" than to an appreciation of Spenser as the most learned poet in English with the possible exception of Milton.

Our difficulty in Spenser's case is complicated because he both wants to use the conventions and then not to use them, as if he did not know what he was about or had a recalcitrant muse. Witness his adaptations from Ariosto and Tasso. A smaller but more pertinent example occurs when he attributes the parentage of the muses to Apollo and Mnemosyne in the first half of the poem and to Jupiter and Mnemosyne in the second half.[2] Scholarly embarrassment over this nod was relieved only when Lotspeich announced that Spenser might have known about Apollo as "dux pater" of the muses by reading it in Natalis Comes, which might very well be true but does not take us very far into what Spenser is doing.[3] The foreclosure of literary questions by mere reference to previous literary examples is dogmatism of a very precarious sort. "This one says it" or "They all did it" or "It was in the air" will not do as argument, unless we know why this one said it or what they all did or why what was in the air had to be included in this

---

2. The Apollonian invocations are *FQ* I.xi.5–7, II.x.1–3, III.iii.4, the Jovian invocations are IV.xi.10, VII.vi.37, and VII.vii.1. The invocation in the Proem to Book I avoids the subject of parentage.

3. Because of the large number of references to classical and Renaissance texts, wherever possible I cite the Loeb Library for classical authors and the two sets of mythographical writers edited by Stephen Orgel and reprinted by Garland Press, as here, Natalis Comes (1616), bk. IV, chap. 10, p. 183: "Fertur idem fuisse musicae & vaticiniorum inuentor, vt est in primo Metamorphoseon Ouidii [I.517–18]. Perutile sane & praeclarum inuentum fuit Apollinis musica, que tanquam solatium quoddam, & ad obliuionem humanarum calamitatum remedium, quibus vita hominum vndique septa est, fuit inuenta, verum illam nunc magis effoeminarunt quam conueniebat, vt chromaticum melos adhibuerunt ad demulcendos animos: nunc magis virilem fecerunt: nunc ex his ambobus modulis fecerunt permistam: sicuti requirebat rerum presentium ratio. Neque rudis omnino aut inurbanus habitus est, qui musicae non fuisset ignarus. Alius fuit musicae modus, cum per numeros animi in bellum essent incitandi, alius modulus fuit in conuiuiis, alius inter Deorum sacrificia. Qui enim modulos recte cognouerit, & quibus ex numeris componantur singuli, ille facile ad omnia tempora musicam rationem accommodabit. Fuerunt hac ipsa de causa Musae in eius tutela creditae, quarum & dux pater Apollo fuit existimatus."

poem. We are still in the infancy stage of Spenserian criticism because we dare not ask the questions: Why would Spenser use this minute and obscure detail of the Apollonian parentage of the muses when he obviously knew—or later learned—of the Jovian parentage? What purpose does the Apollonian innovation serve?

These questions are more than rhetorical, because they pose the problem of how we assess the "facts" of Spenser's sources. In this case, the "fact" of Apollo's paternity ("dux pater Apollo") occurs in the paragraph where Comes is discussing Apollo as the inventor of music and the power of music to soothe the human spirit or to make it more warlike. The crucial sentence is followed by the fabled parentage of Linus, who some say was the son of Amphimarus and Urania, others of Apollo and Terpsichore, and still others of Urania and Mercury, but the main point of the passage is not the truth of the parentage but the fact that Linus excelled all mortals in the glory of his music ("omnes mortales gloria musice antecelleret") and devoted himself to Apollo in song ("Apolline, cui se cantu conferebat"), that very Apollo who was the inventor of music and prophecy ("musicae & vaticiniorum inventor"). To prove this point Comes quotes two lines from Ovid's *Metamorphoses*, which I think explain Spenser's deviant parentage of the muses: "Iuppiter est genitor; per me, quod eritque fuitque / estque, patet; per me concordant carmina nervis" (*Met.* I.516–17: "Jove is my father. By me what shall be, has been, and what is are revealed; by me the lyre responds in harmony to song.") These lines are taken from Apollo's speech to Daphne while pursuing that nymph who was to become the laurel crown of poets. Although the lines in the context of the *Metamorphoses* clearly refer to Apollo himself, in isolation as they are in Comes' text they can become a gloss on the muses themselves, in which the parentage of Jove is admitted only to advocate the necessary agency of Apollo in the creation of true song. It is Apollo who opens up the past, the present and the future in song, and it is for this reason that Comes makes him "dux pater." Comes undoubtedly knew that his predecessor Gyraldi had cited both Eumelus Corinthius and Johannes Tzetzes, in whose commentaries on Hesiod Apollo is named as father of three muses: Cesiphon, Apollonida, and Boristhenida,[4] but such erudition takes us much beyond Spenser's "nod" to Apollo as the father of the muses. It seems to me that Lotspeich was right in pointing

---

4. Lilio Gregorio Gyraldi, *De deis gentilium* (1548), p. 156.

out Comes as the source of Spenser's aberrant parentage of the muses, but it also seems that many more important questions and answers are lost in the bargain. Even if my suggestion is correct, we are no closer to answering the question of why Spenser changes the parentage of the muses to Jupiter in the second half of his poem, unless we are witnessing a shift from the power of Apollo in the first half to the power of Jove in the second half, a shift from private to political virtues, but this is a suggestion that raises more questions than it answers.

Let us turn to the muses themselves and begin with the seven invocations in *The Faerie Queene*. In the Proem to Book I Spenser calls his muse "holy Virgin chiefe of nine" (I Proem 2.1). In Book III he invokes Clio: "Begin, o *Clio*" (III.iii.4), for the first time naming the muse invoked. With one exception the other invocations do not specify a muse by name (I.xi.5–7; II.x.3; IV.xi.10; VII.vii.1), but that one exception complicates the problem by naming two muses: "Mean while, O *Clio*, lend *Calliope* thy quill" (VII.vi.37).[5] As Padelford pointed out many years ago, the line can be read in two ways: either "Meanwhile, O Clio, give way for the moment to Calliope" or "Meanwhile, O Clio, lend thy services for the moment to Calliope."[6] To establish the validity of either reading requires that Clio or Calliope also be the "chiefe of nine" mentioned in the Proem to Book I, and to decide that question we must go back to the very beginning of the tradition.

Hesiod is the "only begetter" of the muses. It is he who first names the nine, and it is his names that resound through more than two millennia of Western literature and art. In spite of the alternative traditions of muses numbering from one to eight with differing names,[7] the dominant tradition adheres to Hesiod's revelation of his muses, which was reinforced when Homer followed Hesiod. It is this tradition that is given pride of place by the medieval encyclopedists and the Renaissance mythographers.

Ταῦτ' ἄρα Μοῦσαι ἄειδον, Ὀλύμπια δώματ' ἔχουσαι,
ἐννέα θυγατέρες μεγάλου Διὸς ἐκγεγαυῖαι,

5. All quotations are from *The Faerie Queene*, ed. Thomas P. Roche, Jr. (Harmondsworth, Eng.: Penguin Books, 1978; New Haven: Yale University Press, 1984).

6. *Variorum* I.507.

7. Cicero, *De natura deorum* III.21; Plutarch, *Moralia*, Table-Talk 9, Question 14: "Unusual observations on the numbers of the Muses," pp. 264–86, but especially p. 270; Gyraldi (1548), pp. 356–58.

Κλειώ τ' Εὐτέρπη τε Θάλειά τε Μελπομένη τε
Τερψιχόρη τ' Ἐρατώ τε Πολύμνιά τ' Οὐρανίη τε
Καλλιόπη θ'· ἣ δὲ προφερεστάτη ἐστὶν ἀπασέων.
ἣ γὰρ καὶ βασιλεῦσιν ἅμ' αἰδοίοισιν ὀπηδεῖ.
(*Theogony* 75–80)

(These things then, the Muses sang who dwell on Olympus, nine daughters begotten by great Zeus, Cleio and Euterpe, Thaleia, Melpomene and Terpsichore, and Erato and Polyhymnia and Urania and Calliope, who is the chiefest of them all, for she attends on worshipful princes.)

Calliope alone is singled out for special notice, and the preeminence assigned her by Hesiod continues through all the permutations of her functions as muse right through the Renaissance.

One of the main difficulties besetting scholarly comment on the muses is the unstated assumption that there is a standard iconography of the nine that can be called upon to fit any situation in which the muses appear. This comfortable but erroneous assumption afflicts art historians as well as literary critics and usually takes the form of restricting muse X to function Y; e.g., Clio is history, Calliope is epic poetry. Often artists or poets will restrict muses to a single function, as we shall see in the case of Spenser, but this simplistic optimism as a general rule of thumb should constantly be reminded of Curtius's description of the multiplicity of the muses:

Unlike the Olympians, the Muses had no well-marked personalities. No one knew much about them. They incarnate a purely intellectual principle, which could be dissociated from the Greco-Roman pantheon. The only figure with whom they were regularly associated was Apollo. Their image was vague even in ancient Greece. From the earliest times there were conflicting traditions as to their number, lineage, dwelling-place, and function. Hesiod's Muses are different from Homer's, those of Empedocles from those of Theocritus. But from of old the Muses had been patronesses not only of poetry but also of philosophy and music. The schools of both Pythagoras and Plato were connected with the cult of the Muses from their beginnings. But the consensus also placed all higher intellectual pursuits under the sign of the Muses.[8]

---

8. Ernst Robert Curtius, *European Literature and the Latin Middle Ages*, trans. Willard R. Trask (New York: Pantheon, 1953), pp. 229–30. One should also see his earlier pieces, "Die Musen in Mittelalter," in *Zeitschrift für Romanische Philologie*, 59 (1939), 129–88, and 63 (1943), 225–74.

With this eloquent proviso in mind, we can proceed with caution to discuss the development of Calliope as the chief muse in the work of Macrobius, Martianus Capella, and Fulgentius at that critical juncture when the "Classical World" became the "Middle Ages" (spatial metaphor becomes temporal metaphor). Their comments on the muses were repeated constantly at least until the end of the sixteenth century.

Macrobius's *Commentary on the Dream of Scipio* was until the nineteenth century our main source of information about the lost *De re publica* of Cicero, that very Cicero who accommodated Greek learning to Roman custom. Macrobius, in reference to Plato's notion that a siren sits on each of the celestial spheres (*Republic* X.617B), transforms Plato's sirens into the muses:

> Moreover, cosmogonists have chosen to consider the nine Muses as the tuneful song of the eight spheres and the one predominant harmony that comes from all of them. In the *Theogony*, Hesiod calls the eighth Muse Urania because the eighth sphere, the star-bearer, situated above the seven errant spheres, is currently referred to as the sky; and to show that the ninth was the greatest resulting from the harmony of all sounds together, he added: "Calliope, too, who is preeminent among all." The very name shows that the ninth Muse was noted for the sweetness of her voice, for Calliope means "best voice." In order to indicate more plainly that her song was the one coming from all the others, he applied to her a word suggesting totality in calling her "preeminent among all."[9]

Macrobius's philosophical precision about the identification of Plato's sirens with the muses should not deter us from seeing that he is treating the muses as they were to be treated throughout their long history—as allegorical names to be plugged into any other convenient series of nines. His justification of this allegory is, of course, the order of the

9. Macrobius, *Commentary on the Dream of Scipio*, trans. William Harris Stahl (New York: Columbia University Press, 1952), bk. II, chap. 3, pp. 193–94. The Latin text is from *Commentarii in Somnium Scipionis*, ed. Jacobus Willis (Leipzig: Teubner, 1970), II.104: "Theologi quoque novem Musas octo sphaerarum musicos cantus et unam maximam concinentiam quae confit ex omnibus esse voluerunt. unde Hesiodus in Theogonia sua octavam Musam Uraniam vocat, quia post septem vagas, quae subiectae sunt, octava stellifera sphaera superposita proprio nomine caelum vocatur; et ut ostenderet nonam esse et maximam quam conficit sonorum concors universitas, adiecit [Hesiod, *Theogony*, l. 79] ex nomine ostendens ipsam vocis dulcedinem nonam Musam vocari, nam Kalliope optimae vocis Graeca interpretatio est: et ut ipsam esse quae confit ex omnibus pressius indicaret, adsignavit illi universitatis vocabulum [*Theogony*, l. 79]." See also J. R. T. Pollard, "Muses and Sirens," *Classical Review*, n.s. 2 (1952), 60–62.

muses as given in Hesiod and the preeminence of Calliope. His allegory also sweeps the formerly earth- or mountain-bound muses into the empyrean, where they will remain for the next millennium.

At about the same time as Macrobius was creating his scientific allegory, Martianus Capella in a different way was also un-earthing the muses in his *De nuptiis Mercurii et Philologiae*. The *De nuptiis*, because of its enormous importance as a philosophical text in the Middle Ages, has not been given sufficient credit for its elegant hilarity as fiction. Modeled on Apuleius's story of Cupid and Psyche, it tells of Mercury, the Cyllenian, who decides that it is time to marry:

> His mother had encouraged him in this inclination when, on his yearly journey through the zodiac, he greeted her in the company of the Pleiades. She was concerned about him, especially because his body, through the exercise of wrestling and constant running, glowed with masculine strength and bore the muscles of a youth perfectly developed. Already with the first beard on his cheeks, he could not continue to go about half-naked, clad in nothing but a short cape covering only the top of his shoulders—such a sight caused the Cyprian great amusement. With all this in mind he decided to marry.[10]

The sly humor of this passage displays Martianus's command of Mercury's iconographical attributes and should alert us to further displays of humor in even the most philosophical passages, such as his discussion of the muses. As Mercury ascends into the heavens to claim his bride, Martianus describes a vision:

> Then the whole world could be seen joining in celebration; for Tellus had seen Mercury the god of spring flying upward and was bright with flowers, and the region of Air shone without clouds in the sight of Apollo. The upper spheres and the seven planetary spheres produced a symphony of the harmonious notes of each, a sweeter song than usually heard; indeed they had sensed the approach of the Muses, each of whom, after traversing the spheres, took her position where she recognized the pitch that was familiar to her. For Urania was attuned to the outermost sphere of the starry universe, which was swept along with a high pitch. Polymnia took over the sphere of Saturn; Euterpe controlled that of Jove; and Erato, that of Mars, which she entered; while Melpomene held the middle region, where the sun enhanced the world

10. *Martianus Capella and the Seven Liberal Arts*, trans. William Harris Stahl, Richard Johnson, and E. L. Burge (New York: Columbia University Press, 1971–77), II.6.

with the light of flame. Terpsichore joined the golden Venus; Calliope embraced the Cyllenian sphere; Clio set up as her lodging the innermost circle—that is, the moon's, whose deep pitch reverberated with deeper tones. Only Thalia was left sitting on earth's flowery bosom, because the swan which was to carry her was indisposed to carry its burden or even to fly upward and had gone to find the lakes which were its home.[11]

This sprightly little fancy was to become one of the most important literary sources for the muses in the Middle Ages and the Renaissance. If Martianus did not know Macrobius's conflation of Plato's sirens with the muses, then both of them derive their spherification of the muses from some earlier source of which I am unaware. I would prefer to think that Martianus had Macrobius very much in mind because of the way in which he insists on the musicality of the situation and the way he elaborates, indeed forces, Macrobius's notation of only Urania and Calliope to the logical conclusion of accounting for all the muses in a way that suited his purpose as well as that of Macrobius. Like Macrobius, Martianus begins with the etymology of Urania's name and associates her with the highest sphere, but because he does not want to make Calliope *concentus sonorum* as in Macrobius, he invents that delightful fantasy about Thalia and her reluctant swan. I do not believe that this is a displacement of Calliope from her position of eminence, because Calliope is associated with the sphere of Mercury, the protagonist of the whole fiction, and also because only Calliope and Urania of all the muses are mentioned in the later sections of the *De nuptiis*.[12] It seems significant to me that an important interpretation of the muses should occur in a very influential handbook on the divisions of knowledge, whose last seven books are devoted to an exposition of the seven

11. Stahl et al., p. 16; "Nam Urania stellantis mundi sphaeram per extimam concinit, quae acuto raptabatur tinnitu. Polymnia Saturnium circulum tenuit; Euterpe Jovialem. Erato ingressa Martium modulatur; Melpomene medium ubi Sol flammanti mundum lumine convenustat. Terpsichore Venereo sociatur astro. Calliope orbem complexa Cyllenium; Clio citimum circulum; hoc est, in luna collocavit hospitium, quae quidem graves pulsus modis raucioribus personabat. Sola vero, quod vector ejus cygnus impatiens oneris atque etiam subvolandi alumna stagna petierat, Thalia derelicta in ipso florentis campi ubere residebat." Martianus Capella, *De nuptiis Mercurii et Philologiae* I.27–28, ed. Ulricus F. Kopp (Frankfurt, 1836), pp. 69–70.

12. At the wedding of Mercury and Philology each of the muses sings a song, the order being: Urania, Calliope, Polymnia, Melpomene, Clio, Erato, Terpsichore, Euterpe, Thalia (Stahl, pp. 40–45). See below for a discussion of this order in Geoffroi Tory's *Champfleury*.

Liberal Arts, the ancient *trivium* and *quadrivium* of medieval and Renaissance education. While it is quite true that these seven Liberal Arts depicted as learned sisters appear in every conceivable form of programmatic display, almost as if Boethius's banishment of the muses in favor of Lady Philosophy at the beginning of *De consolatione philosophiae* had taken instant effect for several hundred years, it is equally true that the muses continued a quiet existence in literary texts and in fact began to draw to themselves some of the attributes of their more spectacular sisters.[13] Hence, their former Greek and Roman occupations forgotten, the muses had to make do with the rented finery of the Liberal Arts—a subject to which I will return shortly.

Part of this assimilation of late classical and medieval educational theory by the muses is owing to Fulgentius, who wrote his *Mythologiae* less than a century after Macrobius and Martianus. His allegory of the Hesiodic names reverses the spherification of the two earlier writers by internalizing the muses as names for the production of human speech and learning. Fulgentius begins by affirming nine as the number of the muses because of the nature of human speech, produced by two lips, four teeth, one tongue, one windpipe, and breath from the lungs. Lest any modern reader be put off by this extraordinary anatomy, we should realize that Fulgentius is merely doing the same act of allegorization as Macrobius and Martianus, except that Fulgentius validates the muses by reference to the microcosm of man rather than to the macrocosm. Although he does not specify the names of the muses for his allegory of speech production, he is quite explicit about the identification of particular muses with *doctrinae atque scientiae modos*, and his arrangement of the names is a variation on Hesiod's order, based for the most part on the etymology of the Greek names. It will be enough for us to know that Clio is derived from *kleos* and Calliope from *optimae vocis*, this last etymology deriving from Hesiod's original singling out of Calliope as the most excellent of the muses and Mac-

13. See the early articles of Curtius cited in note 8. For the influence of Boethius's dismissal of the muses, see Pierre Courcelle, *La "Consolatio philosophiae" dans la tradition littéraire: Antécedents et postérité de Boèce* (Paris: Etudes augustiniennes, 1967). See also L. D. Ettlinger, "Muses and Liberal Arts," in *Essays in the History of Art Presented to Rudolf Wittkower*, ed. Douglas Fraser, Howard Hibbard, and Milton J. Lewine (London: Phaidon, 1967), pp. 29–35, and *The Seven Liberal Arts in the Middle Ages*, ed. David L. Wagner (Bloomington: Indiana University Press, 1983).

robius's making her the *concentus* of the other eight. The last sentence of Fulgentius's allegory is a summation: "Ergo hic erit ordo: primum est velle doctrinam, secundum est delectari quod velis, tertium est instare ad id quod delectatus es, quartum est capere ad quod instas, quintum est memorari quod capis, sextum est invenire de tuo simile ad quod memineris, septimum iudicare quod invenias, octavum est eligere de quo iudicas, nonum bene proferre quod elegeris."[14] The equation between the names of the muses and the steps of learning can be tabulated as follows:

1. to want learning (Clio)
2. to be delighted by what you want (Euterpe)
3. to pursue what delights you (Melpomene)
4. to know what you pursue (Thalia)
5. to remember what you know (Polyhymnia)
6. to invent something similar to what you remember (Erato)
7. to judge what you invent (Terpsichore)
8. to select from what you judge (Urania)
9. to make well known what you select (Calliope)

I have not yet discovered the source of this paradigmatic progression of learning, but it smacks unmistakably of the Rhetorician's Handbook. Be that as it may, Fulgentius's allegory of the muses was probably even more important than Martianus's because it is repeated even more often, right on through the Renaissance.

That the medieval reader would have found Fulgentius in line with Macrobius and Martianus is suggested by the incorporation in the ninth-century commentary on Martianus by Remigius of Auxerre of a Fulgentian interpretation in which Urania is "humanae intelligentiae sublimitas," Polyhymnia is "capacitas memoriae," Erato is "inveniens simile, nulla enim re plus voluntas delectatur quam similium collatione," at which point Remigius unmistakably has his eye on Fulgentius's Erato: "invenire de tuo simile ad quod memineris," to which he adds functions for Terpsichore

---

14. Fulgentius, *Mythologiae*, in *Opera*, ed. Rudolphus Helm (Lipsiae, 1898), pp. 25–27. The popularity of Fulgentius extends as far as Pontus de Tyard at least, because Tyard quotes him in *Le Solitaire premier*, ed. Silvio F. Baridon (Geneva: Droz, 1950), II.54–56. Picinelli, *Mundus symbolicus* (Cologne, 1687), also interprets the muses as "via ad eruditionem" but does not distinguish among them: "Parnassum & Heliconem, montes altissimos, inhabitare dicuntur Musae. . . . Nam ad eruditionem aspirantibus, enitendum est per ardua. Arcem Musae incolunt in sublimi positam, a cajus ascensu absterrentur plurimi, qui propter pigritiam horrent laborem discendi" (p. 164).

and Calliope equally derivative from Fulgentius: "Huic Terpsichore quasi artium delectatio sociatur, cogitationum enim perfectio sine disciplinarum exercitatione fieri non potest. His omnibus omnis humanae locutionis honestas gignitur quae Calliope signatur."[15] Here once more we have the Macrobian view of Calliope as the culmination, or *concentus*, of the previously mentioned muses. But Remigius was well aware that two muses—Clio and Thalia—remained uncommented on, and he hit on the brilliant solution of making them, the last two in Martianus's list, the logical outcome of the process of learning he has just allegorized: "inde Clio, hoc est bona fama, nascitur; sub qua Thalia quasi in ultimo loco, hoc est positio vel germinatio virtutum." Clio, good fame, is born from the process culminating the "humanae locutionis honestas" of Calliope and is based on the development of virtues represented by Thalia. Remigius conflated Martianus and Fulgentius in a way that supports the supremacy of Calliope and introduces the notion of fame as a generating force in the interpretation of the muses,

> the spur that the clear spirit doth raise
> (That last infirmity of Noble mind)
> To scorn delights and live laborious days.

Whether spur or reward, beginning or end, fame was firmly entrenched in the pursuit of the muses, but Clio, despite the etymology of her name (whether priority or finality, it comes to the same thing), did not displace, was not even in conflict with, the supremacy of Calliope.

The last of the medieval sources of the muses I shall discuss is the so-called "De musis inventis," which was regularly included among the minor poems of Virgil in Renaissance editions, thus acquiring enormous circulation and prestige.

> Clio gesta canens transactis tempora reddit.
> Dulciloquis calamos Euterpe flatibus urguet.
> Comica lascivo gaudet sermone Thalia.
> Melpomene tragico proclamat maesta boatu.
> Terpsichore affectus citharis movet impetrat auget.
> Plectra gerens Erato saltat pede carmine vultu.
> Signat cuncta manu loquiturque Polymnia gestu.
> Urania arce poli motus scrutatur et astra.
> Carmina Calliope libris heroica mandat.

15. Remigius of Auxerre, *Remigii autissiodorensis commentum in Martianum Capellam, libri I-II,* ed. Cora E. Lutz (Leiden: E. J. Brill, 1962), p. 102.

> Mentis Apollineae vis has movet undique musas,
> In medioque sedens complectitur omnia Phoebus.[16]

The poem is clearly not Virgilian, nor have I been able to find the original attribution to him; it was included in both manuscript and printed texts of Ausonius through the Renaissance and in the works of Cato as early as the ninth century. It was undoubtedly intended as a mnemonic device for the attributes of the muses, and like most mnemonics is valuable not as an end in itself but for its ability to call up detailed masses of information not included in the device, and thus what was originally intended as a spur to memory becomes for us without that information a potential trap. The fact that some editions begin with Clio and some with Calliope, followed by Clio, is of very small consequence in that the order of listing the muses is never of importance, beginning with Hesiod.[17] The lines in whatever order one reads them are a conflation of several traditions linking the muses with the seven Liberal Arts and the invention, or emergence, of literary genres, first in Greece, then in Rome, and finally much later in the Romance languages of the late Middle Ages. For example, Badius Ascenius in his annotations to the poem included in editions of Virgil, identifies Erato with geometry, Polyhymnia with rhetoric, and Urania with astronomy, while Clio is linked to history, Melpomene to tragedy, Thalia to comedy, and Calliope to letters. The first three are part of the standard list of the Liberal Arts, while the latter four have taken on a life of their own quite distinct from their place in the Liberal Arts. It is a moot question whether Badius's association of Euterpe with the *tibia* and Terpsichore with the *psalterium* owes more to the music of the *quadrivium* or to a distinction between wind and string instruments.[18]

16. The poem is not included in the Loeb edition of Virgil, but it appears in the Loeb Ausonius, II.280, and in *Minor Latin Poets*, p. 634. The variant form attributed to Florus appears on p. 434. Another version of the Latin is quoted in Elisabeth Schroter, *Die Ikonographie des Themas Parnass vor Raffael* (Hildesheim: G. Olms, 1977), pp. 318–19. Bennett's article misprints *mendat* for *mandat* in l. 9 (Freudian slip?). A similar misprint occurs in Lotspeich, although he disclaims knowledge of Bennett's work before publication. I have found no edition of the poem that reads *mendat*.

17. Bennett's and Gregory's insistence on the importance of the order of these lines in Renaissance editions ignores the fact that we really know very little about what the lines mean in the case of each muse, and they blow up out of all proportion the importance of the lines for a Renaissance reader.

18. For the extremely complicated classical preference for string over wind instruments see Emmanuel Winternitz, "The Curse of Pallas Athena: Notes on a 'Contest

In short, without adequate knowledge of the date of its composition or of its relation to at least two other variants of equally ambiguous provenance, one cannot be sure of the program that led to the composition of this mnemonic device.

The point is of some importance because there is a similar poem on the function of the muses in the *Greek Anthology*, which is quoted by both Gyraldi (1548) and Natalis Comes (1616) in their chapters on the muses.[19] Although Comes attributes the poem to Callimachus, its date and provenance are not certain. The Loeb editor lists it as "anonymous." Since modern editions of the *Anthology* are based on the huge manuscript of Constantius Cephalas, which was found in Heidelberg by Salmasius in 1616, it may be useful to point out that until that time the *Anthology* was identified with a fourteenth-century redaction by Planudes Maximus, who reduced the original fifteen books to a selection divided into seven books, which was first published in Florence in 1494 by Janus Lascaris and was followed by Aldus (1503, 1521, 1550), Badius (Paris, 1531), Opsopoeus (Basel, 1540), Brodaeus with commentary (Basel, 1549) and H. Stephanus (Geneva, 1556) among others. It was alternatively known as *Florilegium diversorum epigrammatum in septem libris*.[20] It is very likely that one of these early printed editions of the "Planudean anthology" was the source for both Gyraldi and Comes.

---

between Apollo and Marsyas' in the Kress Collection," in *Studies in the History of Art Dedicated to W. E. Suidas on His Eightieth Birthday* (Phaidon Press for Samuel H. Kress Foundation, 1959), pp. 186–95. For discussions of the Renaissance knowledge of classical instruments see Patricia Egan, "Poesia and the *Fête Champetre*," *Art Bulletin*, 41 (1959), 303–13; Kathi Meyer-Baer, "Musical Iconography in Raphael's Parnassus" *Journal of Aesthetics and Art Criticism*, 8 (1949), 87–96, and her *Music of the Spheres and the Dance of Death: Studies in Musical Iconology* (Princeton: Princeton University Press, 1970). See also the classic studies of Emanuel Winternitz in *Musical Instruments and their Symbolism in Western Art* (New York: Norton, 1967), esp. chap. 13: "Muses and Music in a Burial Chapel: An Interpretation of Filippino Lippi's Window Wall in the Cappella Strozzi," and chap. 14: "Musical Archaeology of the Renaissance in Raphael's *Parnassus*."

19. The Greek version appears as no. 504 among the Declamatory Epigrams of the Loeb *Greek Anthology*, III.278. The Gyraldi translation of the Greek is in *De deis gentilium*, p. 360, and the Natalis Comes in bk. 7, chap. 15 of the *Mythologiae* (1616), p. 403.

20. The most important work on the *Anthology* remains the two books by James Hutton, *The "Greek Anthology" in Italy* (1935) and *The "Greek Anthology" in France* (1946), both Ithaca: Cornell University Press. Also useful are John W. Mackail, *Select Epigrams from the Greek* (London, 1890); and William Smith, *Dictionary of Greek and Roman Biography and Mythology* (London, 1867), s.v. *Planudes*.

Calliope heroi monstravit carminis artem,
Clio dulcisonae citharae modulamina prompsit,
Euterpea chori tragici resonabile carmen,
Melpomene dulci concentu barbita movit,
Grataque Terpsichore calamos instare paravit,
Ast Erato divum iucundos repperit hymnos,
Harmoniam numeris, saltusque Polymnia iunxit,
Uraniae astrorumque chorum coelique rotatus,
Comica vita Thalia tibi est, moresque reperti.

The poem which I here print in the translation of Gyraldi (1548, pp. 359–60; spelling regularized) agrees with the functions assigned to the muses by the pseudo-Virgilian poem only in the cases of Thalia (*comica*) and Urania (*astrorumque chorum*) and possibly Calliope (*heroi carminis*). The other muses are too closely identified in terms of musical instruments that had one function in Greece, another in Italy, and almost certainly none in the Middle Ages or Renaissance.

In this welter of attributes in all of the mnemonic poems there are three muses who are always given the same functions: Calliope, Urania, and Thalia, and this collocation of muses suggests either influence on or derivation from the work of Macrobius and Martianus Capella. For example, the frontispiece to Gafurius's *Practica musica* (1496), discussed both by Seznec and Wind,[21] presents at the top of the page a figure of Apollo, above whose head is a scroll that envelops both sides of the picture. On the right side are eight connected circles representing the fixed stars, Saturn, Jupiter, Mars, Sol, Venus, Mercury, and Luna, and on the left side (similarly in descending order) Urania, Polymnia, Euterpe, Erato, Melpomene, Terpsichore, Calliope, and Clio; that is, the order of the muses as given in Martianus Capella and also associated with the planets specified by him in the passage already discussed. At the bottom of the picture is the triform head of Serapis, whose tail extends all the way up through the cosmos to the feet of Apollo, but the head commands the earthly terrain of the four elements, and beneath is the lonely head of Martianus's un-swanborne Thalia. Even more important for the present discussion is the scroll above Apollo's head, framing the picture, inscribed with the penultimate line of the pseudo-Virgilian poem: "MENTIS APOLLINEAE VIS HAS MOVET UNDIQUE

---

21. Jean Seznec, *The Survival of the Pagan Gods*, trans. Barbara F. Sessions (New York: Pantheon, 1953), pp. 190–211; Edgar Wind, *Pagan Mysteries in the Renaissance* (New Haven: Yale University Press, 1958), p. 46n.

MUSAS," which seems to confirm my suggestion that the poem could be interpreted in terms of the earlier interpretation of Martianus.

We can also see the continuing influence of Martianus in the picture *L'Homme scientifique* in Geffroi Tory's *Champfleury* (1529), discussed by Seznec.[22] It is a picture of a nude man, various parts of whom are assigned to the Liberal Arts, the muses, and so on, by lines pointing to the appropriate portions of the body. Musica is assigned to the brain, Urania and Calliope to the right and left eyes, Polymnia and Melpomene to the right and left ears, Clio and Erato to the right and left nostrils, Terpsichore to the mouth, Euterpe to the right wrist, and Thalia to the genitals. The order is the same as that in which Martianus allows the muses to sing their hymn at the wedding of Mercury and Philology,[23] and even if the order is adventitious, it seems to me significant that Urania and Calliope should be given custody of the eyes (vision being the most important of the five senses) and the comic Thalia the custody of the genitals, the most earthly or perhaps the most comic parts of the body.

Although *L'Homme scientifique* has nothing to do with the pseudo-Virgilian poems, it does bring us closer to the kind of iconographical specification we would like for the muses, and that function is accomplished in the Renaissance by Cesare Ripa's *Iconologia*, first published in 1593. Ripas's discussion of the attributes of the muses is intended for artists who wanted to know how to depict the pagan gods. Even though his descriptions of the gods have been taken as too golden by the art historians as a general statement of the case, his discussion of the muses gives an interpretation of the pseudo-Virgilian lines which is useful to get us out of some of the perplexities surrounding that poem.

Ripa first suggests that Clio is a young woman crowned with laurel, holding a trumpet in her right hand and in her left a volume inscribed *Herodotus*, to honor the first historian, who named each of the nine books of his history after a muse, beginning with Clio as in Hesiod and continuing in his order. Calliope is also a young woman, her head bound with a circlet of gold, holding in her left hand many garlands of laurel and in her right three volumes inscribed *Odyssey*, *Iliad*, and *Aeneid*. Ripa is following the tradition of Clio as history and Calliope as heroic poetry, but more important for the purposes of this essay he

22. Seznec, pp. 142–47 and illustration 49 on p. 136.
23. See note 12.

glosses the attributes in a way that explicitly makes Calliope the first of the muses:

> Se le cinge la fronte col cerchio di oro, perchè secondo Esiodo è la più degna, e la prima tra le sue compagne, come ancora dimostra Ovvidio lib. 5. Fast.
> *Prima sui capit Calliopea chori.*
> E Lucano, e Lucrezio lib. 6.
> *Calliope requies hominum, divumque voluptas.*
> Le corone di alloro dimostrano, ch'ella fa i Poeti, essendo queste premio loro, e simbol della Poesia. I libri sono le opere de' più illustri Poeti in verso eroico, il qual verso si attribuisce a questa Musa, per il verso di Virgilio in opusc.[24]

Ripa then quotes the pertinent line from "De musis inventis": "Carmina Calliope libris heroica mandat." Thus, one important Renaissance encyclopedia, late for Spenser to be sure, read the pseudo-Virgilian lines in a way that leaves no doubt about the primacy of Calliope among the muses.

Bennett's argument that Clio was the chief of the muses on the basis of the primacy of the "De musis inventis" will not hold up. That poem is not the most important source of information about the muses in the Renaissance or earlier. That honor belongs to the combined commentaries of Macrobius, Martianus Capella, and Fulgentius, which form the major part of the commentaries of Herrad of Landsberg, Albricus, and Boccaccio.[25] Even with the explosion of classical sources cited in sixteenth-century encyclopedias such as those of Gyraldi, Natalis Comes, Cartari, Ripa, and in specific works on the muses such as those of Linocier and Lomazzo,[26] there is no suggestion that Clio is anything

---

24. Cesare Ripa, *Iconologia*, p. 196.

25. Herrad of Landsberg (Herrad of Hohenbourg), *Hortus deliciarum*, ed. Rosalie Green, Michael Evans, Christine Bischoff and Michael Curschmann (London: Warburg Institute, 1979), II.55–56; Albricus/Albericus Londiniensis/Alexander Neckham (for discussion see Seznec, pp. 170–83), *Allegoriae poeticae*, Tractatus 3, cap. 3, fols. xxx-xxxii; Giovanni Boccaccio, *Genealogie deorum gentilium libri*, ed. Vincenzo Romano (Bari: Laterza, 1951), II.539–42.

26. Lilio Gregorio Gyraldi (1479–1552), *De musis* (1507), *De deis gentilium* (1548); Natalis Comes (1520–82), *Mythologiae* (1551); Vincenzo Cartari (c. 1520–c. 1570), *Le imagini degli dei degli antichi* (1556); Cesare Ripa (c. 1560–before 1625), *Iconologia* (1593); Geffroi Linocier (c. 1550–1620), *Mythologiae musarum libellus* (from 1583

more than the muse whom Hesiod and the "De musis inventis" mention first, and much to suggest that Calliope is always the principal muse. Cartari is very explicit about the matter in relating the allegory of Fulgentius: "La prima, che è detta Clio significa Gloria. . . . La nona, che è Calliope, tanto importa quanto perfettione di scientia, & è la superiore, & il capo di tutte le altre."[27] Even outside the encyclopedic tradition the primacy of Calliope is maintained, sometimes with and sometimes without footnotes to Macrobius, Martianus, and Fulgentius. To commemorate the death of Petrarch in 1374, Coluccio Salutati planned a "treatise" on the muses, which he did not write; he did write, however, a verse epistle to Maestro Bartolomeo del Reame di Puglia, in which he links the muses with the seven Liberal Arts, beginning with Calliope as music:

> Det tibi sublimis de celi culmine vocum
> Calliopea decus gravibusque retardet acuta,
> Dissonaque harmonico necnon et consona nexu
> Coniungat placide, verborum pondera librans.[28]

These lines because of their insistence on harmony strike me as suspiciously Macrobian, and my suspicion is confirmed by what the editor of Salutati's letters refers to as a fifteenth-century commentary but which is in fact a somewhat simplified version of Salutati's treatment of the muses in *De laboribus herculis*: "Pythagorei atque Platonici . . . Musarum maximam quam Caliopen vocaverunt."[29] Petrarch's teacher, Convenevole da Prato, wrote an elaborate masque of welcome for the visit of Robert of Anjou in 1320. It is complete with speeches by the nine orders of angels, the three theological virtues, the four cardinal virtues, the seven Liberal Arts, and finally the nine muses, ending with

---

printed with Comes); Giovanni Paolo Lomazzo (1538–1600), *Della forma delle muse* (1591). A rough count of the sources cited in the various treatises on the muses makes the point: Boccaccio 17, the 1507 *De musis* 90, which Gyraldi reduced to 50 in the 1548 version. Natalis Comes maintains a modest 20 in both versions, while Lomazzo exceeds all bounds with 120.

27. Cartari, *Imagini*, p. 49.

28. Coluccio Salutati, *Epistolario di Coluccio Salutati*, ed. Francesco Novati (Rome, 1891), p. 347.

29. Coluccio Salutati, *De laboribus Herculis*, ed. B. L. Ullman (Zurich: Thesaurus Mundi, 1951), bk. I, chaps. 9–10, pp. 40–53.

Calliope, *optima vox*, taking the final aria, which ends in a triumphant *laus deo*, only to be achieved by an *optima vox* straight out of Macrobius and Fulgentius.[30]

It should not be surprising that the Florentine Neoplatonists were attracted by these allegories that supplanted Plato's myth of sirens and the celestial spheres, and so we find Ficino at the end of his commentary on the *Ion* taking up the problem of the muses and inspiration:

> Quamobrem ab Ioue Apollo, & Musae ab Apolline, id est, mente animas mundi, chorus musarum ducitur, quia mens illa sicut ab Ioue illustratur, & sic animas mundi sphaerarumque illustrat. Gradus autem quibus furor ille descendit, hi sunt. Iupiter rapit Apollinem, Apollo illuminat Musas. Musae suscitant & exagitant lenes & insuperabiles uatum animas. Vates inspirati interpretes suos inspirant. Interpretes auditores mouent. Ab aliis uero Musis aliae animae rapiuntur, quia & alii, sphaeris sideribus que aliae attributae sunt animae, ut in Timaeo traditur. Calliope Musa uox est, ex omnibus saltans spherarum uocibus.[31]

We need not go into detail about Ficino's assignment of the various muses to the spheres, except to mention that Clio is assigned to Mars "propter gloriae cupiditatem." What Ficino has done is to follow the Macrobian format of placing Urania in the *coelum stellatum* and making Calliope the *concentus sonorum* and then to invent his own allegory based on the figurative etymology of the Middle Ages and Renaissance, hence his placing of Clio with Mars. Let me conclude this section by quoting the short eleventh chapter of the first book of Pico della Mirandola's *Commento* on the canzone of Benivieni. It will speak for itself:

> *Che le anime de le otto Sfere insieme con l'anima del mondo sono le nove Muse.*
>
> Dopo l'anima del mondo pongono e' Platonici molte altre anime razionale, fra le quali ne sono otto principale, che sono l'anime delle spere celeste, le quali secondo gli antichi non erano più che otto, cioè sette pianeti e la spera stellata. Queste sono le nove Muse, da' Poeti celebrate, fra le quali è la prima Callyope, che è la universale anima del mondo, e le altre otto per ordine sono distribuite ciascuna alla sua spera.

30. Convenevole da Prato, *Regia carmina, dedicata a Roberto d'Angio*, ed. Cesare Grassi (Milano: Gruppo Bibliofili Pratesi, 1982).

31. Marsilio Ficino, *Opera omnia*, ed. Paul Oskar Kristeller (Torino: Bottega d'Erasmo, 1962), II.1283–84.

Però dobbiamo dire Callyope essere la più nobile e la prima anima fra tutte le anime e l'anima universale di tutto il mondo.[32]

In spite of Pico's extravagant language it is pointless to belabor the issue further: Calliope, no matter what her position in any listing of the muses, is the most important of the muses and hence should be that "holy Virgin chiefe of nine" invoked by Spenser in the Proem to Book I of *The Faerie Queene*.

The arguments set forth by Bennett as chief of the Cliophilists have subverted the intellectual content of the vastly complicated iconography of the muses. From the very beginning, with Hesiod, the order of listing the muses did not indicate an order of importance. It should also be manifestly clear that the pseudo-Virgilian verses are not the most important source of iconographical information about the muses but an interesting side road that has acquired more importance for Spenserian studies than it has for the rest of the tradition. Nevertheless, Bennett's contention that Spenser and Harvey—and only they—follow the order of the pseudo-Virgilian verses in defiance, or ignorance, of the tradition I have been describing is a possibility that would merit serious consideration if her main evidence did not blow her argument away. Gabriel Harvey wrote a nine-part elegy for Thomas Smith, each part assigned to a particular muse in the order given in the pseudo-Virgilian verses. Song I is assigned to Clio. There is no mention of Clio as the greatest muse nor any mention of her connection with poetry. The seventh song is Calliope's, to which Harvey adds an interesting introduction: "Song VII. *Which is equal to the eight others, and embraces the entire history of almost his whole life, expressed in comparatively few verses.*" This song which is "equal to the eight others" is so by analogy to Calliope as interpreted by Macrobius—*sonorum concors*. Harvey's order of the muses may be pseudo-Virgilian, but the

32. Giovanni Pico della Mirandola, *Comento*, ed. Eugenio Garin, in *De hominis dignitate, Heptaplus, De ente et uno* (Florence: Vallecchi Editore, 1942), pp. 477–78. A translation of the entire commentary is in *Commentary on a Canzone of Benivieni . . .* , trans. Sears Jayne (New York: Peter Lang, 1984), p. 90: "After the World Soul, the Platonists list many other rational souls. Among these there are eight principal ones, namely the souls of the heavenly spheres. (According to the ancients, there were no more than eight spheres, namely seven planets and the sphere of the fixed stars.) These souls are the nine Muses celebrated by the poets; the First Muse is Calliope, who is the universal World Soul, and the other eight Muses are distributed in order, each to her own sphere. Hence we must say that Calliope is the noblest and highest of all souls; she is the universal Soul of the whole World."

ideas informing that order are Macrobian, and therefore Calliope is preeminent.

Spenser's first reference to the muses in *The Shepheardes Calender* suggests the priority of Calliope:

> I see *Calliope* speed her to the place,
>   Where my goddesse shines:
> And after her the other Muses trace
>   With their Violines. ("April" 100–03)

The violins as attributes of the muses seem to owe more to the necessity of a rhyme for *shines* than to any special knowledge on Spenser's part of the iconography of the muses. E. K. comments on these lines: "Calliope, one of the nine Muses: to whom they assigne the honor of all Poetical Inuention, and the first glorye of the Heroicall verse. Other say, that shee is the Goddesse of Rhetorick: but by Virgile it is man-ifeste, that they mystake the thyng."[33] E. K. is, of course, referring to the pseudo-Virgilian line, "Carmina Calliope libris heroica mandat," and wants to dissociate her from the iconography linking the muses with the seven Liberal Arts, in particular, Calliope with Rhetoric, which he might have found in Diodorus Siculus, Phornutus, Plutarch, Gyraldi, or the dictionary of Charles Stephanus.[34] The obvious reason

---

33. *Spenser's Minor Poems*, ed. Ernest de Selincourt (Oxford: Clarendon Press, 1910). See also "June" 57–61: "I sawe *Calliope* wyth Muses moe, / Soone as thy oaten pype began to sound, / . . . Renne after hastely thy siluer sound." These references are to Calliope as leader and harmony of the other muses, the *sonorum concors* of Macrobius.

34. The tradition that makes Calliope the muse of rhetoric is developed from a hint in Hesiod, part of which has been mentioned before. After listing the other muses he writes: "and Calliope, who is the chiefest of them all, for she attends on worshipful princes: whomsoever of heaven-nourished princes the daughters of great Zeus honour, and behold him at his birth, they pour sweet dew upon his tongue, and from his lips flow gracious words. All the people look towards him while he settles causes with true judgements: and he, speaking surely, would soon make wise end even of a great quarrel; for therefore are there princes wise in heart, because when the people are being mis-guided in their assembly, they set right the matter again with ease, persuading them with gentle words" (*Theogony*, ll. 79–90). This hint is elaborated by later writers. Diodorus Siculus associates the muses with the Liberal Arts and says of Calliope that she wins the approbation of her auditors because of her beautiful voice (IV.7.4, Loeb, p. 364). Phornutus is quite explicit: "Calliope est, vocalis, & comptis verbis exornata Rhetorica, cujus auxilio respublicas administramus, populos compellamus, eos persuasione, & non vi, quo volumus, trahimus" (*De natura deorum*, in *Opuscula mythologica*, ed. Thomas Gale [Amsterdam, 1688], p. 160). See also Plutarch, *Moralia*, Table-Talk, bk. IX, question 14; Gyraldi (1548), p. 359, and Charles Stephanus, *Dictionarium historicum, geographicum, poeticum* (Geneva, 1670), col. 1389, s.v. *Musae*.

is that E. K.'s editorializing for the New Poet requires that his poet refer only to the very best sources and that his references be only of the highest valence, poetry being a higher thing than rhetoric. He would have saved us all much time if he had added a line about the primacy of Calliope, but that is the kind of commentator he is.

"The Teares of the Muses" is, needless to say, the logical place to seek out Spenser's knowledge of the muses, but as every critic has pointed out, Clio and Calliope lament in much the same manner. One of the main faults of this poem is its imprecision, imprecise even by Spenserian standards; it is a general and diffuse complaint about the ills of the world, and this same generality and diffuseness is reflected in its diction. The muses as an organizing principle are but the slightest of attempts to impose order. They have a general appropriateness because of their association with the arts and learning, but Spenser is not trying to specify precisely the ills of the world as they exist in the particular province of each muse, even if he knew what those were. The function of each muse in this poem is of only secondary importance, and we are deceived in building an argument about Spenser's muses on a close interpretation of their functions as revealed in this poem.

If we cannot make any discrimination about Spenser's muse from his minor poems, then we are left with a resounding question from all Cliophilists: Why does Spenser bring Clio into his epic poem at all? It is a very good question, to which I think I have a satisfactory answer.

Spenser read his "De musis inventis" quite literally: Clio is the muse of history and Calliope is the muse of heroic poetry. He also saw that epic poets even beyond those he mentioned in the "Letter to Raleigh" often had internal invocations to muses other than Calliope: Virgil, Statius, and in his own England, Lydgate,[35] and on the basis of these two discriminations he invoked Calliope, unnamed except for the learned epithet "chiefe of nine," as the muse of his poem, possibly in imitation of Virgil ("Musa michi causas memora quo numine laeso"), possibly aware that that unnamed muse in the first illustrated edition of Virgil had the name "Calliope" written above her head.[36] This Calliope, worthy of Virgil, was to be the muse of his invented Faerie

---

35. Virgil, *Aeneid* I.8 ("musa"), VII.37 (Erato), IX.77 ("musae"), IX.525 (Calliope), 774–75 ("musis"); Statius, *Thebaid* I.4 ("deae") and 41 (Clio); *Lydgate's Troy Book*, ed. Henry Bergen, EETS, ex. ser. XCVII, p. 2: Calliope is invoked as mother of Orpheus.

36. Sebastian Brant, *Opera* (1502), fol. i.

Land, but at various points in his epic poem he had to make reference to what Northrop Frye has called the "red and white world" of Tudor history, and for this disjunction, if that is the right word for Spenser's distinction, he invoked Clio, the muse of history.

The internal invocations occur before the history of Britain in II.x, in which Arthur reads the history of his kingdom. It is true that Guyon also reads the Antiquity of Faerie Land in the same canto, but that is equally a lesson in history. The continuation of Arthur's history occurs in III.iii with an invocation to Clio, for the first time named. The next invocation occurs before the marriage of the Medway and the Thames (IV.xi) and the last just before the myth of Arlo Hill (VII.vi), in which Spenser is celebrating the locality in Ireland in which he lived. Of these four internal invocations, two refer to temporal events and two to geographical locations. I would like to suggest that they are all related to an actuality of history and geography that Spenser wanted to differentiate from his fictive faeryland, for the purpose of making his poem work as he wanted it to, not as his later critics expected of him.[37]

In each of the episodes preceded by an invocation Spenser wanted to emphasize the factual basis of his fiction, and hence he invoked Clio, "gesta canens transactis tempora reddit," to bring her expertise to his poem in order to supplement the epic stance of Calliope. To invoke one muse is not to un-invoke a previously mentioned one, as if there were only one circuit, because as in a famous Virgilian crux (*Aeneid* IX.525), where Calliope is addressed in the second person plural, the commentators assure us that Virgil is merely showing that to invoke one muse invokes them all and that we should not worry unduly about the territorial rights of the individual muses. If one draws an analogy to devotion to the saints, it should be obvious that although particular saints are particularly right for particular causes, prayer to any one of them, even the wrong Saint Anthony, invalidates neither the prayer nor the possible intervention. It is particularly appropriate that Clio be invoked for the history of British kings and its continuation in the

37. I want to avoid making an opposition between England and Faerie Land because that opposition would falsify Spenser's poem. I also want to avoid making a distinction between *real* and *ideal*, as I did in *The Kindly Flame*, with its unnecessary bow to Coleridge's theory of ideal space, because the Romantic *topos* of real and ideal sets up polarities that violate the subtleties of Spenser's poem. I would also like to avoid getting involved in the oppositions of epic versus romance, because all such post-Hegelian oppositions set up either-or-and-easy-out situations instead of the both-and situation that Spenser was proposing.

prophecy of Merlin to Britomart. From this catalogue of British kings it would have been an easy jump for Spenser to invoke Clio for the catalogue of rivers in the marriage of the Medway and the Thames episode, which is really a kind of spatial history. It seems right and proper that the Cliophilists should find in these invocations references to attributes of Clio, for I agree with them that Clio is being invoked.

It is for this reason that Spenser at the beginning of his myth of Arlo Hill asks, "Mean while, O *Clio*, lend *Calliope* thy quill." Clio is being invoked because the setting of his myth is the specific locale of his home in Ireland ("Who knowes not *Arlo-hill?*"). It may, of course, be objected that the myth of Arlo Hill is not really a catalogue, an objection with which I totally agree, but the point is that Spenser is insisting on a specific locale beyond even the necessary accuracy of a catalogue, simply by asking that rhetorical question. I wager that quite a few readers of the 1609 *Faerie Queene* would have had to admit ignorance of this Irish landmark, which, of course, the reason that Spenser is so insistent about it. He played a similar rhetorical trick when he introduced himself into his vision of the graces in Book VI, Canto x: "who knowes not *Colin Clout?*" An equally large number of readers in 1596 would have had to admit that they did not know that Spenser was referring to himself at the conclusion of his *rota Virgilii* in the persona of the very Colin Clout he had chosen for himself in 1579 at the pastoral beginnings of his poetic career. Apparently Spenser felt no need to invoke muses for the vision of self amid the graces as he did for his reference to Arlo Hill, because he, the poet, is taking control of his destroyed vision, of his fragmentation of his epic plans, as so often has been said of the ending of Book VI. In the vision of Mount Acidale, Spenser did not invoke the muse because he was terminating his epic plans. For reasons we will probably never know, he did invoke the muse in that coda we know as the Mutability Cantos, when he turned from cosmological myth to etiological myth in the guise of pastoral simplicity. I do not think that Spenser ever doubted the reality of either part of his myth of mutability. In this invocation to Clio and Calliope he was indicating a decorum of genre which he needed for the satisfaction of his fiction, as he suggests strongly in the opening of Canto vii:

> Ah! whither doost thou now thou greater Muse
> Me from these woods & pleasing forrests bring?
> And my fraile spirit (that dooth oft refuse

> This too high flight, vnfit for her weake wing)
> Lift vp aloft, to tell of heauens King
> (Thy soueraine Sire) his fortunate successe,
> And victory, in bigger noates to sing.

"Greater muse" and "bigger noates" *almost* suggest the preeminence of Calliope and her role as the harmony of the other muses, but I would like to emphasize the *almost*, not that I doubt that Spenser intends Calliope but that he is so careful to amplify rather than to specify his muse. In the second stanza of the invocation this muse seems to take on the function of Urania, who rules the eighth sphere and in the various versions of "De musis inventis"; "motusque poli scrutatur et astra," "polos octavo limine scandit," "numeris scrutatur sidera mundi," and in Gyraldi's Latin version of the Greek, "astrorumque chorum coelique rotatus." Spenser seems in this second stanza once more to submit to inspiration—I would like to suggest—of a different kind, which goes far to explain his reluctance to be more specific about the name of the muse of his poem.

> Yet sith I needs must follow thy behest,
> Doe thou my weaker wit with skill inspire,
> Fit for this turne, and in my sable brest
> Kindle fresh sparks of that immortall fire.
> Which learned minds inflameth with desire
> Of heavenly things: for, who but thou alone,
> That art yborne of heauen and heauenly Sire,
> Can tell things doen in heauen so long ygone;
> So farre past memory of man that may be knowne.

Just as in the first stanza we are pushed beyond Jove to "heauens King" *in the words of the poem* but must maintain firm control of Jove as the vehicle of the metaphor, so in this stanza we are pushed *by the words* beyond the identification of Calliope or Urania to a reaching after that Holier One Who spoke through the prophets. Spenser contents us merely with that underidentified Calliope—"thou greater Muse"— here at the end of his poem, but she is still the "chiefe of nine"— Calliope, a name from Hesiod and the epic tradition he was imitating. Spenser at the end of the epic tradition could still maintain a fiction of allegiance to the inspiration of the muses, but he yearned for invocations to be fulfilled only in the *Fowre Hymnes.*

His successor Milton could not play that game any more than he could find "king or knight before the conquest . . . in whom to lay the pattern of a Christian hero."[38] Milton's muse is verbally carefully delineated and diabolically hedged about and, if I am not mistaken, deeply influenced by the Uranian overtones in Spenser's final invocation.

> Descend from Heav'n Urania, by that name
> If rightly thou art call'd, whose Voice divine
> Following, above th'*Olympian Hill* I soar,
> Above the flight of *Pegasean* wing.
> The meaning, not the Name I call: for thou
> Nor of the Muses nine, nor on the top
> Of old *Olympus* dwell'st, but Heav'nly born,
> Before the Hills appear'd, or Fountain flow'd,
> Thou with Eternal Wisdom didst converse.
> (*Paradise Lost* VII.1–9)

"The meaning, not the Name I call," but the name is called, and Milton forces the reader to accept two sets of conventions: the classical muse Urania and the Holy Spirit of orthodox theology, in neither of which he believed. "So fail not thou, who thee implores: / For thou are Heavn'ly, shee an emptie dream" (*PL* VII.38–39). It has often been suggested that Milton invokes Urania because of the influence of Du Bartas and other Renaissance poets who tried to make Urania the muse of divine poetry.[39] That may be, but I can see in Milton's choice a knowledge of Macrobius and Martianus, the power of whose Urania stops at the eighth sphere, which is the reason that Milton does not even try to compete with Spenser's struggles with Calliope, so diffident about the name but not the meaning of his muse. Spenser was not so cunning or did not need to be about his muse, because he stood firmly within the classical conventions (whatever they might mean for him): for in the plenitude of Spenser's Christian cosmology, where or how

38. John Milton, *Complete Poetry and Major Prose,* ed. Merritt Y. Hughes (New York: Odyssey Press, 1957), *Reason of Church Government,* pp. 668–69.

39. For discussions of Urania as the muse of "Christian" poetry see L. B. Campbell, "The Christian Muse," *HLB,* 8 (1935), 29–70; and H. G. Lotspeich, "Spenser's Urania," *MLN,* 50 (1935), 141–46.

could muses exist? Convinced that the Holy Spirit did not exist except as a manifestation of God the Father, Milton forces the issue to a semantic crisis, after which there is no place to go but to Byron's comically lofty and empty "Hail, Muse, etcetera." But that is another story, beyond the scope of this essay.[40]

40. I cannot leave the subject of Spenser's muse without making some comment on the fifth invocation (I.xi.6–7), which occurs just before Redcross engages the dragon. This invocation is somewhat different from the others, but its peculiarities have not been discussed. As the battle with the dragon develops, it is clear that Redcross becomes a type of Christ overcoming evil. What then shall we make of the "gentle" rage which Spenser asks of his muse? Why should she "lay that furious fit aside" until she sings of the battle of the Faerie Queene with the Paynim king? And what does "second tenor" mean? The first two questions, I believe, are easily answered and suggest a possible answer for the third. Redcross is fighting the battle of the Christian soul with evil, participating in Christ's redemption of man, the freeing of Adam and Eve from their enemy. The battle of the Faerie Queene and the Paynim king would appear to be the Spenserian equivalent of the Apocalypse, in which evil is finally overcome by good. This supposition is supported by the echoes of Revelation in the last four lines of stanza 6: "dreadfull trompe," "slepe . . . so sound," and the "horrour" of the "scared nations" (Rev. 11:12ff., 20:14–15). The last six lines of the seventh stanza can be interpreted through the old Four Senses of allegory: literal or historical, tropological, allegorical, and anagogical. "The tropological meaning was that which was applied to the individual so that it was frequently moral in application. The allegorical sense was used originally to interpret the Old Testament in the light of the New, or to interpret it as it applies to the Church. The anagogical sense is concerned with the heavenly mysteries" (D. W. Robertson, Jr., and Bernard F. Huppé, *Piers Plowman and Scriptural Tradition* [Princeton: Princeton University Press, 1951], p. 3). Within this scheme the battle of Redcross is clearly tropological. Spenser is asking the muse to descend from the heavenly mysteries to the problem of the soul of man, from the fourth to the second sense. This is the only possible explanation of the word *tenor*. The *OED* lists only one meaning that might apply (II.4. Mus. c.). *Second tenor* is defined as "the next bell to the tenor. Also applied . . . to a string of tenor pitch in an instrument, as a harp." Spenser's other uses of the word *tenor* in connection with the muses (*Shepheardes Calender*, "October" 50, "Teares of the Muses" 367, "Epithalamion" 9, "Hymne in Honour of Love" 13) all seem to combine this musical meaning with the more usual definition as "drift or course of an argument." I believe that Spenser is here transferring the word in a figurative sense to the Four Senses of allegory, with an unmistakable reference to the spherification of the muses I have described.

9
Romance and Empire:
Anachronistic *Cymbeline*

PATRICIA PARKER

One of the most striking features of Shakespeare's *Cymbeline* is its curious anachronism, its superimposition of a "jay of Italy" (III.iv.49) like Iachimo—and language suggestive of a bourgeois setting of Italian and English Renaissance merchants—on a plot and scene that are ostensibly Roman, set at the time of Augustan Rome.[1] Iachimo—the putative Roman noble who betrays and finally bows to English Posthumus—is Italian not only by name but derisively that "slight thing of Italy" (V.iv.64), and most disparagingly, that "Italian fiend" (V.v.210). He himself confesses the origin of his villainy in the play's final scene: "mine Italian brain / Gan in your duller Britain operate / Most vildly" (V.v.196–98). Yet the play eschews its own more contemporary allusiveness. Its setting and primary historical referents justify its characterization as "Shakespeare's last Roman play."[2] And the context for the redoubling of romance plot motifs within it is the opposition between Augustan Rome and Britain in the age of Cymbeline—not Renaissance England and Italy.

The combination, in Iachimo, of Roman noble and Renaissance Ital-

1. The text of Shakespeare used throughout is *The Riverside Shakespeare*, ed. G. Blakemore Evans et al. (Boston: Houghton Mifflin, 1974). This essay is part of a more extended study of Roman and Renaissance imperial themes.
2. David Bergeron, "*Cymbeline*: Shakespeare's Last Roman Play," *Shakespeare Quarterly*, 31 (1980), 31–41.

ian has long been part of the assumed anachronism of this romance—a blurring of times with no apparent purpose or (in a strain of Shakespeare criticism on the lookout for errors of this sort) a quaint blunder to be ascribed to poetic licence, to carelessness, or to a distorted sense of history. Dr. Johnson, among his many complaints against the play, remarks as part of its "incongruity" its "confusion of the names and manners of different times."[3] I would propose, however, a markedly different perspective on this crossing of times, one that would involve deliberate achronicity—a flattening out of two historical times into the single space of the stage—and a series of reversals that evoke a different relation just behind the surface of the play's historically conservative close, the ending in which Cymbeline pays tribute to Rome though British forces have in fact won the day. I want also to argue that this crossing and temporal conflation is accomplished in part by an allusive conflation of texts and that the evocation of a specific imperial text in *Cymbeline's* romance plot[4] not only adds to the sense of "much ado about everything" this late Shakespearean romance is notorious for but makes its central anachronism something very different from either bungling error or historical oversight.

I will start with an evocation the play makes explicit when Posthumus deserts the maligned British Imogen, leaving her behind in a more negative sense than he had in his original departure, as exile, for Rome:

> True honest men being heard, like *false Aeneas,*
> Were in his time thought false; and Sinon's weeping
> Did scandal many a holy tear, took pity
> From most true wretchedness. So thou, Posthumus,
> Wilt lay the leaven on all proper men. (III.iv.58–62; my emphasis)

Imogen's complaint here momentarily identifies Posthumus with that "false Aeneas" who deserted Dido for the higher goal of empire and

---

3. For Johnson's comments, see the Introduction to J. C. Maxwell's New Cambridge *Cymbeline* (Cambridge: Cambridge University Press, 1968).

4. The first to place a principal emphasis on *Cymbeline's* political and historical dimension was G. Wilson Knight, in *The Crown of Life: Essays in Interpretation of Shakespeare's Final Plays*, 2nd ed. (London: Methuen, 1948), pp. 129–202.

Rome. Its aligning of Posthumus with Aeneas by name makes explicit what may already be recalled—to ears familiar with that moment in Virgil's imperial text when Aeneas, looking back (*respiciens*) at Carthage from his ship, abandons Dido—in the earlier description of Posthumus's departure for Rome:

> for so long
> As he could make me with [this] eye or ear
> Distinguish him from others, he did keep
> The deck, with glove or hat or handkerchief,
> Still waving, as the fits and stirs of 's mind
> Could best express how slow his soul sail'd on,
> How swift his ship. (I.iii.8–14)

In leaving for Rome, Posthumus "forgot Britain. And himself" (I.vi.113)—a phrase in which "Britain" stands synecdochally for the abandoned Imogen—and his departure involves both explicit and implicit evocation of Virgil's Aeneas, who abandoned Carthage (synonymous, also by synecdoche, with an abandoned Dido) for Rome. The identification of Imogen with Britain as inviolate isle, yet vulnerable to invasion, is reiterated in the Second Lord's hope for her in Act II ("The heavens hold firm / The walls of thy dear honor; keep unshak'd / That temple, thy fair mind, that thou mayst stand / T' enjoy thy banish'd lord and this great land!" [II.i.61-64]). By the time we get to the play's happier romance ending, however, Posthumus has returned to Britain. And as the older generation, in the person of Cymbeline, voluntarily yields the demanded tribute to Rome in a final scene that echoes the *pax Augusta* achieved by the labors of Virgil's Aeneas, Posthumus is paid tribute to by Iachimo, a repentant "jay of Italy" whose gesture of submission to a British "Aeneas" subtly reverses the British king's gesture of submission to imperial Rome. It is this exchange—and these ghostlier demarcations of the play's famous anachronism—that I propose to chart.

We might start by exploring the possibilities opened up by the explicit association of Posthumus with Aeneas in Shakespeare's "last Roman play." One of them is the link between this principal Virgilian figure for the translation of empire from fallen Troy in the East to the "second Troy" of Rome, and the persistent westering motif that critics of *Cymbeline* have long observed within it.[5] Posthumus himself is compared to the traditionally westering "eagle" of Jupiter (I.ii.70), which will later, in the soothsayer's vision, wing toward "the west" (IV.ii.348–50) in a clear allusion to a Hesperian Britain ("I saw Jove's bird, the Roman eagle, wing'd / From the spungy south to this part of the west, / There vanish'd in the sunbeams"). And at the end of the play, in the "peace" established between Roman and Briton, this omen of westering returns:

> for the Roman eagle,
> From south to west on wing soaring aloft,
> Lessen'd herself and in the beams o' th' sun
> So vanish'd; which foreshow'd our princely eagle,
> Th' imperial Caesar, should again unite
> His favor with the radiant Cymbeline,
> Which shines here in the west. (V.v.470–76)

The relation of *Cymbeline* to the westward translation of empire has already been noted—as have its echoes of the putative Trojan origin of the British and of London's status as the "third Troy" (or "Troynovaunt") after the "second Troy" of Rome. "Troynovaunt" is the original of "Lud's town" in the Queen's nationalistic appeal to the Britons in Act III (III.i.32). The names "Posthumus" and "Innogen" actually appear in Holinshed's chronicles of this history. "Innogen," wife of Brute, Britain's legendary Trojan founder, is not only so close as to be a possible substitute for "Imogen" (Simon Forman's report of an early performance of *Cymbeline* speaks of its "Innogen") but also the name Shakespeare used for the mute wife of Leonato of Sicily in *Much Ado about Nothing*. "Posthumus," successor of "false Aeneas" in Imogen's complaint, appears in Holinshed as the son of Aeneas and Lavinia,[6] the bride whose winning symbolizes the translation of empire from Troy to Italy: the shift from father to son, which within the *Aeneid* provides the central temporal paradigm for the westering of empire, is also the familiar Virgilian instance of *imitatio* with a difference. It has been

5. See especially J. P. Brockbank, "History and Histrionics in *Cymbeline*," *Shakespeare Survey*, 11 (1958), 42–49; and Emrys Jones's review article "Stuart Cymbeline," *Essays in Criticism*, 11 (1961), 84–89.

6. See Raphael Holinshed, "The First Booke of the Historie of England," in *The First and Second Volumes of Chronicles* (1587), p. 7.

further remarked that the play's echoes of the history of the westering of empire—not just from Troy to Rome but from Rome to Britain—would be fitting for a Jacobean play and the reign of a king who presented himself as a second Arthur, in a mythology already exploited by the Tudors, and as a second Brute, since he was the first since the eponymous founder of Britain to unite the whole island under single rule. James I—in a way suggestive for the dominant note of "peace" at the end of Shakespeare's complex romance—was by his own choice designated a second Augustus, the emperor whose *pax* was the culmination of the long and arduous labors recounted in the *Aeneid* and the reign under which Christ, the "Prince of Peace," was born. James's motto, we remember, was *Beati pacifici*.[7]

There are, however, even apart from the general sense of *translatio imperii*, much more specific implications in the identification of Posthumus with Aeneas. In calling *Cymbeline* "Shakespeare's Last Roman Play," David Bergeron joins other critics in observing that the play's Roman atmosphere is underscored through the presiding presence of Jupiter, whose "descent . . . on the back of an eagle in V.iv gives dramatic reality to the numerous references to this god (he is referred to thirty times in the play)."[8] Since Bergeron's primary focus is the figure of Augustus, he reminds us of the association of Augustus with the Temple of Jupiter. But dramatically, Jupiter's striking descent in Act V—in order to forecast the eventual fortunate outcome of the romance plot's exasperating sufferings and delays—has a function that again evokes the homology between Aeneas and Posthumus, both of whom suffer in obscurity, ignorant of the larger plot working to secure that outcome. Aeneas in Virgil is repeatedly described as *ignarus* and put through a series of setbacks and frustrations, unable to share the larger perspective of Jupiter, who in the epic's first book foretells to Aeneas's mother Venus the final happy issue of her son's sufferings—the achievement of a second Troy in Rome and the ultimate Augustan peace. Jupiter in *Cymbeline* descends from the imperial skies in Act V in order to justify to the family of the ignorant and sleeping Posthumus the trials *their* son has suffered. Venus appeals to the fatherhood of

---

7. For this discussion of the Jacobean dimension, as for the associations of Imogen's name, see Jones, "Stuart Cymbeline," pp. 90, 98.

8. Bergeron, "Shakespeare's Last Roman Play," p. 35.

Jupiter, who seems to have forgotten and turned away from the Trojan race (*Aeneid* I.229–53), and asks what "end" Aeneas's misfortunes will have. Posthumus's family appeals to Jupiter as the "father" he should have been to "great Sicilius's heir," asks why Jupiter has "adjourn'd" or delayed "The graces for his merits due, / Being all to dolours turn'd," and supplicates that he "no longer exercise / Upon a valiant race" his "harsh and potent injuries" (V.iv.30–84). Jupiter's answer to Aeneas's supplicant parent is to forecast that plot through which present suffering will finally bring about the glory that is to be Augustan Rome. Jupiter's response to Posthumus's family is to deliver what might be the paradigmatic statement of the trajectory of suffering in both the *Aeneid*—where fulfillment is frustratingly delayed—and the complicated romance plot of *Cymbeline*, where the characters also wander in darkness and where there is a sense of something higher than their bounded perspective, working to realize that much-delayed but finally happier ending:[9]

> Whom best I love I cross; to make my gift,
> *The more delay'd, delighted.* Be content,
> Your low-laid son our godhead will uplift.
> His comforts thrive, his trials well are spent.
> Our Jovial star reign'd at his birth, and in
> Our temple was he married. Rise, and fade.
> He shall be lord of Lady Imogen,
> *And happier much by his affliction made.* (V.iv.101-08; my emphases)

Like Aeneas, laboring in the dark and ignorant of the future outcome of his labors, Posthumus ("to himself unknown," as the text he wakes to find puts it [V.iv.139]) is here at the place of "blindness" (V.iv.189). He will, however, experience this blindness as part of a larger plot finally articulated in Lucius's "Some falls are means the happier to rise" (IV.ii.403), the upward shape of "rising again" which informs the *locus classicus* of Aeneas's own opening speech: "Perchance even this distress it will some day be a joy to recall [*forsan et haec olim meminisse iuvabit*]. Through divers mishaps, through so many perilous chances, we fare towards Latium, where the fates point out a home of rest.

---

9. For this sense in *Cymbeline*, see the discussion of the play in Northrop Frye, *A Natural Perspective: The Development of Shakespearean Comedy and Romance* (New York: Harcourt, Brace & World, 1965), pp. 66–67.

There 'tis granted to Troy's realm to rise again; endure, and keep yourselves for days of happiness" (I.203–07).[10]

Even more specifically in relation to the explicit aligning of Aeneas and Posthumus in *Cymbeline*, we need to recall the context of this famous speech at the beginning of Virgil's imperial poem. Aeneas here has already lost his father, now dead and left behind in Sicily. "Sicilius Leonatus"—the name of the father of Shakespeare's Posthumus—also links *his* dead and buried father with Sicily. Like Posthumus in prison when Jupiter descends to deliver his prophecy of an eventual happier end, Aeneas wishes fervently for death rather than for that afterlife which the present suffering appears to be for the "remnants" of Troy (I.30). There is, that is to say, something initially "posthumus" about Aeneas himself—spared from the death and fall of Troy as a kind of leftover and bereft of his father on Sicily: he calls to those "thrice and four times blest" (*O terque quaterque beati*) whose fortune it was, like Posthumus's older brothers, to die before their father's eyes in an earlier war.

Cymbeline as a whole seems to involve—as does the *Aeneid*—a sense of larger things at stake than the characters themselves can fully grasp, things of whose meaning they (like Aeneas in relation to the shield he bears) are at least temporarily ignorant. Aeneas and others in Virgil's imperial epic are visited with prophecies, signs, and omens that they do not understand and yet must interpret or carry with them on their way. Book III of the *Aeneid*, which tells of their westering journey, is filled with prophecies misunderstood or only dimly grasped in their full future meaning; Book VII includes a prophecy to Latinus, the Italian king, to wait for a "son" from abroad, a foreign suitor for his daughter, and thus to hold off the suit favored by Amata, his queen (a situation not without echo in the two suitors for Imogen—Cloten and Posthumus—in *Cymbeline*). Posthumus, in Shakespeare's play, receives a tablet left by the descending Jupiter, whose riddling text he cannot decipher, though it foretells the future outcome of his present suffering, and whose meaning coincides with the ultimate fulfillment of a plot which, like the *Aeneid*'s, also binds up personal stories and familial struggles into a larger imperial history.

10. The edition used in all citations from Virgil is the Loeb translation of the *Aeneid* (Cambridge, Mass.: Harvard University Press, 1949).

If we are attentive to the echoes of Virgil's epic of empire in a Shakespearean romance that G. Wilson Knight was first to recognize as "mainly . . . an historical play,"[11] we may also begin to notice how many echoes of the *Aeneid*, and of the fall and translation of empire within it, are scattered throughout the play. Cloten, for example, the loutish son ranged on the side of the narrow British nationalism promoted by his mother the Queen, is found in Act IV not only dead but decapitated, anonymous ("what trunk is here? / Without his top?" [IV.ii.353–54]). For readers of Virgil, the visual emblem of a headless trunk would recall, in the midst of a very different dramatic and romance scene, the visual emblem of the Fall of Troy—the headless and anonymous trunk of Priam, "a nameless corpse" (II.558) upon the shore. If this emblem is not recalled for us when we encounter Cloten's headless body, the text of *Cymbeline*, to underscore the association, gives us Imogen's curious momentary assimilation of herself to the mourning Hecuba, wife of Priam ("All curses madded Hecuba gave the Greeks" [IV.ii.313]), when she mistakenly takes this nameless corpse to be Posthumus.

The unmistakable allusiveness of this "trunk" without its "top" forges a curious link between Priam, emblem of fallen eastern Troy, and loutish Cloten, identified with the narrow nationalism of Britain in the West and, mistakenly, with Posthumus. But this headless trunk, linked imagistically and through "madded Hecuba" with the Fall of Troy, is not the only association the nationalistic British forces in this play have with Virgil's epic of the westering of empire and the mingling of races in a single "peace." The British queen herself—anxious to install her son in a marriage with Imogen, the English heir—recalls not only the role of Livia, Augustus's wife and the stepmother who succeeds in getting her son on the throne, as David Bergeron suggests,[12] but also the role in the *Aeneid* of the narrowly nationalistic Italian queen, Amata, who champions the suitor on the Italian side and opposes the Aeneas who will blend eastern and western, Trojan and Italian, into a Hesperian "second Troy." This queen is part of the whole complex of female figures in the *Aeneid* ranged against the fulfillment of the Jupiterian plot of eventual Augustan peace—from Juno, whose project is to

11. Knight, *The Crown of Life*, p. 129.
12. Bergeron, pp. 38–41.

obstruct the achievement of that end, to the Fury Alecto, who introduces discord into the initial amity of Italian and Trojan and hence turns Virgil's epic into the more complicated and extended plot it becomes. In the *Aeneid*, the obstructing queen favors the match of Lavinia with Italian Turnus, representative of the narrower Italian nationalism that would be the western counterpart to the purely eastern empire of Priam, the first Troy. Perhaps now we can begin to see why Cloten, the narrowly western and British suitor in this play, is curiously surrounded by echoes of Priam, fallen representative of the East, or Troy: the separatism of extreme East and far West here come together in a single image of decline and fall, in a play that will end instead with a union of east and west.

The Queen in *Cymbeline* clearly provides the local western and British counterpart to Amata's local western and Italian in the *Aeneid*. Like Juno in relation to the larger Jupiterian plot, which favors the harmony of East and West, however, Shakespeare's Queen can only obstruct, complicate, and delay rather than finally alter the prophesied ending: "Not mine will it be—I grant it—to keep him from the crown of Latium, and by fate Lavinia abides immovably his bride; yet to put off the hour and to bring delay to such great issues—that may I do" (*Aeneid* VII.313–15). Like the female obstructors of the larger imperial project of the *Aeneid*, and like the Italy of Iachimo (III.iv.15), *Cymbeline*'s Queen is also linked with potions and drugs, with a poisonous and destructive element that has ultimately to pass away before the final "peace" can be effected (I.v). And like Amata in particular, she is the queenly opponent of a peace already concluded between a local king and forces from an outside empire. In the *Aeneid*, the Italian king, Latinus, is temporarily ruled by his queen, a situation of temporary obstructionism and overruling mirrored in the inversion of "A father by thy step-dame govern'd, / A mother hourly coining plots" (II.i.57–58) and the Queen's disruption of the promised concord in *Cymbeline*. We might remember that Juno's disruption of an already concluded concord between Italian and Trojan—contracted by Latinus, the counterpart in the narrative of the "second Troy" of the husband, British Cymbeline, in the story of the third—was already presented in the *Aeneid* as a revenge against the "hated race" of Aeneas (a phrase recalled in the suffering of Posthumus's "valiant race"). And it is presented there in terms that might well suggest the frustrated and cruel stepmother figure put forward in such generically overdetermined fashion by the mixture of folktale and imperial themes in *Cymbeline*.

Cymbeline gives us virtually all the redoubled motifs of delay from the traditions of folktale and romance: the echo of this female obstruction from the *Aeneid* adds to it the imperial paradigm of an end that, though long delayed, is finally reached after the demise of an obstructor queen. Jupiter's "Whom best I love I cross; to make my gift, / The more delay'd, delighted," then, simultaneously enunciates the principle of the long labors before the epic achievement of an imperial "peace" and the mainstay of romance. Shakespeare's late romances all in one way or another foreground the quintessential romance strategy of delay—*The Tempest* with its "pow'rs delaying (not forgetting)" (III.iii.73), in a frame that also depends on echoes of the *Aeneid*; *The Winter's Tale* with its "delay'ed, / But nothing alt'red" (IV.iv.464–65), in a plot that extends temporal delay far beyond the accepted boundaries of dramaturgical time; *Pericles*, where delay and evasion enable the structural transformation of the conflated identities of the opening incest to be replaced by more distant familial relations and a more satisfying romance ending. *Cymbeline*, in its combination of folktale and imperial elements, exploits all the romance resources of delay— assumed names, enigmatic riddles, latent identities, and hidden heirs recognized only in a final scene—within a frame whose intertextual allusions also summon up the obstructive delays that made Virgil's epic of empire the hybrid progenitor of so many Renaissance epic-romances. Its "more delay'd, delighted" translates the Virgilian "forsan et haec" into the final resolutions of its complicated romance plot.

The temporary effect of Juno's opposition to Jupiter, and that of Queen Amata to the marriage and concord that will finally produce the line of Rome as second Troy, is to establish the power of a discordant queen over a reigning king. Amata's power over her husband is matched in *Cymbeline* by the temporary rule of Cymbeline's obstructing consort. The link between the *Aeneid*'s Italian queen and Cymbeline's British one is further strengthened in the moment of their deaths—prelude, as well, to the cessation of a local and one-sided opposition to the concord of East and West imaged in a final peace. In the last book of the *Aeneid*, Amata watches as the Trojan forces begin to carry the day, in a passage on the fall of a city which echoes the original description of the fall of eastern Troy. In the *Aeneid* itself, in other words, the singularity of extreme East and extreme West is already aligned, just as Cloten's headless trunk, in an Hesperia now shifted to Britain, recalls Priam's at the moment of Troy's fall. In the larger movement of both *Cymbeline* and the *Aeneid*, singularity cedes to concord and blending.

What such images and parallels suggest, then, is that there is a link between the imperial plot of Virgil's epic and Shakespeare's "last Roman play," beyond the play's explicit identification of Posthumus with Aeneas: even Iachimo's entry into Imogen's chamber, at night and hidden in the trunk presented as a gift, carries with it echoes of an earlier treacherous and invasive gift, the Trojan horse. But before considering the relation of these echoes to the question of anachronism with which we began, we need to look at what happens to Posthumus and Imogen as the narrower British nationalism of Cloten and the Queen is eliminated and the play approaches its final word of "peace" (V.v.485). Posthumus, exiled from Britain, goes to Rome and is numbered among the Romans (in another submerged eagle image) in Iachimo's description in Act I ("Some dozen Romans of us, and your lord / (The best feather of our wing) have mingled sums / To buy a present for the Emperor" [I.vi.185–87]). When hostilities break out between Roman and Briton, Posthumus comes to Britain "Among th' Italian gentry" (V.i 18–19), fighting for an imperial Rome here identified more narrowly with Italy. But he then exchanges his "Italian weeds" for the clothes of a "Britain peasant" (V.i.23–24) and fights on the British side to enable a crucial turning point in the fortunes of battle, before turning himself in as "A Roman" (V.iii.89) for imprisonment in a British jail:

> For being now a favorer to the Britain,
> No more a Britain, I have resum'd again
> The part I came in. Fight I will no more,
> But yield me to the veriest hind that shall
> Once touch my shoulder. Great the slaughter is
> Here made by th' Roman; great the answer be
> Britains must take. For me, my ransom's death.
> On either side I come to spend my breath;
> Which neither here I'll keep nor bear again,
> But end it by some means for Imogen. (V.iii.74–83)

It is in this jail that he falls asleep as his ancestors appear and Jupiter makes the prophecy that this "low-laid" son will ultimately emerge from his "trials," "happier much by his affliction made" (V.iv.108). And it is here that a British jailer makes the pronouncement that anticipates the play's concluding peace: "There are verier knaves desire to live, for all he be a Roman: and there be some of them too that die against their wills. So should I, if I were one. I would we were all of one mind, and one mind good" (V.iv.202–04).

Posthumus—linked explicitly with "Aeneas" in those lines in Act III and surrounded with echoes of Aeneas's labors and ignorance—thus goes through a dizzying series of exchanges of national identity before the play's complex romance plot concludes in the peace between Britain and Rome. Unlike Cloten, he is British and Roman, Roman and British by turn, in a series of chiastic exchanges that finally make him the play's primary combination of both.[13] Commentators on the play have pointed out his combination of "Roman" and "British" characteristics. David Bergeron notes that, though he is technically a Briton, both "in name and in character Posthumus Leonatus seems the most Roman of the British characters," while G. Wilson Knight emphasizes that "he is imaginatively at least a composite of the British and the Roman." His name sounds Roman rather than British, but he comes to symbolize British strength. Robert Miola reiterates the sense that "Posthumus is recognizably Roman" and yet is "un-Roman in a number of important particulars": "The Briton who exercised Roman virtue in British costume, finally, in Roman costume, shows a British capacity for humility and spiritual growth."[14] He is identified with the westering Roman eagle and, at the moment of his confusion with the beheaded Cloten, characterized as a "very valiant Britain," in lines that repeat the sense of movement from east to west:

> This was my master,
> *A very valiant Britain*, and a good,

13. The sense of chiasmus or exchange is also literally enacted in the successive "turns" on the battlefield, in which the place of the "eagles," first occupied by the Roman forces, is taken, as the Romans suffer what is literally a reversal, by the initially "flying" Britons (V.iii.41–43) who then turn and attack, inspired by the example of the "old man, and two boys" (V.iii.52) who, though Britons, vow to be "Romans" in courage to any too cowardly to defend Britain against attack (V.iii.26).

14. See, respectively, Bergeron, "Shakespeare's Last Roman Play," p. 36; Knight, *Crown*, p. 142; and Robert Miola, "*Cymbeline*: Shakespeare's Valediction to Rome," in Annabel Patterson, ed., *Roman Images*, Selected Papers from the English Institute, 1982 (Baltimore: The Johns Hopkins University Press, 1984), pp. 54–56.

That here by mountaineers lies slain. Alas!
There is no more such masters. I may *wander*
From east to occident, cry out for service,
Try many, all good; serve truly; never
Find such another master. (IV.ii.368–74; my emphases)

The "wandering" speaker here is the disguised Imogen, who is finally united with this "master" when he returns from east to west, Rome to Britain. His confusion here with Cloten—the headless trunk whose description recalls the fall of Priam—only underscores the difference within similarity, the eventual distinction of Posthumus as a "valiant Britain" from the narrower British nationalism of the other suitor for Imogen.

At the same time as Posthumus moves through these exchanges— from Britain to Rome, and from British "peasant" to "valiant Roman" to "valiant Britain"—Imogen correspondingly changes sides, becoming, though "Briton born" (V.v.84), a page in the service of the Romans. The play's complicated approach to its own concluding "peace" involves, therefore, not only the demise of the figures identified with a narrow British nationalism—Cloten and the Queen—but a series of exchanges between British and Roman that prepare for the final concord of the two. Its imperial subtext may also help to account for the complex overdetermination of Imogen herself, who, though, like Rosalind, in male disguise, also remains, as feminist readings of the play have seen, finally more passive than her comic counterpart.[15] She is, in the positions required of her in this imperial plot, not just the heroine in search of the husband who has turned against her but, in the kaleidoscopic subplot of the imagery, also an abandoned Dido, a passive Lavinia, and, in Iachimo's entry in the trunk, the potential British counterpart to ransacked Troy.[16] Like Lavinia, she is the object of a

15. See, for example, Clara Clairborne Park, "As We Like It: How a Girl Can Be Smart and Still Popular," in *The Woman's Part: Feminist Criticism of Shakespeare,* ed. Carolyn Ruth Swift Lenz, Gayle Greene, and Carol Thomas Neely (Urbana: University of Illinois Press, 1980), p. 107.

16. Imogen is also linked, as an object to be "voyaged upon," to the other imperial history of mercantile ventures upon new worlds, an imagery that casts her as passive object of male rivalry as well as of commercial venture. I have discussed this other dimension of the play's versions of imperial enterprise, together with its relation to male rivalry, in *Literary Fat Ladies: Rhetoric, Gender, Property* (London: Methuen, 1987), pp. 132–38. Catherine R. Stimpson's "Shakespeare and the Soil of Rape," in *The*

rivalry between two suitors, one identified with a fierce local attachment, the other with the blending of both sides into the concord of a *Troia rediviva*. But unlike Lavinia, whose father has no male heir, Imogen is finally displaced by her father's assumed dead but finally rediscovered royal sons.

The emergence of these long-lost sons into battle is also accompanied by a conflation and blurring of sides and by suggestions that, when caught between the Roman invaders and rebellious Britons associated with the Cloten they have killed, they are of neither extreme. Their temporary period of pastoral latency and nonage is in Wales, associated with the ancient British lore of Arthur. It is even more specifically a pastoral retreat suggestive of a similar pastoral place in the *Aeneid*, the geographically removed residence of Evander who becomes Trojan Aeneas's western ally. Evander's rustic simplicity contrasts with the grandeur of empires, and his house requires that even the great "stoop" to enter: "'These portals,' he cries, 'victorious Alcides stooped to enter; this mansion welcomed him. Dare, my guest, to scorn riches; fashion thyself also to be worthy of deity, and come not disdainful of our poverty.' He said, and beneath the roof of his lowly dwelling led great Aeneas" (*Aeneid* VIII.362–65). Belarius, Evander's counterpart in *Cymbeline*, advises the king's sons:

> A goodly day not to keep house with such
> Whose roof's as low as ours! Stoop, boys, this gate
> Instructs you how t' adore the heavens, and bows you
> To a morning's holy office. The gates of monarchs
> Are arch'd so high that giants may jet through
> And keep their impious turbans on without
> Good morrow to the sun. (*Cymbeline* III.iii.1-7)

Woman's Part, ed. Lenz et al., p. 61, shrewdly notes the blunting of the play's analysis of the consequences of male rivalry by its repetition, through Cloten, in parodic form and the final reunion of Posthumus and Imogen. Coppélia Kahn, in *Man's Estate* (Berkeley: University of California Press, 1981), pp. 126–27, links the plot of male rivalry—and its relegation of Imogen to more passive status—to Posthumus's famous misogynist outburst against "the woman's part" in man (II.v.1–35). Part of the overdetermination of the figure of Imogen—her participation in the sense, in this play, of "much ado about everything"—is her positioning, at different times, as both the Lavinia figure of rivalry between suitors and the "woman's part" to be cast out from a male enterprise, which, like that of the *Aeneid*, strives to leave the female behind.

The lowly roof of Belarius's cave evokes not just a proto-Christian humility anticipatory of the play's final echoes of the British reign into which Christ was born but the image of lowliness and dignity from the whole episode in the *Aeneid* in which Aeneas visits Evander's house, the future site of Rome. In both the *Aeneid* and *Cymbeline*, however, this pastoral place must ultimately be abandoned in the empire and peace that will emerge only after trial.

By the time the intervening trials and battles of Shakespeare's play have culminated in that projected end, two things have happened: Cloten and the Queen, along with the narrow British nationalism they represent, have been eliminated, and Cymbeline—though the British forces, helped by "Roman" Posthumus, have carried the day—has freely offered the tribute formerly refused. In the terms Northrop Frye has suggested for this final gesture, the play's end is a conservative one in which, in a retrograde movement from the westering of empire repeatedly imaged in an eagle's flight, the "third Troy" does voluntary homage to the second Troy of Rome.[17]

This—together with the identification of Posthumus with Aeneas and the play's echoes of plot and motifs from the *Aeneid*'s narrative of first and second Troy—brings us back to the question with which we began: the anachronism in which Augustan Roman setting and imperial Roman theme occupy the same dramatic space as more contemporary references to "Italian weeds" and to the "jay of Italy," and in which ancient aristocratic and Renaissance bourgeois elements stand side by side. What we have been tracing within a play that manages to be at once late romance and Shakespeare's last Roman plot has been a pattern of allusion to the Virgilian text and context of the *translatio* of empire. The ending, then, would seem within this larger history to be a recursive movement in which the already self-conscious Hesperia of Britain, successor to Rome, voluntarily cedes its victory over the Romans in a historically regressive act of tribute to it.

Cymbeline does homage to the Roman envoy, offering the tribute that had been earlier withheld under the influence of the "wicked queen" (V.v.463): "Although the victor, we submit to Caesar, / And to the Roman empire" (460–61). In the putative time of this "last Roman play," this gesture is indeed a conservative and backward-looking one,

---

17. Frye, *A Natural Perspective*, p. 88.

the third Troy doing voluntary homage to the second Troy, even in a victory that has established its right to independence. But there are other echoes and another gesture in this closing scene which superimpose on it another history, and a time that has been present as anachronism throughout. Commentators have noted not only the strong echoes of the *pax Augusta* in the play's concluding "peace" but the fact that it was under Augustus that a new dispensation destined to supersede the Roman was instituted with the birth of Christ—creating, in Augustinian terms, that split in which the Rome achieved through Aeneas and celebrated by Virgil would be definitively surpassed. It has also been remarked how strongly associated Holinshed's Cymbeline is with this transition and transformation, with the new reign marked, for example, in Spenser's chronicle of British kings: "Next him Tenantius raigned, then *Kimbeline*, / What time th' eternall Lord in fleshly slime / Enwombed was" (*FQ* II.x.50–51).

The ending of Shakespeare's Jacobean *Cymbeline* catches precisely that historical moment in which the Rome done tribute to by this British king is about to be superseded. The double reference—of culmination and beginning—at the romance's end already contains the possibility of a specifically temporal exchange and double vision, and hence the form of projection often read as anachronism, a duality of focus inherited not just from biblical typology but from the temporal exchanges within the *Aeneid* itself.[18] The final scene, as we have seen, contains not one but two parallel gestures of submission; and it is the other gesture that complicates the sense of simple recursive or regressive ending or of bungling anachronism in the coexistence of references to "Roman" and "Italian" throughout. In the same scene where Cymbeline, the British king, does homage to the Roman envoy and promises the withheld tribute, Iachimo, the "Italian fiend," bends his knee before Posthumus, who helped the Britons to victory over the Romans. This act of submission on the part of the figure associated throughout with a more contemporary Renaissance Italy joins his earlier tribute to the Britons, after being beaten by Posthumus disguised as the poorest

18. In the double time, for example, of Book VIII, where Aeneas's visit to Evander, with its story of Hercules, and the depiction of the Battle of Actium and other events of Roman history on Aeneas's shield superimpose legendary history, the "now" of the narrative events, and the later time of its writing under the post-Actium reign of Augustus.

British soldier: "If that thy gentry, Britain, go before / This lout as he exceeds our lords, the odds / Is that we scarce are men and you are gods" (V.ii.8–10). The structure of chiastic exchange already charted in the exchanges of identity Posthumus himself performs between Roman and Briton is thus joined by a specifically historical chiasmus, in which the backward-looking gesture of Cymbeline's turn toward the east, his submission to Rome, is shadowed by projection of the later history, of this Italian's submission to a British Aeneas, at a British court, as the ultimate fulfillment of the play's already cited images of westering:

> *Soothsayer.* The fingers of the pow'rs above do tune
> The harmony of this peace. The vision,
> Which I made known to Lucius, ere the stroke
> Of this scarce-cold battle, at this instant
> Is full accomplish'd: for the Roman eagle,
> From south to west on wing soaring aloft,
> Lessen'd herself and in the beams o' th' sun
> So vanish'd; which foreshow'd our princely eagle,
> Th'imperial Caesar, should again unite
> His favor with the radiant Cymbeline,
> Which shines here in the west. (V.v.466–76)

The sense of historical poise—of an end suggestive of the beginning of a new era—which concludes Shakespeare's Roman romance is joined by the sense of historical transumption in which the ultimate reversal of Cymbeline's backward gesture is the final fulfillment of Rome, and empire, in the new Hesperia of the West. Posthumus, as "a very valiant Britain," is finally distinguished both from the "irregulous" Cloten and from Iachimo, representative of the degenerate second Troy, or "spungy south," from which the "Roman eagle" has taken wing.[19] What is accomplished by this end is a casting off of both the insular nationalism of Cloten and the Queen and the Italianate model of Iachimo and, as several readers of the play have suggested, a passing of the true Roman virtues not from Rome to a later Italy but from Rome to the Britain symbolized by Posthumus and Imogen and by the

---

19. As Wilson Knight remarks, without explicitly linking this contrast to the *trans-latio* theme, "As the Roman virtue sinks to the level of Iachimo, the heritage of ancient Rome falls on Britain" (*The Crown of Life*, p. 166).

king's recovered heirs. The play, poised at the moment of the decisive *translatio* that is to go beyond the empire of Rome, also in this more contemporary gesture suggests the overgoing of a later Rome, one associated with the villainy of Iachimo and even, perhaps, in the evocation of a "Romish stew" (I.vi.152), with its complex relation to the Roman church. The ending even manages to suggest an overgoing of the *Aeneid*, its Roman and imperial subtext throughout, as Posthumus's forgiveness and pardon of his great Italian enemy recasts the final lines in which Aeneas almost spares the life of *his* Italian enemy but then kills him in an act of fury far removed from the promised "peace."

To see the play's apparent anachronism as a chiastic superimposition of times and a structural pattern of suffering and delay transformed from Virgil's imperial text would, finally, anchor this Shakespearean romance of empire more historically as well. For James was not only, as we have seen, deliberate in his self-reference as the new Arthur and new Augustus of his realm—combination of the virtues of ancient Britain and ancient Rome—but exploiter of that specifically Hesperian ideology which made him, as monarch of that third Troy, "the Glory of our Western World":

> Great Monarch of the West, whose glorious Stem,
> Doth now support a triple Diadem,
> Weying more than that of thy grand Grandsire Brute.[20]

The Jacobean *pax*, which extended even to negotiations with Papal Rome (part of what is adumbrated, perhaps, in Cymbeline's concluding peace with an already vanquished power) by no means negated the ideology of historical transumption in which Britain, and its king, would be the fulfillment and surpassing of Rome, just as the play's repeated focus on Milford Haven cannot but recall both the western region of Arthur and the landing place of Henry VII, founder of the Tudor and hence of the Jacobean line.[21] The revisions of empire—and

---

20. See respectively Ben Jonson's *Panegyre* (1603), occasioned by James's entry into Parliament, and Dekker's *Magnificent Entertainment* (1603), quoted in Jones, "Stuart Cymbeline," p. 92.

21. Jones, "Stuart Cymbeline," pp. 96 and 93.

the sheer number of allusions to an older text of empire—in this late Shakespearean romance make it even more the "much ado about everything" its detractors have decried. But they also give substance to Wilson Knight's original perception that in this play we have to do with history and romance at once.

10

"Kidnapped Romance":
Discourse in *The Faerie Queene*

HARRY BERGER, JR.

One of the pressing problems that confront critics who belong to the generation of A. C. Hamilton and myself is that of accommodating our now old and at least nominally dated practices to the new agendas that continuously revise and often refresh the scene of interpretation. I still consider myself a New Critic, even an old-fashioned one, but one who periodically subjects himself to the equivalent of what academic departments undergo in the form of five-year reviews. In the steady state of change that characterizes our condition, we reconstructed old New Critics don't find it all that hard to negotiate the leap from, say, the Intentional Fallacy to the Author Function, from the work to the text, from genre to intertextuality, from the virtual speaker or persona to the virtual reader (a very small leap), or from ambiguity to undecidability. Some of these leaps may seem more rewarding than others, but all of them operate according to the same principle and obey the same injunction, the principle and injunction that mark one aspect of the change from modernism to postmodernism: *Only de-estheticize.* We have always, at least since the time of Empson, read "with suspicion," but during the 1960s we learned that our suspiciousness was not sufficiently relevant, and during the 1970s that it wasn't sufficiently reflexive. We were told that we did not inscribe our own presuppositions, our ideological missions, our political positions, into our discourse.

When I use terms like *inscribe* and *discourse* I find myself caught between a feeling of adolescent pride and an impulse to giggle. The sense of achievement that comes from deploying the current lingo like an intellectual hipster or inside dopester is almost as satisfying as it is silly. But such confessional pricklings are irrelevant because the only important question is whether the change of lexical and conceptual landscape makes a real difference, whether the new terms change the scene in a substantive way, whether I can use them to say things I didn't say or couldn't have said before. That malleable and all-purpose term *discourse* is a case in point, and in the present essay I want to explore the hypothesis that such a term, given sufficient conceptual boundaries, *can* make a real difference to an interpretation—an interpretation that may well proceed without it—even if only sparingly used. I shall focus on a particular *topos* within the discourse of love, the venerable *topos* in which erotic relations are formulated in the idiom of hunting, and my evidence will consist of a reading of a text from Book III of the *The Faerie Queene*. But first, before rushing into the secure green world of New Critical interpretation, I should say a few words about discourse.

Discourse as Language-Game

At one extreme the *American Heritage Dictionary* restricts *discourse* to "verbal expression in speech or writing," and from this point the meanings ascribed to the term cut an ever broadening swath from—for example—Benveniste and Ricoeur to Lacan to Bakhtin to Greimas to Foucault, who gives the widest purchase to such terms as *discourse, discursive formations*, and *discursive practices*. The term seems to thrive on a tension between, on the one hand, systolic restriction to the confines of a speech event and, on the other, diastolic expansion to the organlike harmonies (or dissonances) of a broad range of cultural, social, and political practices. This tension is reflected in Catherine Belsey's definition of discourse as "a domain of language-use, a particular way of talking (and writing and thinking). A discourse involves certain shared assumptions which appear in the formulations that characterize it. The discourse of common sense is quite distinct, for instance, from the discourse of modern physics. . . . Ideology is *inscribed* in discourse in the sense that it is literally written or spoken *in it*." And in Belsey's Althusserian formulation, *ideology* is "the sum of the ways in which people both live and represent to themselves their relation to the conditions of their existence."[1] "Common sense" is no less an ideology, no less a social construction, than "modern physics," and the distinction between them is itself part of a discourse that reflects, signifies, and helps to maintain the ideology of a differentiated institutional structure. "The discourse of *x*" is a formula that marks any "domain of language-use" as a social construction rather than a "fact of nature."

Belsey's concise statement of the relationship between discourse and ideology is not very far from the one I find most useful and will put into play as the basis of my own account: Ludwig Wittgenstein's notion of language-game.[2] Wittgenstein writes that "to imagine a language means to imagine a form of life" and that "the term 'language-*game*' is meant to bring into prominence the fact that the *speaking* of language is part of an activity, or of a form of life."[3] But when we confront a text, whatever extralinguistic "activity" or "form of life" we imagine the language to be part of—apart from the activity of the text—we "experience" only through our interpretation of textual activity. Therefore, it would be better to reverse the terms of Wittgenstein's statement that the language-game is "the whole, consisting of language and the actions into which it is woven" (p. 5e), for in literary discourse the actions are woven into the language, though of course since language is itself a form of action there are specifically literary language-games whose boundaries are coterminous with those of genres. So, for example, a discourse or language-game of gender in a particular literary work is embedded in the language-game of pastoral, romance, epic, or lyric. The provenance and scope of a language-game is implied in Wittgenstein's vague phrase, "form of life," which denotes the collectively, socially, culturally, institutionally constructed ambience of language use. The value of the language-game concept for my purpose is that it reverses priorities from mental states to the outward criteria of observable discursive behavior, to the coherence of community practices observable as "forms of life," and to describable kinds of lan-

1. Catherine Belsey, *Critical Practice* (London: Methuen, 1980), pp. 5, 42.

2. Here I follow Keir Elam, who made this connection in *Shakespeare's Universe of Discourse: Language-Games in the Comedies* (Cambridge: Cambridge University Press, 1984).

3. Ludwig Wittgenstein, *Philosophical Investigations*, trans. G. E. M. Anscombe, 2nd ed. (Oxford: Basil Blackwell, 1958), pp. 8e, 11e.

guage-games situated primarily in the culture of the community and only secondarily in the individual.[4]

Wittgenstein gives a clear example of the way this view frames the role of individual intention within language-games:

> 337. But didn't I already intend the whole construction of the sentence (for example) at its beginning? So surely it existed in my mind before I said it aloud!—If it was in my mind, still it would not normally be there in some different word order. But here we are constructing a misleading picture of "intending," that is, of the use of this word. An intention is embedded in its situation, in human customs and institutions. If the technique of the game of chess did not exist, I could not intend to play a game of chess. In so far as I do intend the construction of a sentence in advance, that is made possible by the fact that I can speak the language in question. (p. 108e)

The discourse of chess is a little too sanitized to represent the language-games or contexts of intention with which I am concerned here. These conform to a cruder model that, in one of the more unappealing language-games of contemporary lay (or near-lay) psychology, goes by the name of "the games people play." But Wittgenstein's account is helpful in reminding us that we often can't tell whether, in a given stretch of language use or behavior, the "playing" is intended as well as motivated; the game has its own logic, its own scenario, and plays itself out in the speaker's language or agent's behavior regardless of the cognitive status we ascribe to it. And such a view of discourse as language-game exhibits a commitment to the notion that states of mind "belong" not so much to particular speakers or agents as to the discourses they participate in. The importance of the commitment is that it provides a loophole that allows the reader the option of escaping from the constraints of the disjunctive view that meaning is either intended or unintended, conscious or unconscious. It allows for the broad and strategically fuzzy interpretive force I want to give to the concept of motivation as whatever it is that moves, or moves through, a speaker whether or not she or he displays awareness of it. The concept allows the interpreter to factor the situational ambience of "human customs and institutions" into the analysis of psychological or cognitive phe-

4. See Saul Kripke, *Wittgenstein on Rules and Private Language* (Cambridge, Mass.: Harvard University Press, 1982), pp. 93–113.

nomena. In my lexicon, then, a discourse is both a particular pattern of motivation and the pattern of language from which it is deduced. In its psychological orientation, this definition argues for a Lacanian rather than Freudian approach to literary discourses and the discourses they represent, as I think will be apparent from the reading that follows.

Florimell in Faerie Land

A weird chain of events is set off when the frantic Florimell first blazes into *The Faerie Queene* out of a "griesly" forest (III.i.14) chased by the "griesly Foster . . . / Breathing out beastly lust her to defile," pushing his "tyreling jade" so fiercely

> That from his gorie sides the bloud did gush:
> Large were his limbes, and terrible his looke,
> And in his clownish hand a sharp bore speare he shooke. (i.17)[5]

Guyon, Arthur, and Timias respond instantly to the target of chivalric opportunity this outrageous spectacle offers: the two heroes follow Florimell while Arthur's squire goes after the forester. Britomart, how-ever, passes. Her "constant mind," the narrator earnestly and ap-provingly explains, "Would not so lightly follow beauties chace, / Ne reckt of Ladies Loue" (i.19). This moral commendation may be hi-larious but it is also informative. It differentiates Britomart's reaction from Arthur's and Guyon's in a manner that glances at the ambiguity of the chivalric motive for rescuing damsels in distress; and it tells us that Florimell's distress may owe partly to the beauty that affects even the noblest would-be rescuers.[6]

That Arthur and Guyon set out to rescue Florimell by pursuing her rather than the forester is itself weird, as the contrast to Timias's more reasonable reaction points up. But the weirdest aspect of the episode is what it implies about Britomart; she would only help save another woman from predatory males if she had the same ambiguous motive—if she "reckt of Ladies Loue." We know from an earlier statement that Britomart's constancy of mind is associated with her search for the

---

5. The text cited is the *Variorum.*
6. See Stan Hinton, "The Poet and His Narrator: Spenser's Epic Voice," *ELH*, 41 (1974), 169. I shall return to the narrator.

"louer (loue farre sought alas,) / Whose image she had seene in *Venus* looking glas" (i.8), but here the narrator applauds it as a sign of her health and unwavering commitment to heterosexual pursuits. Perhaps in the "world" of Book III the second constancy is only guaranteed by the first. Perhaps readers think Britomart's refusal to help is unsisterly, especially since she goes out of her way a few stanzas later to save a man from woman's erotic aggression, Redcross from Malecasta. Perhaps they think it only poetic justice that this piece of derring-do makes *her* the object of "beauties chace" and "Ladies Loue." Perhaps, since Florimell's fearful flight is so obvious an icon of Embattled Chastity, they expect the Knight of Chastity to give her a hand and are thus puzzled by her refusal to involve herself with that particular signifier of the virtue she represents.

Where do all these perhapses lead? Granted that the allegorical poem is a great perhapsing machine, its virtual reader a perplexed head-scratcher lost in the mazy deferrals of *Errours den*, at what point does the labyrinth slow down its writhing and vouchsafe a glimpse of the quarry? Perhaps it happens in the fifth canto when Spenser lightheart-edly scrambles the chronology to make Britomart's defeat of Marinell the cause of the flight that preceded it. We then learn that Florimell is not merely in flight from random pursuers but also in pursuit of her beloved. As allegorical sequence diverges from chronological sequence, the construction of "beauties chace" shifts from the objective to the subjective genitive and Florimell's chastity is resituated from a simple context of self-preserving fear to a more complicated context of self-exposing desire. The result is surely that Florimell is more like Brit-omart and more intimately linked to Britomart than we had thought. It is surely significant that just when Britomart steps out of the poem for a few cantos we learn that she was the indirect cause of the chase she would not lightly follow. And surely that avoidance now becomes pregnant with new meaning as her project and Florimell's are brought into alignment, their journeys identical in goal but antithetical in form. Isn't it clear by now that Florimell, who has been called a surrogate of Britomart,[7] displaces something within the heroine, something she avoids and surely fears, something Florimell suffers and carries off like

7. Jonathan Goldberg, *Endlesse Worke: Spenser and the Structures of Discourse* (Baltimore: The Johns Hopkins University Press, 1981), p. 4.

a scapegoat, making all Faerie Land tremble while Britomart marches on and keeps "her readie way," "for all was in her powre" (iv.18)? Can there be any doubt that Florimell's continuing plight is the necessary condition, the cost, of Britomart's "stedfast courage and stout hardiment" (i.19)?

Surely; that is, perhaps; or probably not. There is no temple at the center of the third book's labyrinth, and even the *mons Veneris* atop the Gardens of Adonis is no sooner stabilized in a figure of sight or space than it is unfigured and ploughed back into the rhizomes of the text.[8] A constant mind is no help to anyone following Spenser's chase, and my own sexual preferences make it easy for me to stop reaching irritably after abstract allegorical certainties in order to join Arthur and Guyon, but mostly Arthur, in search of Florimell. Here the spark that jumps the gap between the character's name, the rhetorical conduct of her story, and its narrative design, ignites the great perhapsing machine, which proceeds to generate forests and oceans of commentary. James Nohrnberg's very useful compendium of sources and analogues relieves one from having to thrash about too long in iconographic waters, and the simplicity of the moral he draws should not blind us to its suggestiveness: "The result of these comparisons seems clear: Spenser is consciously re-creating the marine motifs of the Mediterranean epyllion. The poet is showing us that the power of love extends to the kingdom of the sea. . . . The flux of analogies and comparisons makes a related point as well: love takes many forms. As Ovid says . . ."[9] In my lexicon, *consciously re-creating* becomes *representing*, and since I believe "As Ovid says" is part of what Spenser represents, I would raise this to a higher power: the poet is showing us what poets have shown us about the power of love.

Reading the story of Florimell, one is struck not merely by the pastiche of Ovidian motifs and allusions but by "the effect of Ovid." This extends beyond the Ovidian plot and theme to the storyteller's urbane amusement, and here one might also want to describe it as the effect of Ariosto. It is in part, as Paul Alpers has shown so well, a tonal or

8. See Angus Fletcher, *The Prophetic Moment: An Essay on Spenser* (Chicago: University of Chicago Press, 1971), pp. 14–34 et passim.

9. James Nohrnberg, *The Analogy of "The Faerie Queene"* (Princeton: Princeton University Press, 1976), p. 592.

rhetorical effect, "an exploitation of the reader's expectations,"[10] the representation of the poet as a virtuoso storyteller and literary *regisseur*, himself a voracious if skeptical reader of the Great Texts of his culture. The technique of discontinuous narrative produces a flow of isolated, sharply visualized, but highly conventional episodes whose modern theatrical counterpart is the musical comedy or variety show; an art that diverts and debunks, that delights in its witty disenchantment, that flags its commitment not to the portrayal of Life, Society, etc., per se but to the portrayal of the portrayal of Life, Society, etc., in the Literature it emulates or parodies. What I shall try to demonstrate in the following pages on Florimell is that Book III is not merely "influenced" by that art but displays the influence, shows itself seduced, passes its seduction on to the reader, yet at the same time deploys a range of techniques—rhetorical, structural, intertextual— that contain and criticize it. Its message is that the Ovidian/Ariostan artist was himself seduced and failed to get all he could out of his material. And the burden of my argument is that the implications of this message reach beyond the esthetic domain into cultural, social, and political "art."

Spenser's literariness has been exhaustively analyzed by Alpers, who notes that "when Spenser borrows a character from Ariosto, he is interested in a more or less conventional figure who is in a poetically interesting situation, as opposed to an individual with a unique moral nature"; his interest is "not in a character, but in the beautiful maiden who arouses erotic desire and is constantly being pursued" (p. 194). Alpers goes on to show that Spenser's portrait of Florimell conflates aspects of "Isabella, the model of chastity" with aspects of "Angelica, the arch-flirt" (p. 195), but here he only uses this demonstration to argue that for Spenser the different parts of Ariostan episodes "are to some extent interchangeable." In another context, however, Alpers has very good things to say about the complex effect produced by Spenser's "rather light-hearted treatment" of Florimell "as the maiden in distress"; although the "paradoxical quest by flight expresses the sexual fearfulness that is the ambiguous source of her fidelity," we read this not as indicating "a psychological inadequacy" but as conveying the

10. Paul Alpers, *The Poetry of "The Faerie Queene"* (Princeton: Princeton University Press, 1967), p. 33.

message "that fidelity must be the product of erotic desire" (p. 395). This feels right to me, and Alpers could have gone further by noting the peculiarity of the first statement—I would have expected him to say that her fidelity is the ambiguous source of her sexual fearfulness—and by exploring the implication of the idea that sexual fearfulness and erotic desire are equally productive of fidelity. The implication is not merely that fear of sex, the desire to control and delimit one's sexual encounters, is a negative source of fidelity but rather that one fears one's own desire, the desire that makes one attractive *and* vulnerable to others. The lover may be vulnerable, for example, to the beloved she is drawn to, either because he may not be faithful in return or because she fears that the intensity of her desire will impel her to surrender her autonomy and place herself in his *daunger*, which is a threat inherent in the project of institutionalizing true love as marriage. The force of Venus may drive her into the arms of Diana.

These dilemmas are excluded by the reductiveness of such single-valued conventional models as Isabella and Angelica, or Venus and Diana, and if Spenser places them before us either by allusion or by representation, it may be to make precisely that point. Had Alpers brought his two discussions of Florimell into closer contact, and had he treated Spenser's Ariostan borrowings unequivocally as critical allusions—not merely influences—he could have enriched his own thesis by arguing that Spenser's interest in the "conventional figure" and "poetically interesting situation" lies in a revisionary appropriation that foregrounds both the limits imposed by their Ovidian or Ariostan environment and the possibilities released by combining them in new and more complex forms. I agree with Alpers that Spenser's tone and treatment discourage us from worrying about the "psychological inadequacy" of Florimell as an individual character. But I think his antipathy to the focus on individual characters and their psychology prevents him from seeing that Florimell—like Spenser's pastoral puppets—is a kind of experimental model, a site for the inscription and exploration of erotic psychology. The poem predicates psychological inadequacy of the atmosphere that pervades the representation of gender relations in the literature Spenser so conspicuously cites. The effect of Ovid and Ariosto is thus present in the portrayal of Florimell as an effect Spenser critically revises. It is by focusing this literary critique on the contradictions and dilemmas of erotic psychology that the reader assimilates the revision of literature to the revision of the cultural attitudes toward gender the literature reflects. And one of the attitudes Spenser targets is that traditional fantasies about love and gender relations are to be exploited for their entertainment value so that even the poet who cynically debunks them is parasitic on and testifies to their continuing influence.

It remains true nevertheless that one finds it difficult to keep the ear attuned to the grand mythic resonances of the Florimell story when the narrator so clearly enjoys the rhetoric with which he converts her darkest moment to a Monty Python episode, as the fisherman and Proteus, not to mention the reader, dissolve in gales of lubricity. No one manhandles the hapless heroine with more disrespect than the poet, who makes her unwittingly stir up the fisherman with the kind of double-talk one would associate with the False Florimell:

> But thou good man, sith farre in sea we bee,
>   And the great waters gin apace to swell,
>   That now no more we can the maine-land see,
>   Haue care, I pray, to guide the cock-bote well,
>   Least worse on sea then vs on land befell.
>   Thereat th'old man did nought but fondly grin,
>   And said, his boat the way could wisely tell:
>   But his deceiptfull eyes did neuer lin,
> To looke on her faire face, and marke her snowy skin. (viii.24)

Such passages, studded with asides that mimic folk wisdom ("Hard is to teach an old horse amble trew" [viii.26]) and heroic outrage (27–29), seem conspicuously to capsize the ship of Meaning. Florimell's name could just as well have been Pauline or Hazel. As the narrator represents himself succumbing to Ovidian pleasures and giving the tale its head, he inscribes his perspective in the very atmosphere—the atmosphere of dirty jokes in the men's locker room of Western civilization—which the poem is at pains to dispel and deconstruct.

However uplifting modern readers find the oceans of scholarly allegoresis poured over the Florimell/Marinell/Proteus story, they don't easily stay afloat on the currents of Orphic, Neoplatonic, vegetative, and other mythologies when Florimell tells the old fisherman to guide the cock-boat well and, for her pains, ends up with "blubbered face" on a pile of fish. And although the Proteus who comes to the rescue wears an impressive array of mythographic medals and ribbons, although this assignment adequately motivates his appearance as "An aged sire with head all frory hore, / And sprinckled frost vpon his deawy beard" (viii.30), such resonances go up like spume when Spenser closes in with dactylic buoyancy on his "frory lips full softly" kissing Florimell "Whiles the cold ysickles from his rough beard, / Dropped adowne vpon her yuorie brest" (viii.35). At the moment of Florimell's greatest peril the mighty, Proteus reaches new heights of hilarity as he goes the way of all her would-be saviors; first cajoling and then threatening, he exercises his mythic privilege, dances out his Ovidian principle, in a frenzied but futile display of shape shifting (39–41).

One could try to reassure oneself about this episode, insist that it illustrates love's vicissitudes or its tyranny or the triumph of chastity over lust or, in the long run, over mutability or the seasonal death preceding rebirth. But then one brushes up against those softly kissing "frory lips," trips on "Dropped adowne," and all is lost. The grand mythic themes kept in play through names, allusions, analogies, and the network of "deep" symbols are upstaged by condensation into an amusingly visualized episode. This is Spenser at his Ovidian/Ariostan best, deflating mythography and entertaining the reader. The question is whether he manages to overgo the seductions of this mode, whether the mythic themes are recuperated, and whether their hovering presence targets the limits of episodic visualization. If whatever Proteus or Florimell represents can't adequately be represented by condensation into the name-bearing character and its situation, and if that literary inadequacy is a thesis of the poem, where do we look for the indicators that apprise us of this? Had I space enough and time I could approach this project by exploring the intricate network of contrasts and resemblances that link Proteus with other types of the mage, the seer, and the practitioner of the arts of image making; this exploration would enable me to lay out the evidence showing how the poem's three wizards—Merlin, Proteus, Busirane—renew the presence and power of the primal Old Man, Archimago, how the sequence of their appearances registers increasing impotence and aggressiveness, and how Archimago, the figure of the corrupt imagination, returns to haunt Book III as a specifically male figure of the powerful have-not. It is in the problematic tensions between such large patterns (which Spenser ap-

propriately spells "Paterne" in "Hymne . . . of Beavtie" [32]) and the
comic play of episodic visualization that the limits of the latter are
thematized, framing Ovidian art in the critical perspective of a counter-
Ovidian art. But Florimell herself—or itself—is a major site of the
conflict between these two arts and displays it more economically.

Her name is Florimell, after all, not Pauline or Hazel, although in its
early appearances in the Arguments prefacing Cantos i, iv, and v it does
not invite much scrutiny. She is officially baptized at v.8–11 when her
Dwarf tells Arthur (and us) her story. The name helps interpret the
function and effects of her beauty, and we are encouraged to do so by
the Dwarf's account, which suggests that her beauty and its exposure
signify the desire that sends her into the world to find Marinell. This
new information places her in the familiar position of the pursuer
pursued, and her subsequent adventures exacerbate the transformation
of desire into *daunger,* quest into flight. Yet if we explore the implications of her name, that flight betrays a Parthian power—a daemonic
power, in Angus Fletcher's sense of that term, for she is inscribed with
an allegory of natural process. Florimell, "flower-honey," is a human
version of the "aboundant flowres" the earth throws forth in spring to
tempt "all liuing wights" to love (IV.x.45). The power daemonically
inscribed in her name and effects is best expressed in the following lines
from *Colin Clouts Come Home Againe*: the human male's response to
love differs from the animal's in that man

> Chose for his loue the fairest in his sight,
> Like as himselfe was fairest by creation.
> For beautie is the bayt which with delight
> Doth man allure, for to enlarge his kynd,
> Beautie the burning lamp of heauens light,
> Darting her beames into each feeble mynd:
> Against whose powre, nor God nor man can fynd
> Defence, ne ward the daunger of the wound,
> But being hurt, seeks to be medicynd
> Of her that first did stir that mortall stownd. (869–78)

The gradual shift of the male's position from agent and chooser to
feeble wounded victim edges *medicynd* with menace; it is almost too
easy to replace it with *revenged*.

Still other texts suggest the close connection among Florimell,

Cupid, and the moment of vernal awakening described in *Amoretti* 4. The New Year calls forth,

> out of sad Winters night,
> fresh loue, that long hath slept in cheerlesse bower:
>   wils him awake, and soone about him dight
>   his wanton wings and darts of deadly power.
> For lusty spring now in his timely howre,
>   is ready to come forth him to receiue:
>   and warnes the Earth with diuers colord flowre,
>   to decke hir selfe, and her faire mantle weaue.
> Then you faire flowre, in whom fresh youth doth raine,
>   prepare your selfe new loue to entertaine.

The context of persuasion reminds us that the human flower has to play her part, especially since she has been graced with all the celestial endowments conferred by Neoplatonic fantasy:

> Therefore to make your beautie more appeare,
> It you behoues to loue, and forth to lay
> That heauenly riches, which in you ye beare,
> That men the more admyre their fountaine may,
> For else what booteth that celestiall ray,
> If it in darknesse be enshrined euer,
> That it of louing eyes be vewed neuer?
>   (*An Hymne of Beavtie*, 183–89)

But the consequences for Florimell of discharging this obligation might well encourage the kind of reticence connoted in *enshrined*. Though the speaker of the *Hymne* deplores the opinion of "ydle wits" that "beautie is nought else, but mixture made / Of colours faire" (64–66), his own effort to promote the "fleshly bowre" and "comely corpse . . . endewed" with true beauty (123, 135) reveals that the latter does not eschew "colours faire" and that it is sometimes hard to distinguish true from false beauty as easily as he would like, especially since he insists at some length that even true beauty is in the eye of the beholder (211–59). Arguing on similar grounds that Florimell is "illusory, or at least elusive," Isabel MacCaffrey notes the "irrational behavior" she causes and "the readiness of virtuous as well as wicked characters to substitute a false version for the true."[11] Florimell is no less a male inven-

---

11. Isabel MacCaffrey, *Spenser's Allegory: The Anatomy of Imagination* (Princeton: Princeton University Press, 1976), p. 297.

tion than the False Florimell. Both equally project and reflect male
desires, and their effects sometimes converge, just as Neoplatonist fantasies easily slide into Petrarchan fantasies. From this standpoint, the
False Florimell is truer insofar as she is more explicitly an engine built
out of the parts invented by "ydle wits." The stress on artifice in
Spenser's images of Florimell frequently edges her in that direction:

> All suddenly out of the thickest brush,
>   Vpon a milk-white Palfrey all alone,
>   A goodly Ladie did foreby them rush,
>   Whose face did seeme as cleare as Christall stone,
>   And eke through feare as white as whales bone:
>   Her garments all were wrought of beaten gold,
>   And all her steed with tinsell trappings shone. (i.15)

> What mister wight (said he) and how arayd?
>   Royally clad (quoth he) in cloth of gold,
>   As meetest may beseeme a noble mayd;
>   Her faire lockes in rich circlet be enrold,
>   A fairer wight did neuer Sunne behold,
>   And on a Palfrey rides more white then snow,
>   Yet she her selfe is whiter manifold. (v.5)

> With that adowne out of her Christall eyne
>   Few trickling teares she softly forth let fall,
>   That like two Orient pearles, did purely shyne
>   Vpon her snowy cheeke (vii.9)

> Tho gan she gather vp her garments rent,
>   And her loose lockes to dight in order dew,
>   With golden wreath and gorgeous ornament (vii.11)

Such passages suggest a figure not reducible to the nature-function
inscribed in her name, one whose form wavers with the varying pro-
ductions of male desire in Neoplatonist, Petrarchan, Ovidian, and Lucretian tropologies. And just as the corrupt sonneteer's fantasy de-
taches Florimell's form from her Neoplatonic and Lucretian functions
to create False Florimell, so she too goes astray in Book III.[12] Since her

---

12. But why is it a witch, another anxious mother (Cymoent was the first), who
creates False Florimell to divert her lovelorn son, building a hilarious flirtation machine
out of the materials manufactured by Petrarchan sonnetry, and commissioning a male
spright to operate it? A demonic antithesis of Venus constructs a demonic antithesis of
the unattainable virgin out of maternal solicitude for the wretched "comfort of her age
and weary dayes" (vii. 12).

chief assignment is to arouse desire when seen, her continuous exposure and flight intensify unruly responses, and these are reflected back into herself: "The original motive for flight—her love for the wounded Marinell—is changed to fear,"[13] and it is while fleeing compulsively *from* vain fear rather than *toward* Marinell that she activates the witch, her son, her monster, the old fisherman, and Proteus. In this way she helps make her fantasy a reality, just as the "rauenous beast" of the simile at vii.1 becomes a narrative fact at vii.22.

Though Florimell's beauty expresses her desire, announces the readiness of woman for love, and thus opens Cupid's season in the forest of male desire, the force she embodies transcends its embodiment, and Spenser's language suggests the danger of "the burning lamp" she bears. Her flight threatens to set the woods on fire with the flowery flames of "her faire yellow lockes" that stream behind her

> All as a blazing starre doth farre outcast
> His hearie beames, and flaming lockes dispred,
> At sight whereof the people stand aghast:
> But the sage wisard telles, as he has red,
> That it importunes death and dolefull drerihed. (i.16)

Perhaps the foregoing discussion will suggest why the locks of the terrified Florimell are compared (in a simile generated from the etymology of *comet*) to a terrifying male figure interpreted as an evil omen by another male, the "sage wisard" whose perspective may well be that of Spenser's Archimago figures, his mages and seers, his embittered and therefore antierotic elders. Florimell is inseparable from the destructive force she carries, and that force is male in origin. The potential prey is a predator and her pursuers are her prey.[14]

Some of this meaning rubs off on the description of the forester at i.17. The indefinite reference of "his gorie sides" momentarily assimilates the horse to the man, suggesting self-inflicted wounds that increase his pain. His angry gesture is comically inappropriate, but the

---

13. Thomas P. Roche, Jr., *The Kindly Flame: A Study of the Third and Fourth Books of Spenser's "Faerie Queene"* (Princeton: Princeton University Press, 1964), p. 155.

14. See the brilliant discussions by Michael J. B. Allen in "The Chase: The Development of a Renaissance Theme," *Comparative Literature*, 20 (1968), 302–05; and Leonard Barkan, "Diana and Actaeon: The Myth as Synthesis," *ELR*, 10 (1980), 349–52.

perverse symbol of virility he brandishes indicates that his pain charges his lust with vengeful and destructive anger.[15] The Adonis in the tapestry we see thirty stanzas later prefers boar hunting to love, but in the forester the two forms of venery are confused. At the outset there seems to be no prospect of his succeeding, since his "tyreling jade" and "clownish hand" are obviously no match for the great heroes setting out to rescue Florimell. As long as lust is represented in so pure and simple a stereotype, personified in so rude a form, it is bound to be self-defeating. The battle between Beauty and Beastly Lust is too one-sided. Lust's continuance and power depend on its ability to free itself from the forester and insinuate itself into more competent psyches. And this is what happens.

The forester pursues Florimell, Arthur and Guyon pursue Florimell, and Timias pursues the forester. In every case, the pursuit transforms the pursuer into a predator who in various ways is or becomes the prey of his prey. Superficially, it does not seem to make much difference whether Arthur or the forester does the pursuing or whether the heroes pursue Florimell or the forester. Thus at iv.45–46 Spenser confuses the two pursuits: "in chace of beautie excellent," Arthur and Guyon pursue "that same foster strong" with "fiery zeale" so as

> To reskew her from shame, and to reuenge her wrong.
>
> Through thick and thin, through mountaines and through plains,
>> Those two great champions did attonce pursew
>> The fearefull damzell, with incessant paines.

With like pains the forester chased her "Through thicke and thin, both ouer banke and bush" (i.17)—a more modest and rustic itinerary but undertaken with the same fiery zeal. "Pursuer" seems to be a role that has built into it a constellation of motives that affect anyone who fills it. Nevertheless, Spenser indicates by various means that the choice of prey does make a difference.

---

15. Nohrnberg (p. 447) suggests that *foster* can mean "parent" and cites the interesting connection Spenser makes between Florimell and Myrrha. Though I find it hard to believe that the description of the forester is meant to encourage readers to fix on the parental sense of the term, I agree that the idea of generational conflict and confusion is central to the poem.

From the start he places in question Arthur's impulse to save Florimell by pursuing her rather than her assailant:

> Full of great enuie and fell gealosy,
> They stayd not to auise, who first should bee,
> But all spurd after fast, as they mote fly,
> To reskew her from shamefull villany.
> The Prince and *Guyon* equally byliue
> Her selfe pursewd, in hope to win thereby
> Most goodly meede, the fairest Dame aliue;
> But after the foule foster *Timias* did striue. (i.18)

By coupling Arthur with Guyon, Spenser makes it clear that while the
"goodly meede" they aspire to is not sexual, it is oriented in a self-
directed manner toward a beautiful woman as the spoils of competition, a trophy bringing honor to the winner. Yet this chivalric motive is
not entirely free of sexual desire, which lurks under the contentious
anger intended in the phrase "great enuie and fell gealosy," and we are
not surprised to find Arthur's "goodly fire" (v.1) of honor modified by
the process of pursuit, so that when he loses the track he comes to wish
that his own love, Gloriana, "were such, as shee." Florimell's unwitting
complicity in this process is underlined: she flees "as light-foot hare
from vew / Of hunter swift," and Arthur obligingly assumes the predator's role by assaying "to win so goodly pray" (iv.46) and feeling
deprived when "cursed night . . . reft from him so goodly scope"
(iv.52). *Scope* means not only "sight" but also "target" or "prey," the
object of pursuit or desire. Arthur submits to the self-fulfilling logic of
Florimell's fugitive *daunger:* by fleeing she unwittingly encourages the
pursuit, arouses the desire she fears, and thus increases her fear; her
beauty, exposing itself to view, ambiguates even the noblest intentions.
Whoever follows her, whether "to save or spill," provisionally steps
into the role of hunter her preylike behavior creates and, in yielding to
her "guidance," effectively becomes her prey, since she makes him
swerve from his first intent.

As the forester's lust turns to anger during pursuit, so Arthur's
honorable anger subtly modulates into desire; to arouse the former is
to kindle "sensuall desire" along with it, since both flame from the
same source, the love that diversely "doth his pageants play, / And
shewes his powre in variable kinds" (v.1). But the prince rides out of

Book III in v.12 none the wiser, having shifted the blame for the "thousand fancies" that "bet his idle braine" (iv.54) from himself to Night, "foule Mother of annoyance sad" (iv.55): "Thou are the root and nurse of bitter cares, / Breeder of new, renewer of old smarts" (iv.57). A demonic negative of the Great Mother who will appear in Canto vi, this mythic projection is held responsible for the same kind of pain Britomart earlier blamed on her love for the image of Artegal. Arthur, with a little help from Florimell's dwarf, regains his confidence before riding off, but when he carefully reminds himself that "ill weares he armes, that nill them vse for Ladies sake" (v.11) he doesn't ride off scot-free, since the words also remind us that his sense of chivalric honor was forced to compromise its purity in order to cloak or justify its swerve toward another meaning of "for Ladies sake."

The narrator's sense of the experience is that the goodly fire has had to struggle to keep the prince on the right path. But the very words that express this sense reenact the swerve in spite of themselves, because the pursuit of Florimell has shown that the "sensuall desire" the narrator assigns to "the baser wit" in v.1 contributes to the force lifting the prince up and pushing him forward, the force the narrator identifies with the "goodly fire" of honor:

> Ne suffreth it vncomely idlenesse,
>   In his free thought to build her sluggish nest:
> Ne suffereth it thought of vngentlenesse,
>   Euer to creepe into his noble brest,
>   But to the highest and the worthiest
> Lifteth it vp, that else would lowly fall:
>   It lets not fall, it lets it not to rest:
>   It lets not scarse this Prince to breath at all,
> But to his first poursuit him forward still doth call. (v.2)

After the episode to which this passage refers, "first poursuit" is studiedly vague: is it the pursuit of Gloriana or of Florimell? Is it honor or desire? Is it primarily for their sakes or for his?

The reader beating a way through the maze of these uncertain passages is tempted to put the allegorical perhapsing machine into higher gear. Perhaps, as Arthur leaves the third book, Timias becomes his surrogate, just as Florimell, Belphoebe, and Amoret have been thought to be surrogates for Britomart. Perhaps Arthur's final words confer on

Timias the unenviable task of representing the effect of the prince's swerve on his sense of honor: returning to the quest of Florimell he complains of

> The want of his good Squire late left behind,
> For whom he wondrous pensive grew in mind,
> For doubt of daunger, which mote him betide;
> For him he loued aboue all mankind,
> Hauing him trew and faithfull euer tride,
> And bold, as euer Squire that waited by knights side. (v.12)

Arthur's estrangement from Timias may illustrate no more than the threat to "homosocial" bonding posed by woman and the onset of desire. Yet the contradictions of a chivalric quest that proposes Gloriana and glory as its twin goals suggest a more intimate alliance of squire to prince. The reduction of Gloriana to glory or honor, of a powerful and desirable woman to a male objective and attribute, serves the hero's chivalric project but is threatened by the appearance, power, and claims of Florimell. Though Timias had appeared before Book III, he is first named—and abruptly introduced—in connection with Florimell at i.18. Arthur's squire, that is, receives the name of Honor and separates from Arthur when the chivalric quest modulates into an erotic quest. His response to Florimell's plight enfolds him in his own story and brings Belphoebe into the field of pursuit. The split between Gloriana and Belphoebe returns to the foreground to preside over and be mirrored in the split between Arthur and Timias. Perhaps, then, his elevation to an independent figure makes him more fully a personification, a model magnifying the effect of the chivalric hero's momentary lapse on the sense of honor "he loued aboue all mankind."

This effect is registered in the opening lines of the next stanza:

> Who all this while full hardly was assayd
> Of deadly daunger, which to him betid;
> For whiles his Lord pursewd that noble Mayd,
> After that foster fowle he fiercely rid,
> To bene auenged of the shame, he did
> To that faire Damzell. (v.13)

"Who all this while": the simultaneity of these two diverse yet parallel actions correlates them in what may be causal or at least functional interdependence. This correlation may be a signal to the reader to be on the lookout for other correlations between the parallel (if superficially opposed) pursuits of Arthur and Timias and the parallel (if superficially opposed) flights of Florimell and the forester. The perhapsing machine continues to generate possibilities that break down the barriers between one character and another and between internal and external events.

Earlier, after telling us that Arthur and Guyon "did dispart" themselves when they "came vnto a double way"—the division between knights parallels the division growing within Arthur between chivalric honor (or "temperance") and predatory desire—Spenser had turned briefly to Timias. The prince's squire

> That Ladies loue vnto his Lord forlent,
> And with proud enuy, and indignant ire,
> After that wicked foster fiercely went.
> So beene they three three sundry wayes ybent. (iv.47)

Whether the prefix in *forlent* has an intensive or a renunciatory force,[16] the second line, which parallels Arthur's "great enuie and fell gealosy," does not seem to be directed exclusively toward the forester; "proud enuy" combines nuances of disdain, desire, and emulation, implying (1) that he frowns on the motive expressed by the prince's choice of prey and (2) that he might have liked to make the same choice but knows it is not his place. Hence the rhetoric suggests that something more than the forester arouses "indignant ire."

Timias's vengeful anger increases during his pursuit and communicates itself to the forester (v.15–16), producing a situation in which the two briefly exchange roles in the hunter-prey relationship. Thwarted lust is intensified by restraint (cf. vii.32–33); the forester's predatory lust changes to lustful predation as he mobilizes his two brothers to ambush Timias at a swollen brook in the forest. There, Spenser tells us, the squire "labour'd long in that deepe ford with vaine disease" (v.19) before receiving his thigh wound. The phrase has an allegorical sense imparted by the reference to the "ouerflowne" ford "Through which it was vneath for wight to wade" (v.17), since in Book III sloth and lust are associated with the damp humor aggravated by the "humid night"

16. See OED, s.v. *for-*, senses 3 and 8.

on which Arthur had just blamed his own misfortune at the end of
Canto iv. If we take "with vaine disease" to mean not only "accompanied by futile discomfort" but also "against the (forester's) vain
disease of lust," we may feel the momentary identity of Timias and his
foes, of honorable anger and the desire against which it fights.

Timias is thus susceptible to the disease before he actually catches it
from the "cruell shaft, headed with deadly ill" (v.20).[17] The logic of
pursuit allows me to play on *catch*, for if he pursues lust successfully,
he catches it and is therefore defeated or infected by it. In translating
allegory to event, Spenser marks the displacement that conceals the
nature of the infection from the victim. What Timias suffers is physical
hurt; the "passion of vnwonted lust, / Or wonted feare of doing ought
amis" (I.i.49) burrows underground and festers in reserve. Spenser's
descriptive details signal the displacement. The culprit arrow "did light
/ In his left thigh, and deepely did it thrill: / Exceeding griefe that
wound in him empight" (v.20).[18] Although Spenser, unlike Shakespeare, does not use "thrill" in its strictly modern sense, he often conflates its primary sense, penetration, with the sense of the particular
affect it causes, in this case the "griefe" of physical pain.[19] But as we
know, weapons and wounds are always potentially significant as double displacements in Spenser's allegorical force field: they can symbolize either the effects of Cupid or the impotence produced by penetration, which places the male victim in the position men assign to
woman.

The question this reading raises is how Timias's plight is related to
the next episode, his encounter with Belphoebe, in the allegorical

17. Echoes of details in the Malecasta episode give this passage the nuance of erotic
displacement: cf. the overflowing "bancks" and "secret darts" of i.51 and the "fountaine by some couert glade" of i.35.

18. The shaft is identified as an arrow in line 5 of Stanza 20 and in Stanza 24; this
identification is important for the association of the episode with the arrows of Cupid
and Belphoebe.

19. At iv.15, hearing Marinell's challenge, Britomart is "Ythrild with deepe disdaine
of his proud threat." This passion allows her to relieve her love longing by turning it
outward in the form of aggression (iv.13). Here, *Ythrild* acquires a suggestion of erotic
passion even as it signals its transformation. Previously "penetrated" by the image of
Artegal, she is now excited to disdain by Marinell, who is a limited prefiguration of
Artegal and whose misguided antierotic stance represents a male obstacle to her love
quest.

scheme of things. Belphoebe finds him by following the traces of the fresh blood she thought would have led her to "some wild beast, which with her arrowes keene / She wounded had" (v.28). When "with melting eyes" she views him lying bloody "in deadly swownd"

> All suddeinly abasht she chaunged hew,
> And with sterne horrour backward gan to start:
> But when she better him beheld, she grew
> Full of soft passion and vnwonted smart:
> The point of pitty perced through her tender hart. (v.30)

Characteristically, the gaps in Spenser's explanation leave the meaning of her response indeterminate. Does the final couplet fully account for the violence of her reaction? The metaphor of penetration suggests the boomerang effect that makes the predator her own prey. It is an odd reversal of the Actaeon motif with which she is persistently associated, and, in addition, it connects her "vnwonted smart" to the effect she will have on Timias. Yet "when she better him beheld" suggests that the thrill of pity is not the sole cause of her sudden horror, leading me to speculate that she starts back because she thinks *she* is responsible for Timias's plight.

The point of this speculation is not to try to penetrate Belphoebe's consciousness, since "she" doesn't have very much of that commodity (or only has it when it is strategically useful for Spenser's purposes), but to argue that the confusion aligns her effect on Timias with that of the three foresters. In the allegorical scheme healing one wound only to open up another means undoing the displacement of the original wound to a physical injury and transferring it to Timias's mind so that the lurking infection breaks out in a more complex "Malady" (v.43) of guilty desire:

> Still as his wound did gather, and grow hole,
> So still his hart woxe sore, and health decayd:
> Madnesse to saue a part, and lose the whole. (v.43)

Since *hole/whole* is a possible homonymy produced by orthographic variation, the convention barring identical rhyme words yields the possibility of a pun at either rhyme site. The innuendo this produces at *whole* is less interesting (except as an index to the narrator's delight in sending up his little "tragedy") than the implication of *hole*: the wound she opens up is the wound she heals. The effect of this wordplay on Belphoebe is equally interesting. It is true that the erotic nuance of "soft passion and vnwonted smart" is quickly defused by "point of pitty," but the danger of her entrapment in an unwanted (or at least unlooked-for) erotic encounter remains. Her problem, indeed, her function in the poem, is to represent woman's autonomy, her rights over her own sexuality, by imposing constraints on male desire. It is a problem because in order to demonstrate this power, she has to arouse male desire, and this is also her function. Whatever consciousness she and Florimell may be said to possess, they have this in common: though one spends most of her time in flight and the other in her forest retreat, the meaning of both is centered on their visibility, and both are described in such a manner as to emphasize their awareness of being on display.

Belphoebe's entanglement with Timias comes metaphorically alive when she tries to heal his thigh wound and hurts

> his hart, the which before was sound,
> Through an unwary dart, which did rebound
> From her faire eyes and gracious countenaunce. (v.42)

Like Florimell's, her *daunger* and care are undone by the fact that she is another embodiment of destructive Beauty, "Darting her beames into each feeble mynd." Regaining consciousness, Timias lifts his eyes "toward the azure skies / From whence descends all hopelesse remedies"—remedies not hoped for, remedies *for* hopelessness, and remedies *producing* hopelessness—and spies "The goodly Mayd full of diuinities" (v.34). The important thing about the "unwary dart" is that it *re*bounds, and does so not once but twice: beauty darts beams into his eyes and heart, his heart sends back the dart as desire, and the dart glances back from her eyes as *daunger*. *Unwary* displaces to the dart their mutual unawareness of the complex action metaphorically concentrated in the figure of the rebounding weapon. From its narrative context this figure precipitates the following information: the wound is partly self-inflicted; in Belphoebe the beauty of Diana has the effect of Venus, therefore the armed *daunger* that unwarily deflects (rejects) his desire is inseparable from the beauty that unwarily aroused it; *daunger*

transcoding

is an offensive as well as defensive weapon—it adds force to the rebound and thus intensifies the victim's pain; Belphoebe's *daunger*, penetrating Timias's heart, becomes his own concern so that the battle he fights within himself is a battle on her behalf. His heart assimilates her *daunger* to his sense of honor, but at the same time the presence of beauty together with the constraint of internalized *daunger* increases the force of desire. A failing Anteros figure, his warfare against Cupid is simultaneously supported and undermined by the beautiful embodiment of feminine *daunger*—or the *daungerous* embodiment of beauty, who (like Florimell) does Cupid's work in spite of herself.

In Timias's encounters with the forester and Belphoebe there is continuous dissonance between the claims of rhetoric and those of narrative, the former calling attention to itself in a way that decelerates the reading process, the latter encouraging readers to move swiftly on. To respond to the dissonance is to feel that the text is richer than the story, that more goes on than meets the "ear" of one whose reading simulates the aural reception of twice-told tales and who conceives the reader's task primarily as the visualization of narrated events.[20] The effect of dissonance is produced partly by the continuous play on *wounds*, the conspicuous transcoding of more complex psychic events into the simpler vehicle of physical events. And the effect in turn ensconces the characters in a panoply of innocence that protects them from the textual ambiguities their language and behavior manifest. So, for example, we assume that Timias and Belphoebe don't know what we know: that their story is shaped by the generic transference of Petrarchan tropes from the register of the male subject's lyric complaint to that of his narrative situation, from the scene the conventional poet-lover imagines to the scene poor Timias inhabits, and from a hyperbolic fantasy of victimization to its narrative enactment.

For us to recognize this is also to recognize that the story is itself a hyperbole, an externalization of the lyric fantasy whose perspective and interests remain those of the male subject. This recognition enhances our sense that romance as a story is a pastoral reduction of the

if subjected to analysis (+ abstraction)

transcoding (metonymy)

what happens when the reader ≠ male?

20. See John Webster's very interesting hypothesis that Spenser produces this double response by contrasting use of oral-formulaic style and the rhetorical complexity that demands close reading: "Oral Form and Written Craft in Spenser's *Faerie Queene*," *SEL*, 16 (1976), 75–93.

complex into the simple—of the complex psychological interactions I
have been describing in the previous pages to the simplified puppets
that model the interaction. In this respect Spenserian romance uses the
effect of Ariosto not only to make urbane fun of its own indulgent
literariness but also to draw attention to a serious critique of the ideology inscribed in the conventional forms of literariness it represents.
The narrativization of Petrarchan tropes works to parody the self-
serving, self-subverting character of the androcentric fantasy inscribed
in the lyric genre. Maureen Quilligan has shown how this discloses the
seriousness of the misperceptions to which the fantasy gives rise. She
notes, for example, that Britomart and Marinell "err when they interpret by Petrarchan metaphor."[21] But the case of Timias and Belphoebe
is more interesting because the critique is directed only at the Petrarchan ideology, not at the characters. Their ardors and innocence
are merely amusing: while Timias hurts and complains, Belphoebe, as
Alpers says, "remains the simple country girl: she keeps on applying
her medicines and wonders why Timias does not get better" (p. 189).

The tension between innocence and the psychologcal edginess of the
moment in which the male becomes victim of the Petrarchan love strike
is conveyed with wonderful humor in stanzas 35–36. After Timias
addresses Belphoebe in Aeneas's words—"Angell, or Goddesse do I
call thee right?"—he asks what "seruice" he can do to repay her for
healing his "sinfull" wounds, and offers to kiss her "blessed feet."[22]
Arthur's squire is surely not to be confused with his opposite number,
the Squire of Dames, who might exhibit what service means to him by
proceeding to kiss his way up the divine body. Nevertheless, the confusion of motives passed on from the preceding episodes affects the interplay of *service* with *sinfull* and provokes in the reader a wicked
"thought of vngentlenesse" (v.2). Surely Timias aspires to protect the
gentler meanings of his words from such a thought, and surely the

21. Maureen Quilligan, *The Language of Allegory: Defining the Genre* (Ithaca:
Cornell University Press, 1979), p. 83.

22. The Virgilian echo adds further to the complications in which our innocent hero
and heroine are ensnarled and thus enhances our sense of their innocence, their entrapment in the pastoral reductiveness of Spenser's narrative. The allusion linking
Belphoebe to Venus disguised as Diana is more predictable than the effect of the linkage
of Timias and Belphoebe to Aeneas and his mother. Since this, together with
Belphoebe's staging of another of Spenser's little pietàs, suggests maternal solicitude, the
rhetoric of Neoplatonized Petrarchism is beset by hints of forbidden desire.

gentle reader shares that aspiration and feels relief, feels gratitude, when Belphoebe clears the air. Or does she?

> Thereat she blushing said, Ah gentle Squire,
>   Nor Goddesse I, nor Angell, but the Mayd,
>   And daughter of a woody Nymphe, desire
>   No seruice, but thy safety and ayd;
>   Which if thou gaine, I shalbe well apayd. (v. 36)

Surely the humble maiden blushes only because she hears herself unduly apotheosized, not because she is flattered, not because she detects a sexual innuendo. Yet innuendo thrives on conspicuous exclusion. In another part of the Petrarchan forest the blush might register responsiveness to flattery and the same words might have the force of a mild rebuke delivered by one who worries lest her motives be misconstrued, one who feels called on to protest that she is not a courtly mistress fishing for hyperboles and proposals of service but a virgin dedicated to worthy causes and Diana's woody games. The elliptical syntax of the long first clause generates a hint of cautious recoil by nudging the verb toward the imperative mood: the easy graciousness of "I desire no service" is challenged by the prohibition "you must desire no service."

Trapped in the voyeuristic medium of the storyteller's transaction with readers, the energetic Belphoebe is not much better off than the enervated Timias. She has trouble keeping her self-representation from being breached by just those nuances it is her function to fend off. The narrator's mischievous mimicry makes it impossible for the characters to say, do, and be only what they want to say, do, and be, impossible for them to escape from the constraints of the generic roles they perform. But as I have noted, if this makes for an ironic effect, it is not at the expense of the characters. Whatever power Belphoebe has over men is a power ceded to her by the men who have power over her in the sense that she is their fantasy. Her power is not fully explained either by the analogy of Elizabeth or by Alpers's thesis that she is the product of "the perpetual spring of the pastoral world" (pp. 390–91). For the particular pastoralism her appearance, behavior, and speech reflect is that of the erotic Diana shaped and cloistered in the Petrarchan subject's mind: the "pleasant glade" of her valley retreat is encircled by mountains and shaded by "mighty woods" (v.39)—the haunts of the male enemy—just as her innocent reponse to Timias is encircled and shaded by unwanted meanings. The wild surround makes her valley resemble "a stately Theatre . . . / Spreading it selfe into a spatious plaine": the *hortus conclusus* is not only marked as a site of performance and self-display but also breached by a frisson of erotic invitation, made broader by the echo in the second line of the description of Malecasta's castle (i.20). Her retreat is infiltrated by the displaced tokens of male desire, now conveniently domesticated into an idyll of languid and pleasant pain. The sonneteer's woe is reduced to "a little riuer" that only gently complains of the restraint imposed by "pumy stones": those evoke a thought of the hard-hearted lady, and *pumy* conveys both the attritional and the refining effect of her *daunger* on the lover. Her grove has myrtles for Venus and laurels for poetry, but here the lady's worshipful and tormented sonneteers are transformed as if by Circe to harmless birds who "prayse" the god (Cupid?) and enjoy their "sweete teene" (v.40).

One might easily be tempted to brand the Spenser who describes this scene a misogynist and voyeur, on the grounds that he furtively stocks Belphoebe's chaste preserve with all the signs of the Cruel Lady's erotic power and that by thus practicing on his innocent, well-meaning heroine he deviously reasserts the power and enacts the revenge of the Petrarchan poet. He is a more benign Petrarchan than the one described by Louis Montrose: "The Petrarchan lover worships a deity of his own making and under his own control; he masters his mistress by inscribing her within his text, where she is repeatedly put together and taken apart—and, sometimes, killed."[23] But Spenser not only conveys his admiration and even his desire of the deity he constructs (as in II.iii.22–31), he also endows her with so many additional good qualities—pity, courtesy, kindness—that, for this and other reasons, he has been praised for privileging "a female vantage point" in Book III.[24] Still, one could argue that his treatment of Belphoebe is only superficially benign, and actually insidious, in that everything about

23. Louis Montrose, "The Elizabethan Subject and the Spenserian Text," in *Literary Theory/Renaissance Texts*, ed. Patricia Parker and David Quint (Baltimore: The Johns Hopkins University Press, 1986), p. 325.

24. See Maureen Quilligan, *Milton's Spenser: The Politics of Reading* (Ithaca: Cornell University Press, 1983), p. 186 and pp. 185–99 passim, and Lauren Silberman, "Singing Unsung Heroines: Androgynous Discourse in Book 3 of *The Faerie Queene*," in *Rewriting the Renaissance: The Discourses of Sexual Difference in Early Modern Europe*, ed. Margaret W. Ferguson, Maureen Quilligan, and Nancy J. Vickers (Chicago: University of Chicago Press, 1986), pp. 259–71.

her—appearance, behavior, speech, and habitat—conforms to the needs of the self-refining male subject whose *object* she remains: "The Petrarchan poet writes of a mistress who is unattainable so that his own perpetual longing provides subject matter for his poetry and the occasion for his assuming the vocation of poet" (Silberman, p. 260). That Belphoebe has no meaning apart from the longing she is created to arouse and resist is evident from Spenser's insistence on depicting a sensibility totally, exclusively permeated by the dangers of arousal and resistance; even when she seems to intend kindness and "Platonic" friendship, the poet undoes her with wordplay.

Is Spenser, then, the lady's friend, a species of closet feminist, or is he a run-of-the-mill Elizabethan misogynist? I would gladly pledge allegiance to the former, even if that meant sacrificing the nastier and more bracing pleasures of the latter. But I am not persuaded that either view has very much to do with what is going on in *The Faerie Queene* because I don't think the views can be attributed to "Spenser." The reason for this opinion has been developed in the preceding interpretations, and if it isn't yet clear, that may be because those interpretations presuppose a peculiar form of fictiveness or virtuality, a category of representation, that I have yet to dignify with a name. The category has already been described but not put into play, and this is what I shall try to do in the final section of the essay.

Discourse in *The Faerie Queene*

It is with considerable pride that I call attention to the fact that the word *discourse* did not appear once in the preceding section. I could have used it on several occasions—when, for example, I mentioned Neoplatonist, Petrarchan, Ovidian, and Lucretian *fantasies, tropologies,* and *functions,* or the contradictions of the chivalric *quest. Discourse* could be substituted for all the italicized terms. But what difference would it make? How would the practice of close reading be affected by a change to Neoplatonist, Petrarchan, Ovidian, Lucretian, and chivalric *discourses,* or *language-games*? Would a change of terms also be a change of conceptualization? Would it produce a different interpretation? I submit that it would, and in this concluding section I shall try to show why.

I begin with some comments on romance by Northrop Frye, who observes that when the quest romance is translated into dream terms it becomes "the search of the libido or desiring self for a fulfilment that will deliver it from the anxieties of reality but will still contain that reality."[25] In his attempt to revise Frye's "modal" view of genre, Fredric Jameson criticizes its essentialism, that is, its assumption of a "generalized existential experience behind the individual texts." Jameson finds "Frye's assimilation of the 'world' of romance to nature" symptomatic of this tendency, and he objects, predictably, to "the implication that this 'nature' is in any sense itself a 'natural' rather than a very peculiar and specialized social and historical phenomenon." After discussing some problems and possibilities in Frye's emphasis on the traditional oppositions and "categories of character" in romance, he states that "the modal approach to genre must be pursued until, by means of radical historicization, the 'essence,' 'spirit,' 'world-view,' in question is revealed to be . . . a historically determinate . . . complex which can project itself variously in the form of a 'value system' or 'philosophical concept,' or in the form of a protonarrative, a private or collective narrative fantasy."[26] Frye of course had already followed this recommendation to some extent in *The Secular Scripture*. He noted, for example, that in Spenser's day, if not in ours, *"The Faerie Queene* was regarded as pandering to a middlebrow appetite for stories about fearless knights and beauteous maidens and hideous ogres and dragons," and he added that "Spenser knew very well what he was doing with his ogres and dragons: he was trying to get imaginative support for the Protestant revolution of his time." The example is used to illustrate Frye's notion of the "kidnapped romance": "In every period of history certain ascendant values are accepted by society and are embodied in its serious literature. Usually the process includes some form of kidnapped romance, that is, romance formulas used to reflect certain ascendant religious or social ideals." The formulas that are kidnapped tend to express a "more uncritical kind" of "social mythology," one that "may be intense but is not deep, and is founded on prejudice and unexamined assumptions."[27]

25. Northrop Frye, *Anatomy of Criticism* (1957; rpt. Princeton: Princeton University Press, 1971), p. 193.

26. Fredric Jameson, *The Political Unconscious: Narrative as a Socially Symbolic Act* (Ithaca: Cornell University Press, 1981), pp. 107–08, 111, 112, 115.

27. Northrop Frye, *The Secular Scripture: A Study of the Structure of Romance* (Cambridge, Mass.: Harvard University Press, 1976), pp. 28–30, 168.

For me, to think of *The Faerie Queene* as a kidnapper of romances is—following Frye's suggestion—to think of it as always in some measure a critique of its victims, and this idea can be given more historical determination in a social as well as literary context by bringing together Frye's comment on social mythology with his reference to the poem's early reputation as a pander. I submit that the "middlebrow appetite" for stories in several genres is something the poem represents by its mimicry of those genres, by its critique of the "value system" sedimented in one or another mode of "collective narrative fantasy." Thus Spenser's poem is not merely the representation of quest romance but also a representation of the way quest romances have been represented and, by implication, of the readerships whose tastes and values they appeal to. And just as the kidnapper's project is often complicated by some unaccountable attraction for the one kidnapped, so the poem does not always maintain its critical distance but frequently weakens, melts, embraces the kidnapped forms. The fluid variations between distance and embrace are, however, consistently sustained within the perspective of analysis and critique, and this means that whenever embrace dominates, the critique becomes reflexive; the narrator archly performs his mimicry for our amused contempt, displays the susceptibility his mastery of the forms allows, shares with us his delight in being seduced by his endless inventiveness and improvisatory surprises.

Frye's kidnapped romance and Jameson's "collective narrative fantasy" together define what I mean by *discourse*. The most important aspect of this notion is that it drives a wedge between our naïve reception of the story as a first-order fiction and our more suspicious response to the story as a pastiche of parodied forms we are encouraged to scrutinize with a squint eye. Thus it isn't enough to say that the first two books of *The Faerie Queene* represent the chivalric hero's quest as the medium and subject of an allegorical poem. In both, the tropes of Christian and classical ethic (Book I dominated by the former, Book II by the latter) are deployed in a manner that makes them as well as the two heroes the objects of serious parody. The critique is focused on the dangerous egocentricity of the quest formula and on the way those cultural tropologies provide resources—of self-justification, self-evasion, self-deception, and self-protection—that reinforce heroic innocence, resources that repress or defer and ultimately exacerbate guilt, despair, and self-doubt. Both books target the reliance of this discourse on simplistic images of feminine power which, whether benign and supportive or wicked and seductive, threaten the masculine hero's autonomy.

The hero's discourse is inseparable from discourses of gender, thus in I and II all the ingredients are already in place for the shift of emphasis to the latter in Book III. At the outset the self-deceptions of chivalric discourse are exposed with Ariostan fanfare and mirth when the hero's antierotic defense of manly Temperance is overthrown by a woman's magical arms. And when Britomart appropriates the hero's position the possibilities for discursive parody are greatly enhanced. In particular, as the instability of masculine power and desire become prominent, as this prominence is correlated with the disruptive power of mothers, witches, and even the most helpless of beautiful virgins, male fantasies modulate into the familiar discourse of victimization and revenge. Spenser concludes by assigning power over the Ovidian, Petrarchan, and courtly varieties of this discourse to Busirane, the *busy reign* of masculine imagination trying ever more busily—because ineffectively—to dominate, violate, and terrorize the feminine "cause" of pain. Kenneth Gross describes the House of Busirane as "Spenser's vision of a human subject wounded in both mind and body by poetic conceits," and the phrase is suggestive because it implies that poetic conceits do Cupid's work—that Cupid symbolizes investments of desire mobilized by and productive of poetic imagery whose power over lovers and readers transgresses "a merely aesthetic commitment to that imagery."[28] Spenser dramatizes this transgression by literalizing metaphors in narrative enactment. He not only brings the fantasies "to life" but also marks the stages of transgression and thereby gives the victim/revenger's discourse citational status—places it, so to speak, in quotation marks.[29]

28. Kenneth Gross, *Spenserian Poetics: Idolatry, Iconoclasm, and Magic* (Ithaca: Cornell University Press, 1985), p. 163. Gross credits Thomas Hyde with this idea, which is important because it suggests that poetic conceits are functions of cultural and not merely literary discourse, so that even an apparently "aesthetic commitment" can be fraught with political as well as psychological implications. See the classic discussion of this theme in Renato Poggioli's "Tragedy or Romance? A Reading of the Paolo and Francesca Episode in Dante's *Inferno*," in *The Spirit of the Letter: Essays in European Literature* (Cambridge, Mass.: Harvard University Press, 1965), pp. 50–102.

29. Spenser touches briefly on the limits of the Neoplatonic discourse of sublimation—the male's attempt to preserve autonomy by diverting desire from woman to the

The psychological complexity of Book III is extraordinary but it is not focused on the "psyches" of major characters in a way that invites readers to invest much affect in them, to attack or adorn individual psyches with psychoanalytic fervor. In saying this, I am only saying what commentators of the poem have always said: Spenser's stenographic portrayal of character seems to solicit reactions that are diffuse and fundamentally nondramatic. One such reaction is the pursuit of psychomachian simplicities, the impulse to course the wandering, densely overgrown path of the text in search of decidable moral conflicts. This is the reaction of traditional commentary. Reader-response criticism has reinforced the intuitions of several New Critics and myth critics that if this is not a correct reaction it is nevertheless not a wrong reaction *tout court* but a "wrong" reaction, since the poem offers the reader temptations homologous to those confronted by characters: escape from difficulty, ease after toil, and sometimes ease before toil. What I have called the conspicuous irrelevance of the poem's local texture contributes to this reaction by encouraging readers to divide the poem into ornament and argument, fable and allegory, pictures and messages, "poetry" and "truth," "pleasure" and "morality," etc. One alternative—the New Critical reaction to this traditional reaction—was to take the conspicuousness seriously and try to subdue Spenser's

---

divine—in his account of Timias's torments (to which I shall return) and his mention of the heavenly Venus in vi.12. The dangerous power invested by male fantasy in Venus is suggested by that mention: Neoplatonic narcissism cannot escape the feminine power that motivates its upward flight; it is also suggested by the metamorphosis of Venus first into the goddess of courtly pleasure (vi.22) and then into a Lucretian figure of maternal nature in the Gardens of Adonis, a figure who takes on suspiciously Malecastan and Acrasian overtones in the "gloomy groue" and secret "pleasant arbour" of "sad louers" (vi.44–46). If, as Gross suggests, Cupid represents the power of fictions—"poetic conceits"—that have been naturalized or deified, Venus represents both the object and cause of Cupid's power. She personifies the desirable, the beautiful, as a female power of love that seduces and threatens the male. As in the case of Cupid, her personification is a metonymy of displacement transforming the effect of male fantasy into its cause. The specious power and autonomy granted to Venus in the discourses of gender suggests that feminine desire is itself an invention of masculine imagination, that Venus is Cupid's daughter rather than his mother. Venus and Cupid together preside over discourses that both threaten and supplement the organization of gender relationships in the patriarchal system of marriage. As alternatives to marriage they support and are supported by it in parasitic mutuality. Spenser's sensitivity to the problems such a symbiosis creates is shown by his revising the scene of Amoret's captivity and torture from the premarital to the postnuptial relation.

so-called dualism by making the first term in each pair the subject of interpretation and the second the means. This division produced a more suspicious mode of reading dominated by the tendency to "thicken" the imaginary world of the fable and, in some cases, to follow the traces of intricate verbal and narrative designs into the lair of the individual character's psyche.

Much of my earlier work on Spenser was dominated by this project, and I think the flaws inherent in its general assumptions about fictional character were decisively analyzed by Alpers in *The Poetry of "The Faerie Queene."* His critique has persuaded me that the New Critical approach to the psyches of fictional subjects may not be any more helpful in reading Spenser than the psychoanalytic approach that probes fictional psyches as if they were the properties of empirical subjects. Yet I am by no means prepared to go all the way with Alpers in his axiomatic disjunction between the criteria of fictional consistency and those of the coherence of the reader's responses. I think it is important to register the *effects* of character, place, event, visualizable drama— effects that compose into the larger effect of a fictional "world"— precisely because they are not "consistent," because they are intermittent and variably stressed. They are, so to speak, temporary "condensations" of meaning effects into effects of scene, character, event, etc., and one of the dominant consequences of the subtle tonal play of the poem's addresses to the reader—its rhetoricity—is to problematize its condensation of meaning into "vision" or self-contained fiction.[30] The value of Alpers's intervention (for others as well as myself) has been to force us to revise ingenuous New Critical commitments to character per se, fiction per se, and vision per se.

From all this I conclude that the best approach is neither psychomachian nor psychological but *metapsychological.* I use the term loosely to include several of the senses given to it by Freud and others: (1) an "attempt to construct a psychology 'that leads behind conscious-

30. See, for example, my "Busirane and the War between the Sexes: An Interpretation of *The Faerie Queene* III.xi-xii," *ELR,* 1 (1971), 114–17, and "The Discarding of Malbecco: Conspicuous Allusion and Cultural Exhaustion in *The Faerie Queene* III.ix-x," *SP,* 66 (1969), 149–54. For a fine survey—compact and lucidly organized—of changing approaches to *The Faerie Queene,* see A. C. Hamilton, "*The Faerie Queene,*" in *Critical Approaches to Six Major English Works: "Beowulf" through "Paradise Lost,"* ed. Robert M. Lumiansky and Herschel Baker (Philadelphia: University of Pennsylvania Press, 1968), pp. 132–65.

ness' . . . as compared to the classical psychologies of consciousness";
(2) an "endeavor to redress the construction of 'metaphysics,'" or mythology, that is, of *psychology projected into the external world*"; (3)
the construction of "an ensemble of conceptual models which are more
or less far-removed from empirical reality."[31] In the present context,
empirical reality would refer to the object aimed at by the complex
psychological analysis of the individual character and "consciousness,"
while *conceptual models* would be virtually synonymous with *discourses* or *language-games*. We may then describe Spenser's approach
as metapsychological in the sense that it centers on the roles, positions,
and interactions inscribed in an ensemble of traditional discourses
rather than in the players or agents. The metapsychological perspective
reduces characters to "actantial" functions: what happens *to* them is
less important than what happens "in" them and "through" them, for
the simplified or typified mode of portrayal shifts attention from dis-
crete individual psyches to their positions in the discourses that traverse and "subject" them, the discourses they model.

It may already be apparent that when *metapsychological* is predi-
cated in this matter of Spenser's practice it means much the same as
allegorical, especially if the field on which metapsychology operates is
viewed in Lacanian terms as "the whole structure of the language"
animated by "the agency of the letter" (i.e., the agency of the "material
support that concrete discourse borrows from language").[32] Many of
the features of Spenserian allegory picked out by Angus Fletcher display this metapsychological orientation: the "daemonic" character of
narration that "accepts and depicts the irresistible drives of men's actions"; the generative contribution of punning to this daemonic narrative; the uses of parody and collage in "drawing attention to the *materials* of art and life" and in denying "the neutrality and transparency of
the medium"; the tendency of allegories to function as "mirrors of
ideology"—or, as I would prefer to say, as distorting mirrors that

31. Jean Laplanche and J.-B. Pontalis, *The Language of Psycho-analysis*, trans. Donald Nicholson-Smith (New York: Norton, 1973), p. 149. The idea of using "metapsychology" in this context was suggested to me by my colleague, H. Marshall Leicester, Jr., from whose forthcoming study of the discourse of gender in *The Canterbury
Tales* I have greatly profited.

32. Jacques Lacan, "The Agency of the Letter in the Unconscious; or, Reason Since
Freud," in *Écrits: A Selection*, trans. Alan Sheridan (New York: Norton, 1977), p. 147.

target the ideological implications of the discourses they represent.[33] To conceive allegory in these metapsychological terms is to recognize the dominant structuring function played by the Lacanian algorithm

$$\frac{S(\text{signifier})}{s(\text{signified})},$$

and thus to reverse the approach of traditional allegoresis.

This reversal has been emphasized by Maureen Quilligan in *The Language of Allegory*, which bases itself on Fletcher's account but essays a more restrictive definition of the genre. She argues that the genre to which *The Faerie Queene* belongs consists of works whose "particular emphasis [is] on language as their first focus and ultimate subject," works that have their "source in a culture's attitude toward language" and that generate "narrative structure out of wordplay." Thus Spenser "forces his reader to attend to the problematic relationships between the metaphorical and literal meanings of words, and to witness the nearly fatal mistakes characters (and readers) make when they confuse the two." In Book III he shows how characters "err when they interpret by Petrarchan metaphor," whose limitations he "consistently keeps before the reader."[34] Quilligan agrees with C. S. Lewis that in this book "Spenser plays profoundly with a whole tradition of allegory," the "allegory of love," but she replaces Lewis's emphasis on "the subject of love" with an emphasis on "the more particular subject of love's language" (p. 85). Yet when Lewis argues that Spenser is his "collaborator" in telling "the final stages of the history of courtly love,"[35] he is at least thematically concerned as much with the literary language as with the subject of love, since courtly love as a cultural discourse is dominated by literary texts, and its concepts are not merely conveyed but controlled by an iconographic repertory of tropes and images. Lewis is neither a close nor a reliable reader of *The Faerie*

33. Angus Fletcher, *The Prophetic Moment*, pp. 55, 99–106; *Allegory: The Theory of a Symbolic Mode* (1964; rpt. Ithaca: Cornell University Press, 1970), p. 368.

34. Quilligan, *The Language of Allegory*, pp. 15, 22, 80, 83–84. For a germinal anticipation of this thesis, see A. C. Hamilton, "Our New Poet: Spenser's 'well of English undefyld,'" in *Essential Articles for the Study of Edmund Spenser*, ed. Hamilton (New Haven: Archon Books, 1972), pp. 488–506.

35. C. S. Lewis, *The Allegory of Love: A Study in Medieval Tradition* (London: Oxford University Press, 1936), pp. 298, 338.

Queene; nevertheless, I think the line of analysis he develops offers more flexibility than Quilligan's approach because it centers on a distinction between the poem as an allegorical discourse and the discourses the poem represents. Quilligan's project of overcoming another distinction—"our traditional insistence on allegory's distinction between word said and meaning meant" (p. 26)—occasions inattentiveness to this one.

The misadventures of Book III are often linked to misinterpretations, and Quilligan is right to insist that they are occasioned by verbal ambiguity, but it is neither wordplay nor language per se that produces the "subtle sophismes" whose "double senses" lead the fictional interpreters astray. If, for example, "the pun on chase . . . [is] a profound structuring principle at work throughout the book," one that encourages readers to play with the *chased/chaste* homonym and the etymological pun on *venery*, it is because the rationale of Ovidian discourse guides interpretation. The metapsychological reading bears on the psychological drama situated in and between the positions created by the discourse (predator and prey, for example) rather than on the characters who fill or model the positions. But as I tried to show in the preceding section, it also bears on the rhetorical situation, the play of language, that interprets the drama it represents. Quilligan's thesis, slightly modified, is that the allegorical genre as illustrated by Spenser foregrounds "the agency of the letter" in generating the dynamic interplay of discourses and their daemonic operations on the subjects they constitute.

Lewis focuses on courtly love and Quilligan on Petrarchism, but because both tend to ignore or minimize other discourses in the poem their readings obscure the effect produced by mimicry, multiple contexts of allusion, pastiche, and the constant interplay of several diversely weighted language-games. A metapsychological reading would connect the interplay and diversity with the meaning of the third book's titular virtue and its embodiment in a woman. It would explore their relation to the relaxed narrative control noted by Jonathan Goldberg in his comment on "all the erosion of the quest structure in Book III that keeps Britomart from seeming to be the kind of hero that the Red Crosse knight and Guyon appear to be," including her four-canto absence, "her insubstantial victory" over Busirane, "her repeated wounds," and her puzzling allegorical connections to the parade of surrogates (Florimell, Belphoebe, Amoret) that model aspects of Chastity while she is gone.[36] Where the Temperance of Book II remained more or less tightly furled around the sexually polarized figure of an embattled, repressed, and repressive hero, the Chastity of Book III flutters uncertainly from one to another of several figures of both sexes. There is apparently something about this virtue as Spenser conceives it that can't be adequately represented by a quest scheme consistently oriented on a single exemplar. More so than in the case of Britomart's two predecessors, the "or" in the title of Book III may connote disjunction rather than indifference:

THE LEGEND OF BRITOMARTIS

OR

Of Chastitie

The Chastity in question may paradoxically have to be weaned from the stable contours and "glorious pourtraict" of the individual hero, shadowed "in colourd showes," psychologically diffused and diffracted "In mirrours more then one." Such diffraction and diffusion are represented even within *Britomartis*—generated within the name by the intersection of two narratives, one intratextual and the other intertextual, the first looking forward and the second backward, the first the tale of a virgin's loving search for her future husband, the second the tale of a virgin's fearful flight from attempted rape, the first contextualized in Tudor history and Elizabethan genealogy, the second in the Ovidian tradition of classical myth.

The classical sources of the name are compactly summarized by Nohrnberg, who, in addition, shows how the imitation of Ovidian and quasi-Ovidian motifs organizes the stories of Britomart and Florimell, Venus and Adonis, and the Malecastan episode in a network of analogies (*Analogy*, pp. 446–48). He notes, for example, that "one part of the [classical] Britomartis story appears in the flight of Spenser's Florimell," and suggests that Florimell represents "an aspect of the chastity of Britomartis" (p. 446). Does she also represent an aspect of the chastity of Spenser's Britomart? Several of the metaphors applied by Glauce and Britomart to the latter's love pains in Cantos ii (stanzas

---

36. Goldberg, *Endlesse Worke*, pp. 3–4.

40 and 41), iii (stanza 18), and iv (stanzas 7–10) are actualized in
Cantos vii and viii as "literal" dangers confronted by Florimell. One
could argue that Florimell suffers everything Britomart experiences as
fantasy, and controls, but that since she controls it by wounding Marinell, she is the cause of Florimell's plight and displaces to Florimell
her own Ovidian torments.

All this reactivates the perhapsing machine. Perhaps Britomart is
purged of her Ovidian inheritance at Florimell's expense; perhaps the
appearance of Florimell represents the condensation and exorcism of
that inheritance. Yet there is an odd congruence in the effects they
produce by their contrary forms of quest. One effect of Britomart's
actions is to lower male resistance to love: she unhorses Guyon and
Marinell, two self-protective Anteros figures, and refuses to help a
woman whose fugitive beauty inflames heroes as well as blackguards.
That she tolerates Malecasta's advances because of "self-feeling of her
feeble sex," safely experiencing the male's role as object of a desire like
hers, and that she saves Redcross from woman's *maisterie* and promis-
cuity, indicate her desire for a constant union with a hero who will
neither resist her love nor betray it. The same impulse sends Florimell
flying through Faerie, where she collaborates with Britomart by kind-
ling "goodly fire" in "braue sprite" (v.1) so that, like a whiffler, she
begins to clear the way to the "saluage" (IV.iv.39) heart of Britomart's
beloved. While she does this, Britomart trots through Faerie Land
masquerading as a man in the armor of "a Saxon Virgin."

Perhaps, then, that masquerade is the equivalent of Florimell's flight
from beauty's chase. Perhaps it is Britomart's way of fleeing from men
and avoiding that chase. Perhaps the two narratives inscribed in the
name *Britomartis* are separated and placed in complementary relation,
with Florimell being assigned the ancillary function of carrying off the
classical burden in order to purge and secure the success of Spenser's
new myth of "this royall Maid of yore," Elizabeth's Briton forebear.
But on the other hand perhaps Florimell and her story nest within
Britomart and her story, constituting a psychomachian parenthesis
within the narrative of the heroine's quest. Or perhaps Spenser's digression to beauty's chase dramatizes his continuing fascination with
the Ovidian discourse that diverts Britomart and the poem from their
forward march toward Artegal, Elizabeth, and glory. Perhaps this di-
version only reflects what Louis Montrose has called "the interpenetra-

tion and mutual contamination of sexual and political codes" characterizing the "collective discourse of Elizabethan power that we call
'Queen Elizabeth,'" a discourse construing England's "royal virgin"
not only as Diana and Astraea (Belphoebe and Gloriana) but also as
her subjects' mother, lover, and beloved.[37] "But yet the end is not":
since I see no way to shut down the perhapsing machine, I resign myself
to the conclusion that the two discourses struggling within *Britomartis*
remain tangled in rhizomatic embrace to this very day. From this com-
forting if evasive closure I move to another that will summarize the
thesis I have tried to develop in the preceding pages.

In his representation of Ovidian discourse, Spenser's conduct of the
motif of the chase picks out the paradoxical element embedded in the
structure of this version of male aggression: the reversibility of the
positions of predator and prey. The vulnerability of the male predator
is ascribed not only to Acrasian figurations of Venus but also to her
more benign manifestations in mothers and chaste lovers, and not only
to the multivalent fluidity of Venus but also to the fixed ambivalence of
Diana. Montrose traces this sexual problematic back to the Proem of
Book II, noting that when "Spenser conjoins 'the Amazons huge river'
and 'fruitfullest Virginia' . . . he is invoking not only two regions of the
New World but two archetypes of Elizabethan culture: the engulfing
Amazon and the nurturing Virgin." When these are later "conjoined
again in Belphoebe" it is in the shade of "an ominous epic simile
comparing her both with the goddess Diana and with Penthesilea, 'that
famous Queene / Of *Amazons*, whome *Pyrrhus* did destroy,'" and of
this Montrose remarks that even as "it personifies and celebrates
female power, the simile works to incorporate a reaffirmation of the
male capacity to master that very power: the poet destroys the subject
of his celebration in a parenthetical phrase."[38] But if this move enacts
such a compensatory reaffirmation, it does so in response to an archetype the male poet and his culture have empowered; its aggression is in
that respect self-directed against a fantasy expressing man's fear of
having the tables turned, the fear that woman might "usurp" man's
"rightful" place and power.

37. Montrose, "The Elizabethan Subject," pp. 330, 317.
38. Louis Montrose, "*A Midsummer Night's Dream* and the Shaping Fantasies of
Elizabethan Culture: Gender, Power, Form," in *Rewriting the Renaissance*, p. 79;
"Elizabethan Subject," p. 329.

The destruction of the alien as Amazon is relatively easy; it can be achieved "in a parenthetical phrase." It takes a little longer to destroy another version of the alien, Acrasia and the Bower of Bliss. Guyon's "self-defining violence," writes Montrose, is enacted against a "female other" who "is represented as threatening the male subject with more than sexual enthrallment: the climactic image of the bare-bosomed witch cradling the slumbering youth in her lap makes it evident that she is also threatening him with maternal engulfment" ("Elizabethan Subject," p. 329). As "self-defining violence" suggests, Acrasia is also a male fantasy of weakness refashioned as feminine witchcraft, displaced, visualized, and condensed for easy disposal in a fictional episode. Guyon's victory dispels her spell but only occludes or represses its source. The fear of being undone by predatory desire, and by one's own objectifications of desire, breaks out in more subtle and varied displacement in the metapsychological plot of Book III. There, the male imagination transforms the fear of vulnerability into images of the other that are virtuous in every sense of the term, images essential to the continuation of institutionalized male authority, and images the male clings to in order to defend against his susceptibility to the more salacious projections whose Acrasian glitter directly assaults that authority.

After the bachelor hero of Book II has been unhorsed, the chivalric love quest is restored in a complex new form that makes Virgin power, and especially the power of the loving virgin, even more central than in Book I, and more dangerous to men—not only to those who are overthrown by chastity's spear or beauty's chase but also to those who suffer the ignominy of having to be saved or replaced by powerful virgins.[39] With its shift of focus to the virgin-hero and the beginning of her love quest under patriarchal auspices (Merlin and Britomart's father temporarily control the specular power of Venus), generational and sexual politics come to the fore. And with its varied repetitions of the pietà, its new emphasis on the dangers of engulfment by overpowering maternal eroticism or erotic maternalism, Book III winds its readers through episodes whose turnings again and again expose the

---

39. At vii.52 Spenser briefly mentions "a faire virgin, that in martiall law, / And deedes of armes aboue all Dames is deemed." Her name is Palladine, which may be translated into Pallas-power, or Virgin-power.

Archimago

precariousness of masculine identity, generating an ingenious diversity
of threats to male power which motivate the *busy reign* of terror. The
dangers that confront loving virgins are functions not of their weakness
but of their power, a power bequeathed by the dominant male fantasies
inscribed in traditional discourses of gender.

As I suggested earlier, I think the arch-poet of those discourses can
be associated with Archimago, the *Old Man*, or *vetus homo*, whose
metamorphic magic and image making in Book I are ascribed in anti-
papist terms to the religious idolatry and self-damning despair of the
unregenerate nature. His name authorizes a cultural imagination cor-
rupted by its own impossible aspiration toward "wholeness"/"holiness," toward heroic autonomy and tyrannical power, and
thus torn by deprivation, anger, and the perpetual fear of impotence.
Archimago hates Una "as the hissing snake," and he is mentioned in
Book III just at the point at which Britomart gives way to Florimell,
who is replaying Una's flight through the woods. His links to Merlin,
Proteus, and Busirane are established by several allusive echoes of
Book I, so that in Book III the power and impotence of the Old Man
are more specifically androcentric and gerontocentric.[40]

Spenser represents his versions of Ovidian, courtly, and Petrarchan
discourses as the work of an Archimagian fantasy that splits its feminine construct into mirroring contraries—Una and Duessa, Diana and
Venus, true and false Florimell, militant and fugitive virgins. The series
reveals the self-divided structure of what is essentially a dream of male
parthenogenesis. The two sides of this structure are coupled in the
responses of the old fisherman and Proteus to Florimell and of
Scudamour and Busirane to Amoret; in the sequence that leads from
Malbecco's torments to Busirane's aggression; and, most interestingly,

40. Compare I.i.34–37, III.iii.7 and 14, and III.xii.31–36, also I.ii.9–10 with
III.viii.41. The analogies between Una and Florimell have been traced by Nohrnberg,
who also discusses the more explicit linkage of Archimago to Proteus and suggests a
connection between Archimago and Merlin (pp. 114, 570, 444). The analogy between
Merlin and Busirane, both of whom—like Archimago—use or consult magical writing,
has been noted by Gross (pp. 152–53). These analogies make the single reference to
Archimago at III.iv.45 seem less anomalous. The momentary blurring together of Britomart, Una, and Florimell at that juncture, the earlier appearance of Redcross at Malecasta's house in an episode that bears some resemblance to his bad night at Archimago's (I.i), and the mention of "Duessaes traines" in the Argument prefacing III.i,
compose into a strong allusion to the problems and dangers of Book I.

in the strange contradictions that crisscross Spenser's portrayal of Merlin, hatching his prophetic power within the shadows of his sinister birth, his magical fiend binding, and his enthrallment to the Lady of the Lake. That his prophecy inscribes Britomart's love in a political myth illustrates the power and value of the virgin's chastity: whether erotic or antierotic, it is a virtue prized by, necessary to, male control of the institutional cornerstone, marriage, on which the preservation and continuity of patriarchal order is founded. Merlin's own fate reinforces the lesson that since men are weak they need to inseminate strong women with the fidelity and capacity for chaste love required to guarantee what has been called "transmission of the phallus." His exhortation to Britomart to "submit thy wayes vnto his [Artegal's] will" (iii.24) assumes ironic force against the background of his own susceptibility to the Duessan wiles—"that false Ladies traine" (iii.11)—that proves his undoing.

Such, then, are the consequences of Spenser's new conception of chastity. It is new in that it is represented as an ambivalent rather than a single-valued structure, one that derives its meaning within the project of desire rather than in opposition to it, and one that presides over the struggle of "true love" to emerge from the reactionary framework of discourses that threaten to block or divert it. The legend of chastity is thus about beginnings in two senses. First, it is about the onset of desire, the formation of gendered identity, and the early stages of a quest destined to end in the marriage of true lovers who will found a national dynasty. Second, it is about the emergence of this new idea of chastity from a discursive field whose language-games are alien to it. Spenser's primary focus is on the metapsychology of those language-games rather than on the individual characters or psyches they traverse. He shows how they endanger the new idea by locking up traditional forms of desire in a chase that imprints gender relations with the languages of warfare and conquest, gaming and hunting, idolatry and iconoclasm, voyeuristic dismemberment and sadomasochistic fantasy. These are the tropologies of traditional discourses that are at once literary and cultural practices, at once conventions of poetry and attitudes toward—or strategies of—sexual politics. Since they not only *represent* but also *organize* relations between genders and between generations as struggles for power, it may be more accurate to follow Foucault's example and call them *discursive regimes*. They dominate the literary culture Spenser aspires to rewrite and the literate rhetorical culture of the elite readers (aristocratic, courtly, mercantile) he writes for, and to, and about, and against. Book III enacts its own submission to those discursive regimes, shows itself not only wary of but also diverted by their literary blandishments, dramatizes their resistance *and* its own to the project of expropriating their language in the service of a "purer" discourse of love.

For such a complex and ambivalent enactment to succeed, the poem must in some manner persuade readers both to embrace the "kidnapped" discourses and to reestablish the critical distance that acknowledges—and questions—their appeal "to a middlebrow appetite for stories about fearless knights and beauteous maidens," not to mention stories about Ovidian hunts, gynarchic pastoral, and Petrarchan sadomasochism. One device Spenser uses to encourage this divided response is the occasional comment on the story that promotes the narrator from the role of teller to that of reader and interpreter of the tale he tells. I subscribe to a currently prevailing opinion that the narrator's expressive or interpretive interventions are not authoritative guides to reader response, and to this opinion I add my own, which is that the reason they aren't authoritative is that Spenser uses the commentator as the voice of the discourses, the voice of the kidnapped genres parodied in *The Faerie Queene*.[41] To support this opinion I shall devote my concluding discussion to the narrator's treatment of and response to Belphoebe in Canto v.

41. Even a partial listing of studies devoted to this topic will reveal the diversity of opinions about Spenser's deployment of the narrator function: my book *The Allegorical Temper* (New Haven: Yale University Press, 1957), pp. 161–66 and passim, which I now think is badly flawed; Paul Alpers, "Narrative and Rhetoric in *The Faerie Queene*," *SEL*, 2 (1962), 27–46; Robert Durling, *The Figure of the Poet in Renaissance Epic* (Cambridge, Mass.: Harvard University Press, 1965); Alpers, *Poetry*, esp. chaps. 1–4 and 9, passim; Kathleen Williams, "Vision and Rhetoric: The Poet's Voice in *The Faerie Queene*," *ELH*, 36 (1969), 131–44; Jerome S. Dees, "The Narrator of *The Faerie Queene*: Patterns of Response," *TSLL*, 12 (1971), 537–68; Thomas H. Cain, "Spenser and the Renaissance Orpheus," *UTQ*, 41 (1971), 24–47; Hinton, "The Poet and His Narrator"; Judith H. Anderson, *The Growth of a Personal Voice: "Piers Plowman" and "The Faerie Queene"* (New Haven: Yale University Press, 1976); A. Leigh DeNeef, *Spenser and the Motives of Metaphor* (Durham: Duke University Press, 1982), pp. 91–141. I have found the caveats and problems raised by Alpers, Dees, Hinton, and DeNeef most helpful, though—with the exception of DeNeef—their agendas differ markedly from mine.

In the opening stanzas of Cantos iii and v the narrator gives voice to the conventional pieties of romance reinforced by Neoplatonizing sentiments. Here, as in Cantos ii and iv, he plays the advocate of chivalry and courtesy who joins with his protagonists in the effort to redress the wrongs done to women. As a courtier he stresses the long view leading to Artegal, Gloriana, and Elizabeth but conspicuously evades what the text just as conspicuously reveals in its metapsychological analysis of the discourses being staged in Faeryland. The incompatibility between what the narrator says and what the text of his narrative shows is most striking in his praise of Belphoebe. To appreciate the force of his chivalric allegiance we must first glance at the passage in Arthur's lament which prefigures Belphoebe's appearance:

> For day discouers all dishonest wayes,
>   And sheweth each thing, as it is indeed:
> The prayses of high God he faire displayes,
>   And his large bountie rightly doth areed.
> Dayes dearest children be the blessed seed,
>   Which darknesse shall subdew, and heauen win:
> Truth is his daughter; he her first did breed,
>   Most sacred virgin, without spot of sin.
> Our life is day, but death with darknesse doth begin. (iv.59)

The pressure of the speaker's desire for relief qualifies these commonplace hyperboles in a significant way: turning from the evil matriarchy of Night to the good patriarchy of Day, Arthur speaks less of a virginlike truth than of a truthlike virgin. When this truth image ultimately emerges as the sun's daughter, Belphoebe (Arthur's terms are echoed and amplified at vi.1–2), the ambivalence that produced it will be mirrored in the product, with its values reversed: they will be one-sidedly feminine, and Belphoebe will admit the male into her charmed circle only as her victim, patient, or servant. The feminine ideal of spotless purity will receive a more complex genealogy in Canto vi, but here it originates in male fantasy as an ideal that will help protect the heroic quester from his own susceptibility to the "darknesse" of "sensuall desire," the blame for which he displaces to the Mother.

As Timias and the reader draw closer to Arthur's remote, pallid, and half-abstract "sacred virgin," her full fleshly complexity emerges into

view,[42] never more compellingly than when the narrator registers his
own admiring response to Belphoebe's chastity and exhorts women to
follow her example:

> That dainty Rose, the daughter of her Morne,
>   More deare then life she tendered, whose flowre
>   The girlond of her honour did adorne:
>   Ne suffred she the Middayes scorching powre,
>   Ne the sharp Northerne wind thereon to showre,
>   But lapped vp her silken leaues most chaire,
>   When so the froward skye began to lowre:
>   But soone as calmed was the Christall aire,
> She did it faire dispred, and let to florish faire.
>
> Eternall God in his almighty powre,
>   To make ensample of his heauenly grace,
>   In Paradize whilome did plant this flowre;
>   Whence he it fetcht out of her natiue place,
>   And did in stocke of earthly flesh enrace,
>   That mortall men her glory should admire:
>   In gentle Ladies brest, and bounteous race
>   Of woman kind it fairest flowre doth spire,
> And beareth fruit of honour and all chast desire.
>
> Faire ympes of beautie, whose bright shining beames
>   Adorne the world with like to heauenly light,
>   And to your willes both royalties and Realmes
>   Subdew, through conquest of your wondrous might,
>   With this faire flowre your goodly girlonds dight,
>   Of chastity and vertue virginall,
>   That shall embellish more your beautie bright,
>   And crowne your heades with heauenly coronall,
> Such as the Angels weare before Gods tribunall. (v.51–53)

After noting that in the first stanza "Spenser most fully presents and
evaluates the form of chastity Belphoebe embodies," Alpers adds that
we "feel very keenly the attractiveness and naturalness of the rose as
part of a pastoral garden of love, and when the rose becomes frankly
metaphoric in the subsequent address to the ladies, it gets its strength

42. Her relation to the sun is figuratively established when she is introduced
("*Belphoebe* was her name, as faire as *Phoebus* sunne" [v.27]) and this relation becomes
more than figurative in Canto vi.

from these feelings" *(Poetry,* p. 193). But if *we* feel the attractiveness it is only because the narrator registers his own attraction to it. His response to Belphoebe resembles Arthur's to Florimell. The imagery of "a pastoral garden of love" transparently veils and so draws attention to the symbolic center of what is simultaneously sexuality and virginity—or, rather, sexuality as virginity, since the latter is only a state or subclass of the former. "That dainty Rose" echoes two demonstrative phrases in the previous stanza, "that sweet Cordiall" and "that soueraigne salue," which Belphoebe "did enuy" to Timias "and to all th'vnworthy world forlore" (v.50). By synonymy, therefore, the rose at first signifies virginal chastity less directly than the erotic "salue" or "cordiall" chastity denies. This impression is enhanced by the concrete but ambiguous adjective "dainty" (pleasant, choice, delicate, rare, precious, fastidious) and by the spelling of "chaire," which adds a French meaning to its obvious sense ("charily"), that is, "her most fleshly silken leaves." It is also enhanced by the allusion to the *Roman de la Rose,* about which Quilligan makes by far the most useful comment: "Spenser rewrites that text of deflowered virginity into a paean for Elizabeth's chastity."[43] But if there is an *effect* of rewriting, or of *writing against* the *Roman,* it is produced only by a conspicuous allusion to the prior text, an allusion that activates its subversive implications. Yet the narrator's rhetoric carefully muffles these implications. Even as he verbally caresses the rose, his nature metaphors are referentially obscure enough to diffuse the impact of the erotic image. His weather report is at once so evasive and so detailed as to be funny. "Lapped vp her silken leaues" and "did it faire dispred" clearly denote actions. But just what actions do they denote? There is something oddly voyeuristic in these displacements. They are, one might say, "chaire," as if his fleshly desire is occasioned by her fleshly beauty, her chariness by his desire, his chariness by hers—once again, the rebounding dart of desire and *daunger.*

43. Quilligan, *Milton's Spenser,* p. 189. For a different reading, see Roche, *Kindly Flame,* pp. 139–42. My view is closer to that of Alpers (pp. 390–91) and Donald Cheney in *Spenser's Image of Nature: Wild Man and Shepherd in "The Faerie Queene"* (New Haven: Yale University Press, 1966), pp. 101–104, except that their focus remains on Belphoebe's limits and complexity whereas mine is shifted to the narrator's reaction as a device that exhibits the ambivalence and evasiveness of the discursive strategies Spenser mimes.

The Actaeonic danger hinted at in all Belphoebe's appearances is here affixed to the narrator's viewpoint. As the first reader of his story, he dramatizes the temptations of Ovidian entrapment and signals the danger by following the voyeuristic innuendo of the "dainty Rose" stanza with four stanzas of fervent praise and exhortation. This pattern duplicates that of Arthur and Timias. Like them he recoils from the erotic glimpse and attraction of the virgin's sexuality into a Neo-platonizing mode that spiritualizes the flower, then goes on in Stanza 53 to make amends for his lapse by paying the Ladies a chivalrous compliment and enthusiastically recommending the advantages of the virtue Belphoebe models.[44] Yet the particular way in which he defines and endorses that virtue betrays a more complex reaction to Belphoebe's rose than is acknowledged by his impassioned sweep through the stanza. Alpers argues that if Belphoebe "is an unsatisfactory image of human erotic desire," it is because she "has no erotic desire" (*Poetry*, p. 390), but this remark misses the point that if she is unsatisfactory it must be because she arouses and then frustrates desire: she is in the poem partly, as Quilligan observes, "to define the queen's erotic power as unpossessable woman" (*Milton's Spenser*, p. 182), and, I would add, Queen Elizabeth is in the poem to focus the political aspect of that power and danger.

The subtext of the stanza is that erotic skills are political skills: "chastity and vertue virginall" is a euphemism for sexuality displayed and withheld in order to subdue men. Quilligan sees this passage as one of Spenser's many addresses in Book III to "female" or "woman" readers (pp. 188–89), but here, at least, the class of addressees is more restricted: these are "Ladies" and "Faire ympes of beautie," women who—being desirable—have something men want and who are presumed to be socially well placed and politically ambitious. Their adviser speaks as a courtly and Petrarchan insider. He knows from bitter

---

44. He resumes the advocacy undertaken in the opening stanzas of Cantos ii and iv. The defense of women's rights stridently aired in those stanzas is hardly feminist. It is simply an exaggerated display of chivalric courtesy, a gesture entirely appropriate to the romance code. Thus if, as Quilligan argues, "the male perspective" in those passages is "radically censured" (*Milton's Spenser*, p. 188), the censure is itself a reaffirmation of a traditional male perspective. I would not necessarily attribute this to Spenser *tout court*, as I have already noted. Rather the passages model the contradictions inscribed in the traditional discourse of gender and its literary reproductions. The uproarious rhetoric of outrage in iv.1–2 by its melodramatic fervor marks the parodic status of this discourse.

experience, the experience of Timias or Arthur, what it takes for a woman to become a Lady, that is, to dominate men while playing by the rules of a man's game in a man's world. The message his speech conveys under its Neoplatonizing rhetoric is that women should use their power judiciously, should learn when it is profitable to "faire dispred" the rose and when to withhold it. The message undermines the narrator's rhetorical investment in the pattern of descent and ascent (from "Eternall God" to "Gods tribunall") that characterizes Neoplatonic discourse: it converts the discourse to a smoke screen that mystifies an appeal to political interest as an appeal to ethical and religious aspiration. At the same time, the strategy of sublimation marking his retreat from his encounter with the rose reveals his own interestedness. He makes a bid to regain power over women by speaking as their disinterested servant, admirer, advocate, and counselor, one who knows and is willing to share the secret that will help them advance their careers and dominate such men as himself.

What I have been trying to suggest in these comments on the narrator is the way Spenser uses this figure to dramatize the limits, contradictions, evasions, and self-deceptions inscribed in the different literary versions of the traditional discourse of gender. The narrator speaks the familiar literary language and expresses the familiar sentiments of the more "refined" or polite traditions of love lore. His response to the story is one that minimally registers its textual complexities and uncritically endorses an ideology of gender that the text again and again places in question. His falsifying simplifications, his pious clichés appealing to the *bien pensant* among Spenser's readers, throw the critique of that ideology in high relief. I have argued elsewhere that E. K. serves a similar function in *The Shepheardes Calender*: his commentary provides a coherent epitome of the traditional attitudes toward love and poetry which the *Calender* cautiously criticizes. E. K. brings to life the divided sensibility of traditional pastoral, the sensibility of *puer senex* torn between the delights of youth—poetry and love—and the embittered age of the Stoic Censor.[45] Like E. K. in the *Calender*, the narrator is the first reader and interpreter of *The Faerie Queene*. That his interpretation is at once conspicuously inadequate and conspicuously con-

---

45. Berger, "Orpheus, Pan, and the Poetics of Misogyny: Spenser's Critique of Pastoral Love and Art," *ELH*, 50 (1983), 53–58.

ventional drives the wedge deeper between the radically revisionary discourse of Spenserian romance and the maze of interpenetrating discourses it revises. The narrator is there to state the claims of those kidnapped discourses, and the statement fails to persuade. By showing us how not to read *The Faerie Queene*, he opens up another way to read it.

11

Lady Mary Wroth: Female Authority and the Family Romance

MAUREEN QUILLIGAN

Fredric Jameson finds the origin of the ethical polarities endemic to romance in the chansons de geste, popular when central authority had collapsed and "marauding bands of robbers and brigands range[d] geographical immensities."[1] Romance, according to Jameson, can be understood as an "imaginary solution" to the "real contradiction" that arose when these bands formed into the feudal nobility, a single social class with a coherent ideology. Romance thus becomes "a symbolic answer to the perplexing question of how my enemy can be thought of as being *evil* (that is, other than myself and marked by some absolute difference), when what is responsible for his being so characterized is quite simply the *identity* of his own conduct with mine, the which— points of honor, challenges, tests of strength—he reflects as in a mirror image" (p. 118). An unidentified black knight rides into the lists, refusing to say his name, until, victorious (or vanquished), he says his name and is revealed to be—a knight: "he becomes one more among others and loses all his sinister unfamiliarity" (p. 119). That is, unless he is revealed to be a woman, that irreducibly other "other" romance favors as a representation of evil in its magically powerful and dangerously unassimilable difference. Romance had, of course, its ways to render

1. Fredric Jameson, *The Political Unconscious: Narrative as a Socially Symbolic Act* (Ithaca: Cornell University Press, 1981), p. 118.

even this female other the same, and in this particular drive it tends toward family romance. Mordred is the son of Arthur, incestuously begotten on Arthur's own sister, Morgan le Fay. In the more comic mode available to Renaissance romance, Ariosto makes his female knights Bradamante and Marphisa the sisters of known heroes, Rinaldo and Ruggiero. In its pastoral vein, unidentified foundling females are found proper, aristocratic families (Spenser's Pastorella; Shakespeare's Perdita).

Given the reliance of romance on family connections, there is a certain generic logic to the fact that, in the history of English literature, the first work of prose fiction published by a woman should be Lady Mary Wroth's romance *The Countesse of Mountgomeries Urania* (1621), for Wroth was the niece of Sir Philip Sidney. Neatly, one of the first voices of the female other to be heard in English literature is in a text that fully reveals romance to be grounded in family connections.[2] Although it is also much more, Wroth's *Urania* is, in its inception, a rewrite of Sidney's *Arcadia*; it is therefore a rewrite of a father's brother's literary romance, a text that itself deals with two cousins' protracted and comic courtships of two sisters, which was dedicated to and, indeed, published by the author's sister: *The Countess of Pembroke's Arcadia*.[3] The countess of Pembroke was Wroth's aunt, and the example of Mary Sidney's authorship may have influenced the niece's brave decision to write at all. Contemporaries (such as Jonson, Chapman, and Davies) saw Wroth's writing as part of a family practice, and while the three Sidney siblings, Philip, Mary, and Robert (Wroth's father) were all writers, it is—not surprisingly—her uncle Philip's text to which Worth appeals most directly in the opening scene of her *Urania*.[4]

2. Lady Elizabeth Carey had published her closet drama, *Mariam, Faire Queene of Jewry*, in 1613, and Aemilia Lanyer had published her long poem on Christ's passion and Eve's defense of women, *Salve Deus Rex Judaeorum*, in 1611. The inclusion of the sonnet cycle "Pamphilia to Amphilanthus" at the end of the text of the romance makes Wroth the first female author in English in that (Sidneyan) genre as well. For excerpts from Carey and Lanyer, see Betty Travitsky, ed., *Paradise of Women: Writings by Englishwomen of the Renaissance* (Westport, Conn.: Greenwood Press, 1981).

3. For a discussion of the countess of Pembroke's part in the publication of the revised *Arcadia*, see A. C. Hamilton, *Sir Philip Sidney: A Study of His Life and Works* (Cambridge: Cambridge University Press, 1977), pp. 169–72.

4. Josephine A. Roberts quotes some of the contemporary notices of Wroth's writing in *The Poems of Lady Mary Wroth* (Baton Rouge: Louisiana State University Press,

Because the niece's rewrite of the uncle's text recasts a scene he had already revised, it will be useful to begin with Philip Sidney's totally new opening to the *Arcadia*. In the opening scene of the revised *Arcadia*, Sidney presents two shepherds, Strephon and Claius, who lament the absence of Urania, a woman whose love has elevated them from their baseborn state as pastoral tradesmen to the status of true poets: how can they "leave those steps unkissed wherein Urania printed the farewell of all beauty?"[5] As one of them rhetorically asks the other: "Hath not the desire to seem worthy in her eyes made us, when others were sleeping, to sit viewing the course of the heavens; when others were running at Base [a game], to run over learned writings; when others mark their sheep, we to mark ourselves? Hath not she thrown reason upon our desires and, as it were, given eyes to Cupid? Hath in any but in her, love-fellowship maintained friendship between rivals, and beauty taught the beholders chastity?" (pp. 63–64). Urania's lack of presentness in this text, like Laura's, like Stella's, underwrites male writing. Her absence here also marks a new authority for Sidney's revision.[6] Love of her has so ennobled Strephon and Claius that Musidorus, even in the midst of his frenzy that Pyrocles has been lost in a shipwreck, notices their distinct and unshepherdlike nobility. They have shifted class, raised into nobleness by their love of her. As a new muse of revision and in her very absence—by her recall and remembering—Urania, muse of the stars, may therefore name the heroizing leap in class Sidney's *Arcadia* makes from (unpublished) family comedy to fully public, heroically ambitious narrative.[7] The new opening scene substitutes for the straight narrative description of Basilius's protocomic withdrawal from political activity in the *Old Arcadia*, a withdrawal Urania's mimics, but here without the problematic emphasis on a *senex* who is illegitimately withholding his daughters from a

---

1983), pp. 7–26. Robert Sidney's verse was never published until 1984, in an edition by P. J. Croft, *The Poems of Robert Sidney* (Oxford: Clarendon Press); Croft lists Wroth's verbal echoes of her father's poems in Appendix C.

5. Sir Philip Sidney, *The Countess of Pembroke's Arcadia*, ed. Maurice Evans (Harmondsworth, Eng.: Penguin, 1977), pp. 62–63.

6. For a discussion of Sidney's rewrite of the opening of Jorge de Montemayor's *Diana* in the scene with Strephon and Claius, see Hamilton, pp. 126–29.

7. Sidney left the unfinished "new" *Arcadia* with Fulke Greville, who elected to print this version as being more worthy of publication than the "old," unrevised *Arcadia*. See Hamilton, pp. 169–70.

proper traffic in women—a *senex* therefore vulnerable to any machinations the comic heroes might think up to circumvent his folly (cross-dressing, lower-class disguise). In the revision, Virgil's Fourth Eclogue leaps to mind rather than Plautus: Urania's absence, unlike Basilius's, indicates politically serious prophecy rather than private pastoral shenanigans.

In the opening scene of *The Countesse of Mountgomeries Urania*—which runs to 558 pages in its printed section and is continued in another unpublished part (now in the Newberry Library) about two-thirds as long—Wroth recasts her uncle's opening yet again. This time Urania is not absent but present; it is the shepherdess herself who appears, alone in the pastoral landscape. In a soliloquy marked by unstable pronouns, she laments the lack of a self: "Alas Urania said she . . . of any misfortune that can befall woman, is not this the most and greatest which thou art falne into? Can there be any neare the unhappinesse of being ignorant, and that in the highest kind, not being certaine of mine own estate or birth?"[8]

Where Strephon and Claius celebrate their high-aspiring knowledge while lamenting their Urania's absence, Wroth's Urania loses the base of her identity by learning that she is highborn: "Why was I not stil continued in the beleefe I was, as I appeare, a Shepherdes, and Daughter to a Shepherd? My ambition then went no higher then this estate, now flies it to a knowledge; then was I contented, now perplexed. O ignorance, can thy dulness yet procure so sharpe a pain? and that such a thought as makes me now aspire unto knowledge? How did I ioy in this poore life being quiet? blest in the love of those I took for parents, but now by them I know the contrary, and by that knowledge, not to know my selfe" (p. 1). Where Sidney's shepherds gain from an absent Urania a self-awareness that is the truest sign of humanist discourse—because it carries a sense of self-worth beyond class—Wroth's shepherdess Urania discovers a knowledge that knows it does not know itself. Wroth places the female character center stage but has her speak a complete lack of self-presence. She does not know her family: and if she does not know her family, she does not know herself.

The details of the two scenes are so coherent in their pointed rever-

8. Lady Mary Wroth, *The Countesse of Mountgomeries Urania* (London: John Marriott and John Grismand, 1621), p. 1.

sals that one is tempted to assume that Wroth was fully conscious of the specificity of her insertion of gender difference into the text. Urania specifically asks if hers is not the worst "Of any misfortune that can befall *woman*." What can we expect from this Perdita-like beginning? That Urania will rush off into her narrative, armed like a pastoral Britomart with a desire to find not a male lover but her female identity, possibly cross-dressed or protected by her lower-class disguise? The first thing Urania does, in fact, recalls Britomart. She immediately comes upon a knight, who is, like Scudamour, lamenting his lost beloved. She stirs him out of his sobbing passivity into heroic action. But she does not accompany him on his quest or engage in any further female questing of her own. Instead, a far more conventional narrative makes its way to the privileged pastoral spot where Wroth, like Sidney before her, has opened her text. Thirty pages into the romance we learn that there is a most royal Prince—indeed the hero of the story—who, along with all his noble confreres, seeks a lost sister. Urania, one of them guesses, cannot but be she, and indeed she is, just as Marphisa is Ruggiero's sister, and Bradamante, Rinaldo's. Shortly after this abrupt short-circuiting of what we anachronistically expect in this female-authored quest, Urania is not only found, she is lost again. Like Marphisa and Bradamante, Urania has a brother; unlike them (or Britomart) she is no female warrior cross-dressed in armor, disguised as a male. Instead, Wroth shuts her up in Venus's Tower of Love once her paramour Parselius (the confrere who found her) momentarily loses sight of her importance to him. In his spurious vision of heroic achievement and male bonding, Urania is lost to the text entirely. Imprisoned in her tower, she remains absent from the narrative for a hundred pages until her brother, the renowned Amphilanthus, and his most loyal lady, Pamphilia, arrive on the isle of Cyprus and release her from her enchantment (p. 142).

As such a plot suggests, Wroth is not only rereading her uncle's arcadian romance, but also rewriting Spenser's *Faerie Queene*.[9] Wroth specifically rewrites the Spenserian scene she echoes in her second episode, in which Urania urges a knight to revenge his beloved. At the

9. Wroth is also continuing contemporaneous Scots and Continental romance tradition, which had become something of a prose fashion at James's court. See Roberts, pp. 28–29.

climax of the printed Part I, Pamphilia, the actual heroine of the romance and author of the sonnet cycle appended to the text of *Urania*, is treated to a vision of her beloved Amphilanthus's torture, which distinctly recalls the torture of Amoret. In the culminating episode of Book III of *The Faerie Queene*, Britomart finds Amoret chained to a pillar with her heart ripped out of her chest cavity while the enchanter Busirane, a sadistic sonneteer, writes strange characters with her heart's blood. In Wroth's version the victim is male, the torturers female. Britomart is, of course, successful in her rescue; Pamphilia is not, her impotence resembling that of Scudamour, who cannot pass the flames. Wroth's rewrite of Spenser is just as specific as her rewrite of Sidney:

> Pamphilia adventured, and pulling hard at a ring of iron which appeared, opned the great stone, when a doore shewed entrance, but within she might see a place like a Hell of flames, and fire, and as if many walking and throwing pieces of men and women up and downe the flames, partly burnt, and they still stirring the fire. . . . the longer she looked, the more she discernd, yet all as in the hell of deceit, at last she saw Musalina sitting in a Chaire of Gold, a Crowne on her head, and Lucenia holding a sword, which Musalina tooke in her hand, and before them Amphilanthus was standing, with his heart ript open, and *Pamphilia* written in it, Musalina ready with the point of the sword to conclude all, by razing that name out, and so his heart as the wound to perish. (p. 494)

Wroth's rescripting of Spenser's already literalized set of conceits, making the written name "Pamphilia" visible on Amphilanthus's fleshly heart, is authorized by Spenser's own practice in the first poem of the *Amoretti*, where his beloved reader is asked to read what is written by tears in "hart's close bleeding book." We may have to struggle harder to find out where the bits and pieces of fried male and female lovers' flesh come from, but the dismembering tradition of the Petrarchan blazon may be an influence on this baroque scene of torture.[10] What is

---

10. What Wroth has done is to literalize not only the "flames" of passion which "burn" a lover's heart but also the elaborately celebrated body parts from the tradition of the blazon Spenser himself mocks, for instance, in the scene with Serena and the cannibals in Book VI of *The Faerie Queene* (VI.viii.39). For a discussion of the blazon as implicit dismemberment, see Nancy Vickers, "Diana Described: Scattered Woman and Scattered Rhyme," *Critical Inquiry*, 8 (1981), 265–79.

most striking about Wroth's revision of Spenser's scene is that the moral values are completely reversed. Pamphilia tries vainly to come to Amphilanthus's rescue but she is unable to, not because she may, like Scudamour, be implicated in some way in the torture or because she has no powers of aggression (like Britomart's magic—and some have thought phallic—lance), but because only *false* lovers are able to enter such an arena. She is *too* true and constant (read "chaste") to have an impact:

> So with as firme; and as hot flames as those she saw, and more bravely and truly burning, she ran into the fire, but presently she was throwne out again in a swound, and the doore shut; when she came to her selfe, cursing her destinie, meaning to attempt again, shee saw the stone whole, and where the way into it was, there were these words written:
>
> > Faithfull lovers keep from hence
> > None but false ones here can enter:
> > This conclusion hath from whence
> > Falsehood flowes, and such may venter. (pp. 494–95)

The entire pressure of the narrative of the *Urania* insists upon the moral virtue of constancy (the titular virtue for the incomplete seventh book of Spenser's epic). Pamphilia is heroine because she is the truest, most constant lover, the most all-loving, that is, "Pam-philia." In Wroth's text women are, for the most part, better lovers than men. The hero is named for the principle of falsity, "Am-philanthus," "lover of two." Wroth's huge romance, then, rewrites Spenser's satirical Squire of Dames dilemma as well as the constancy test of the Argalus and Parthenia episode in the *Arcadia*—with this twist: how do the two women who love and are beloved by the same man remain true to each other?[11] Strephon and Claius can remain rivalrous poets and lovers

11. The Squire of Dames seeks chaste women with little success. The story of Argalus and Parthenia, the first new story Sidney interpolated into his revised *Arcadia*, tests male versus female constancy. The story of Parthenia's disfigurement may be a reference to Sidney's own mother's tragic facial scarring by smallpox, so severe that Lady Sidney left court. Parthenia's magical healing may represent the son's wish to erase his mother's pain—as well as, of course, providing the exemplary test case of Argalus's constancy and his refusal to accept a perfect look-alike who is not in fact Parthenia herself. For an argument assuming this familial referentiality in the Argalus episode, see Margaret P. Hannay, *Philip's Phoenix: Mary Sidney, Countess of Pembroke* (Oxford: Oxford University Press, forthcoming). The possibility that Sidney's episode is a familial roman à

because Urania is not only wonderful but also absent: she is then the typical bond "between men." Female jealousy takes on different coloring.

Before going on to examine a compelling episode of female jealousy in the *Urania*, we should recall that moment in the *Arcadia* when Pyrocles humorously mocks Musidorus for having himself fallen in love in spite of all his earlier misogynist lectures to Pyrocles about how the passion does "womanish" a man. It is a remarkable pretext for Wroth's exposition of feminine jealousy, because at this point in the *Arcadia* Pyrocles is, of course, cross-dressed as Zelmane the Amazon, so that the text refers to him with feminine pronouns:

> "Why, how now dear cousin," said she, "you that were last day so high in the pulpit against lovers, are you now become so mean an auditor? Remember that love is a passion, and that a worthy man's reason must ever have the masterhood."
> "I recant, I recant," cried Musidorous.

Zelmane at first thinks Musidorous is merely mocking her/his own passion but soon believes and soon after becomes "racked with jealousy," fearing that Musidorous has fallen in love with her/his own lady Philoclea, sister to Pamela. Thus, when Musidorous mentions the love he feels at the sight of the two sisters, Zelmane's jealousy bursts forth:

> "At which sight?" said Zelmane, not able to bear him any longer.
> "O," said Musidorous, "I know your suspicion. No, no banish all such fear; it was, it is, and must be Pamela."
> "Then all is safe," said Zelmane. "Proceed, dear Musidorous."
> (pp. 170–71)

Wroth grants us a savvy—and, as far as I know, culturally unique— female viewpoint on the stage convention of male cross-dressing. She notes in passing that a male character is so unmoved by a female character's pleas that "he was no further wrought, then if he had seen a

---

clef (a possibility that could have been assumed, if anywhere, within the Sidney family) would have provided added authority for Wroth's autobiographical account of her own experiences in the story of Lindamira in the *Urania*, especially as her story begins with an apparent description of her parents'—Robert Sidney and Barbara Gamage's—courtship. For a discussion of the parallels, see Roberts, pp. 30–31.

delicate play-boy acte a louing woman's part, and knowing him a Boy, lik'd onely his action" (p. 60). That Wroth is here commenting on a *female* character's unpersuasive pleas broaches the problematic issue of role playing open to either gender in Elizabethan and Jacobean court society and also subtly comments on the potential unreality of Sidney's basic plot device, that is, Pyrocles' cross-dressing, which fools all but the potentially evil Gynecia.

The episode of female jealousy in Wroth's *Urania* is unprotected by the theatrical distance allowed by Pyrocles' disguise; it is far less comic than the scene in the *Arcadia*. It occurs after Amphilanthus has brought a lady he has rescued, Antissia, to Pamphilia's court for safekeeping. The episode's quotation of the *Arcadia* is a complicated collapsing of the two separate conversations between the princes Pyrocles and Musidorus when at different moments each confesses that he has fallen in love. It is, I suspect, no less conscious a rewrite than the other two scenes I have described.

Having retreated to a private garden to mope, Pamphilia writes a sonnet on a tree, beginning "Beare part with me most straight and pleasant Tree / And imitate the Torments of my smart" (p. 75). This is, of course, a lament very close to Pamela's "Do not disdain, O straight upraised pine, that wounding thee my thoughts in thee I grave" (p. 650). Soon after she has written this poem, Pamphilia is startled by a noise in the bushes and perceives Antissia "close by her," just as Musidorous had eavesdropped on Pyrocles/Zelmane, who had been reciting his poem on his cross-dressed predicament: "Transform'd in show, but more transform'd in mind" (p. 131). Unlike Musidorous, Antissia already knows Pamphilia is in love. With the sensitivity wrought by fellow suffering, she recognizes all the signs in Pamphilia, who is reputed to be above such folly. What Antissia wishes to know is not whether Pamphilia loves but *whom* she loves: "My curiositie . . . was, and is, lest it should bee hee whom I affect," that is, Amphilanthus (pp. 67–78 [*sic*]). Pamphilia, the most discreet of princesses, heroic in her silent suffering, refuses to confess that she loves Amphilanthus beyond his just deserts as a most worthy prince—but even if she should, theoretically, love him, she asks,

> What then? were it any more then my extremest torment, when I should see his affections otherwise placed? the impossibility of winning him

from a worthy love, the unblessed destiny of my poore unblessed life, to
fall into such a misery; the continuall afflictions of burning love, the fier
of just rage against my owne eies, the hatred of my brest for letting in so
destroying a guest, that ruines where he comes; these were all, and these
alone touching me in all disquiets. What need should they have to molest
you, since so perfectly you are assured of his love, as you need feare no
occasion, nor any body to wrong you in that, wherein he will not wrong
his worthy choice and constancy? (p. 79)

The conversation ends when Antissia confesses, "I am contented." And
the scene ends when, "So rising, and holding each other by the arme,
with as much love, as love in them could joine, they tooke their way
backe towards the Palace."

Antissia is only momentarily satisfied by Pamphilia's evasions and
has not, in fact, been taken in by Pamphilia's act; she still suspects what
is all too true, that Pamphilia loves Amphilanthus and is beloved by
him. She witnesses a secret meeting in this same garden between Pamphilia and a man whom she takes to be Amphilanthus (that is, Urania's
brother) but who is actually one of Pamphilia's four brothers. This
brother of Pamphilia has been engaged in a Musidorus-like courtship,
dressed as a servant; he has returned in secret to his father's court,
where he wishes to remain unknown, or rather, known as the Unknown knight (he has been so commanded by his lady). Pamphilia
needs therefore to act as messenger between her disguised brother and
their father, the king of Morea, who—with a considerable difference
from noncomic literary tradition—remains remarkably mute and remote in this text. An episode demonstrating the king's lack of immediate authority over his progeny occurs when Dalinea arrives at his court
to announce her prior marriage with Parselius, his son, and the birth of
their child. The king is distressed to hear of this marriage which Parselius has not mentioned, for he has been paying bigamous court to
Urania. The king calls his son in to explain. Before Parselius can lie to
his father, Dalinea announces herself, reminding him of their marriage.
Parselius does not say anything directly to her, but asks his father to
call in Leandrus, Dalinea's brother. He then confesses all, to both his
father and Leandrus: "This Sir is true, and humbly I aske pardon for
my fault, which I had meant more priuately to have confess'd; and you
Leandrus pray now pardon me, your Sister hath lost nothing by this
match, nor shall have reason to complain of me, if true affection and a

loyall love can merit love's requitall from her breast" (p. 203). The king
for his part "forgave them, and with fatherly affection wept, and kissed
her, and the babe: then did Leandrus embrace them both, shee asking
pardon, and Parselius too he did forgive, and so all were content."
Urania for her part is "untouch'd with love or anger"; the narrator
comments with characteristic cynicism, "Mourning was cast aside and
all the joy express'd that clothes or Triumphs could produce." Pamphilia "admiringly" (that is, in some puzzled wonder) "beholds her
brother and Urania" and prays, "Protect me from such distress."

It is impossible to overstress the strange plethora of brothers and the
even more bizarre patriarchal silence of fathers in the *Urania*. In this it
differs radically from the *Arcadia*, where, if Basilius is the bad father of
daughters who withholds them from a proper traffic in women, then
Euarchus is the patriarch par excellence, exhibiting his governorship
most pertinently at the point he would sentence unto death his own son
Pyrocles to satisfy the exigencies of the law, that is, until saved by the
comic deus ex machina of Basilius's resurrection when the misad-
ministered love potion simply and finally wears off. In the *Urania*,
Parselius owes as much to Leandrus's forgiveness as he does to his own
father's: the responsibility for patriarchal order is shared between fathers and brothers, and the general pressure of the narrative grants the
brother the greater share of power to trade women.[12] The women
silently suffer not only their wayward lovers but their brothers' wayward actions.

For all their exquisite heroines and evil queen mothers, cross- or
down-dressed princes and foolish old men, Sidney's arcadian texts are
a paean to the patriarchy, revealing how in spite of all their play with
crossing gender and class, the heroes will grow up to be proper patriarchal replacements for their own fathers. As Leonard Tennenhouse
has argued, the political plot of the *Arcadia* pivots on a conflation of a
"strictly patrilineal system of inheritance where power is always embodied in the male, and a bi-lateral system where power descends
through the daughters of the first son."[13] Seen in this light, the *Arcadia*

12. I am indebted to Gwynne Kennedy for suggesting to me that the subject of the
Urania is the traffic in women.
13. Leonard Tennenhouse, *Power on Display: The Politics of Shakespeare's Genres*
(London: Methuen, 1986), p. 25.

in effect continues Sidney's consideration of the problematic Tudor traffic in women, begun so inauspiciously for his court career in "The Lady of May," and continuing in the infamous "Letter concerning Monsieur" to Queen Elizabeth. Sidney kept insisting on his male right to advise the queen on whom she might and might not marry, acting, that is, the patriarch to her female lack of freedom to dispose herself where she might wish. Lady Mary Wroth was herself the offspring of a marriage between Robert Sidney and Barbara Gamage which Queen Elizabeth had tried to stop—but her letter interdicting the match arrived a couple of hours too late.[14] The Sidneys always managed to evade her patriarchal powers.[15] If even Queen Elizabeth could not control the traffic in women in her own court, far be it from such as Mary Worth, or Urania, or Pamphilia to think of doing so. No one ends up with the "right" person in the second part of the *Urania*.

In her study of identity and difference in *The Subject of Tragedy*, Catherine Belsey has argued that women in Britain for most of the sixteenth and seventeenth centuries were not fully any of the things posited of the subject of liberal humanism—unified, autonomous, author of own choices. Able to speak, indeed to write, they were "permitted to break . . . silence [only] in order to acquiesce in the utterances of others. . . . [They] were denied any single space from which to speak for themselves."[16] The confusing contest for control over the "subject position" of women at this period and its troublesome impact on even so self-conscious an author as Mary Wroth may be signaled by the bizarre pronoun slippages marking, as we have seen, Urania's opening soliloquy. As Wroth's representative of the self-possessed "poet," however, Pamphilia writes not only more self-consciously but more coherently than does Urania. Wroth, in fact, stages an interchange between the two women characters about the issue of self-possession,

---

14. Roberts, p. 5.

15. The marriage between Sir Philip Sidney and Frances Walsingham took place without Elizabeth's sanction. When she objected, Sir Francis Walsingham excused himself by arguing that the birth of the two parties being so low, he did not think it necessary to alert the queen to the existence of the match. For a copy of his letter to Christopher Hatton defending his silence (and an example of his probable hypocrisy), see Mona Wilson, *The Life of Sir Philip Sidney* (Oxford: Oxford University Press, 1932), pp. 214–15.

16. Catherine Belsey, *The Subject of Tragedy: Identity and Difference in Renaissance Drama* (London: Methuen, 1985), p. 149.

which may have bearing on the different degree of authority each possesses both as a writer and as "author"of her own choices. We will not, though, understand the peculiar pressures on Urania's position (or what, finally, Wroth might be about in positing a contrast between the two women) unless we take into account Urania's peculiarly dramatic experience of her brother's culturally granted power to "trade" her, that is, to help her select a suitable suitor.

Urania is less upset than she might have been when Dalinea comes to claim Parselius because, prior to this revelation of his unfaithfulness to her, Urania has been cured of her love for him. The cure aptly dramatizes the power given to brothers in the romance. After rescuing his newfound sister Urania from her imprisonment on Venus's island, Amphilanthus sets about obeying an obscure prophecy. He takes Urania to the island of St. Maura, where, he has been told, he must pitch her into the sea: "Deerest Urania, I must throw thee into the Sea; pardon me, Heaven appoints it so. My deerest brother, sayd she, what need you make this scruple? You wrong me much to thinke that I fear death, being your sister, or cheerish life, if not to joy my parents; fulfill your command, and be assured it is doubly welcome, comming to free me from much sorrow, and more, since given mee by your hand. . . . he tooke her in his armes, and gently let her slide, shewing it rather to be her slipping from him, then letting her fall, and as shee fell, so fell his heart in woe, drownd in as deepe an Ocean of despaire" (p. 192). There is no need for sorrow, however, as shortly thereupon Urania is rescued by "two men in a boat," who dive in after her: one of them is Parselius, and the other Steriamus, destined to be Urania's husband. After all three are rescued from the waves, "Amphilanthus embraced them, and with teares of joy welcom'd his sister, and his friends, who now well understood the operation of that water; for Parselius knew nothing of his former love to her, only the face of Urania, and being assured of her neernesse to him in blood [they are first cousins], rejoyced with them. . . . Urania's desires were no other, then to goe into Italy to see her father" (p. 193).

Women are the bonds between men, the cultural glue, as it were, that holds society together as they are exchanged between groups of men; here Urania moves (if as yet imperceptibly) from Parselius to Steriamus (who has begun to forget that he has been in love with Pamphilia, Parselius's sister, as he moves on to Urania, Amphilanthus's sister). If fathers trade in both sons and daughters—that is, arrange matches for both—the gendered (as opposed to the generational) nature of patriarchy becomes clearest in the very different relations of power between brothers and sisters. Both fathers and brothers can trade in their female relations. Indeed, if it had been Wroth's conscious intention specifically to focus on the gendered nature of patriarchy, the way it treats females differently from males, she would have had almost programmatically to distinguish between the authority of fathers and that of brothers. Patriarchy allows fathers to traffic in upper-class youth of both genders—and William Burleigh, for one, notoriously manipulated the system of wardship in male heirs to his personal profit. But patriarchy does not merely allow one generation to traffic in another, it allows males to traffic in women. By multiplying the number of brothers and sisters in her text, Wroth points to that brother-sister relationship which most specifically marks the gendered nature of the system of transfer. If fathers trade both sons and daughters, only brothers trade sisters. Sisters do not trade brothers.[17]

The humane warmth and affection of the interchange between Amphilanthus and Urania show how deeply Wroth accepts the affective bond between brother and sister as natural. The intimacy and strength of the tie, the sense of physical connectedness between the two, demonstrate the richness of most human structures, a richness Wroth fully dramatizes. This does not mean, however, that she is incapable of catching a glimpse of the problematic position in which the brother's far greater power puts sisters such as Urania, who are happily willing to die at their brothers' hands. Wroth directly critiques the traffic not through the figure of Urania but through the (perhaps equally problematic) position of Pamphilia. In a sense the initially orphaned Urania

17. For a Marxist reading of the anthropological argument and a Lacanian analysis of the psychological effects of such transfers, see the now classic article by Gayle Rubin, "The Traffic in Women: Notes on the Political Economy of Sex," in Toward an Anthropology of Women, ed. Rayna R. Reiter (New York: Monthly Review Press, 1975, pp. 157–209). Elizabethan and Stuart England had, of course, very different kinship structures from the tribal societies usually studied by anthropology. As Jack Goody has argued in The Development of the Family and Marriage in Europe (Cambridge: Cambridge University Press, 1983), these structures had changed under centuries of pressure from the Church to open up an exploitable freedom for women to choose their own mates. Wroth seems to have understood what Goody describes when she notes in passing that "Parents hav[e] (were it not for Christianity, I should say), a cruel and tyrannical power over their children" in the choice of marriage partners (p. 35).

is the character Wroth uses to analyze the experience of the female caught in the web of family relations, while Pamphilia, in her royal isolation (she is a queen in her own right), allows Wroth a focus on the singular female "self." Before we can understand the specifics of the critique Wroth mounts in the contrast between the two women's experiences, however, we need a better sense of the specifics of Wroth's unusual family situation.

The central and overarching relationship of mutual passion in the *Urania* is between two first cousins, Pamphilia and Amphilanthus. Josephine A. Roberts, the recent editor of Wroth's poems, has persuasively argued that this pairing is a reflection of Wroth's long-term affair with her own first cousin, William Herbert, the son of the countess of Pembroke, a notoriously amorous young man to whom she bore two illegitimate children. Some have also identified Herbert as Shakespeare's Mr. W. H. the "only begetter" of the sonnets. The identification of William Herbert with Amphilanthus, however, rests on rather more solid ground than the other, not merely because of the similar family relationship but also because Wroth makes Amphilanthus the author of a poem that was identified as Herbert's in a number of contemporaneous manuscript collections, a verse beginning "Had I loved butt att that rate."[18] This poem is, however, given only in the *unpublished* manuscript second half of the romance. Thus, although he is famous for his poetry throughout the entire text, Amphilanthus never actually produces a poem in the published volume, almost as if Wroth could neither risk identifying him in public nor deny the identification by supplying him with a poem of her own. In the private segment of her work, though, Wroth does risk the familial identification.

It is difficult to assess whether or not the affair between Wroth and her cousin would have been thought to be actually incestuous; it did, however, produce the two illegitimate children, a girl and a boy. There exists a letter from Robert Sidney, Wroth's father, to Barbara Gamage, her mother, which praises Gamage for sending Wroth's boy away from Penshurst. Because illegitimacy was not necessarily a problem in itself with this class at this time—Penelope Devereux (Sir Philip Sidney's

18. Roberts prints the poem on p. 217; for the argument as to identification, see pp. 43–44.

Stella), for example, had five illegitimate children whom she raised quite openly with her lover Charles Blount—we may wonder at Robert Sidney's motives for sending little William away. Statutes passed under Henry VIII had decreed first-cousin marriage to be licit in the Church of England. But the Catholic church and, more important, continental Protestant churches still prohibited it. The Sidney family's strong Protestant convictions may have made them less than easy with the situation.

I would like to suggest that whether or not it was felt to be actually incestuous, the non-exogamous relationship between Wroth and Herbert was very discursively empowering. In loving her first cousin, Pamphilia is granted a choice of her own sexual partner that runs counter to the prevailing social norm. The movement of the traffic is thereby stalled, so to speak, at the place where the woman speaks her own active sexual desire. The very activity of that desire is, of course, the tabooed social fact: an actively desiring woman is more difficult to trade at will. The transgression of the taboo on desire is, however, marked by its focus on the possibly tabooed male family member. At the place of halt, at a boundary line of licitness, the discursive space for the female opens. That the rules for female behavior enjoined the repression of language along with sexual control we know from the triple injunction to be chaste, silent, and obedient.[19] To enforce the one is to enforce the other; to refuse the one is to refuse the other. And thus female texts are marked by sexual scandal as the fundamentally authorizing verbal move.

Urania attacks Pamphilia for loving her brother Amphilanthus not because it is an unsuitable match but because she loves too constantly. As Amphilanthus has been constantly inconstant to her, so Urania reasons, Pamphilia should be allowed a change in her affections. Urania argues against Pamphilia's willfulness: "'Tis pitie said Urania, that ever that fruitlesse thing Constancy was taught you as a vertue, since for vertues sake you will loue it, as having true possession of your soule, but understand, this vertue hath limits to hold it in, being a

---

19. For the triple command as the burden of the majority of books aimed at women during the period, see Suzanne Hull, *Chaste, Silent and Obedient: English Books for Women, 1475–1640* (San Marino, Calif.: Huntington Library, 1982).

vertue, but thus that it is a vice in them that breake it, but those with whom it is broken, are by the breach free to leave or choose againe where more staidnes may be found" (p. 400). Urania does not, of course, single out herself as a happy instance of those who find greater contentment in change, although Amphilanthus saved her sorrow by pitching her over the cliff, drowning out memories of her unsuitable love. For her part, Pamphilia insists on the willful activity of her desire, irrespective of anything Amphilanthus might do. Her position seems at first to be masochistic, but actually her intransigence demonstrates that she has a will of her own and exercises full command over it in order to institute her own unresponsive desire as her possession of herself: "To leave him for being false would shew my love was not for his sake, but mine owne, that because he loved me, I therefore loved him, but when hee leaves I can do so to. O no deere Cousen I loved him for himselfe, and would have loved him had hee not loved mee, and will love though he dispise me. . . . Pamphilia must be of a new composition before she can let such thoughts fall into her constant breast, which is a Sanctuary of zealous affection, and so well hath love instructed me, as I can never leave my master nor his precepts, but still maintaine a vertuous constancy" (p. 400). As paradoxical as it may sound, Pamphilia's point is that if she loved Amphilanthus only as a return for his loving her, her desire would have its origin in the male; then female desire would remain a mere reflective repetition of male desire. In order to locate an active desire in her female self, she needs *it*—her own will—to be autonomous. While she appears to depend on Amphilanthus, taking her identity from him, she in fact insists upon her identity as opposed to his. Her constancy is an act of willful self-definition. She "will love though he dispise me."

The willfulness of this position, though melancholy, is highly productive of discourse. Like Amphilanthus, Pamphilia is famous for her poetry within the fiction of the romance; she complains of his infidelity and insists in poem after poem on her own constancy. Pamphilia gains her authority from her refusal to respond to the fluctuating demands of the social situation. It is an active desire that looks like paralyzed stasis. She will not budge, even when—possibly because—her desire is not fulfilled. She fills the social emptiness with poems. Wroth has reformulated a potentially transgressive active female desire but dressed it up in a former female virtue, patient constancy. Out of this maneuver, she creates Pamphilia's authority, institutionalized in the poems of the sonnet cycle appended to the *Urania*.

As the first Englishwoman to publish a work of prose fiction and the only one to publish a sonnet cycle during the Renaissance, Wroth confronts herself not merely as a writing subject but as an author. In staging that authority as a regendered imitation of her uncle's various texts, she imitates in her fiction the erotic choice she made in her life: she refused to be traded out, staying, instead, within the confines of a family that somehow managed to authorize its females' desire to write.

If we look briefly at three portraits of Sidney family members from different moments in the family's historical development we may be able to make better historical sense of the difference between Sidney's and Wroth's divergent familial plotting. Because Wroth's public presentation as author proclaimed her Sidney family membership, it will be useful to see, if we can, the peculiar impact that membership had on her authority. The portraits offer us evidence that underlines the radical significance of gender in the experience of the Elizabethan family. Most specifically, we see again the quite literally central importance of the sibling male in Wroth's gendered experience of her family.

A first painting most useful for glimpsing Sidney authority is the portrait that represents Sir Philip as a soldier, dressed in partial armor, one hand on his hip and the other on his sword (Figure 1).[20] Here, he is more soldier than courtier, and, indeed, in the end he himself apparently placed more faith in soldiery than in his service to the queen. It was as a soldier, after all, that he died and as a soldier that he had become a legend by the time of his niece's adolescence. (Mary Sidney Wroth was probably born in the year of his death.) Sidney's figure looms, unlocatable in any background, untrammeled by any social context, a singular hero. What is striking from a modern perspective is that the portrait gives no sign of the poet-lover whatsoever. The portrait gives the lie to the argument of *Astrophil and Stella* and emphatically agrees with

20. The crooked-arm, hand-on-hip pose is a quotation of a distinct classical position representing triumph and is to be seen in many portraits of the period. I am indebted to Professor Paul Watson of the University of Pennsylvania Art History Department for this information.

FIGURE 1. Sir Philip Sidney. By an unknown artist. Reproduced by permission of the Viscount De L'Isle VC. KG., from his private collection.

Greville's estimation of the man as a soldier-statesman beholden to no party beyond his own individual conscience.[21]

The portrait of the family of Robert Sidney (Figure 2) offers an entirely different representation of authority. Although the father (Philip's younger brother) is absent from this picture, we see a trace of the Sidney posture in the eldest son and heir, who stands at the very center of the picture. The father's absence is notable.[22] The two sons are still dressed in infantile skirts, but their mother's hands rest on their dynastically important bodies. Most significant is the position of Mary Sidney Wroth—second from the right—holding hands with her younger sister, in a paired group that finds its echo in the other set of marginalized sisters on the left. Antissia and Pamphilia walk back to the palace holding hands just as Mary and her sister do in this family portrait, and another major coupling in the text of the *Urania* is the friendship between Urania and Pamphilia. In the portrait, the only element that connects the pair of sisters on the right to the main grouping is the elder brother's thin sword, a distinct bright red in the oil painting. The sword is visually important, its hilt ending the sweep the eye makes across the dynastically significant arc inscribed by the mother's hands and arms, down the shoulder and jauntily crooked arm of the heir. It functions as both bar and link, bar because it transgresses the integrity of the figure of Lady Mary, and link because it is the only thing that forms the group into a whole. In the context of this portrait's representation of Mary holding her sister's hand, it is interesting to realize that Susan Herbert, the countess of Montgomery, for whom Wroth wrote the *Urania*, was a sister-in-law to William Herbert.

21. Nicholas Hilliard's famous miniature *Young Man among Roses*, which Roy Strong identifies as "probably" a portrait of Robert Devereux (c. 1587), offers an alternative model of the lover. See Roy Strong, *The English Miniature* (1983; rev. ed. London: Thames and Hudson, 1984), p. 102, fig. 125. See also Strong, *The English Icon: Elizabethan and Jacobean Portraiture* (London: Routledge & Kegan Paul, 1969), pp. 34–37, for a discussion of the shift in portraiture from public to more private, affective poses. For a persuasive discussion of the political "argument" in *Astrophil and Stella*, see Arthur F. Marotti, "'Love is not Love': Elizabethan Sonnet Sequences and the Social Order," *ELH*, 49 (1982), 396–428; for the relationship of sonnets to miniature portrait painting, see Patricia Fumerton, "'Secret Arts': Elizabethan Miniatures and Sonnets," *Representations*, 15 (1986), 57–97.

22. Historically at least, the absence is easy to explain: Robert Sidney, who had inherited his elder brother's hard-won title of governor of Flushing, was often away in the Netherlands. The portrait could have been painted for him as a memento of his absent family.

FIGURE 2. Barbara Gamage, countess of Leicester, and her children. By Marcus Gheeraerts the Younger. Reproduced by permission of the Viscount De L'Isle VC. KG, from his private collection.

The family picture portrays a group that may temporarily lack a patriarch; but patriarchy is fully present in the figure of the elder brother, especially as that brother's martial accoutrements make contact with and control the spatial placement of the figure of his older sister. The narrative implied by the picture, indeed, matches the narrative of Wroth's romance. Both limn a story of the traffic in women controlled most directly by brothers. Women do not grow up to inherit their father's stations, and their mothers are only taller versions of their own status as miniature adults, just as Barbara Gamage herself is only a slightly larger version of her children, who all wear clothes of the same light cream color. The startling distortion of Barbara Gamage's body, while obviously accidental, implies a certain carelessness about the integrity of her person; her historically specific head does not fit well onto her generic mother's body: indeed, so specifically unromantic and particular was the match that Robert Sidney and Barbara Gamage may never have seen each other before the day they were quickly married. The children are also identified by their adult names, inscribed at a later date. Thus, Wroth is titled "Mary Wroth"; the portrait thereby identifies her not as she was at the time, a member of this family, but by the name she bore after she had been given to another family; that is, after she had been "trafficked in."[23] Seen in the perspective offered by this portrait, Elizabethan and Stuart patriarchy, while remarkably fatherless, is crowded with sisters and brothers.[24] In the same way, Urania has no story of her own: it is tied directly to her brother's story.

The portrait of the adult Lady Mary Wroth (Figure 3) shows a woman standing next to a gargantuan archlute, sign of her status as a poet. This picture represents aristocratic woman as Stuart artist; the lute is a sign of the poethood her solider-uncle eschewed in his portrait.[25] This portrait of the adult Lady Mary seems to claim for Wroth

23. I am indebted to Professor Susan Snyder for this point.

24. Because the actual perspective of the painting may have been the father's, so that the viewer is made to inhabit Robert Sidney's position, it thus may represent how his family would look to him. We may, however, still ask what it was like to be seen—as woman and as children—in such a contextualizing perspective: the actors presented to the patriarchal gaze (of both painter and patron) still take their positions linked by the brother's martial ornament.

25. No other painting of a woman in Strong's collection *The English Icon* represents such an object. Women are usually portrayed holding fans or gloves.

FIGURE 3. Mary Sidney, Lady Wroth. By John de Critz. Reproduced by permission of the Viscount De L'Isle VC. KG., from his private collection.

that stable, autonomous status which Belsey argues did not exist for women at this time. The text of *Urania* suggests, however, that the story this autonomous subject tells is not only the painful achievement of that status as an author, but also what it was like to experience the position revealed in the earlier family picture. The sister's story is only tellable as the brother's tale; the only social identity possible for a woman at this time is established through the link with the brother, that is, the male who specifically represents gender difference (not generational difference). If we think of Giovanni and Annabella in Ford's *'Tis Pity She's a Whore* or of Ferdinand and his nameless sister, the Duchess of Malfi, we may begin to perceive how central to the seventeenth century the brother-sister tie is for representing changes in its cultural code.[26] What Wroth appears to have represented in the character of Urania is the seventeenth-century female experience of the traffic in women. In Pamphilia she achieves the portrait of an autonomous author, one who wins a space for her writing at the cost of all social movement. If Wroth can be said to have returned to a fundamental tenet of romance, an emphasis on the brother-sister tie that had previously helped the genre to remake the other as the same, she does so with a practice that specifies how difficult and unstable the position of that other was. She reveals indeed how profoundly her romance was shaped by the authority of her family.

26. For a discussion of Ferdinand's incestuous obsession with his sister as a sign of cultural anxiety about class mobility, see Frank Whigham, "Sexual and Social Mobility in *The Duchess of Malfi*," *PMLA*, 100 (1985), 167–86.

12

Caves, Labyrinths, and
The Faerie Queene

WILLIAM BLISSETT

I

Its image of the catalyst may not work as well as it pretends, and its tone may be too judicial for our taste, but "Tradition and the Individual Talent" through most of the twentieth century has struck its readers with the force of a revelation and stayed with the durability of a dogma. "The existing monuments form an ideal order among themselves, which is modified by the introduction of the new (the really new) work of art among them. The existing order is complete before the new work arrives; for order to persist after the supervention of novelty, the *whole* existing order must be, if ever so slightly, altered; and so the relations, proportions, values of each work of art toward the whole are readjusted; and this is conformity between the old and the new." How much more adequate and elegant is T. S. Eliot's way of seeing old and new, ancients and moderns, than the simple image of a dwarf standing on a giant's shoulders, or the articles of war in the Battle of the Books, or the obsession with past and present in the nineteenth century, with its vast accumulation of historical knowledge, its triumphalism, its dismay, or the radical clearances and accelerating cultural revolutions of the twentieth. And yet is there not something unsatisfyingly static about the presence of the immobile observer, the anonymous "introduction" of the new work, the instantaneous "readjustment" of the equation? Surely the whole process must have a temporal dimension, the experience an element of suspense. Through these changing vistas, with ever nearing, ever delayed access to a point of vantage, moves the persevering reader, the questing critic—perhaps even a company of questers, a readership large enough to constitute a public. So restated, literature as it unfolds is apprehended as a continued allegory or dark conceit. Socrates said it about an inconclusive discussion of kingship but clearly meant it to apply to thought, to life, to literature, and to *The Faerie Queene*: "At last we came to the kingly art, and enquired whether that gave and caused happiness, and then we got into a labyrinth, and when we thought we were at the end, came out again at the beginning, having still to seek as much as ever."[1]

For some years—since the publication of *The Anathemata* in 1952—I have been trying to readjust relations, proportions, and values of existing works (the ones I know) to the new work of David Jones, which is itself an imaginative and discursive meditation on the order of creation and the order of history. I early realized that the cave and the labyrinth are key images for the understanding of this twentieth-century William Blake. The chief outward event of his life took place in the trench-labyrinth of the Great War, his later years being spent in a single room, a cave of making. The world of his art is of labyrinthine intricacy, often as if inscribed on the uneven frameless surface of a cave; and the world of his writings has as its dominant features the dugouts and trenches of *In Parenthesis*, the winding history-paths of *The Anathemata* and *The Sleeping Lord*, and their caves, ranging from blackest pits and funk-holes to the cushiest redoubts, from the most primitive retreats of the Great Mother to the most intricate bureaucratic complexes of empire, and from Bethlehem, the House of Bread, to the upper room, the Cave of Bread, in which the Eucharist was first celebrated.[2]

Such is the origin of my interest in the present subject. There are many other ways in, occasioned by the introduction of the new, the

1. T. S. Eliot, "Tradition and the Individual Talent," *Selected Essays* (London: Faber and Faber, 1951), p. 15; Plato, *Euthydemus* 291B, trans. Jowett.

2. David Jones, *In Parenthesis*, 1937; *The Anathemata*, 1952; *Epoch and Artist*, 1959; *The Sleeping Lord*, 1974; *The Dying Gaul*, 1978 (all published in London by Faber and Faber); *The Roman Quarry* (London: Agenda, 1981). See also my article "Himself at the Cave Mouth," *UTQ*, 36 (1967), 259–73.

really new, in twentieth-century writing. Think how caves avail in the mental landscape of Freud, labyrinths in that of Jung; recall Nietzsche's application to himself of the story of Theseus, the place of the artificer Daedalus in the labyrinthine works of James Joyce, the reverberation of the Marabar Cave in E. M. Forster's *A Passage to India*, the mazes of Franz Kafka, Jorge Luis Borges, Alain Robbe-Grillet, Umberto Eco. The secondary literature is vast and intricate. W. H. Matthews's *Mazes and Labyrinths* (1922), so clear and useful, so rich in illustration and lore, is again in print; and the enquiring reader will know Rachel Levy's *Gate of Horn* and Jackson Knight's *Cumaean Gates*. It is possible to consult, and to be enthralled by, four large, copiously illustrated books—in Italian, Portuguese, English and German—the last being Hermann Kern's magisterial *Labyrinthe*. A book in honor of Northrop Frye has recently appeared under the title *Centre and Labyrinth*, and its final essay, by the noted Spenserian and student of allegory Angus Fletcher, bears the title "The Image of Lost Direction" (Frye's descriptive phrase for the labyrinth). The twentieth-century mind and sensibility enters readily into caves and labyrinths. It is newly alert to the many labyrinthine literary constructs of the past, from *The Arabian Nights* and the *Roman de la Rose* and *Orlando furioso* to Sterne and Balzac and Proust. May not *The Faerie Queene* belong in this company? It is time to cross the threshold and find out.[3]

II

The episode by which Spenser chooses to plunge his reader into his poem must be unique in literature for its amalgamation of cave and

3. William H. Matthews, *Mazes and Labyrinths: Their History & Development* (1922; rpt. New York: Dover, 1970); G. Rachel Levy, *The Gate of Horn* (London: Faber and Faber, 1948; republished 1968 as a Harper Torchbook under the title *Religious Conceptions of the Stone Age*); W. F. Jackson Knight, *Cumaean Gates* (Oxford: Blackwell, 1936), included in *Vergil: Epic and Anthropology* (London: Allen & Unwin, 1967); Paolo Santarcangeli, *Il libro dei labirinti* (Florence: Vallecchi Editore, 1967); Lima de Freitas, *O labirinto* (Lisbon: Arcadia, 1975); Janet Bord, *Mazes and Labyrinths of the World* (New York: Dutton, 1975); D'Orsay Pearson, "Spenser's Labyrinth Again," *Studies in Iconography*, 3 (1977), 70–88; Hermann Kern, *Labyrinthe* (Munich: Prestel, 1982); Angus Fletcher, *The Prophetic Moment* (Chicago: University of Chicago Press, 1971), and "The Image of Lost Direction," in Eleanor Cook et al., eds., *Centre and Labyrinth: Essays in Honour of Northrop Frye* (Toronto: University of Toronto Press, 1983), pp. 329–46.

labyrinth and its concentration of evils therein. It is a tangle or thicket of whatever is deep, dark, dangerous, devious, hidden, complicated, malign, grotesque, unnatural, bestial—yawning, devouring, vomiting. The Redcross Knight and his companions leave the plain to shelter from a storm in a "covert grove" with many turnings:

> At last resoluing forward still to fare,
>> Till that some end they finde or in or out,
> That path they take, that beaten seemd most bare,
> And like to lead the labyrinth about;
> Which when by tract they hunted had throughout,
> At length it brought them to a hollow caue,
> Amid the thickest woods. The Champion stout
> Eftsoones dismounted from his courser braue,
> And to the Dwarfe a while his needlesse spere he gaue.

(The cave allows no vehicle or mount, no weapon but one with shortest range: all encounters there must be at close quarters.) The Lady Una cries, reinforcing the identification of labyrinth and cave, "This is the wandring wood, this *Errours den*." The monster Errour when she appears is herself an embodiment of both cave and labyrinth as well as a denizen of a cave within a labyrinth; her "huge long taile . . . in knots," its "folds," its "endlesse traine" are labyrinthine; cavelike her devouring mouth, her maw, her teeming womb with progeny that will in turn devour their dam. This quasi dragon has no adversarial dignity, being allowed no good association and performing no useful service. She is not coiled about a World Tree or Sacred Mountain, nor does she guard any secret or treasure. She is a mouth and a gut containing other mouths and guts. Appetite, destruction, nothingness as enemy of the Word, the first monster of the poem is full of libels as the last, the Blatant Beast, is to be full of slander.[4]

This strongly defined and limited effect Spenser chose for his open-

---

4. *The Faerie Queene*, I.i.11, 13, 15, 16, 18. I use the annotated text of A. C. Hamilton (London: Longman, 1980), which reprints the Oxford text of 1909. There is hardly an extended study of Spenser that does not give due attention to this passage; this is therefore the place for me to say, with regret, that I have had to keep the citation of secondary material to a minimum in order to prevent the essay from becoming an annotated bibliography. The gratitude that all Spenserians feel for one another's work will be suffused throughout the forthcoming *Spenser Encyclopedia*.

ing scene. Involved in such a choice was a vast and variegated hoard of personal and cultural experience. Consider his primary human endowment, and ours—the book of the body: this tenement of clay is the first and richest treasury of images. Mouth, rib cage, belly, womb, heart, skull are all caves, empty or full, profane or sanctified. Three of these have cave mouths: the oral, place of discourse and music or lies and noise, of dining or devouring; the vaginal, place of joy and fruitfulness or of violent intrusion or sensual domination; the anal, place of necessary ejection, normally out of sight and out of mind but asserting itself at times in the ambience of mucky pelf, stink, and the wrong-way intestinal spiral, *à rebours*. Likewise, though less obviously, the body may present labyrinthine aspects: the curls or tangles of hair, the outer and the inner ear (appropriate receptor of the amazing intricacies of music), the coils of the bowels, the convolutions of the brain. The human being as microcosm is thus equipped to encounter the caves and labyrinths of the world outside.[5]

A cave combines the elements of earth and air. It is a breathing space largely enclosed by earth or rock. The presence of water or fire is incidental: dragons are optional. As a defined position fortified by nature, usually covert or secret, it serves as a base for retreat or sortie. By extension, under *cave* may be included any hollow structure from the simplest den or delve or bower or arbor to palaces and fortresses and underground kingdoms, provided only that the verbal context demands or allows some relevant association with the elemental notion. Its range of association within those limits is immense: it can be a place of emptiness or bareness, of fullness or repletion; the locus of wealth and growth or of hoarding and usury; the place of psychological consolidation or regression, of wisdom or illusion; equally a seed place and a place of bones and ashes, the place of honorable or dishonorable love. The cave will take what meaning the context gives it.[6]

5. See Richard B. Onians, *The Origins of European Thought about the Body, the Mind, the Soul*, . . . (Cambridge: Cambridge University Press, 1952); Leonard Barkan, *Nature's Work of Art: The Human Body as Image of the World* (New Haven: Yale University Press, 1975).

6. The idea of the world as cave is at least as old as Empedocles: "We have come into this roofed cavern" (frag. 120); we recall Plato's allegory of the cave and Porphyry's on the cave of the nymphs in the *Odyssey*. Modern studies of prehistoric thought and art have greatly reinforced the association. See Levy, passim, and Siegfried Giedion, *The Eternal Present* (New York: Pantheon, 1962).

While the cave is primarily a natural formation, it is quite exceptional for the labyrinth or maze to be so. Some cave systems with winding
connecting passages do exist, and some rivers do meander above or
below ground, but the labyrinth or maze is typically artificial, planned,
a work of human skill, displaying (or betraying) some evidence of
deliberate care (or deliberate malice): it is plotted. "Labyrinth or
maze," I write, as if the terms were synonymous. They have both,
indeed, been in the language for many centuries, and no distinction of
meaning has ever been made to stick in common usage. For purposes of
this discussion I shall adopt a threefold distinction, but naturally I can
impose it only on myself, not on quoted material. There are three kinds
of structures, occasioning three types of experience in the person moving through them: the *transit maze, center-seeking labyrinth*, and the
there-and-back labyrinth.[7]

The transit maze seeks an exit. This exit is usually across on the far
side, but it may be quite randomly located, even next door to the
entrance. Such a maze is always *multicursal*: choices of direction must
continually be made. Anyone keeping consistently to the right wall (or
the left) is guaranteed of a passing mark; the only way to do better than
that, to hasten the course, would be to follow correct instructions or to
intuit the plan after trial and error. The duration of the transit may be
felt simply as more of the same or as an interesting variety of episodes,
but what matters is the leaving, late or soon, whereby one moves out of
an unintelligible world to a further shore or a new life or, at the very
least, something that is not a maze, or not this maze. Most maze
puzzles are of this type, as are the mazes derived by psychologists for
rats.[8]

---

7. The earliest English witness to the word *labyrinth* (Trevisa, 1385, "laborintus,
Dedalus house") refers particularly to the Cretan structure and only gradually takes on
extended meanings: "dangerous labirinthes and snares" (1548), "laws . . . la-
birunthyall" (1550), the sense of a garden maze (Coryat, 1611), "a mazey laberynth of
small veines and arteries" (Crooke, *Body of Man*, 1615). The OED gives "the Maze" in
the (obsolete) sense of delirium, delusion, disappointment, as the earliest (1297) appearance of the word *maze*, with the transitive verb (to stupefy, daze, craze) virtually
contemporaneous. Both noun and verb soon entered the limits of the labyrinth, and
have never been evicted. In *The House of Fame* (ll. 1920–21) Chaucer refers to "that
domus Dedali, / That *Laborintus* cleped is," but in *The Legend of Good Women* (ll.
2012–14) he writes: "the hous is crinkled to and fro, / And hath so queinte weyes for to
go— / For hit is shapen as the mase is wrought."

8. The distinction between unicursal and multicursal, and many other basic observations, derive from Matthews. See especially chap. 21.

The center-seeking labyrinth is *unicursal*: there is no choice but to go on, and if, as is sometimes the case, doors close or rocks fall to block return, it presents a formidable image of the irreversibility of time. Lack of choice permits the maximal use of space, and so such labyrinths are symmetrical, architectural, fourfold, cruciform, when their pattern is laid out. The corridors, or stages, will be felt as of comparable length and the turnings expected. Such labyrinths often have a three-dimensional, hence spiral, character—an infernal descent or a purgatorial climb, usually with a strong ethical cast. At the end is a sense of an ending, not simply an exit or release: one penetrates a mystery, moves to an encounter, arrives at a great good (or bad) place, the heart of the matter.[9]

The labyrinth involving a journey there and back, of which the original story of Theseus and the Cretan labyrinth is the archetype, shows the curious anomaly of being experienced as unicursal on the way in and multicursal on the way out. The descent into the testing place at the center seems to require only courage and perseverance: from antiquity all representations of the work of Daedalus show a neat, orderly, symmetrical, fourfold structure, strictly unicursal. Once, however, the Minotaur—Theseus's other self, the half brother of Ariadne—has been overcome, a guiding thread is needed for the return (a different person) to the original starting place.[10]

The cave is spatial, a position; both maze and labyrinth are temporal, a process; at least the eye, if not the feet, must go their course. Borges, writing on one of his favorite themes, says this: "The steps a man takes from the day of his birth until that of his death trace in time an inconceivable figure. The Divine Mind intuitively grasps that form immediately, as men do a triangle." So he underlines the fact that we can never instantaneously apprehend the labyrinth even at its most pictorial: rather, it challenges and frustrates every impulse to make of its intricacies a *Gestalt*. It is this quality of delay, together with the

---

9. The fourfoldness of the typical labyrinth (cf. maze) is strongly impressed on anyone who ponders the pictures in Matthews, Kern, and the other illustrated books.

10. See John Ruskin, *Fors Clavigera*, XXIII; J. Hillis Miller, "Ariadne's Thread: Repetition and the Narrative Line," in Mario J. Valdés, ed., *Interpretation of Narrative* (Toronto: University of Toronto Press, 1978) pp. 148–66; Angus Fletcher, "The Image of Lost Direction," pp. 329–46; and Philippe Borgeaud, "The Open Entrance to the Closed Palace of the King: The Cretan Labyrinth in Context," *History of Religions*, 14 (1974), 1–27.

rapid loss of a sense of direction, that has permitted the application over the centuries of the same pair of words, without hopeless confusion, to unicursal and multicursal mazes and to labyrinths seeking a center and labyrinths seeking a return. Necessity or choice, even destination, however important in the individual instance, are never crucial to the whole concept: the essential idea is loss of bearings, followed by advance or delay, whether one moves from outside to center or from one point to another. One must make the journey, with eyes or feet: *hoc opus, hic labor est.* Thus, the labyrinth always combines confusion and order, hope and wanhope, the pleasure and the anxiety of the riddle. It is suspense, solidified. Be it never so devious and subtle, it remains a synecdoche, a simplification, the amazing part for the whole temporal world. It is the opposite of "the intense moment isolated, with no before and after."[11]

A Londoner by birth and upbringing, Edmund Spenser may never have entered any notable cave, though it is highly likely that he knew of at least two, since they were among the sights of England, visited by travelers from abroad and described in topographical accounts. Michael Drayton in his *Poly-Olbion* and John Selden in his learned notes to that immense "chorographical" poem only half a generation later than *The Faerie Queene* make much of Wookey Hole in Somerset, for its grandeur of scale and natural architectural features, and, for a grotesquerie to match its name, the Devil's Arse in Derbyshire—to be given a full Rabelaisian celebration by Ben Jonson in *The Gypsies Metamorphosed*. However, Spenser was undoubtedly alert, as we shall see, to literary caves and imaginative extensions of the cave idea.[12]

Closer to his own experience than the natural cave would very probably have been the artificial labyrinth in some of its forms. Simple turf mazes in gardens and churchyards were common in his day, some of

11. Quoted in Ana Maria Barrenechea, *Borges the Labyrinth Maker*, trans. Robert Lima (New York: New York University Press, 1965), p. 63; *hoc opus, Aeneid* VI.129; T. S. Eliot, "East Coker" pt. V.

12. William Worcestre, *Itineraries* (c. 1478, not published until 1778), ed. John H. Harvey (Oxford: Clarendon Press, 1969), pp. 69 (Devil's Arse), 291 (Wookey Hole); Michael Drayton, *Works, IV: Poly-Oblion,* ed. J. W. Hebel et al. (Oxford: Shakespeare Head Press, 1933, 1961), pp. 55, 65 (Wookey Hole, poem and Selden's note), 531–32 (Devil's Arse). Ben Jonson's imaginative use of caves and labyrinths in his masques invites comparison with Spenser: see *Pleasure Reconciled to Virtue,* 1618, and *A Masque of the Metamorphosed Gypsies,* 1621.

them perhaps dating from Roman times. The great churches of England did not follow continental practice in having very elaborate pavement labyrinths the tracing of which in devout prayer would symbolize an undoing of the bondage of sin and serve as a surrogate for a pilgrimage to Jerusalem, but there were some smaller versions in English churches. More specifically, as a London child of seven, Spenser may well have seen Queen Elizabeth's coronation procession winding its way through the narrow streets of the capital—an allegory in motion. One famous station at the Little Conduit in Cheapside presented Truth the daughter of Time, emerging from a cave of incarceration or safe concealment. "And Time hath brought me hither," commented the young queen. He would certainly have had ample opportunity thereafter to see many elaborate civic and royal processions and the movements of great personages and their train. (*Train*, a favorite word with Spenser, has the sense both of enticement or allurement and of what follows behind, a procession.)[13]

Quite as important as any actual experience of cave or labyrinth must have been Spenser's entrance at an early age into the realm of literary imagination in which he was to spend his life as a poet. No exhaustive account can be attempted here: enough if we look briefly at Virgil, Ovid, and the Bible, with a preliminary mention of Homer and a promise to touch on Ariosto and Tasso later. How convenient it would be if we could be sure that Spenser knew any Homer at first hand. Of course, he knew the outline of the epics, the reputation of the poet, the echoes in Virgil. Just conceivably he might have seen Chapman's translation of Achilles Shield (*Iliad* XVIII) before it was published in 1598. If so, he would have found in the dedication a question congenial to his allegorical purposes—"for what is here prefigurde by our miraculous Artist but the universall world"—and in the text itself Vulcan, described as a "huge monster," recalls his nine years in an undersea cave before going on to forge the great shield, the details of which, as a vision of human society in war and peace, are lovingly described, culminating (after a description of a pastoral scene) thus:

13. Kern, chaps. 8 and 9; Fritz Saxl, "*Veritas Filia Temporis*," in Raymond Klibansky and H. J. Paton, ed., *Philosophy and History: Essays Presented to Ernst Cassirer* (Oxford: Clarendon Press, 1936), pp. 197–222; Daniel M. Bergeron, *English Civic Pageantry, 1558–1642* (Columbia: University of South Carolina Press, 1971), esp. pp. 19–21.

> In this rare Shield the famous Vulcan cast
> A dauncing maze, like that in ages past
> Which in brode Cnossus Daedalus did dresse
> For Ariadne with the golden tresse.

The dance of the youths and maidens concludes the account of the shield. If Spenser was unaware of this passage when he wrote, at the end of his pastoral episode, of the dance on Mount Acidale, the coincidence of sensibility is the more impressive. Likewise, any acquaintance with the *Odyssey* will introduce the spellbound reader to the "arching caverns" of Calypso and her sweet insistency, to the horrifying cave of Polyphemus, to the paired dangers Scylla and Charybdis, a cave-riddled rock and a whirlpool labyrinth, and to the mysterious cave where the Nymphs weave dances. And as the young imagination stretches to encompass the marvelous story, how can it not explore further reaches of meaning as Odysseus wanders in the trackless maze of the sea or discern the shadow of a labyrinth in Penelope's long delay of weaving and unweaving her web?[14]

With Virgil we come to a poet that Spenser possessed as he cannot be said to possess Homer. Virgil and Spenser are perhaps the two poets—the first directly influencing and subtly pervading the second—in whom caves and labyrinths are most in evidence. Some Homeric episodes directly reappear in Virgil—Scylla and Charybdis, the Cyclops, Circe weaving in her secret grove, the hero's pathless journey, the forging of arms in the cavern-smithy of Vulcan; but the brief passage about the labyrinthine dance on the shield of Achilles has been greatly amplified by Virgil in two extended passages—in the description of the Troy-game led by Ascanius in Book V and in the *catabasis*, or descent into the lower world (prepared for by carefully placed reference to the Cretan labyrinth), that occupies most of Book VI. These have always been recognized as major episodes, but some smaller details are no less germane to our enquiry. The Cave of Aeolus near the opening of the poem stands at the head of the development of physical or "meteorological" allegory: the image there of tempest and earthquake, first

---

14. *Chapman's Homer*, I: *The Iliad*, ed. Allardyce Nicoll (New York: Pantheon, 1956), pp. 543 (Dedication), 557 (ll. 291–94 of "Achilles Shield," 1598). See also George de F. Lord, *Homeric Renaissance: The Odyssey of George Chapman* (London: Chatto & Windus, 1956).

contained and then breaking forth destructively, carries over to the hollow fatal Trojan horse and also to the tempest of weather and passion that drives Dido and Aeneas together in a cave and differentiates their uneasy love from the easy union of Odysseus with Circe and Calypso. Both cave and labyrinth are explored in their most sinister aspects by Virgil, to the benefit of Spenser: Allecto's cavern of spite and malice and the cave of the giant Cacus, enemy of Hercules and of civilization, are well on the way to being allegorical *topoi*; and at the end of the poem Juturna leads the doomed antagonist Turnus through a maze as debilitating as Aeneas's *catabasis* had been edifying.[15]

Ovid was a poet every schoolboy did study and might enjoy; he was

15. The passages in the *Aeneid* germane to my discussion can be briefly listed: I.52–63 (the cave of Aeolus), 166–68 (the fresh-water cave of the nymphs in Libya), II.13–20, 50–53 (the hollow, cavernous Trojan horse), III.381–83 (the "trackless track" or pathless journey to Italy), 420–32 (the abyss of Charybdis, the cavern of Scylla, with the warning that it is best to go the long way round), 443–44 (the Sibyl to be sought deep in a rocky cave), 558 (avoiding Charybdis), 617 (Cyclops cave), IV.165 (the cave marriage, planned by Juno, 124), V.575–604 (the Troy-game, explicitly related to the Cretan labyrinth, 588–91), VI.10, 42–43, 77–78,98–99 (the cave of the Sibyl), 27–34 (the representation of the Cretan labyrinth on the temple doors), 126–29 (easy descent, difficult return), 200, 237, 575–79 (cavern-jaws of Avernus, Hydra, Tartarus), 268–72 (the dark descent of Aeneas and the Sibyl), 519 (the Trojan horse pregnant with soldiery), VII.10 (Circe weaving in her secret grove), 568–71 (the fury Allecto disappears into the jaws of a cavern), VIII.94–96 (journey up the winding river with overarching greenery), 193–280 (the evil cave of Cacus, enemy of Hercules), 416–25 (the cavern-forge of Vulcan), 630 (the mother wolf, foster mother of Romulus and Remus, outstretched in the green cave of Mars), XII.908–18 (Juturna leads Turnus through a maze). Other cave references in Virgil include Eclogue IV.50, the world's massive dome, V.5–6, 19, VI.13, 74, IX.41, Georgic IV.333–34, a bower of the nymph Cyrene beneath the river's depths, 418–22, the vast cavern of Proteus, 467, the jaws of Taenarus, the portals of Dis. See also Raymond J. Clark, *Catabasis: Vergil and the Wisdom-Tradition* (Amsterdam: B. R. Grüner, 1979), esp. pp. 204–11; Mario A. Di Cesare, *The Altar and the City: A Reading of Vergil's "Aeneid"* (New York: Columbia University Press, 1974), esp. pp. 64–65 on Aeneas's journey to discover the purpose of his journey; J. G. Fitzgerald, "Nisus and Euryalus . . . ," in John R. C. Martyn, ed., *Cicero and Virgil: Studies in Honour of Harold Hunt* (Amsterdam: Hakkert, 1972), pp. 114–37, esp. 122–23 n. 10 on emptiness, *inanis*, and 125 n. 14 on the labyrinthine woods of death; S. K. Heninger, Jr., *A Handbook of Renaissance Meteorology* (Durham: Duke University Press, 1960), esp. p. 131 on wind, cave, earthquake; Jackson Knight, *Cumaean Gates*, passim but esp. p. 143 on Aeneas "reading" the picture of the labyrinth, p. 156 on labyrinth as delaying action, p. 167 on Sibyl and Calypso, p. 272 on Aeneas and Dido in the cave; Michael C. J. Putnam, *The Poetry of the "Aeneid"* (Cambridge, Mass.: Harvard University Press, 1965), esp. pp. 6–8 on the Trojan horse, 12 on Aeolus, 59 on Nisus and Euryalus, 141 on the cave of Vulcan.

accessible to anyone literate in Latin and indeed to the English reader from the publication of Arthur Golding's translation of the *Metamorphoses* in 1567. The simple juxtaposition of a few passages in this translation should be sufficient to remind us of Ovid as a poet of cave and labyrinth. From the second book, the cave of Envy (761–66):

> She goes me straight to Envies house, a foule and irksome cave
> Replete with blacke and lothly filth and stinking like a grave.
> It standeth in a hollow dale where neyther light of Sunne,
> Nor blast of any winde or Ayre may for the deepenesse come.
> A dreyrie sad and dolefull den ay full of slouthfull colde,
> As which ay dimd with smoldring smoke doth never fire behold.

From the third, Diana's bower (155–62):

> There was a valley thicke
> With Pinaple and Cipresse trees that armed be with pricke.
> *Gargaphie* hight this shadie plot, it was a sacred place
> To chast *Diana* and the Nymphes that wayted on hir grace.
> Within the furthest end thereof there was a pleasant Bowre
> So vaulted with the leavie trees, the Sonne had there no powre:
> Not Made by man or mans devise, and yet no man alive,
> A trimmer piece of worke than that could for his life contrive.

From the seventh book, the entrance to the lower world (409–16):

> There is a cave that gapeth wide with darksome entrie low:
> There goes a way slope downe by which with triple cheyne made new
> Of strong and sturdie Adamant the valiant *Hercle* drew
> The currish Helhounde *Cerberus*: who dragging arsward still,
> And writhing backe his scowling eyes because he had no skill
> To see the Sunne and open day, for verie moodie wroth
> Three barkings yelled out at once, and spit his slavering froth
> Upon the greenish grasse.

From the eleventh book, the Cave of Sleep (592–602):

> Among the darke *Cimmerians* is a hollow mountaine found,
> And in the hill a Cave that farre dooth ronne within the ground,
> The chamber and the dwelling place where slouthfull sleepe dooth cowch;
> The light of *Phebus* golden beames this place can never towch.

A foggye mist with dimnesse mixt streames upwarde from the ground,
And glimmering twylyght evermore within the same is found.
           Yit from the Roches foote dooth go
The ryver of forgetfulnesse, which ronneth trickling so
Uppon the little pebble stones which in the channell lye,
That untoo sleepe a great deale more it dooth provoke thereby.

And from the eighth book, the Cretan labyrinth (157–75):

                     This shamefull infamie,
This monster borne him by his wife he mindes by pollicie
To put away: and in a house with many nookes and krinks
From all mens sights and speach of folke to shet it up he thinks.
Immediately one *Daedalus* renowmed in that land
For fine devise and workmanship in building, went in hand
To make it. He confounds his worke with sodaine stops and stayes,
And with the great uncertaintie of sundrie winding wayes
Leades in and out, and to and fro, at divers doores astray.
And as with trickling streame the Brooke *Maeander* seemes to play
In *Phrygia*, and with doubtfull race runnes counter to and fro,
And meeting with himselfe doth looke if all his streame or no
Come after, and retiring eft cleane backward to his spring
And marching eft to open Sea as streight as any string,
Indenteth with reversed streame: even so of winding wayes
Innumerable *Daedalus* within his worke convayes.
Yea scarce himselfe could find the meanes to winde himselfe well out:
So busie and so intricate the house was all about.[16]

Beyond Ovid, two other classical writers require mention here. One
is the elder Pliny, who in his *Natural History* mentions the labyrinth as
"quite the most abnormal achievement on which man has spent his
resources, but by no means a fictitious one." He goes on to describe the

---

16. *Shakespeare's Ovid: Being Arthur Golding's Translation of the "Meta-morphoses"* [1567], ed. W. H. D. Rouse (London: Centaur Press, 1961). Standard book and line references have been supplied with the quotations; the page references in Golding are 59, 66, 147, 232, 164. Charles Paul Segal, *Landscape in Ovid's "Metamorphoses"* (Wiesbaden: Franz Steiner, 1969), esp. pp. 20–23, on the mysterious, numinous, ominous qualities of Ovid's caves and cavernous hollows. Lancelot P. Wilkinson, *Ovid Recalled* (Cambridge: Cambridge University Press, 1955), pp. 184–86, finds it appropriate to render Ovid's Cave of Sleep in Spenserian stanzas.

dimensions and design of four labyrinths—the Egyptian, the Lemnian, the Cretan, and the Italian or Etruscan, the last being the tomb of King Porsena. He is unique in showing no interest in the purpose of the commissions or the meaning of what occurs within them, returning at the end to his first thought, of conspicuous waste and "vesana dementia"—insane folly, like an eighteenth-century *honnête homme* deploring the architectural "follies" of his age.[17]

Sir Thomas North's translation of Plutarch's *Lives* appeared in 1579, the year of the *Shepheardes Calender*. An ample, beautifully produced volume that would have been a boast to own, a privilege to borrow, it is also a repository, a chrestomathy, of historical anecdote and political wisdom sufficient to edify a gentleman or noble person through the major occasions, private and public, of a lifetime. The very first biography in this long book, of Theseus (paired with Romulus), bears on our concern. The secret of the royal parentage of the child Theseus is hidden under a stone, which he removes when he comes to age and strength, to find his father's tokens, a sword and a pair of shoes—a prefiguration in miniature of his descent into the stone labyrinth, his walking through it, fighting the Minotaur, and thereby qualifying for royal power. Plutarch thus describes the main event: "Furthermore, after he arrived in Creta, he slewe there the Minotaure (as the most parte of auncient authors doe write) by the meanes and helpe of Ariadne: who being fallen in fansie with him, dyd give him a clue of threade, by the helpe whereof she taught him, that he might easely winde out of the turnings and cranckes of the Labyrinthe." And he adds this further description of the ritual dance called the Crane, which recalls and acts anew the emergence from the labyrinth: "Theseus then departing from the Ile of Creta, arrived in the Ile of Delos, where he did sacrifice in the temple of Apollo, and gave there a little image of Venus, the which he had gotten of Ariadne. Then with the other young boyes that he had delivered, he daunced a kinde of daunce, which the Delians keepe to this day, as they say: in which there are many turnes and returnes, much after the turninges of the Labyrinthe."[18]

In mature years Spenser will have read more widely and more deeply

---

17. Pliny, *Natural History* XXXVI.xix.84–93.

18. Plutarch, *The Lives*, vol. I, trans. Sir Thomas North (London: Nonesuch, 1929, reprinting edition of 1579), pp. 13, 16.

than this brief sampling implies. I have been concerned with large probabilities and analogies as much as with demonstrable influence. One major constituent in the structure of his imagination remains to be outlined. Spenser was not an exegete or a hermeneut, but he was clearly a strong supporter of the Elizabethan Settlement and well instructed in the Protestant faith, and that implies a good knowledge of scripture, probably absorbed more through the set readings of the lectionary—the epistles and gospels of the successive weeks and seasons, and the Old Testament, New Testament, and Psalms appointed for matins and evensong for each day—than through private study, in which, if he resembled his fellow Christians in every age, he paid more attention to Genesis and Exodus than to Leviticus and Numbers, more to the judges and early kings than to the later, more to the major prophets than to the minor; and such a natural human predilection must be reinforced by a poet's attraction to whatever fires the imagination—the Psalms, the Writings, the Gospels, and the Book of Revelation.

Literal caves in scripture are few but metaphorical extensions are manifold; the words *labyrinth* and *maze* never appear, but the *way* and its opposite, *wandering*, pervade the whole. Consider first the cave, with its related terms, den, hole, pit. Moving from the literal to the figurative, one finds burial caves for Sarah and Lazarus; iconographically if not literally the stable at Bethlehem and the Holy Sepulchre are caves. When the wicked perish, they are said to go down into the pit; Joseph when thrown by his brothers into the pit suffers a kind of death, and Egypt is a kind of labyrinthine land of the dead. The cave is a shelter, real or vain: David hides in a cave and on a later occasion spares the sleeping Saul in one—the scene of that favorite Elizabethan text "Touch not the Lord's anointed." Foxes have holes, but the Son of Man has not where to lay his head; on the last day, when prophets no longer wander in caves, the reprobate will seek to hide in dens and rocks. The cave is the natural habitat of robbers and predators: the phrase "den of thieves" and the story of Daniel in the lions' den spring at once to mind. Some, however, who do not belong there find themselves entrapped, the cave-pit symbolizing pestilence, harlotry (though not witchcraft, in spite of the later iconography of the witch of Endor), prison, and hell. The frequent combination of the pit and the net—both images taken from hunting—encourages amplification to a dangerous labyrinthine cave.[19]

The Bible is the book of the Way, which is a divine Name. Wandering in the wilderness, a perverse desire to wander, wandering in the sense of playing the harlot or departing from true understanding—all these are contrary to the Way. The imagery is, however, not completely locked in iron: in the book of Ecclesiasticus, Wisdom appears as an educator and takes the young soul at first "by crooked waies." If the forty years wandering in the wilderness were punitive, the forty days temptation in the wilderness are redemptive, and the chosen of God are "strangers and pilgrems" in this world, with "no continuing citie." Nevertheless, though forms of *amaze* are used a dozen times in Scripture in the sense of a great arrest at a manifestation of divine power, it has no overtone of *maze*. Calvin speaks for Christendom when he observes that "God, the maker of the worlds is manifested to us in Scripture, and his true character expounded, so as to save us from wandering up and down, as in a labyrinth, in search of some doubtful deity."[20]

The final suppression of religious orders in England took place less than twenty years before Spenser's birth, and so he could have absorbed (along with the usual scandals and calumnies) a sense of the difference between the monk's life of stability in his cave-cell and the

19. Biblical references to *The Geneva Bible* (1560), ed. Lloyd E. Berry (Madison: University of Wisconsin Press, 1969): Burial caves, Gen. 23:19, John 11:38; the pit, Ps., passim, Num. 16:30, 33; Joseph, Gen. 37:20, 24; David's caves, 1 Sam. 24:3, 7, 8, 10, 22:1, 2 Sam. 23:13; foxholes and dens, Matt. 8:20, Luke 9:58; prophets in caves, 1 Kings 19:9, Heb. 11:38, Isa. 2:19, 21, 51:1, cf. Rev. 6:15; den of thieves, Jer. 7:11 (cf. den of dragons, 9:11, 10:22), Matt. 21:13, and Mark 11:17; lions' den, Dan. 6:7, cf. Nah. 2:12; entrapment, Josh. 10:16–18; pestilence, Ezek. 33:27; harlotry, Prov. 22:14, 23:27; prison, Isa. 24:17, 18, 22; hell, Isa. 14:15, 19; pit and net, Ps. 9:15, 10:9, Isa. 42:22, Prov. 1:12, 17, Jer. 48:43, 44. See also Nicholas J. Tromp, M.S.C., *Primitive Conceptions of Death and the Nether World in the Old Testament* (Rome: Pontifical Biblical Institute, 1969).

20. The Way, John 14:6; wandering in the wilderness, Num. 14:33, Ps. 107:40, Job 12:24, Jer. 14:10, 2:20, Prov. 21:16; Wisdom teaches, Ecclus. 4:17–20; wanderers, Ps. 107:4, Hos. 9:17; strangers and pilgrims, 1 Pet. 2:11; no continuing city, Heb. 13:14; John Calvin, *Institutes of the Christian Religion*, trans. Henry Beveridge (Edinburgh, 1875), I, chap. vi, 65. See also George H. Williams, *Wilderness and Paradise in Christian Thought* (New York: Harper, 1962), passim on wilderness, pp. 36–38 on the sacred caves of the Nativity and the Entombment.

friar's holy errands in the labyrinth of the world—a difference indeed inherent in church life from the time the apostle John retired to Patmos and the apostle Paul embarked on his missionary voyages, or when the Desert Fathers took to their caves and the Celtic Wanderers sailed their watery wilderness. This distinction is matched in the secular world of medieval romance by the difference between footfast castellan and footloose crusader. Such considerations as these may have helped to determine Spenser's choice of errantry as the controlling metaphor in his continued allegory or dark conceit. The winding course made visible is especially insistent in the case of the wandering knight on a quest, the knight errant as he moves through places (sometimes, explicitly, caves) of danger, testing, encounter, and judgment. Romance literature, popular and courtly, lay ready to hand for such treatment.[21]

What Spenser supplied to a higher degree perhaps than any of his predecessors except Tasso (and Tasso supplied it largely after the fact) was a sense of overview, and here I should like to suggest a probable source in the cultural experience of the poet. Deriving from the Continent but achieving high development in Renaissance England are topiary knots and mazes in the gardens of palaces and great houses, including the royal palace at Greenwich and Lord Burghley's house at Theobalds. They are intended quite as much for the viewer as for the promenader. The view of the garden from an upper window or balcony has been devised to please the eye with patterns, to implicate the eye with complex patterns, to trap the eye with enticing and puzzling patterns, to amaze the eye with labyrinthine patterns. Thus any drawing of a labyrinth or overview of a garden will convey a sense of controlled near-symmetry, of assured reward to patience. It does take patience—time is of the essence, as we noted—but the viewer can see round corners and is to that degree godlike. So Aeneas must have "read" the representation of the Cretan labyrinth before he was called from his reverie by the stern Sibyl to prepare his descent. Very different from this overview will be the experience of actually entering the labyrinth, leaving theory for practice. The wayfaring and warfaring Chris-

---

21. This is not to imply that everyone, even the most part of the good characters in *The Faerie Queene*, is always on the move: only that characters in movement make things happen in the poem.

tian must tread it and thread it, and *hoc opus, hic labor est.* Latin could play on *labor* and *labyrinth* as English can on *travel* and *travail.*[22]

On entering the labyrinth, even if it has but a single course based on simple alternation of direction, one soon loses one's bearings. Chaos yawns: the yawn of anxiety in the walker being matched by a projected yawn of voracity in the successive portals. A sense of abandonment floods in, the anxiety of impeded movement, of the narrow place (*angustiae*, straits, narrows, from which three languages derive *anguish*, *angoisse*, *Angst*). Entering, as distinct from surveying, the labyrinth is thus always dangerous, riddled with anxiety, and all the more so if the appearance of choice is added to the appearance of necessity. Hemmed in by wanhope, simply to continue is to hope. The concrete image of Appearance is the only reality while it lasts. The characterization of the labyrinth as "the image of lost direction" is an excellent one, provided it is made to apply to kinesis and process, not to stasis and overview. In a wilderness, direction would really be lost—were it not for the pillar

22. The importance of the view of garden patterns, especially mazes, is not much stressed by the authorities I have consulted, in spite of their emphasis on the Renaissance garden as architecture. See David R. Coffin, ed., *The Italian Garden* (Washington: Dumbarton Oaks, 1972); Terry Comito, *The Idea of the Garden in the Renaissance* (New Brunswick, N.J.: Rutgers University Press, 1978): "a sense of the garden as the scene of those privileged moments when the self takes possession of the world" (p. xi); Sir Frank Crisp, *Mediaeval Gardens*, 2 vols. (London: John Lane, 1924), esp. I.vii, knots and parterres, and I.viii, labyrinths and mazes; John Dent, *The Quest for Nonsuch* (London: Hutchinson, 1962), summarizing Anthony Watson ms. *Briefe and True Description*, c. 1582–92: the royal apartments "look out one way on the riches of the courtyard, and the other way on the perplexing twists of the maze and the scented beauty of the garden" (p. 59); Teresa McLean, *Medieval English Gardens* (London: Collins, 1981): hermits' huts, pp. 39, 52, Rosemund's bower, a maze at Woodstock, and imitations of it, pp. 100, 117; Roy Strong, *The Renaissance Garden in England* (London: Thames & Hudson, 1979): the gardens described in Francesco Colonna's *Hypnerotomachia Poliphili*, pp. 16–17, knots and mazes, pp. 40–43, the maze at Theobalds, pp. 46, 52–53, the terrace for viewing knots at Kenilworth, p. 51, Fynes Moryson (1590s) on grottoes, pp. 78–79. I had the pleasure of hearing a paper (Conference on Renaissance Theatre, Waterloo, Ontario, 25 July 1985) by Alan R. Young, "'In gallant Course, before ten thousand eyes': The Tournament and Elizabethan Drama," which impressed upon me the fact that the sovereign's view from the window or balcony of her "fortress of perfect beauty," overlooking the tiltyard at Whitehall, would be quite analogous to her view of topiary mazes from the *piano nobile* of other great houses. Eduard Norden, *P. Vergilius Maro "Aeneis" Buch VI* (Darmstadt, 1915; 4th ed. 1951) on *Aeneid* VI.37, "hic labor ille domus et inextricabilis error," notes that *labor* and *labyrinthus* were thought in antiquity to be etymologically related. He does not explicitly apply this to *hoc opus, hic labor est* (*Aeneid* VI.129).

of cloud by day and pillar of fire by night. It is trackless, as no labyrinth can be: indeed, a unicursal labyrinth is all track. An infernal labyrinth, such as Dante's or that evoked at the end (and in retrospect the whole) of Beckford's *Vathek*, is, paradoxically, no labyrinth at all. Since it has no desirable and possible end, it has no path, no way: all hope abandon, ye who enter here. From the beginning its denizens have finished their course and lost their race. In any true labyrinth, movement is not bootless: to continue is an act of patience and of hope. However the walker may grope and grumble, the eye of faith tells him or her darkly what the overviewing eye could see in plain daylight, that the thing has a meaning beyond lost direction—even that it may prove to be a cruciform four-square mandala. What the protracted act of moving through the labyrinth does, positively, is to impose order, sequence, and deliberate speed on the progress toward a goal, impressing on the seeker the difference between intention and completed act in the world of spirit no less than in the world of action.[23]

The reader of *The Faerie Queene* frequently possesses the sort of general overview just described, the characters more rarely. An experience of an erratic or errant course is usual in the virtuous knights as they pursue their quests and is intermittently shared by readers whenever they abandon their vantage point and enter into this tight corner or that. It is time to look more closely at the poem. A circumstantial account may be desirable because of the great number of caves and labyrinths there—much greater than in Homer, Ovid, Ariosto, or Tasso and, in frequency though not perhaps in emphasis, than in Virgil. It will be possible to say something about each book of the poem in these terms.[24]

III

There can be no question of guilt (as there will be in Guyon's descent with Mammon) when the Redcross Knight and Una enter the wander-

23. Knight, *Cumaean Gates*, p. 156, on labyrinth as delaying action. "The image of lost direction" is Northrop Frye's phrase, *Anatomy of Criticism* (Princeton: Princeton University Press, 1957), p. 150. Patricia A. Parker, *Inescapable Romance* (Princeton: Princeton University Press, 1979), in "The Dilation of Being" (pp. 54–64) associates dilation, deferral, and temporizing with the labyrinth in *The Faerie Queene*.

24. One speculates that perhaps the ideal reader, the queen, is complimented as being able to see the whole action in overview while the rest of us join in the quests and errors.

ing wood: it is only sensible to take shelter from stormy weather, and doing so entails no deviation from the true faith or swerving from the true quest. The Knight's victory over Errour (in line with the lesson of the Legend of Holiness and indeed of the whole *Faerie Queene* as we have it) is real but not final. We are not yet out of the woods: the way thence to the final battle will be multicursal. The "little lowly Hermitage" of Archimago, "downe in a dale," proves no less than Errour's den to lead downward, to the Cave of Morpheus "amid the bowels of the earth." As Book I continues, the false Una and the wanton Squire are seen "in a secret bed, / Couered with darkenesse"; and the mortally injured Sans Loy first is "hid in a secret shade" and then with the aid of Night, who dwells in "darkesome mew," is conducted through the "yawning gulfe of deepe *Auernus* hole," to be cured by Aesculapius in the cave in which he is imprisoned, "Deepe, darke, vneasie, dolefull, confortlesse." The giant Orgoglio, as the son of Earth's "hollow womb" by blustering Aeolus, is himself cavelike, a "monstrous masse of earthly slime, / Puft vp with emptie wind and fild with sinfull crime." The clear moral allegory here is combined with physical allegory: such phenomena (or "meteors") as windstorms and earthquakes were long thought to be engendered in caves, the locus classicus being the cave of Aeolus in *Aeneid* I.[25]

After the Redcross Knight is rescued from the cave-dungeon of Orgoglio, he meets his most insidious enemy, Despair, who is inseparable from the gloomy, bone-littered cave that is his mind's place, and who leads the Knight into a maze of sophistical argument. And finally, he encounters the grossest of open enemies, the great Dragon huge as a hill, whose "deepe deuouring iawes / Wide gaped, like the griesly mouth of hell, / Through which into his darke abisse all rauin fell." The evil at the end of the book involves that of the beginning, like a serpent swallowing his tail, but the Knight by now has been through the toils and can stand apart, armed and aided by a power divine.[26]

Even in the first book, where cave and labyrinth, taking their rhetorical coloring from the opening scene, are overwhelmingly negative in their associations, the poet allows some positive valency to coexist in them. Places of spiritual restoration can be cavelike: in the House of

25. *FQ* I.i.34, 39, ii.3, v.15, 20, 31, 36, vii.9, viii.24 (cf. III.ix.15).
26. *FQ* I.vii.15, ix.33, xi.12 (also 21, 41).

Holiness, the Redcross Knight is cured in a "darkesome lowly place farre in," and a holy housling fire is lit at the nuptials of the Knight and Una and kept burning within the "secret chamber." So too with labyrinths, though to a lesser degree. True, Archimago, having "searcht his balefull bookes" (themselves a riddling obfuscation), separates the Knight from Truth so that Una wanders into woods and forests and the Knight, more culpably, wanders "astray" in company with Duessa. The powers of evil know more of wandering by the way; the soul of the wounded Sans Loy so wanders, belonging as it does near the "yawning gulfe of deepe *Auernus* hole." (A cave mouth with a spin and charged with water, it may be noted parenthetically, is a *gulfe*, or whirlpool-labyrinth, and a *train*, as we have seen, is a coiled deception.) The "craftie cunning traine" of Duessa brings the Redcross Knight to Orgoglio's Castle, his dungeon being the dead end of "mens wandering ways." Quite different, however, is Una's search. To save her Knight from his "wandering perill" Una would herself have wandered "from one to other *Ynd*." If she has "wandered through the world" (the word *stray* is even cleansed of its bad character and boldly given her), it is to guide him to the House of Coelia, where Mercie continues her work of guidance "In all his wayes through this wide worldes waue."[27]

The Legend of Holiness is the book of the Way: that is, for most of its course, of wandering and error. It is marked by that necessary delay in its action (and in our scanning of that action) which we have observed as characteristic both of continued allegory and of labyrinths viewed or trodden. The Legend of Temperance is the book of the *via media*, and a similar necessary delay must occur with the adventures of Sir Guyon. His two main adversaries, Mammon and Acrasia, otherwise so different, menace him with astonishment and amazement, with petrification and loss of bearings, cave and labyrinth: to be drawn into the world of either would be as if to gaze on "Medusaes mazefull hed."[28]

The most fully presented underworld in *The Faerie Queene*, the domain of Mammon, is entirely sinister. Sir Guyon, errant in the wilderness, happens upon an old man counting his gold in a "gloomy

27. *FQ* I.x.25, xii.37, ii.2, 9, 12, v.13, 31, vii.1, 23, vi.32, 2, iii.27, x.9, 34.
28. "Epithalamion" 189–90: "And stand astonisht lyke to those which red / Medusaes mazeful hed."

glade." The miser, startled, furtively pours his coins into a hole in "hollow earth," and then entices the knight to descend to see his subterranean haunt, a "womb" and a "tomb" and a "secret mew," which proves to be a vast realm of work and wealth—work for gain alone, wealth for no good purpose. In this Plutonian kingdom all imaginable riches are fraught with the utmost danger, and every turn taken in this descent makes it seem more of a closed cave, for entrapment is embodied, animated, and moralized in the figure of the fiend that dogs Guyon's footsteps and will tear him to pieces if he touches anything offered him. This temptation in the wilderness Guyon barely survives: he had allowed himself, out of self-reliance and curiosity, to follow the downward spiral, whereas Jesus, given an overview from the top of a high mountain, rises above the temptation because he is about his Father's business as Guyon is not.[29]

The immensely long canto of the voyage and the Bower of Bliss is differently unfolded. Everything, except the resolved will of Guyon and the Palmer, is prearranged by the enchantress Acrasia, the spider at the center of the web. The earliest manifestation of her power is a watery maze, the Gulfe of Greedinesse, with the "huge abysse of his engulfing graue"; the Wandering Islands and the Quicksand of Unthriftyhed menace the navigator's mind with allurement or dismay, but the culminating peril of the deep, "threatning to devoure all," is the Whirlepoole of Decay, the tentacles of whose imagery encompass more than mere bankruptcy, which is its meaning in moral allegory:

> On th'other side they see that perilous Poole,
>   That called was the *Whirlepoole of decay*,
>   In which full many had with hapless doole
>   Beene suncke, of whom no memorie did stay:
>   Whose circled waters rapt with whirling sway,
>   Like to a restlesse wheele, still running round,
>   Did couet, as they passed by that way,
>   To draw their boate within the vtmost bound
> Of his wide *Labyrinth*, and then to haue them dround.

The word *labyrinth* here supplies the suggestion of a devouring monster at the center, to reinforce the more overt allusion to the whirlpool Charybdis.[30]

29. *FQ* II.vii.3–65.
30. *FQ* II.xii.77 (cf. vii.28), 5, 21, 20.

The voyage to the Bower is preparation and forewarning of the Bower itself: the reader there is steeled to resist the later "wanton wreathings intricate" of the witch's world of seductive illusion. Acrasia's victims are "captiu'd eternally in yron mewes and darksom dens" and (same thing) Cymochles lies "in Ladies lap entombed," but in keeping with the deceptiveness, against which the reader is continually warned, the Bower of Bliss is presented as a sunlit arbor easy of access. It is essential that Acrasia should not look spiderlike and that her bower should not call to mind the hollow at the hub of a web. This arachnid must make it seem a place of sweetness and light.[31]

The most elaborate structure in Book II, or indeed in the whole of *The Faerie Queene*, is the House of Alma. While it makes full use of the architectural analogies to the human body, only a very minimal cavelike character is allowed, even where one would most expect it, in the hollows of trunk and skull. It is rather the villainous enemies of the House of Alma that mill about and scramble out of rocks and caves. As Spenser moves from gross anatomy to fine anatomy to physiology to psychology to ethics in his edifying account of the edifice of the soul, he has no need to spell out analogies that elsewhere function better as part of his poetic spell.[32]

In the middle books or heartland of *The Faerie Queene*, concerned as they are with personal and social relations and reticulations, the actions are necessarily delayed as the characters in courtship or friendship enter (following Petrarch) the labyrinth of love or come to know (anticipating Yeats) the labyrinth of another's being. A new intricate manner of narrative comes into play now that is easy to describe metaphorically in terms of a maze or knot. This is the place for a digression on digression (an exercise in imitative form, if you like) and for the promised observations on Ariosto and Tasso.[33]

Ovid's shunting method of moving from story to story may be likened to a unicursal labyrinth, but he does not himself remark on this resemblance beyond comparing the relation of a story to the spinning of wool. "Yarn" for both tale and thread goes back to Old Norse and has always been a basic metaphor—from the simple idiom of keeping to or losing the thread of a story or argument to elaborate analogies to

31. *FQ* II.xii.53, v.27, 36.
32. *FQ* II.ix.24, 29, 50, 55, 13.
33. Petrarch, *Rime* CCXXIV; Yeats, "The Tower."

tapestry or the figure in the carpet. The Fates and the Norns weave the story of life; Penelope's web matches Odysseus's wanderings in Homer's yarn; and Ariadne's thread enables Theseus to return to the land of the living. Indeed, so familiar is the pattern of thought that we are all too ready to deny its inmost nature and try to apprehend it instantaneously, without the necessary delay. Two examples of this. Francis Quarles in a poem on the Christian's pace through the labyrinth of the world attaches a well-known emblematic picture, which shows the pilgrim with hat and staff making his way along the top of a labyrinth wall. He holds taut in his hand a string, the other end of which is held by an angel atop a tower in the distance. The course of the labyrinth is perfectly plain, and the gate to the tower of heaven is in plain sight, and so the possession of the thread does not protect and does not guide but simply comforts, and yet it is possible to read the poem and the emblem indefinitely without seeing that. Again, everyone thinks he understands the riddling words of Blake:

> I give you the end of a golden string,
>   Only wind it into a ball,
> It will lead you in at Heaven's gate
>   Built in Jerusalem's wall.

A spool of thread or a ball of wool is itself a labyrinth, capable of being extended and simplified to trace a constructed labyrinth. Ariadne gave Theseus the ball and held the end of the string herself. The giver here, or Giver, must already have threaded the labyrinth and been to Heaven's gate, leaving the thread along the path: it follows that the end of "your" quest is not a place of danger or testing but pure reward. This cannot be understood without stopping and taking thought. Everything to do with the labyrinth, from the *Roman de la Rose* at its most amplified to Blake at his most terse, necessitates delay.[34]

The myriads of interrupted flights and pursuits and "errors" make *Orlando furioso* the most intricate in construction of the world's ma-

---

34. Ovid, *Metamorphoses* IV.54; Francis Quarles, *Emblems Divine and Moral*, ed. Augustus Toplady and John Ryland (London, 1839): Book IV, emblem II, on Ps. 109:5, "O that my ways were directed to keep thy statutes." For the original emblem, reversed, see Kern, p. 300; William Blake, "Jerusalem," *Complete Writings*, ed. Geoffrey Keynes (Oxford: Oxford University Press, 1966), p. 716.

jor poems. So rich in everything else, it has only one notable cave, the cave of Merlin—the direct source of Spenser's—and only two overt allusions to the labyrinth—the labyrinth of the giant Atlante and the labyrinthine wood. The poem itself is enough of a maze. It is as notable for the absence of loose ends as *The Faerie Queene* is for their presence, and this is not simply because the one is complete and the other incomplete: in a poem where everyone wanders and no way seems straight, the plot finally resolves like a game of cat's cradle.[35]

Tasso's *Gerusalemme liberata* is constructed on the model of the Virgilian epic, not an Ariostan intrigue. Its substance, not its form, would have encouraged Spenser's use of the complex of ideas and images that is our interest. The entire poem moves on the literal level toward the liberation of the holy city of Jerusalem at the center of which is a sacred cave, the Holy Sepulchre; and what impedes this movement is the open and resolute infidelity of the paynim champions and the crafts and subtleties of the devil and his magicians, projected as illusion in the enchanted forest and as allurement in Armida's bower, which is really a dungeon. The magician Ismeno occupies a cave and maze as his habitat: so too "in hollows vast" sounds the trumpet of Satan, whose "yawning mouth" gapes like a whirlpool; and there is also mention of a cave-entry (built by Herod) to a secret path and blind byways through which wandering outlaws may reinforce their hold on captive Jerusalem. The Christian knights, likewise, whenever untrue to their profession and misled by enchantment, wander astray. A major contrast is built up between the pagan enchantress Armida and the Christian hermit by whose counsel she is overcome. Armida is commissioned by the infernal powers to weave a web to entrap the Christian knights, to induce them to follow her "wanton pilgrimage" into deserts and wildernesses. The bower in which she holds Rinaldo (and loses her heart to him, thereby making herself at the end redeemable) is no cave in outward appearance, but rather a *locus amoenus* in which Zephyrs play, nor is the enchanted wood seen as a labyrinth: they are, however, in context, as dangerous and dismaying as if their perils were on display. Necessary instruction is provided by a good hermit in his lovingly described sweet cave, and two rescuing knights forewarned by him sail

35. *Orlando furioso* III.10, XIII.79, XVIII.192. See Parker, pp. 16–30, "Ariosto and the 'Errors' of Romance."

a watery wilderness to arrive at Armida's inmost hold. It is the rescued Rinaldo, after he confesses that he has strayed and erred and wandered, who can withstand the phantoms and voices of the enchanted wood and make straight the way for the conquering army.[36]

Spenser in his middle books reminds the reader at many points of Tasso's characters and incidents and tone of feeling and reminds the reader throughout of Ariosto's style of narrative. Seemingly incidental phrases are germane: the hunt for glory "through wastefull wayes," the following of "false Ladies traine," the seas "hollow bosome" and "greedie gulfe," the "wandring forrest," and "miswandred wayes"; Satyrane "rangd abroad to seeke aduentures wilde," and the Squire of Dames must "wander through the world abroad at will," and "walke the world around." In all these phrases a note of randomness is struck, quite different from the directed quests underlying the errantry of Redcross and Guyon. The inset Trojan history tells of the "fatall errour" (echoing Virgil's words) of Aeneas and the "wearie wandring" of Brute, while Paridell sets his "traines" to entrap Hellenore, whose subsequent life is to be a wandering in ever more wasteful wildernesses.[37]

This phase of the poem brings with it an equipoise between the positive and negative associations of caves. The magic mirror in which Britomart first sees Artegall "round and hollow shaped was, / Like to the world it selfe, and seem'd a world of glas." Here the cave element of earth has been refined and given the transparency of air, or the two cave elements have interpenetrated so as to combine the solidity of one and the transparency of the other. Whatever reservations we may have had about Guyon's following Mammon underground, we can have none about Britomart's act of close attention and self-commitment, her entering the world of glass. However, in the ensuing description of Merlin's "deepe delue," his "hideous hollow caue," his "balefull Bowre," imprisonment in which has been caused by his following "false Ladies traine," we are quite sufficiently reminded that the nega-

---

36. *Jerusalem Delivered*, trans. Edward Fairfax (1600) (New York: Colonial Press, 1901). (Fairfax's translation is strongly influenced by Spenser.) Holy Sepulchre, Book I, Stanza 1; magician's cave, II.2; vast hollows and mouth, IV.3, 7; Herod's path, X.29, 55; Armida's web, IV.24, 26, 27; her bower, XV.53–66 (cf. VII.48, her dungeon, and XVI.1–28, her inmost hold); the hermit's cave, XIV.36–XV.2; confession of errancy, XVIII.6–9.

37. *FQ* III.i.3, iii.11, iv.22, vi.26, vii.18, 30, 54, 56, ix.41, 48, x.11.

tive valency continues concurrently with no abatement of imaginative power. *The Faerie Queene* remains as multiplex as a labyrinth even when seen as a globed compacted thing, single as a cave of glass.[38]

In the story of Florimell and Marinell the cave is ostensibly a shelter, really a prison, for both. Marinell has been fostered in a cave; his mother's lethal solicitude for him is early adumbrated by the phrase, "the sea's hollow bosome" and "greedie gulfe," as the sea nymph hides her son from prophesied danger, but no rococo grotto can shelter him from the chances of life. Concurrently, the fugitive Florimell, after being pursued by a hyena called from a hidden cave by a witch, is held in the bower of Proteus, a "hollow caue" that also proves to be a "dungeon deep." This dungeon-cave of Proteus, "under the hanging of a hideous clieffe," "a sea-walled fort," is described a second time, to make the liberation of Florimell the sweeter when it comes. Ultimately perhaps, this cave is the whole sublunary world of change considered as a place of confinement of the fugitive soul, as Merlin's world of glass contains within it all the challenges that the determined and collected soul must face.[39]

The sinister quality developed in Mammon's dismaying realm of riches (with some carry-over to Marinell's "rich strond") continues through the motif of buried treasure in the story of Malbecco, who at the beginning mews his wife Hellenore in close bower and at the cramped end of his career of gripe and grudge crawls into "a caue with entrance small," beaten by billows, and himself becomes a sort of stalactite image of Jealousy. But this is peripheral: at the heart of the Legend of Chastity lies the Garden of Adonis, the "wombe" of all life, and in the core of that, in an "arbour" in "thickest couert" lie the lovers who are the parents of all things that are born to live and die. The delay of the labyrinth—here slow gestation ensuing in birth—is all to the good. True, Time is active in the Garden, and (what is the same thing) the boar is penned beneath it in a rocky cave, but the impression of replenishment is far stronger than that of entropy. Amoret is fostered there, and she grows to womanhood in the Temple of Venus, a similar place but more open, airy, and spacious. The Temple's many rooms involve delay in access to its inmost penetralia, and so have that iner-

---

38. *FQ* III.ii.19, iii.7, 8, 11.
39. *FQ* III.iv.22, 43, viii.4, 37, 41, 44, IV.xi.3, xii.5, 18.

adicable quality of the labyrinth, but they are in themselves "delightfull bowres," in sharpest contrast to Busirane's gloomy chambers and to the caves and dungeons that proliferate in the Legend of Friendship. These latter may be listed as on a witch's infamous beadroll: Ate's "darksome delue farre vnder ground," the "deepe *Abyss*" or "Chaos" of the underground house of the Fates (to which the loving Agape descends to plead for her sons' souls), the cavelike cottage of Care where Scudamour endures a sleepless night, the cave-dungeon of Lust, the dungeon of Corflambo, and of course the cave of Proteus.[40]

The House of Busirane and the Temple of Venus are, in their negative and positive ways, places of enchantment, riddles made architecture, first to be penetrated and then either abolished utterly or enjoyed without anxiety. Busirane's three rooms may seem simple enough, but they are made mazelike by the bewildering pageant that passes through them, at the climax of which, at the end of the "traine," is something monstrous, a magician tormenting a woman, first having netted her attention by an elaborate choreographical artifice. When Britomart forces Busirane to release Amoret, the unsaying of his spells undoes her bonds and unbuilds the house of bondage.[41]

Earlier in time but later in the narrative, Scudamour has approached the Temple of Venus, as spacious and airy as the House of Busirane is airless. What is there a drawn-out torment is here delay in access. Its profusion of plurals and pairs leads up to a phrase which in any other context would certainly sound tainted and menacing but here stands safe under the sign of innocency, ardor, and self-discovery:

> Fresh shadowes, fit to shroud from sunny ray;
>   Faire lawnds, to take the sunne in season dew;
>   Sweet springs, in which a thousand Nymphs did play;
>   Soft rombling brookes, that gentle slomber drew;
>   High reared mounts, the lands about to vew;
>   Low looking dales, disloignd from common gaze;
>   Delightfull bowres, to solace lovers trew;

---

40. *FQ* III.x.57–58, vi.36–44, 48, IV.x.24, i.20, ii.47, v.33, vii.8, viii.51.

41. *FQ* III.xi.21–55 and xii. Though called a "castle" when Scudamour and Britomart approach it, Busirane's place is not a great house with a social life and hierarchy: it is rather a "secret den" (III.xi.10) and an elaborate, though strangely insubstantial, theater, a grotto wrought with "wilde Antickes" (51).

    False Labyrinthes, fond runners eyes to daze;
    All which by nature made did nature self amaze.[42]

Every good work of justice issues ultimately from Astraea's cave of instruction, in which the goddess, before leaving the earth, nurtures the boy Artegall to be her champion and vicegerent. Successive generations of readers of Spenser's fifth book, the Legend of Justice, have wished that Artegall had returned there for a refresher course. Very curiously, the strongest critics and the greatest admirers of the system of law have always agreed that some measure of delay in attaining its ends, and hence something labyrinthine, is of its essence. This delay is shown positively in such a phrase as "due process of law" or in the insistence that justice must not only be done but be seen to be done; it is shown negatively in the phrase "the toils of the law," in Hamlet's lament at "the law's delay," in the Circumlocution Office in *Bleak House*, in the cat-and-mouse game between arrest and execution in Kafka's *Trial*. Spenser hardly availed himself of any of this in his fifth book. Artegall is merely in the right, his justice is summary, without conveying any sense of deliberation, and he achieves none of the political wisdom compressed in Bacon's observation that all rising to great place is by a winding stair. At no point is the jury out, nor does the judge ever retire to his chamber to ponder the case.

Caves in the Legend of Justice are few and entirely negative: the empty rooms of Dolon's "loathed bower," a metaphoric mention of the "dreadfull mouth of death," the prison of Radegund in which Artegall is held captive, Adicia's "wicked bowre," the cave of Malengin, and the repeated reference to the monster lurking under the Idol's altar at the center of Geryoneo's power. In these Spenser adds little to what he has already organized and expressed in the figure of the cave. Apart from one mistake, which reduces him to the woman's work of spinning thread in Radegund's treadmill (a subdued labyrinth image), Artegall is the least erring of knights, but in his story there are occasional reminders of the maze symbols used earlier in the poem: the caves of Dolon and Adicia just mentioned have their mazelike aspect, and even Arthur and Artegall devise how to lure Malengin from his den and "ensnarle" him.[43]

In the Legend of Courtesy the Wild Man dwells in a forest home made of good earth filled with good air; the Hermit's cell, in contrast, is located on the plain and is likened to "a little cage." Both of these footfast characters are eremitical, in contrast to the footfree Palmer of Book II, who belongs on pilgrimage not in hermitage, in a labyrinth of action, not a cave of contemplation. The one great evil cave of the book is the "hellish den" of the Brigands, from which, after penetrating to "the secrets of their entrayles," Calidore rescues Pastorella. The main action, however, the pursuit of the Blatant Beast, never takes Calidore into a cave or even under cover, though the Beast's origins are emphatically stated so as to link it with many another monster of the poem: it was begotten of Echidna by Typhaon "in fearefull darkenesse," "mongst rocks and caues."[44]

The Knight of Courtesy moves in marked contrast to the Knight of Justice: compliant, unhurried, errant to the point of aberrancy, his delays are of leisure not business, *otium* not *negotium*. The Proem to the sixth book tells of ways through the land of Faerie, and as the action begins, Calidore must "tread an endlesse trace" in pursuit of the Blatant Beast (whose insensate lunges and darts are suggested by the name of his prototype in Malory, the Questing Beast). Following their "strange waies," the characteristic movement of Calidore and of Calepine is deeper into the forest; their negative counterparts, the Brigands and the Saluage Nation, carry Serena and Pastorella into tenebrous thickets. It is this groping "through the worlds wyde wildernes" that makes the pastoral episode such a marvelous breather, culminating as it does in the vision of the dance of the Graces on Mount Acidale. The ground on which the Graces dance is described as "hollow." This word may mean no more than reverberant, but it flashes upon us that what would be dark groping if it took place in the hollow chamber below is unimpeded intricate movement in the open, above. The dance itself is the memory of the labyrinth in clear air and full sight—a labyrinth for the feet of the dancers, for the eyes of the specta-

---

43. *FQ* V.i.6., vi.35, iv.12, vii.37, ix.1, 6, x.29, xi.21, v.23, ix.9.
44. *FQ* VI.iv.13, v.38, x.42, xi.3, 41, vi.11 (see i.8 for an alternative genealogy, also involving conception in "darkesome den").

tors, a maze without menace, time and space in friendship, the knot that holds but does not constrain, the fully answered riddle, the poem signed and delivered.[45]

There we might end at the high point of the last book. *The Faerie Queene* envisaged in the "Letter to Raleigh" is conceived as a gigantic center-seeking labyrinth, having many adits, but with Cleopolis and Gloriana as center and goal and reward. In the process of writing, it becomes ever less unicursal and more multicursal. If the Mutability Cantos are, as I think they are, a detached retrospective commentary and conclusion to the whole, the "existing monument" must be reconsidered. Mutabilitie herself is a Titanesse, a child of earth, but is not chthonic or cave-dwelling, her whole aspiration being upward. Arlo Hill is an everted cave, and Mutabilitie's procession is a spiral labyrinth without impediments. What a vast difference between her sunlit, orderly, delightful procession of times and seasons and creatures and the coiled monster at the threshold of Book I! It is difficult to remember Gloriana and Cleopolis here. But this is not quite the end. Nature's doom silences Mutabilitie and turns her cantos and the whole poem into a transit maze—up and out through an exit surprisingly placed and suddenly disclosed.[46]

45. *FQ* VI Proem 1, 2, i.6, 37 (cf. vi.4: "careless bird in cage," "this worldes unquiet ways"), vii.37, x.10 ff. (the dance on Mount Acidale). Elaborate designs of knots were made by Renaissance artists, among them Leonardo and Dürer, often with the artist's name or pseudonym at the center. It is tempting to think of Spenser so signing the name of Colin Clout to the intricately woven description of the Dance of the Graces. See Marcel Brion, "Le Thème de l'entrelace et du labyrinthe dans l'oeuvre de Léonard de Vinci," *Revue d'Esthéthique*, 5 (1952), 18–38; Ananda K. Coomaraswamy, "The Iconography of Dürer's 'Knots' and Leonardo's 'Concatenation,'" *Art Quarterly*, 7 (1944), 109–28.

46. See my article "Spenser's Mutabilitie," in *Essays in English Literature from the Renaissance to the Victorian Age, Presented to A. S. P. Woodhouse*, ed. Millar MacLure and F. W. Watt (Toronto: University of Toronto Press, 1964), pp. 26–42, reprinted in A. C. Hamilton, ed., *Essential Articles for the Study of Edmund Spenser* (Hamden, Conn.: Archon, 1972), pp. 253–66.

Contributors

JUDITH H. ANDERSON is Professor of English, Indiana University. She is author of *The Growth of a Personal Voice: "Piers Plowman" and "The Faerie Queene"*; *Biographical Truth: The Representation of Historical Persons in Tudor-Stuart Writing*; and articles on medieval and Renaissance literature.

W. W. BARKER, Assistant Professor of English, Memorial University of Newfoundland, is Research Editor of *The Spenser Encyclopedia*.

HARRY BERGER, JR., is Professor of English, University of California, Santa Cruz. He edited *Spenser: A Collection of Critical Essays*, and is author of *The Allegorical Temper: Vision and Reality in Book II of Spenser's "Faerie Queene"* and of many articles on Spenser and others.

WILLIAM BLISSETT is Professor Emeritus of English, University of Toronto. He is author of many articles on Renaissance literature and Co-Editor of *The Spenser Encyclopedia*.

DONALD CHENEY is Professor of English at the University of Massachusetts, Amherst. He is author of *Spenser's Image of Nature* and essays on Elizabethan literature; translator of Boccaccio's *Filocolo*; and Co-Editor of *The Spenser Encyclopedia*.

ALASTAIR FOWLER is Regius Professor of Rhetoric and English Literature (Emeritus), University of Edinburgh, and Visiting Professor of English, University of Virginia. He is author of *Spenser and the Numbers of*

Time; *Kinds of Literature: An Introduction to the Theory of Genres and Modes*; *A History of English Literature*; and many other works.

NORTHROP FRYE, Chancellor of Victoria University in the University of Toronto, is author of *Anatomy of Criticism*; *The Secular Scripture: A Study of the Structure of Romance*; and many other works.

ROBERT B. HEILMAN, Professor Emeritus of English, University of Washington, has written a number of books, including *This Great Stage: Image and Structure in "King Lear"*; *Magic in the Web: Action and Language in "Othello"*; and *The Ways of the World: Comedy and Society*.

A. KENT HIEATT is Professor Emeritus of English, University of Western Ontario. He is author of *Short Time's Endless Monument: The Symbolism of the Numbers in Edmund Spenser's "Epithalamion"*; *Chaucer, Spenser, Milton: Mythopoeic Continuities and Transformations*; and many other works.

CAROL V. KASKE is Associate Professor of English, Cornell University. She is author of articles on Renaissance literature and coeditor and translator of Marsilio Ficino's *De vita*.

GEORGE M. LOGAN is Professor and Head, Department of English, Queen's University. He is author of *The Meaning of More's "Utopia"* and coeditor of *The Norton Anthology of English Literature* and of *Utopia*.

PATRICIA PARKER, Professor of English and Comparative Literature, Stanford University, is author of *Inescapable Romance: Studies in the Poetics of a Mode* and *Literary Fat Ladies: Rhetoric, Gender, Property*. She is coeditor of *Lyric Poetry: Beyond New Criticism*; *Literary Theory / Renaissance Texts*; and *Shakespeare and the Question of Theory*.

MAUREEN QUILLIGAN is May Co. Professor of English, University of Pennsylvania. She is author of *The Language of Allegory: Defining the Genre* and *Milton's Spenser: The Politics of Reading*, and coeditor of *Rewriting the Renaissance: The Discourses of Sexual Difference in Early Modern Europe*.

THOMAS P. ROCHE, JR., is Professor of English, Princeton University. He is author of *The Kindly Flame: A Study of the Third and Fourth Books of Spenser's "Faerie Queene"* and *Petrarch and the English Sonnet Sequences*, and editor of *The Faerie Queene* (Yale English Poets).

GORDON TESKEY, Associate Professor of English, Cornell University, is author of articles on Renaissance literature.

A. C. HAMILTON, Cappon Professor of English, Queen's University, is author of *The Structure of Allegory in "The Faerie Queene"*; *The Early Shakespeare*; *Sir Philip Sidney: A Study of His Life and Works*; *Northrop Frye: Anatomy of His Criticism* (forthcoming); and many articles on Renaissance literature. He is editor of *The Faerie Queene* (Longman Annotated English Poets) and *Essential Articles for the Study of Edmund Spenser*, and is General Editor of *The Spenser Encyclopedia*.

Index

Library of Congress Cataloging-in-Publication Data

Unfolded tales : essays on Renaissance romance / George M. Logan and
Gordon Teskey, editors.
    p. cm.
    Includes bibliographies and index.
    ISBN 0-8014-2268-X (alk. paper)
    1. English literature—Early modern, 1500–1700—History and
criticism. 2. Romances, English—History and criticism.
3. Spenser, Edmund, 1552?–1599—Criticism and interpretation.
I. Logan, George M., 1941– . II. Teskey, Gordon, 1953– .
    PR428.R65U5 1989
820'.9'003–dc19   88-47920